THE LATE SHOW

Other Avon Books by
Helen Gurley Brown

SEX AND THE SINGLE GIRL

THE LATE SHOW

Helen Gurley Brown

AVON BOOKS NEW YORK

Consult your physician for individual medical problems and before trying any of the dietary or exercise regimens given here. Carefully read all instructions and warnings on medicines before using.

The lyrics to "A Little Night Music" on page 62 are reprinted courtesy of Revelation Music Publishing Corp., A Tommy Valendo Publication.

The food chart that appears on page 166 is copyright © 1989 by Sam Grossman. From the book WIN THE FOOD FIGHT and reprinted with permission from St. Martin's Press, Inc., New York, New York.

The *Cosmo* newsletter quiz that appears on page 352 is reprinted courtesy of Debbie Kronenberg.

AVON BOOKS
A division of
The Hearst Corporation
1350 Avenue of the Americas
New York, New York 10019

Copyright © 1993 by Helen Gurley Brown
Cover photo courtesy of Francesco Scavullo
Published by arrangement with William Morrow and Company, Inc.
Library of Congress Catalog Card Number: 92-2386
ISBN: 0-380-77654-5

The William Morrw edition contains the following Library of Congress Cataloging in Publication Data:
  Brown, Helen Gurley.
    The late show : a semiwild but practical
  survival plan for women over 50 / Helen Gurley Brown.
     p. cm.
    Includes index.
    1. Middle aged women—United States—Life skills guides.
  I. Title.
  HQ1059.5.U5B78 1993
  646.7'0082—dc20

First Avon Books Printing: April 1994

AVON TRADEMARK REG. U.S. PAT. OFF. AND IN OTHER COUNTRIES, MARCA REGISTRADA, NHECHO EN U.S.A.

Printed in the U.S.A.

RA 10 9 8 7 6 5 4 3 2 1

For Janet A. Kennedy

ACKNOWLEDGMENTS

Thanks to my brilliant editor, Jeanne F. Bernkopf, who will never see the finished book but knew how grateful I was for her help; she died shortly after completing work on the manuscript. To my intrepid editor at William Morrow and Company, Victoria Klose; to my angel assistant Susan Schreibman, who typed and typed and *typed* (for six long years); to *Cosmo* buddies Roberta Ashley, Guy Flatley, Diane Baroni, Betty Kelly and their colleagues, who made coming to work every day a joy; to super-agent Irving Paul Lazar, whose confidence in me and this book never faltered.

Contents

Introduction

I had been aging—or at least *accepting* aging—very badly. I use the past tense because I'm better now but what a mess there for a while! I never expected to be such a poor sport about age because I never expected to *be* old. If I thought about it at all, which was almost never as the years went by, I expected to go on forever being the *jeune fille* ... *always* younger than others in the room, at least younger by far than *somebody* in the room ... the serious, studious, small-boned little waif-girl right into my nineties. On days of clear vision (this is called Facing Things) I knew age probably *would* arrive. I thought nobody, including me, would be able to tell I was older, because I was Doing Everything Right—maniacal exerciser (over an hour a day), nut-case dieter (a steady 105 pounds—four pounds skinnier than when I was seventeen), making regular "payments" to save the *outside* (silicone injections, face exercises, a little cosmetic surgery) as well as investing in the *inside* (estrogen supplements, vitamins, veggies)—so how could I age?

I think age arrived for me the night Broadway producer Robert Nederlander wouldn't talk to me at a party. Maureen McGovern, a pretty singer who had just been entertaining the group, and I were chatting when Bob came over. "Where did you grow up?" Bob asked. "Little Rock, Arkansas," I said. "Tulsa, Oklahoma," Maureen said. From that moment, Bob never acknowledged by word or glance that I was anywhere closer than Little Rock but chatted animatedly with Maureen. I finally skulked away—and resisted, when I got home, burning the new red Oscar de la Renta dress I'd been so in love with.

1

Then there was the Bus Incident. A pretty Hispanic girl of eighteen or twenty asks if I would like her seat on the Number 30 Madison Avenue bus. It is the second time somebody has asked. The first time I convinced myself the offender "knew who I was" and wanted to be accommodating to a celebrity. This girl didn't have a *clue* ... she simply saw a woman much older than she who probably ought to sit down. Another woman of about forty was standing nearby but *she* didn't get asked. I was so incredulous that I would look like somebody who needed to sit down on the bus, I just stared stupefied at my "benefactress" for about fifteen seconds before saying no, I was getting off at the next stop. I *wasn't* getting off at the next stop; I went and hid in the front of the bus.

In recent years I had been seeing a shrink only a couple of times a year—on "special occasions" (budget crisis at *Cosmo*—staff all wants big raises, management thinks I'm already giving the store away; usual worries about my invalid sister). When my beloved shrink died, I just hadn't started up with anyone new but this seemed to be the right time. My friend Faith Stewart-Gordon, who owns the Russian Tea Room, found me a new helper. On first visit to my new psychiatrist everything came tumbling out ... the rage, sorrow, disgust at being sixty-four years old ... at being *perceived* as sixty-four years old instead of adorable and cute and *young!* Having men introduce their girlfriends to me as though I were some kind of icon, never *mind* men not making passes anymore (passes being a sure sign of one's attractiveness even if the man is a *joke*), having to nap all the time, needing more notice before a trip, forget spur-of-the-moment almost *anything,* having anxiety fits on the way to the airport, requiring more fillings, manicures, hairdressers ... not being as "notorious" as I was at the beginning of my stay at *Cosmo,* fresh from *Sex and the Single Girl* bestsellerdom. I told Dr. Janet Kennedy too many people who were merely little twigs then, some of whom *worked* for me, were now as famous as I or more so.

The psychiatrist let me sob my brains out, occasionally handing me Kleenex, and when I finally stopped whining, she said, "But you want to be *young!*"

"Of *course* I want to be young," I said to this dense person. "What kind of breakthrough is *that?!*"

"Ah, but you can't be," she said. "Older is what we *get.*"

Dr. Kennedy was seventy-three at the time. If she'd been forty, I think I would have hit her.

We kept exploring my refusal to go *along* with being older, *me*—who has always prided herself on living in the Real World, never being assy! We decided I had been trying to negotiate with age! "Listen," I had said to my nemesis, "this isn't working *out* for me, so why don't we not go into business just yet? I'll do some really admirable things—stop being so self-centered, give more of my Adolfo suits to charity before they are in tatters, spend more time uncomplainingly with bores—whatever you say, age, but let's just forget this nasty body-and-brain-going-to-mush business for a while, Okay?"

No dice! Age keeps marching along like a World War II German storm trooper. But you see, when you are used to fighting and *winning*—after a few blood-soaked rounds—no matter who the adversary, you are not equipped to *deal* with something like age, where you can't win no matter *what* you do. Warming to my task, I explained poignantly to Dr. K. that I've always been so little and cute and, well, *young.* From childhood, I have liked being with people *older* than I and that, of course, makes *you* feel younger. In Little Rock during the Depression, my father died when I was ten and my mother, sister and I had very little money. I learned that by being charming to the parents of rich-kid friends, I was always invited to their houses for wonderful lunches and dinners . . . "Bring that little Gurley girl home with you after church," they would say, "She's so sweet." (Early mouseburgering . . . use whatever you've got to get what you need . . . in my case great food, attention from strong, stable adults.)

My widowed mother lived for my sister and me, gave us all she had, but she was often depressed and terrified. With older people I always felt safe and snug, and since most older people seek the company of the young, getting yourself a bunch of older-than-you friends was never a problem. One reason I think I never wanted children is that *they* would be the younger petted darlings of the older crowd, and horrible little competitors! So, always managing to be the "youngest" (I didn't menstruate until age sixteen) in my twenties, thirties, forties, I just assumed I would be the youngest sixty, seventy, eighty, or *any* age. When age finally arrived, it would seat itself unobtrusively like somebody late to a concert who slips into the back row and nobody notices. Hah!!

I explained to Dr. K. how I had got away with "youth" all these years. With a husband six years older than I and no killer problems with him and girls—thank *God* . . . having your man fancy other women in bed and *do* something about them has got to be the most ego-destroying happiness-basher there is and I don't believe I could stand it—age had really kind of left me alone. I sailed through my fifties paying little attention to how old I was getting; my fiftieth birthday was spent on board a private plane en route to Palm Springs for a bikini-clad weekend. I felt so *special.* Great job, darling man, plus all that stuff I was doing to stay young, how could this grisly thing be happening to *me?*

Shrink listened, said I reminded her of Scarlett O'Hara, stamping her foot and screeching, "But Ashley loves *me*, he will *not* marry Melanie!" (he marries Melanie), or of a condemned man being led to the guillotine screaming, "I'm innocent!" but he has to put his head on the block just the same. Beginning to get the hang of it, I said I was maybe like the employee who refuses to be fired! Sometimes a just-fired person will sit around and *argue* with you—as though you and he were on equal footing; by refusing to *accept* the firing, the fired one pretends it hasn't happened or can be undone, but eventually he has to go clean out his desk.

So after ten sessions (that many!) with Dr. Kennedy, I began to accept the *cause* of my depression: loathing aging. I still couldn't see many *laughs* in the situation. Dr. Kennedy kept trying to cheer me, dredging up names of ancient actresses, doddering writers, Dior-dressed society doyennes who were accepting aging better than I. "Oh, for God's sake, *them,*" I kept shrieking . . . "Who wants to be *them?!*" (The cripple not wanting to associate with *other* cripples . . . the passenger figuring if he stays *off* the deck of the *Titanic* and goes back to his stateroom, maybe the ship won't sink!) Some people don't mind being older, Dr. Kennedy claimed. I told her they are lying! Since old is closer to death and nobody wants to die, what's to *like?* As for future compensations—you can sleep late, repot the hydrangeas, reread the classics, bake brownies, see all those people you never had time to see—everybody *knows* sleeping late makes you groggy, nobody can reread classics for more than three days without getting a headache, brownies are better baked by Greenberg's and there was a *reason* you didn't see all those people: they were *boring!* I refuse to give an inch.

After going on in this vein for several weeks—I really was inconsolable—I finally cave in and ask my shrink what I *am* going to do to feel better.

"Write a book," she says.

I write books of *cheer,* I tell her. *Sex and the Single Girl* told single girls they have better sex lives than married ones; *Having It All* said mousy girls can own the world if they dig in and work hard. Feeling as I do about age, what possible cheerful thing could I say? "Tell people you *mind* it," she said. "The ones who feel the same way you do will at least know they're not alone." "People want to be perked *up,* not dragged down," I tell her. "Try it," she persisted.

Well, pain does sometimes connect you with other people. When you really hurt, you lay down your armor, the façade crumbles and you let others get to *know* you. And books certainly do help the people who write them, that's for sure! A writer may kid herself she is doing it for *them*—"all those unfortunates out there who need my message"—but you actually hang on like a mongoose to his cobra and *choke* a book into being because you want the world to pay attention to you; pure killer ego produces books.

So I began to write while the psychiatrist continued her relentless "older is what we get" barrage (like the telephone weather report recording that repeats and repeats if you don't hang up). "You can respond to age two ways," she hammered away. "By being depressed and 'hiding out' or by doing the best you can with what is left of your life." If she gave me that "you see the glass half empty; why not look at it as half full?" routine twice more I thought I really *was* going to belt her (and why didn't she feel *worse* than I—she's eight years *older!*).

"Be thankful for what you have *had,*" she drummed into my dear little ear. "No one can take away your success . . . that is history. Pleasurable things will continue to happen to you even if they are different from before. And you are, for God's sake, to stop thinking one is only womanly if she is fucking her head off"—my shrink's language got worse when I came into her life—"or somebody is trying to get her to. You are *still* a woman."

And so during the next year I make this rapprochement with age. I would not pretend I was getting younger or even staying the same if *age* would acknowledge that I am an *exemplary* older person, still trying to grow and not close down the shop. I mercilessly make my body do things no sixty-four-year-old body should have been asked to do: climb stairs, even at airports, schlepping my luggage, flat-out run as much as a block for a bus, walk instead of ride, continue stuffing my brain with "knowledge," asking it to *remember* the stuffing (sometimes it does, sometimes it doesn't). And I have found that age is a careless jailer. There are hours, days, even weeks when age doesn't seem to hang around much to check up on you. During those times, you are the same whizzy you you have always been, in some ways better. Since beginning to write, these things have happened.

I debated at Oxford, I went into a tank at the New York Aquarium and swam with the dolphins, I interviewed Elizabeth Taylor for *Cosmo*—my first print interview with a celebrity and it came out fine. David and I visited Morocco, Istanbul, the ruins at Ephesus, and I opened new *Cosmo*'s in Taiwan, Korea and Portugal (we have 27 foreign editions now). I made a television pilot and got inducted into the Publishing Hall of Fame along with DeWitt Wallace and Henry Luce who founded *Reader's Digest* and *Time;* the Hearst Corporation (my bosses) endowed a chair in my name at the Medill Journalism School at Northwestern; I've made some speeches people showed up for and recently did my best television interview ever, I think (with Richard Heffner on *Open Mind* for Public Broadcasting). *Cosmo* celebrated its twenty-fifth anniversary with me as editor; we had a razzle-dazzle twenty-fifth anniversary issue and party at the Rainbow Room, and I've now written this, my seventh book.

So I'm feeling perky (and conceited?) enough about age to put down the things I've been thinking about it. If these thoughts should ring true for you, too, that would be my greatest pleasure.

THE LATE SHOW

chapter one

Basic Us

This stuff happens to all of us when older, no matter how adorable we are: The stomach pooches even with those hundred sit-ups you do every day.

Regardless what you do for your upper arms, the under part (from armpit to elbow) hangs there somewhat like *draperies*.

Hair falls from once densely populated areas where it *never* fell before. Like Mother H.'s cupboard, your temples are getting *bare*.

The skin on your face, once thick and waxy, is now papery and fragile.

Your body is not the same color all over anymore. Little red, blue, brown and yellow tidbits have shown up here and there along with tiny streaks and mottling.

You are apparently the only person in the restaurant, unless you brought an "ancient" friend with you, who doesn't think deafening is pleasant. If the decibel level got any higher, you'd have to write *notes* to the waiter, but "youngsters" all around are happily yapping at each other.

You listen determinedly to MTV and rock stations to "keep in touch," then, giddy with relief, cave in and turn to your beloved music station.

You prefer sleep to 40 percent of the things anybody offers you to do, nap as easily as a cat.

You are now "pacing yourself," being more sensible about what you can fit into one day, one hour. Some things (staying up until three—or two?) are being left *out*.

You ask about a little boy you used to play with in your neighborhood and hear that he has retired. Or died.

People selfishly keep dying on you ... not the "golden oldies" but *contemporaries.*

They ask you to dance because they have to, not because they want to, and you want to dance a whole lot longer, not necessarily with the one who asked you but with somebody *good.* It mostly never happens.

You try to make love and *he* can't or *you* can't. (More later.)

You buy the beautiful clothes you longed for as a girl and can now afford and they don't do as much as a slip-dress on a twenty-two-year-old.

You look quite decent headed for lunch or a party but an hour later, glancing in the mirror, you see you've "collapsed."

Okay, a girl of twenty could get together her own list of gruesomes and so could a thirty-six-year-old. I just wanted to jot down *my* little gruesome-list of how we *look* and a few other things that are happening to get them off my chest (I don't want anything pushing down my chest ... it needs all the pushing *out* it can get) so we could get on to other matters ... like what are we like *inside* these days now that we're older?

Same as we were when younger—present-day us is created half by genes, half by environment (family, peers, teachers). Oh, you *learn* things ... like not to leave your luggage in the middle of the British Airways terminal while you go make a phone call, not to force a too-small ring up past your knuckle just to see how it looks. You also know, if you want your husband to diet, you deny him sex, conversation and food for as long as it takes to get him started. (There are other methods but not as effective.) Instincts sharpen. You take the paper, present, ribbon, box *home* to gift-wrap because you can tell the three wrappers behind the counter are going to be slower than waiting for a bad haircut to grow out ... things like that.

But personality and nervous system *stay.* I am still this high-strung little person sitting on the floor of the Holiday Inn bathroom in Shawnee, Oklahoma, screaming her lungs out because she can't get a water bug the size of Venezuela to stay in a Kleenex and be taken out of doors to be freed instead of squirming his way out yet one more time—exactly the way I would have reacted at thirteen. Next time I want to come back *casual* ... with limpid, listless, even *lazy* genes.

So why do we consult gurus, pore through books, listen to tapes, trying to change even *now* when we know we can't? Because we irritate ourselves to death sometimes and would *like* to get things fixed—be happier. Fine in theory, but in a scrappy, secret, almost arrogant way we also don't *want* to change, especially at *our* age. We are set in concrete and blasting would be uncomfortable. I am semimiserable at parties. Why don't I come off it and learn to enjoy myself? Because I've just had too many years of "successfully" hating parties, of "knowing" I'm not a good raconteur, gleaning that men would rather talk to each other or a Madonna look-alike than to me, believing whatever anybody says at a party is banal, etc., etc. I am *comfortable*—if unhappy—as a party-phobe!

To use a far more dramatic case of not changing, why doesn't a woman who is driving her children to despise her stop with the whining, complaining and laying on of guilt so her kids will *like* her? Because she gets some "pleasure" (i.e., comfort) out of being just as she is. The self-destructive tendencies must be in our genes, reinforced by early life-experience.

So do we just go on and on being "unsatisfactory"? No, I think we keep facing *down* the goblins, if only for the sake of people who have to live with us. Some goblins we do rout, some we live with—but I don't think you ever stop trying. These are the ones I battle:

1. **Shyness.** Is half the world shy? A lot of people you'd think *wouldn't* be *say* they are. Mark Goodson, the billionaire game-show creator, Richard Snyder, chairman and CEO of Simon & Schuster—both tiger cats—Bernie Leser, bon vivant president of Condé Nast Publications, all told me at a party the other night *they* were. Actors and actresses are notoriously shy. Brilliant on the screen or in the play, then they're plunked down at a party without a script and it's back into little Susan Beth Israelson from Flatbush or Paul Blobenschuk from Kleinsborough, Kan-

sas, trying to cope with only an ordinary brain and repartee. I've never taken any solace from other "fortunate" people's shy-problems. Cher tongue-tied wouldn't help *me*. From hiding out in the ladies' room to clinging like lint to one party companion for fear I'll never get another, it does seem to me people fall away from a shy person like needles coming loose from a twelve-week-old Christmas tree.

At a really *fancy* party you can feel sort of like a big puffy *germ!* You bravely join a group of four and first thing you know there's just you and the seediest person in the group left. You can tell yourself the others planned to leave anyway but *did* they? The only ones who *never* leave are the widows and mousy wives or girlfriends of successful men who dropped them the minute they came in the door and went off to chat with the boys. So this is a nice person left with me, you say to yourself, and I am going to stay right here and talk to her, but you see the glitterers across the room and think, oh, shit, here I am again with a fellow (social) loser! I don't think age has anything to do with shyness . . . I was even worse when I was younger. And I *know* big parties and receptions were invented for people to move from one group to another, but I never feel I'm the group being moved *to!* At parties or anywhere I *make* myself talk to strangers just for the discipline but, of course, there's a catch to coming out of your shell. You are *stuck* with the person you came out for.

I am about to climb over the man in the aisle seat to take my assigned window seat on a flight from Memphis to New York, when I see many rows of empty seats, and ask the attendant if I may move to one of those. Fine, she says. Thinking the man I am leaving might feel rejected ("She takes one look at me and asks to move her seat!") and fighting "shy," I say sweetly, "Listen, I'm going to *miss* you but I have a lot of papers I need to spread out. I'll be right here in the row behind." First he looks stunned. "What does she mean, she's going to miss me?" Five minutes later he thinks he's figured it out and, as I am asking the flight attendant for two miniature bottles of brandy to take off the plane with which to make vanilla, he leans over the seat and leers, "Gonna drink that later in your room, little lady?" I don't want to play anymore. I've done my Get Out of Your Shell routine just as he's warming *up!* For shy people to continue a conversation bravely started is worse than starting . . . older doesn't make you better at going the distance.

Perhaps all us shy folks need a good whammo kick in the behind or a course in not taking ourselves so seriously. Describing Stephen Tennant, a notoriously shy but showy English dandy of the 1930s, someone said that "the shyness wasn't so much a wish not to be seen as a wish to be applauded on sight." Maybe that's what all us shy people secretly long for. I do know we need to take *risks.* A tape I listened to about shyness suggested you make eye contact with somebody for two minutes . . . *two minutes!* What a great exercise. It said other people are, indeed, what's scary but also what add glamour and excitement to our lives . . . you can't *get* those things without other people. There is a tiny bit of good news about shy and *older.* You can usually talk to strangers without their thinking you are a flake. A twenty-eight-year-old girl who starts a conversation with an "unknown" may be thought to be Asking For It. Nobody figures a sixty-eight-year-old woman is doing that though she *may* be. (See Chapter Three.)

As for how you can be on television and be shy, all talk-show hosts need guests. In a way you are their livelihood, so they shut up and listen, unlike people at parties. Going in you think you are going to pass *out* with fright, but then you don't and pretty soon you're actually having a good time. A celebrity panel is something else. I have been climbed over, talked on top of, laid out cold by the *best* of them—Betty White, Dick Cavett, Wayne Newton, Rosemary Clooney—you'd think they'd quiet down when it's *your* turn but I guess polite isn't how you get ahead in show business. One day I am going to get un-shy and *deck* one of them.

2. **Hurt feelings.** I still get those. I don't think you ever lose your touch for hurt feelings, do you? David (my husband) and I are invited to the beach house of dear friends for the weekend—our ninth summer there. That

same weekend we are *not* invited to a surprise birthday
party for a Wall Street "player" to which everybody this
side of the local sanitation crew plus a starry cast of
"twinkies" has been summoned. Our beach house hosts
call to say *they* have been invited—could we pick another
weekend for our visit? Double hurt feelings! Fortunately I
have a husband who won't put up with indefinite moping
but gets right into his "What's Important in Life" lecture,
which is so boring it gets me out of the mopes right away.
The only reassurance about hurt feelings is that
everyone—*everyone*—there *are* no exceptions—gets them.
They come, they go, and it's got nothing to do with age.

3. **Envy? Jealousy?** I'd have thought to have routed
both of them by now but I'm "better" than ever! Just this
morning I heard how tenderly Michael Caine regards his
beautiful Guyanese wife, Shakira ... seems she sat on
his lap in a crowded car coming home from a party and he
was all puppyish and excited ... and that got me going. I
don't know why stories about these two always give me
the wincies. Anyway, I'm glad they live in London. I'm
about through my Diane Von Furstenberg phase. Years ago
when she told me she had been made love to by Warren
Beatty and Ryan O'Neal both in one day, I thought that
wasn't *fair* ... listen, my criteria for envy aren't under discussion, okay? One night when I had come straight from
the office in heavy winter togs to have dinner with Diane
at her flat, she sent me to her dressing room to find something to slip into. Well, one whole *wall* was lingerie drawers with two or three each devoted to peach, plum,
persimmon, apricot, poppy, shell, mauve—about fifteen
colors in all, plus racks and racks of dressing gowns. I
went home and put all my pantyhose with runs, and the
raveled T-shirts I'd been saving for exercise clothes, down
the incinerator. The night Barry Diller, until recently CEO
and chairman of Fox, Inc., gave Diane twenty-nine diamonds loose in a matchbox for her twenty-ninth birthday,
I hit bottom. But you see, it doesn't last forever. A few
years ago, Diane—who has always been a darling, generous friend, incidentally—fell in love with a somewhat dif-

ficult Frenchman who occasionally gave her a bad time and that got me off her case.

Listen, other people are just as bad as I am. My super-agent friend, Sue Mengers, once told me she would like to be Princess Di. *Di?!* I'm not in a position to criticize anybody else's choice of who to want to be but Di was chosen to marry the Prince in the first place to be a broodmare (she's doing fine there—two royal colts already) and she has to live this structured life and never get mad at her mother-in-law—I mean, would you want to be *her?* (Maybe Susie has changed envy-objects since all that press about Diana's anorexia and depression.) I think many of the top newswomen of the world, I mean tippy-*top,* resent Diane Sawyer's glamour combined with brains. Resent means they're jealous. I debated Angela Newman, White House correspondent for NBC, and Judy Meserve of ABC News on *Good Morning America* on that subject. They said Diane shouldn't have been photographed sexily on the cover of *Vanity Fair* by Annie Liebowitz because "it hurts the image of newswomen everywhere." I suspected the girls wouldn't have turned down the same photography offer if anybody had asked but nobody asked. I could be wrong. An executive of Cosmair once told me Ralph Lauren was devastated by the success of Calvin Klein's Obsession fragrance. (Ralph Lauren fragrances are in Cosmair's Lancôme division.) Obsession had shaken up the industry and shaken up Ralph. How could this attractive genius of the design world, rich beyond counting, be jealous of anybody?

Stage actress Jane Alexander said on the Donahue show she was wistful about Meryl Streep's very visible, industry-rewarded success. I adored her for admitting that—most *don't*—and could see what she meant. My beloved friend Polly Bergen confided in me one night she envied a certain young beauty who had married a Texas oil baron and "he isn't even old or ugly!" I told her she was crazy. The new baroness is an ex-hooker whose whole life is spent getting fitted in her next Christian La Croix. Here was Polly, a beautiful and accomplished singer and recording star, a respected actress who appeared in thirty hours of *War and Remembrance,* television's most ambitious drama, herself (at the time) married to somebody young and handsome and successful and if she had wanted to marry a zillionaire at the ex-call girl's age she could have married *twenty!* A television mogul told me that "having a private airplane or yacht doesn't mean much anymore." What sends *him* spinning, he says, are the appointments of the playthings of his peers. "Donald Trump's airplane isn't much. Trump picked it up cheap from a company under pressure from its stockholders to get rid of its air force but the *Nabila* [Trump's luxury yacht purchased from Adnan Khashoggi, name changed to the *Trump Princess*] with its elephant skin corridors and 18k gold bathroom fixtures . . . now that can unravel my day every time!" I should have called him when Trump had to sell the yacht *and* the plane.

Note of cheer: Your "objects" frequently get unenviable if you stick around awhile. Could I now envy Caroline Lindemeyer, the belle of my John H. Francis Polytechnic High School graduating class for whom there was a three weeks' waiting list to get a date? Last time I saw Caroline, tiny little lines had sprung up all over her face—it looked like pleated chiffon—and her husband kept a turtle in the bathtub. Another high-school beauty who maddened us all with her class and elegance is managing a cheese shop. Nothing wrong with managing a cheese shop, except if you knew Leonia in 1939, you wouldn't have figured she'd wind up doing that. Leonia rode to *hounds,* for God's sake! I can see her now in her jodhpurs, fresh from a romp with Tasha, her chestnut mare to whom she bore a strong resemblance, rich-girling it over us all.

4. What about dealing with the **Just Plain Crazies?** Do you ever look down at your doggie's paws and think your feet are just like his . . . the nails and pads and tiny foot bones and ankles and tendons, like you are part dog and they are part you . . . I mean, we're all in this *together?* I have identified with the horses who pull carriages in Central Park for years, felt their struggle, their wish to do it right but they're so *tired.* Maybe this isn't too crazy, but I feel I have to help people with their pamphlet

distribution on street corners. I don't necessarily get in there and help pass out right along *with* them, but so many passersby won't accept leaflets, I always reach for one and will even take twice from the same person if I pass him on a return trip.

Do you empathize with inanimate objects? It never occurs to me that bobby pins, hair curlers and paper clips do not have feelings. When a couple of paper clips you are trying to separate cling together, I am sure they are in love. And when you try to pick one little clip from a stack but a different clip gets loose and falls out across your papers instead, you know that is an ambitious paper clip . . . take me, take *me!* I think about the kamikaze little lives of paper clips, some of them giving only once, then plop into the wastebasket (not in *my* wastebasket, of course—I recycle). I believe their happiest moments are when they are all shiny new, clustered together in friendship in a box waiting to "serve." I'm convinced bobby pins, rubber bands, vitamins, aspirin *all* want to be the ones chosen even though it's the end of their lives for the vitamins and aspirin. I've always felt this way. Age hasn't really contributed though I may be mainlining now.

5. **Eccentricity?** Maybe not quite as federal as the crazies, but you do get *more* eccentric as you "harden." On a recent flight from Los Angeles to New York, I tried to degrease my salad greens (a death threat couldn't have persuaded me to *eat* all that slime or to give up the salad) by wiping them along the napkin tray. Airplane tray cloths, being made of grass shreds and pulverized glass slivers, are not absorbent, so I *folded* the greens into a little paper napkin saved from cocktails and squeezed out the oil. Better. Then I ate the greens with my fingers. The man sitting next to me watched quite a lot of this, then stared straight ahead. And who *couldn't* empathize (sympathize isn't strong enough) with the late New York society belle Babe Paley who had her secretary cut the pinked edges off all postage stamps so they would be neater?

6. Does **uncontrollable anger** sometimes zap you? You surely don't feel *less* as you get older. Last week a taxi didn't go the way I had in mind from my house to the

office. Actually, his way would have got us there the following afternoon. Since explaining, beseeching and, finally, screeching couldn't get him pointed in the right direction, I said something obscene, jumped cab and took off to find another. (He is probably still trying to find me to pay the meter drop.) I actually *hit* a cab driver the other day, a *big* Oriental—you don't see many like him, they are usually small and compact like me. He was another one headed in the wrong direction and so abusive and *determined* to go fifteen blocks out of the way to get me to work, plus drop me on the wrong side of the street, I couldn't think of anything else to do *but* hit him to make an impression. It wasn't a language barrier—he kept saying "You crazy, lady, lady, you crazy" even *before* I hit him—just on the shoulder—as he went barreling off toward Ninth Avenue instead of heading down Broadway where my office happens to be located and where I have gone for the past twenty-seven years so I know the way.

One day my taxi turned into a street where two trucks, one on the left, one on the right, were double-parked, blocking the street. Other cars had followed us in so there was no escape. Truck drivers nowhere in sight, so I left the cab, walked up to the driverless trucks, rang a few doorbells nearby. Nothing. Finally the drivers sauntered out, slow and easy, but seemed to have no intention of getting on with the day's work. "You can't park here," I tell them. "Nobody can get *through.*" By now about ten cars were in our stalled caravan. No action from the drivers yet, just those patronizing looks New York workmen have perfected to deal with overwrought New York women. At this point I started to tug at a sack of gravel on the open platform of one of the trucks, managed to drag it over the side where it splattered deliciously on the pavement. I was going for my second sack when the men decided to start unloading the rest themselves, me yelling at them to hurry.

It gets worse. I recently screamed at a *baby* on an airplane—a *baby!*—who had been screaming at *me* or at *something* from Oklahoma City to La Guardia Airport in New York, two hours and forty minutes of straight screaming and my nerves had had it. You never saw such shocked parents—or fellow passengers—and for a minute the baby let up. *He* couldn't believe you would scream at a baby *either.* I figured if that's how much the kid hated flying, the parents should have given him a sedative or something—all that exertion couldn't have been good for his little lungs.

I find airports and airplanes are big scream launchers. One night I got to the airport an hour before flight time with a preboarding pass and seat assignment. Nobody at the gate, plane delayed three *hours* because of weather so I hung out at Eastern Airlines Club; Continental didn't have one. When my flight was finally called, I started to board with my pass but they said the boarding pass was not valid, all seats were gone. Grace Kelly ladylike perseverance *might* have produced action but something told me, this being one overbooked mother of a flight, and the last one that night to Houston where I had to give a speech early next morning, a few little screams would be more effective. After placing myself just outside the Boeing 727 door and screeching for about fifteen minutes straight, someone was taken off the plane and his seat given to me. That poor removed-from-the-plane-nonscreamer is probably still talking about what happened to *him* but I mean, what is a boarding pass *for?*

Pouting doesn't get you much of anywhere on airplanes or anywhere else—don't you agree? You are just one big oozy, whiny mess, yet frequently people don't even know what it is you *want.* Occasionally pouting may work with a loved one—he or she gives in because he can't stand your hostility one more second—but I think outright showy anger is much more effective. You get it over with, get on with your life and let him get on with his. Sometimes you drive your anger *inside,* of course. I am awaiting—patiently wouldn't be the right word to describe the wait—news from my agent, mighty Irving "Swifty" Lazar, as to when and whether we have sold this book. Irving, his wife, Mary, David and I are having dinner at Spago on the Sunset Strip. Irvin begins telling me expansively what a sensational writer Joan Collins is, that he has just sold *her* (yet unwritten) book to the United Kingdom for three million dollars ... "and, honey, they haven't seen a *word!*" What *is* it with this dense person I have known, respected and adored for thirty years but am not cozy enough with to wring his tiny neck or tell him please to get to the point?! I begin folding teaspoons. You simply bend the handle down to the spoon part ... takes a little struggle but gets your mind off your troubles ... for the moment. Three bent teaspoons later, Irving finally tells me the book has been sold.

Bent teaspoons sometimes do it, but other times I feel confrontation the only satisfactory action. Earlier this year, after a bus driver wouldn't let me on at the Pottery Barn on the southeast corner of Fifty-seventh and Eighth Avenue (he'd already closed the door and wouldn't open it again even though I was banging on it), I *ran* all the way to Sixty-first Street and Central Park West—four bloody blocks—to catch him at his next stop. I made the four blocks before the bus because the streets were jammed with cars, bicycles, pedestrians, dogs, baby carriages, street musicians, but it was still heart-attack time. Gasping like a guppy, I had the pleasure of climbing the bus stairs, dropping in my token and telling him he was an absolute asshole not to have let me on at the last stop. He didn't agree he should have. Other passengers hid behind newspapers, looked out windows—you know how everybody acts when some lunatic is arguing with a bus driver.

That's about enough about anger! As long as we get angry at idiots instead of just about *life,* I think it's okay.

7. Now let's spend a minute on **depression,** from which some of us suffer and, yes, we "know better" but that doesn't help. I think my own recurrent depression probably comes from early "indoctrination." My mother was melancholy a great deal of the time and, though she loved me and didn't realize what she was doing, influenced me to see the world her special way—through rain forests of tears. There were days in high school when she would pick me up at the doctor after my twice-a-week visit to have acne pustules opened, and we would drive around the Los Angeles streets in our little black Pontiac

and just cry up a storm ... about acne, about my sister, Mary, being in a wheelchair, about our not having a daddy, about money problems and life's general sadness. Sometimes she would lie on the bed with her face to the wall, weeping, and I would lie down beside her, wedging myself up against her back, spoon fashion, and try to find out what was the matter. Usually it was a case of seriously hurt feelings caused by a relative or neighbor or maybe by Mary or me. Sometimes she just cried from general loneliness. Whatever set her off I learned about depression early and well and I can always slip into it as comfortably as a kimono. (No, I don't blame her. While "teaching" me depression, she also nurtured and loved me and taught me to use my brain.)

I had a nice meeting with two "members of the club" in Martha's Vineyard last year—Art Buchwald and Mike Wallace. Neither of them was depressed at the moment but I *was* and they were good enough to tell me about their own bouts. Buchwald's wife, Ann, had been seriously ill, which worried him a lot, and Wallace had gone through a traumatic lawsuit when General William Westmoreland sued both Wallace and CBS for a *60 Minutes* segment unflattering to the general; both said they were very good at getting depressed *without* cause. My friend Ann Ford Johnson, divorced wife of the late car czar, Henry Ford, and now happily remarried, told me she had been in a funk for almost a year because a friend she cared about dropped her when she was unable to attend a pre-party for a big charity function the friend was chairing: Ann was having a party the same night and couldn't dump her own guests to attend. The charity chair refused to discuss the matter but simply cut Ann out of her life. May not sound like a tragedy to *you* but it caused a serious depression in the rejected one. First Lady Barbara Bush reports suffering a severe depression after returning from China with George in 1976. "I know I should have gone to the doctor. I probably had a small chemical inbalance and I could have cured it immediately. But I didn't. I gutted it out."

Most depression is triggered by a real problem, but even when the problem is solved, depression may come back with a new "reason" in its jaws. A depressed person is sort of out trolling all the time! People who don't have the Big D don't *have* it, of course. They get unhappy over life events but they don't have this blue disgusting sleazy sludge oozing through their brain. After her husband died, my friend Bobbie Ashley wouldn't *let* herself "go upstairs and cry about Wilson," though she adored him. She *never* cried or self-pitied. I sent her to my shrink just in case she needed help in her bereavement, but he saw her only once and said she was going to be fine on her own. She pulled *herself* together, went on with her life, married again. She has Wilson's ashes in the trunk of her Cadillac . . . "I think it's friendly." Harold, her new husband, doesn't mind. Depression isn't for *everybody.*

So, how do you get depression fixed if you have it? What doesn't seem to work is going through your Be-a-Little-Grateful-for-What-You've-*Got* routine. We go *through* the routine but the gratitude never gets anywhere near our *gut.* As for getting cheered up by the "important" things in life—a child's smile, tangerine sunsets, autumn leaves—they bring cheer only if you're feeling fine already. "Snapping out of it," as highly recommended by all our bored-with-us friends, is about as possible as snapping out of a crushed pelvis. I, world class at self-discipline, have never "snapped out of it" *yet.* (Can you get novocaine out of your jaw in time for lunch? A green banana to ripen in the oven?) Other people's problems help a *little.* A friend telling you a tragic story sometimes says, "Oh, but I don't want to depress you!" Is she kidding? No matter how much you like this person, she doesn't belong to you, her troubles aren't *yours* and they tend to soothe! If your depression is about aging, which mine was at one time, you may be cheered by encountering a friend you haven't seen for a while who is "older" (like you) but not really "worse," as you have convinced yourself *every* older person has to be. Actually this one is *better.* Running into an ex-lover or male friend who corroborates your femaleness helps. Somebody young may make a pass at you! I've never gotten cheered up by a book, a television show or lecture, have you?

Depression does finally go away. Writer William Styron, a chronic sufferer, says, "Depression's saving grace (perhaps its only one) is that the illness seems to be self-limiting. With or without treatment, the sufferer usually gets well." Fine, but you can be a hundred and five and have felt like a bruised tarantula too many mornings. I go for a fix! A soul chat with a friend may get the boulder off your back for a moment, but, of course, they *know* you so what do *they* know . . . contamination by association! When things are really bad, I go to my psychiatrist. It may seem dopey to see a professional for something you could figure out yourself but that's just the point: You *do* figure it out but you don't *listen.* A shrink helps you see that you are perceiving yourself and life quite inaccurately, distorting the truth . . . at least there's another way to look at things. The professional may even have some *advice!* I *always* listen to my shrink and do what she says. I go just once or twice during a serious Big D bout. A complete analysis might get rid of my mother's legacy of depression permanently, but spending that kind of time right now just isn't for me. My depression isn't any worse than when I was young and mostly it's contained. Do you suppose some of us are worry junkies because it feels so good when the pain's gone? God knows, lots of people have no sense of appropriateness about worry. A darling friend of mine had a lumpectomy, then spent an anxious year of radiation treatments and doctor visits until they determined she was indeed cancer-free; now she is wild with worry at not being able to lose the weight gained because she gave up smoking. Another woman, whose husband was about to be indicted for fraud, was almost equally up the walls because her housekeeper of twenty years was going back to Portugal! If there's nothing *decent* to get an attack about, we find something *indecent.* Relief never lasts as long as it should, of course.

I think, aside from occasional shrink fixes, what works for all this stuff—shyness, hurt feelings, anger, depression, worry, jealousy—is that you have to keep doing something that makes you feel worthy of admiration, maybe even a little superior to others. It can be *anything*

. . . terrific job, philanthropy, kids turning out well, giving great parties, growing the best rhododendrons . . . as long as you know you do it the *best*. Doing it also takes your mind off yourself—a totally superior idea if you are over sixty. And exercise. For me that is as necessary to banish the gloom as breathing is to living.

At our age I don't think we have to take *criticism,* "worthy" as we are! Tell them it's too late, they've missed the boat. Or they've had a free ride on the boat but now they have to get off. Everybody *gets* criticized, of course. I have heard people attack Gloria Steinem and Beverly Sills, two of the best women I have ever met. Out there somewhere, I'm sure is somebody having a go at Charles Kuralt, a major pussycat, Dolly Parton or Vartan Gregorian, the president of Brown University who previously got the New York Public Library back on its financial feet with energy, guts and charm, or even at Mother Theresa. I'll bet *somebody* doesn't like Audrey Hepburn, Jimmy Stewart or Phil Donahue—certifiable "lovers."

I'm not actually attacking—not my style—but *I* fail to see the magic of writer-broadcaster Garrison Keillor, though it's seen by millions of others. Virtually *all* politicians give me a megapain because they are so phony; if they tell the truth ("I did once go to a psychoanalyst" or "I *did* once spend the night in a motel with my secretary"), they won't be back next year. I suppose one should criticize the system that *makes* politicians so deceitful. Criticism! It is always unfathomable to me that somebody shouldn't like *me* . . . nice, adorable *me!* In all my years at *Cosmo* and writing books I have never read the hate mail or responded to nasty phone calls—not once (unless it was an advertiser)—so don't bother to write or call! Once in a while on the social scene a hater scores. The other night at a party somebody's *wife* said sweetly, "I don't *keep* my girls from reading *Cosmo* . . . I put it right out there on the coffee table with *Playboy* . . . You just have to trust children to do the right thing." What was *that* supposed to mean? . . . as if I didn't *know!* To heck with even constructive criticism—if there is such a thing—at our age. People can *advise* you—if asked—and drop in a suggestion or two about the right and wrong way to go about having a confrontation with a slow-paying tenant or deranged hairdresser based on your particular capabilities, but delineating inadequacies or faults is *out!*

Should we actually *like* ourselves? I guess I think "liking yourself" is one of those "worthy" instructions like "Take time to smell the flowers" or "Slow down, you'll live longer" that make *me* want to go out and do just the opposite. Besides, anybody who actually goes around liking herself visibly and audibly is probably seriously asking for a shove in front of a minivan. "Accept yourself" is probably a better idea. Accept faults and all. You shouldn't criticize *yourself* very much. That's something my shrink works on with me. She says sometimes, "Helen, for God's sake, would you let up on yourself ... show a little human charity!" and I back off a little. Kitty Carlisle wrote in her book: "You must ... forgive yourself for your sins. When I wake up in the morning, I run down the litany of my transgressions of the day before and if I have been unkind or made a tactless remark or done one of the thousand things that cause me to blush at the memory, I say, 'Well, Kitty, I forgive you—just try to do better next time.' "

Basic us isn't *so* bad, right?

chapter two

Marriage

Marriage. In theory, that would seem the ideal state for an older woman. (Actually, of course, the ideal state for an older woman is *younger.*) Widows and divorcées feel if they could only find another husband, life would be meaningful. "Just as Sam and I were really beginning to learn how to live together, he *went,*" says my friend Selma. " 'I could kill you for doing this to me,' I kept crying on his coffin. He was so great." (Have you noticed how many husbands get greater after they're no longer here?)

A *good* marriage when you're older (*or* younger) is swell but, as I never tire of pointing out, all marriages have flaws (is the Pope Catholic?) and marriage isn't what makes you happy anyway; you have to do that yourself. Some of the unhappiest women I know age fifty and older do indeed have *living* husbands. I asked my ninety-four-year-old role-model philanthropist-friend, Mildred Hilson, if she had had a happy marriage. "I can't remember," said Mildred. "I was so busy doing for Eddie, living life just exactly the way he wanted us to, I really don't know whether I was happy or *not.*" We've come a long way, baby. I don't know whether Mildred was happy *all* the time—I'm sure she got the blues—but she sure was glamorous and popular and beloved. She still is *beloved.* Mildred had a stroke a year or so ago that is keeping her home. Marriage is okay but so is single.

Anyway, here are my thoughts about marriage:

1. It's best to be married to someone your own age, I think—two to six years' difference in either direction is about right. The *same* age is okay. I don't know why so

many people think *older* is best in a man. Maybe it's because everybody knows we mature faster than men, and if we marry somebody older, his brain will have had a chance to catch up with ours! As for needing guidance and protection from a person more mature than us, are they kidding? That requirement probably goes back to a time when women were thought to be childlike. Jesus! Yes, we know men like to *look* at younger women, and younger doesn't challenge their brain as much, and younger is more fecund. Fine. All reasons for a man to marry younger but no reason at all for us to marry *older.* As for wanting somebody, say, twelve years our senior so he won't leave for a younger woman, he can *leave!* Somebody out there is still *younger.* (Think how director John Derek kept trading them in! Are Bo Derek's days numbered?)

I think the reasons to have a husband not far from your own age when you are *older,* aside from it's being soothing not to get blank stares when you mention Dick Powell, Ronald Colman and Kay Francis, is that you can break down *together.* In your sixties—at least that is when it started happening to me—you really do begin to creak just a *little.* You know how to do everything better but each disagreeable task takes more out of you. A bad employee confrontation upsets me for days. More start-up juice is required to get the tough stuff done. I get cross with dumb people sooner, have less patience with friends who can't decide between the spaghetti carbonara and the crab cakes in a restaurant (is this a life-threatening decision?) and that's just the mental stuff. Physically I go as hard as ever, maybe harder, but then it's collapse city; I have to nap almost every day.

If a husband is considerably older than you, this condition is going to hit him *sooner* and his crossness and forgetfulness and short-fusedness are going to grate on you a lot more if *you* haven't *got* there yet. Sure you can philosophize—so *this* is what it's going to be like for me twelve years from now—but who needs a blueprint for disagreeable? Sufficient unto the day, etc., etc. Sexually, you at sixty and him at seventy-two are not so wonderful. Him at eighty, you at sixty-eight? Please! If there's going to be an age difference, why not let *him* be the younger one! Oh, dear, why am I carrying on so? You've already married whom you married (or are divorced or widowed) and he's whatever age he is. We don't need *me* saying it is/was the wrong one! Speaking of who marries whom, I'm never much surprised—are you?—when meeting somebody's mate. The matchups seem quite logical. You've got to know any young Hollywood actor with screen credits isn't going to be married to a klutz, and an investment banker's *second* wife is going to be beautiful, and his first wife, if he is still with *her*, will probably be self-assured from living with all that money even if she's a bit dowdy, etc., etc. Even young people you would think might marry wild don't much jump out of line to marry out of their class: they match up pretty well in terms of looks, money, jobs, background.

2. Marriages that started out great have just as much chance of going bye-bye as marriages that started out less great, so maybe it doesn't really *matter* whether you pick the totally "Right One." People who hang *in* aren't usually married to any better people than those who hang *up*. You can grow stronger as a team with a question-mark person just as you can grow to loathe an adored one ... marriage is to take a chance on, though I *don't* understand why you would have babies until you saw how things were going ... maybe three or four years in ... unless having babies was your main reason for *getting* married. We know children do nothing to make a weak marriage stronger. Of course, I'm not the one to comment on children because I never had any and can't appreciate the joy they are supposed to bring. David's son Bruce was seventeen when his father and I married; he had been fond of his *last* stepmother and wasn't too keen about *me*—probably I wasn't gifted in getting through. After he left home, went to college and married, we got to be better friends.

I'm sure I missed something *big* by not having kids. They're wonderful to look at ... even a nonparent can see *that* ... and watching the little goslings grow into big quacking geese must be to watch a miracle unfold, but when they're grown, they're often so *mean* to you, have you noticed that? You're frequently the *last* person they want to be with ... is that resuscitating? Divine Ann Getty once told me she went white-water rafting just so she could have dinner with her boys a few nights, *and* they brought along friends so it wouldn't get too boring. I mean, risking your ass for dinner dates with your kids?! And, so far as I can see, most of the grown ones keep coming back home for money and other fix-ups. I hardly know a well-off parent who isn't subsidizing a kid's house. Aren't they supposed to buy their own toys when they grow up? Listen, it's lucky the kids got you instead of me for a parent. I'd be asking what happened to the $250 I loaned you *last* year and what's the matter with renting? (*Somebody* will bury me, don't you think? There *are* services for things like that, aren't there? ... I mean, you can find anything in New York City.)

3. Figuring "you can always get a divorce" is a perfectly okay way to go into marriage. Otherwise you could fool around trying for a totally perfect person forever! How can anyone say divorce makes you a failure? You took a chance. You tried. Nobody *meant* it not to work. Sure you "work at marriage" like they tell you to, but no amount of work is going to return you to loving somebody you have grown virtually to despise. Divorcers should think of themselves as people with courage. Extricating yourself from marriage is about as comfortable as getting yourself removed from a tub of wet cement ... and a lot more expensive. Let the ones who *never* marry or never marry *again* feel like the failures, not us plungers.

4. Nevertheless, a lot of people who divorce might be just as well off not doing so. "There is so little difference between husbands you might as well keep the first," said writer Adela Rogers St. John, who had five. People stay married because they *want* to, not because their particular marriage is the greatest. Unless he is *too* big a rat—which probably nobody should put up with—or is about to irritate you to death or keep you from achieving—I agree with Adela, you might as well keep *this* person. I'm thinking of a woman over fifty. Earlier, I suppose you can dabble around a bit with new husbands, even if you don't

know what you are doing. Myrna Blyth, editor of *Ladies' Home Journal,* married to foreign correspondent Jeffrey Blyth for thirty years, says, "I can imagine murder but never divorce!" My sentiment exactly!

5. Good men often marry the worst women and *sometimes* vice versa and then they meet somewhere in the middle. Whoever started out better gets worse and *occasionally* somebody awful improves. Barbaralee Diamonstein, the author, and Carl Spielvogel, head of Backer Spielvogel Bates, the giant advertising consortium, both got better—their one and one add up now to about seventeen. (He's in his sixties, she in her fifties.) Nice. Milton Petrie, the specialty-shop billionaire, became a philanthropist after he married Carol de Portago who decided that would be a good thing for him to do. He is eighty-seven, she late sixties. Both had been married three times before. Nice again. Mike Tyson and Robin Givens both got *worse.*

6. Married when you are older (divorced, widowed) you don't really have to *get.* Why are so many older single women *frantic* to do so? Companionship, yes, but marriage?! I don't plan to marry again if I'm alone. A husband is a *social* convenience—people would rather ask the two of you than the one of you, and it's hard to break them of the habit. But never mind social convenience, he can be a living *inconvenience,* your life bounded and proscribed by him. My friend Monica says some of her happiest moments are when Clyde goes off to the Bahamas where they own two hotels. "I know I *have* a husband, he loves me and I love him and it's very comforting—but when he's not here I'm different. . . . I don't know what it is exactly . . . I don't get into trouble but I'm *free* . . . I'm *me* . . . I just do stuff I really like." If there were lots of princes to choose from, *maybe* . . . grab a prince . . . but with the chances of doing that rather slim, what's wrong with single?

Think of it this way: If you marry somebody younger, would you want to support him? If he's older, do you want to be a nurse? Of course, an older single woman should have men in her *life,* not just for companionship—your most enjoyable times are probably with your own sex—

but to remind you you *are* a different sex from men and life is more interesting comprised of opposites. Don't think this is sexist but men also bring more stimulating conversation from jobs they hold or held. They are *semi*necessary for sex (there's always masturbation). If *I* were alone and *sexually* needy and no single man was available (likely), I would borrow a husband—preferably of a wife I didn't know—just as I did when I was single and younger.

7. Okay, married—if you are older—you *can* get if you insist. You have to bring something to him he hasn't already got, or got *enough* of. *Fun* could be the thing. They say Fort Worth billionaire Sid Bass married Mercedes Kellogg, late forties, because she was really *serious* fun and allowed him a swinging life-style he didn't have with his first wife. Outstanding ability to take care of his creature needs (repairing the house, *running* the house, laundry, meals ... in other words you're a servant ... ugh!) might do it. (If you have household help, then you're the *executive* housekeeper ... ugh again!) Some men like a little stardust in their lives, so add fame to the list of negotiable assets. We *can't* say you'll enhance the lives of his children and grandchildren because mostly they're dead set against the marriage (as endangering their inheritance).

I've left the most important reason for him to marry you to last: money. Wealthy women can usually buy not-wealthy husbands just as men buy "poorer" wives and that's okay. Supporting a husband gives you power over the man, and a lot of my friends do it, even without *lots* of money, but I know *I* wouldn't care for it. Anyway, I'm just mentioning some outstanding reasons a man might marry us at our age with so many others out there to choose form. Hope you don't think I'm being too analytical. There's *love* of course.

8. Even if you should acquire one, you have to note that extremely wealthy men are frequently not wonderful to their wives even if the wives are smart and attractive. The men are simply spoiled with all that attention—profiled in *Fortune, Forbes, Business Week,* mobbed at

parties by admiring males, fawned over by women. Of all the attributes for a wealthy wife to have in order to be retained, Good in Bed is probably the most important. I have said a million times that if you are the one who has cuntpower for him, you can pretty much count on his loyalty and a lot of his worldly goods. Some sexually besotted wealthy men go banana-village over a girl. Shah Jahan built the Taj Mahal for his beloved Mumtaz; press lord William Randolph Hearst created a whole fairy-tale Bavarian town in the Northern California redwoods for his inamorata, Marion Davies. But, alas, Good in Bed, as recognized by *him* at least, as we've already mentioned, is more likely to be the talent of a second (or third) wife or a girlfriend.

Some wealthy men stay married because of religious convictions, some because they are dynasty-minded (twelve generations of Kottswilligers!), some out of laziness: It is a giantburger chore to divorce and start up again. Probably most often of all, they stay because getting out would be prohibitively expensive (split up a billion dollars?! Give *her* the beach house and the Chagalls?!). Okay, a few darlings don't want a different wife. Good for them! When I mentioned to my real-estate mogul friend, Alice Mason, that a wealthy couple we know were extremely loyal to each other, Alice said married people being loyal simply means they are *stuck* with each other. Alice!

Summing up, about the only way to *marry* a really wealthy older man is to be much younger than he and pretty. Trying to marry a wealthy older man when you are his age is like expecting eyelashes to grow in bushy when they were never anything but skimpy little wisps in the first place. The columnist Aileen Mehle, who knows a lot of rich older men, says you have to have a strong stomach to be married to one anyway. Okay, remembering that should mitigate any disappointment you might encounter in your search.

Random further thoughts about marriage:
1. Surely nobody old or young could seriously want

to be married to an actor—even to Tony Randall who was adorable to his wife of forty years or Paul Newman who is even *faithful—now!* You starve while they are making it and after they do, you have to hang on by your fingernails to keep from being traded in (true of *any* man who becomes famous or rich later). There is that ego business—*his* profile, *his* voice, *his* wardrobe, *his* next role. The wife of a megastar told me that trying to be warm and tender with her husband was like trying to cuddle up to a store mannequin. Most actors don't work at *all,* you know, and during all that unemployment they have to try to continue to like themselves (requiring dedication just this side of mad King Ludwig of Bavaria building all those castles as playpens for Richard Wagner). I suppose one should have *some* compassion since we all need actors to enhance our lives, but I'd just as soon let somebody else *marry* them.

2. Who could love a politician mate except a saint or a masochist? The world revolves around *him.* You have to present an image not any racier than Florence Nightingale's with nothing in your past more alarming than having skinny-dipped in Lake Wachahatchka when you were thirteen. You must raise money, campaign to get him elected (then *re*elected), then never see him. You almost never get well known except as a helpmeet. How many politicians' wives do *you* know who ever shone as brightly as their mates except maybe Eleanor Roosevelt, Elizabeth Dole and Jackie Kennedy, two of whom did it after their husbands *died?*

3. There should be—ideally—one oral and one anal partner in marriage. If both are one persuasion, not good. Two free spenders often blow security—wind up floating loans. Two cheapies will give friends endless opportunity for derision. We have two well-off friends who never—NEVER!—pick up a check. When he was a famous Hollywood director, he got used to having *everything*—furniture, cars, servants—*paid* for and just hasn't got the hang of buying anybody a simple lunch or dinner. David and I—this "ideal" couple—represent one oral and one anal. When we flew to Shawnee, Oklahoma, to visit my sister last Thanksgiving, David flew first class ("Don't give *me*

'It's only a three-hour trip'—I'm going the way I always go"). I am in economy. He *could* have come back and visited me (he didn't). I wasn't allowed in first class. Well, I don't see why anybody should sell *out*.

4. Couples who have been married for a long time develop little stories they tell on social occasions. Listening, you know this isn't the first time Evalina has described "the night Patty and I got locked in the ladies' room of the country club and had to crawl out through the window" or her husband has detailed shooing twelve mallard ducks out of the swimming pool, but you don't mind these little planned performances. *My* standby story is about sneaking on board a TWA flight to Los Angeles when they had given David's and my seats away and *no* seats at all were available and refusing to be removed from the arm of our *assigned* seats until they found some more space on the plane for the people who were now sitting in them. (Throughout my occupation David cowered outside at the ticket counter—somebody told him there was a crazy lady on board causing a Big Ruckus.)

David's favorite story is about losing his passport two hours before flight time, trekking all over Paris to find it, with Darryl Zanuck insisting he'd left it at Madame Claude's (famous brothel) the night before where David said he hadn't *been* and finally finding it at Le Drug Store. Dr. William Cahan, cancer surgeon nonpareil at Sloane-Kettering, likes to talk about his wife, Grace Mirabella, then editor of *Vogue*, taking him to the Paris openings where *she* sat in the front row, while *he* had a seat farther back marked Mr. Mirabella. He also says that if doctors have a chair in their name at the hospitals, psychiatrists should have a *couch* in their name. Sweet. (You *know* it isn't the first time *he* has made that observation, but I'm happy for him to get the good out of it.) David and I frequently recall our day with Jean Paul Getty at Sutton Place—just him, us and the attack dogs—or how when I was out promoting *Sex and the Single Girl*, Khrushchev was sending tankers around the coast of Florida and I got preempted on every one of my scheduled television shows. I sometimes wish David would lay off our private meeting with Ferdinand Marcos at Malacañang Palace; I never felt it played particularly well at the time and it's playing less well every minute.

Younger married people have stories, too, of course, as do singles, but usually smart young single women shut *up*. Nobody can stand burble burble burble me-at-the-mad-center-of-it-all from youngish women who haven't had enough raconteur experience to do it well. A husband can sometimes cut short a wife's too-long story by five or ten minutes ("Let's get *on* with it, Pauline"). Mostly *she* can't do the same thing, however, as he drones into the ninth inning.

5. Older married couples are honor bound, I feel, to look as though they are having a good time when out on a date in a restaurant even if they are just discussing whether to have the Doberman spayed or the patio bricked in. You know how single women are kind of shiny and animated in a restaurant.... I feel it's something for *us* to shoot for. Letting him explain one more time why he thinks the NFL ought to change the rules for trading players will usually perk him up as will news that a good friend is having job or money problems. One reason (about twentieth on the list) for a woman to have a job, I've always felt, is so she'll have stuff to talk about with her husband at dinner. If things are getting sludgy (he's beginning to gaze at the salt or a blonde), I ask David to tell me once more about his experience during World War II at Officers' Candidate School when he had negotiated all the tests and felt he had high marks, then was leading his men back to camp on the last day of training and discharged them at the wrong barracks. He could see the officer writing, "Doesn't even know where his men are *quartered!*" David remained an enlisted man until he was finally commissioned a first lieutenant without going through OCS but that story always makes him chuckle.

6. Faults of older married men are not only innumerable but almost unendurable to a wife, yet, by some miracle, never seem to quite outdistance the man's goodness. (Have we grown numb? Terrified of being alone?) Charlotte Salisbury, married to Pulitzer Prize–winning

journalist/author Harrison Salisbury, says, "Harrison is passionate about the *Chinese*—wants to track every step of Chinese Communism. The other day we were having a little family lunch for just eight people, somebody drove up and four Chinese dissidents got out of the car—they'd been at Tiananmen Square. I took one look and said, 'Harrison, I'm going up to my bedroom and you can call me when this is over.' " (She adores him.)

Wives have faults, too, of course. My publisher friend, the late Steve Birnbaum, said that when his wife, Alex, turned on the stove, he used to check to see which of two things she was doing: putting her head in the oven or drying pantyhose. . . . "She certainly wasn't *cooking!*" I know a wife who has effectively separated her wealthy mate from *two* sets of children by earlier wives—they're *out!*—as she spins her web and nails down the inheritance. But I want to deal only with *their* faults right this minute.

May I tell you about those of *my* beloved? He is a packrat of the rattiest type. He will not throw out a place card from somebody's nice dinner, a newspaper clipping thirty-five years old, program notes from a charity event in which he is listed along with 275 other cochairmen, almost *any* greeting card ever received. David seems to think of this collection as Living Things, deserving nurture and respect. He's a loser—keys, glasses, glasses' case, comb, tickets, Amex receipts, tie clip, you name it, he's lost it—usually just as we are leaving the apartment. I flatten myself against the wall, hoping not to get maimed as he searches, flailing about like a propeller cut loose from a helicopter. Driving to the country, David takes his foot off the gas pedal and puts it back on dozens of times. "Just a habit," he sheepishly explains as I am grossing *out* on nerves. A famous Hollywood producer, handsome but no longer young, said while driving with David one night, after about the twelfth foot-off-the-gas-pedal, back-on-again time, "David, you drive like I *fuck!*"

David says having jewelry is just asking to get robbed or killed, so I buy my own—with his money. He then pleads with me not to wear it! Good luggage also gets you robbed, he avers. "Vuitton is just *asking* for it!" I get the impression he would like me to carry my clothes for a trip in shopping bags or cardboard boxes. No understated travel decorum for my beloved, however. His tipping is obscene. "Take no change" (keep the five, the ten, the twenty) is his motto at airports. Porters stampede to get to him, happily fishing him out of his limousine—"Let *me* get that, Mr. Brown"—as other people and their luggage are abandoned at the curb. David's tipping in restaurants is ... how shall I put this? ... in questionable taste. (How else I could put it is that it's *vulgar,* not to mention budget-blasting.) When I entertain people at a business dinner, David likes to pay the check but will, if I insist, get me a receipt for my expense account. Big help! What company in the world is going to reimburse a $400 bill that breaks down as $235 for dinner, $165 for tips?

If punctuality is the courtesy of kings, we are royal. We not only get the hostess out of the shower, she hasn't decided what to *wear* and is forced to jump into something she possibly hates because she has *us* on her hands. To David, 7:30 means roughly 7:15—"Don't want them worrying whether we're going to show." Six-to-eight cocktails should have you at the door by 6:10. Getting David *out* of a party is roughly the challenge of extricating a dinosaur from the La Brea Tar Pits. A longtime aide of Senator Lloyd Bentsen of Texas says the senator likes to pick his wife up, throw her over his shoulder and walk out. Would I could get David over my shoulder.

When we receive plants or flowers, they must be taken immediately to the second floor and placed beside the glass door to the terrace "so they can get plenty of light and sunshine." I have explained for the two-hundredth time the sun doesn't do *cut* flowers any *good,* but he still feels they are happier in the sun. The only way you can enjoy a bouquet somebody sent you is go up there for a little visit.

David applies the Albert Schweitzer philosophy about animals *(none* should be snuffed our by *us)* to plants. On the tiny terrace outside our kitchen, weeds grow majestically and are left to do that for long stretches because burglar-preventing bars on the kitchen window keep anybody from climbing out to kill them. Also David thinks they are *pretty*. About once a year he grudgingly takes two bars off the window, leaving just enough space for me to squeeze out to the terrace with my weed-eradicating equipment: bare hands and paper sack. How such strong weeds can grow in such tiny little dabs of soil twenty-two stories above the street nobody knows. It isn't even "soil"—just sand mixed into the cement that holds red tiles together. Anyway, on a recent "squeeze-out," I pulled and cursed for an hour, this time managing to take some of the tiles along with the weeds because weed roots were deeply imbedded *under* tiles. One month later, weeds right back in place—healthy, green, happy. "I can't keep doing this," I moan. "Next time I'm using weed killer!" "You are *not*," says my mate. (Pulling apparently is *humane;* chemical killing is genocide.) "You just don't like them because they aren't *designer* weeds." (Weeds at this writing doing fine, wife cursing.)

Politeness is an issue in our marriage, not with each other but outside. I think David's attitude is *unreal,* not to mention irrational. Having been brought up in the South by a diffident and polite mother, not being nice, no matter what's going on *inside,* I usually wouldn't consider (unless it's a taxi, airport or bus situation like those described). Nevertheless, David thinks my manners are somewhere between gutter and late Cro-Magnon. The subject comes up most frequently when I have said something a tiny bit—just a tiny bit, mind you—cross to one of our apartment-building employees in time of stress.

Last Friday, for example, the stuff I send home from the office for the weekend—clothes, manuscripts, memos, books—maybe four canvas totes and a garment bag—doesn't arrive. I ask Raoul, the doorman, if he's seen them. They didn't come in, he says. Are you sure? I ask. He's sure. I spend most of Saturday on the telephone with the four *Cosmo* people who had something to do with dispatching the messenger, plus the office-building folks who take over after my ladies relinquish the bags plus the owner of the messenger service who has given up his golf game to come into the city from Brooklyn to search. No luck. Sunday afternoon the bags are delivered to my door. What happened? Raoul forgot he'd left his post for five minutes Friday evening to go to the john, the relief man took bags in and, not knowing tenants too well, mistakenly sent them up to a man on the twentieth floor where they languished for two days until tenant came home and found them. I had *asked* Raoul Friday night if somebody else *could* have taken in the bags instead of him. "No, Ms. Brown," he said. "I was here all the time." So I had a tiny—only tiny, mind you—fit as I explained to Raoul what an aggravation this temporary loss had been to me and a lot of other people. David said it wasn't a tiny fit at all but a *hissy* and insisted I go back downstairs and apologize to Raoul. Apology graciously accepted . . . I even got a warm smile. I think people can maybe get *too* polite.

So let's continue one more minute with husband (my husband) faults—I'm on a roll. My darling's depressions, usually short-lived, thank God, are cataclysmic. They roll through the apartment like bolts of soggy gray flannel, enveloping everything in sight including the furniture, certainly including *me*. Not infrequently David's blues have something to do with work. The movie industry, he tells me, is frustrating, occasionally agonizing; I have been hearing this frustration and agony (never mind the industry has rewarded him *well)* for thirty-one years, minus two spent in the publishing business, which, while not *as* irritating, was not ten on a scale of ten either.

Finally, when his pain has caused *me* such pain I can't stand it any longer (smoothing his brow, supper on a tray, rubbing his feet get you nowhere), I tell him *I'm* ready to jump. Then I'm in for the summer-soldier, sunshine-patriot, good-only-for-the-good-times lecture. "Can't I ever tell you bad news?" he asks. "What am I supposed to do . . . pretend to be happy, wear a vacant smile just so *you* won't be inconvenienced?" You know, I honestly can't answer that except there is something so pervasive about David's gloom that expecting to stay objective would be like asking an egg to stay separate after it is dropped into a bowl of pancake batter.

Nobody but me ever *knows* David is depressed . . . he

is upbeat, charming, smooth as satin at dinner parties no matter *what's* going on in his head. I sometimes think of the man who emotionally batters his wife while other people see only the bon vivant. Well, one day David's gloom goes away (though there have been times when it's lasted a few months ... brrr!). You tentatively crawl out from under your flannel tarpaulin and take a chance on smiling again though you feel a bit hammered out like a chicken breast for paillard or a dismantled clock. I *know* people can't help depressions ... I've *been* there ... but it's funny to have someone else's affect you worse than your own. Psychiatrists Mildred Newman and Bernard Berkowitz say, "In marriage, or any partnership (1) Don't expect to be sane all the time. (2) Don't expect your partner to be sane all the time. (3) But only one of you can be crazy at a time!" Marriage!

So, may I stop complaining and tell you how I met and married this complex paragon I adore? It wasn't love at first sight for *me*. It was love *before* first sight. I had fallen in love with his credentials: forty-two, brainy (people said he was brilliant), glamorous movie executive, good-looking, terrifically charming. I never felt I could afford to marry just a nice ordinary man I might have to help support along with my family—I needed a *prince*. When we met (this was in Los Angeles), David turned out to *be* princely, thank God, and physically attractive. Having him a turn-off would have screwed up everything.

I met David through my friend Ruth Schandorff, who worked with David's wife and often talked about David during the two years she and I took Saturday morning walks in Griffith Park. When she reported he'd officially come on the market—divorced—I asked to be introduced. Not yet, Ruth said ... he has to get through his starlet phase. I waited a *year* and, finally, after a few episodes reported faithfully by Ruth—with the mother of his twenty-two-year-old girlfriend trying to seduce him and his having to squirm out of buying lynx and sapphires for other ladies who expected them because of being Famous Actresses—Ruth thought he was ready for "a nice sensible girl like you." Hah! She had us both for dinner: arugula salad, baked ham, candied sweet potatoes, French-cut green beans, homemade cinnamon rolls, pineapple sherbet—it was her *cooking* that *got* him!

The man was certainly not rendered giddy by his blind date—you can tell—but I got the impression he was quite taken with my having just paid cash for a Mercedes-Benz 190 SL sports car, now parked at the curb. I still don't know how I had the courage to *do* that—clean out my bank account—so uncharacteristic of anal little me. Perhaps some primal instinct told me I was going to meet a man on whom all cash would make a big impression. Anyway, as he walked me to the car and put me in it, love wasn't gleaming in his eye but respect, I think, *was*. In those days not too many working girls bought expensive sports cars. Relief was there also. If he got involved with this one, she might not be a financial burden. Was there a touch of resignation in his soul also? Perhaps. The wife who had *left* was a "driven career woman" and here, God rest us, was possibly another . . . couldn't he ever get it right?

During the year and a half we dated, I sometimes felt I was dealing with a dolphin—friendly and lovable one minute, swimming out to sea the next. After the night I glimpsed him in his Chrysler 300 with a blonde smashed up against him—we had both pulled up to the same stoplight, me coming from group therapy, for God's sake!—I said I didn't feel smashed-up blondes were appropriate at this stage of our friendship and he quit seeing any of them—so far as I know—but he was miles from marriage. "Why can't we go on like *this?*" he would plead, the subject of marriage always introduced by *me*. "We're happy together; I'm faithful. I've lost twice in marriage; why would you even want to take a *chance?*" "Because it's *time,*" I would say. It wasn't time for *him,* he would explain and, at the end of one year, I delivered the ultimatum—marriage or nothing. He chose nothing. I left. He thought I would be back. I knew I wouldn't.

It *is* the way to get married (to a holdout). You have to say marriage or nothing and mean it. If you go back to him figuring you'll give it one more shot, just a little more time, he *knows* he doesn't have to marry you and *won't!* A holdout may *not* cave in. David did. After three cavings in (he would agree, then refuse to set a date, and I'd have to do it all over again . . . very tedious!), we finally got married by a judge at the Beverly Hills City Hall with his assistant Pamela Hedley, Ruth Schandorff, who had introduced us, and his son as our only witnesses. I hadn't had the pleasure of telling anyone about my approaching nuptials because the man might back out again—who knew whether there'd ever really *be* a ceremony?

All this is to say that some marriages that start out quietly with only hope, affection and attraction to go on grow to be solid, wonderful and passionate. In the thirty-three years I've been married to David, divorce has never entered my mind for more than five seconds. Though I could sometimes kill him, I would never divorce. I certainly couldn't find another David.

Let's talk about sex. Marriage is the bran muffin of sex, you might say: good for you but you can't get too excited about it. Being legally in the clear is *antithetical* to sexual bliss. There has to be a little fear, a little danger, a little risk and a little new—a *lot* of new is best—for sex to be what sex can be, I think. Marilyn Monroe once said, "Husbands are chiefly good lovers when they are betraying their wives." There is no way eight or ten or twenty years in to feel tapioca-headed, nervous as a chipmunk and sick to your stomach with desire as you did in the rapturous beginning of a love affair.

So how are you supposed to stay faithful and never feel that rapture again, like which there is nothing in the world, especially if you marry young? Beats me. Even if you don't stray, everybody *looks* at an attractive other person and thinks "What *if?*" Magazine articles say you can rekindle the flame. Check into a motel with your beloved without any luggage or kids. (Naturally you wouldn't check in with *your* kids—*they're* thirty-five and forty respectively.) Meet your husband at the door in lacy teddies and with a pitcher of margaritas. Read *The Joy of Sex* together. Rent *Debbie Does Dallas*. Listen, dirty movies are surely more of a turn-on than piling everybody into the pickup and heading for Disney World, and being greeted by your wife in Fernando Sanchez satin tap pants beats being greeted by her in her jogging costume, but this stuff is for people who haven't been married forever. My husband prefers me to greet him at the door in something that looks as though you are going to *cook* in it and, being as prissy as I am about booze, I'd have to use the margaritas to pour *over* him because he would have fainted on seeing the pitcher.

Guy de Rothschild said in his memoir, *The Whims of Fortune,* "When the fire dies down, the gleam of flames no longer illuminates but the embers remain alive and provide even greater warmth." Fine—if you go in for embers. Married people *do* still make love, of course, and enjoy it a lot even if they're not floating in a sea of gardenias and Dom Pérignon, but we're talking about the absence of white heat here. In upper-class European marriages both parties, wanting more than embers (i.e., everyday sex), cheat, with tacit permission, and the marriage endures. In many American marriages, both parties (especially him) cheat, with or without permission, and everybody lies and pretends it isn't happening. Some people cheat and marry the new love.

I do think having your man involved with another woman physically makes you feel about as bad as you can feel and you *always* know unless you have been living in a little hut in the Serengeti Valley or have no girlfriends—always good at reporting infidelity. Probably it's idiotic to feel such devastation. Of *course* he still loves you. And of *course* this is just a "thing," and the act of sex per se—two bodies squashing together—has not much more significance than the crushing of grapes for Chablis but you can't be *sure* it's just grape crushing—he might feel something for her in the head and probably *does*. I don't think I know anybody who doesn't go a little crazy with pain when confronted with infidelity ... if she still *cares* for her mate. I never used to be able to stand it when I was single and I don't think I could stand it *now*. Having married at thirty-seven I got a lot of the play—about twenty years of play—out of my system so I feel no deprivation at being faithful all these years, but obviously everybody can't or wouldn't want to marry late to "beat the system." I really don't know what system is best: marriage with fidelity (no new little red Ferrari of sexual thrills at the curb of life ever again), marriage and cheating (people get hurt), marriage and cheating and marry the new person (the left-behind person *still* gets hurt). Sometimes I think *no* system is best, no matter what age you are.

Okay, shall we progress to sex, possibly *without* a husband, or with somebody else's?

chapter three

Sex

How much sex should we have at our age?

None, if you don't want it, I guess, and lots of women *don't,* but if you masturbate, that means your *body* feels desire so whom are we kidding? I've always thought when you stop having sex is when you are officially old; your last sexual act is the official cutoff date of young. No, old isn't a disgrace (I think I've convinced myself of that) and having sex doesn't make you seventeen, but I'm afraid I think there's a chasm between people who do and people who don't still do it as wide as Sunset Boulevard. Having somebody make love to you keeps you one of the girls. We've already lost *some* validation of femaleness. We don't menstruate. We don't have babies. If you are still sleeping with somebody even occasionally, you can say to yourself, never mind this thinks-he's-Julio-Iglesias creep I am talking to at this party who is responding to me with all the warmth a twelve-year-old boy reserves for his math teacher, *somebody* (husband, lover, tax accountant, *somebody)* still likes me in bed! Maybe you think validation of womanliness is not necessary . . . you're happy to let it go bye-bye. ("Thank God I don't have to bother with *that* anymore!") Germaine Greer said in a book proposal I sneaked a look at that her desire was "to reassure women that they do not have a duty of sexual attraction but a duty of living with dignity and grace." Fine. That possibly sounds better than what I propose—that you gamely (grimly?) hang in there and have sex, even if you aren't aflame with desire!

"Sex is one of the easiest things to contain," says my psychiatrist friend Janet Kennedy. "Priests, nuns, even civilian men and women remain virgins all their lives without apparent physiological harm—emotional is something else. We can't survive starvation or inadequate shelter from hostile elements but the *sex* drive is *not* necessary for the survival of the individual." A sexually *participating* woman may go for longish periods (years?) without sex when she is between men. No, we don't hunger or thirst for sex the way we do food and water, so I could be wrong, very wrong, to push sex for older ladies. I just think being the opposite of another sex is still one of life's more interesting conditions. Unisex sucks. I feel the actual *act* of sex—and I'm not talking orgasm here ... orgasm is easier by masturbating ... but sex with a man somehow removes you from being a prim, stuffy, puffy, correct, respected, respectable, *finished* old person! You're still womanly.

So how much sex are older women actually *having?* My gynecologist, a darling Park Avenue practitioner with sophisticated clientele, says, *"All* my sixty-five to eighty-year-old patients are having some sex and would like *more."* That's what I've found among my friends and a lot of women I talked to: participating but not as much as they'd like. "Sometimes I feel the real me is a beautiful big animal," says my friend Ginny. "Probably a leopard—living in rooms above our living quarters. At night he prowls back and forth, back and forth, stalking remembered prey, bumping against walls, rubbing against furniture and sometimes he howls, asking himself, 'What am I *doing* here? They feed me and fill my water pan but I belong in the *jungle!'* "

Yet sex is on the increase for older woman. Clinical psychologist Ethel Person says, "Women are increasingly allowing themselves to *be* sexual at a later age. For such a long time the thinking was that women were finished after menopause and we went along with that foolishness to the point of virtually *becoming* nonsexual. That is beginning to change. Women are letting themselves out of the closet so to speak ... being more flirtatious, more open to sex." *Cosmo*'s former beauty director Mallen de Santis declares, "There aren't many women left anymore who close their eyes and think of England or mentally rearrange the spice rack during The Act . . . most women in their sixties these days really *want* sex." Dr. Person tells me of an eighty-year-old client who recently flew to Los Angeles "to have sex with her boyfriend." Isn't that encouraging? My friend Claudia, a busy decorator with frequent assignments in Europe, is often joined by her doctor-lover. Claudia is sixty-seven. Another pal in her mid-sixties is sent off to the opera, ballet, philharmonic by a husband who "doesn't like that bullshit" and says, "Why don't you take Clarence?" She takes Clarence and they have a sexual rendezvous at his flat before he takes her home. They tell Claudia's mate they were at dinner. One of my friend's *mothers* has begun an affair at sixty-six with a car salesman. "She brings him culture, he brings her rapture," says Yvonne. God *knows* Elizabeth Taylor is still having at it (and always *will* from what she told me in an interview a couple of years ago). My darling friend Gloria Vanderbilt is *never* without a lover. We hear there is sex all over retirement homes as widows and widowers discover the fascination of a body different from the body they knew so long and have the leisure and freedom from stress to explore , . . hooray for Hollywood!

To document this sex activity a bit further, Helen Singer Kaplan, director of the Human Sexuality Program at New York Hospital-Cornell Medical Center, says, "There is a widely held belief in our society, shared by the general public and health professionals alike, that sex is among the first biological functions to fall prey to the aging process. But this is a myth. Sexuality is actually among the last of our faculties to decline with maturity. In all the scientific studies of sexual behavior of American men and women between the ages of fifty and one hundred in the past forty years, investigators found without exception that providing they are in good health, the great majority of people remain sexually functional and active on a regular basis until virtually the end of life. Or, to put it more succinctly, 70 percent of healthy seventy-year-olds remain sexually active, and are having sex at least once a week." Let's hear it for Dr. Kaplan's *research!* In the slightly *younger* category, owner-manager Russell Reed Reeves of the famous Chicken Ranch brothel in Pahrump, Nevada, says, "My oldest lady is forty-four and she is the most popular."

How much of that sex is going on in *marriage?* Some couples are still active. My friend Clarissa says, "We've got more time and money to be romantic now. The sex is just fine." When I chatted with Clarissa, she and George were on their way on a slow boat to Honolulu to celebrate their fiftieth—*fiftieth!*—wedding anniversary. Another near-seventy friend swears she and Wilkie "are still doing it twice a week!" (I think she may be counting hugs and fanny-swats as sex acts but are we going to demand a polygraph?) Letty Cottin Pogrebin, one of the founders of *Ms.,* says she and her labor-attorney husband have a marvelously satisfying sex life after twenty-five years of marriage (though Letty is only fifty).

Other marrieds are not so active. Caroline (I've changed *some* names but real people belong to all these stories) says, "For twenty years sex *cemented* our marriage. We both married for a second time at forty but in the last two years sex has been so pallid—about one ninetieth of what we used to have—we just quietly stopped." "We were always horizontal," says Peggy, "boats, beds, hammocks, floors, but now we go to bed to sleep and you can forget those magazine articles that tell how to get it back if you've lost it. When sex goes dead in a marriage, it doesn't come back." Well, sex surely doesn't go dead in every marriage. My *very* unofficial estimate: About 60 percent of long-married couples have *some* sex with each other, 40 percent don't. (I don't know which camp twice a year falls into!) Marital sex stops because of boredom, too many fights, too many problems, children who turn out badly and, for God's sake, if he is in his *seventies,* he is not that virile.

Poor darlings. Mother Nature started diminishing *their* sexual prowess from about age sixteen. If we can *nab* somebody, we can *do* it. Vaginas can be lubricated with Vaseline, Astro-Glide, K-Y jelly or Premarin cream (please read labels carefully) and we can stroke and blow penises with a lifetime of learned skill—so if your desire has slackened, who *knows?* The older man has more of a challenge. His penis is only semi-hard; it cannot thrust. (Do you suppose it's like trying to slide a slightly-filled-with-water rubber glove under a closed door?) We will probably never *know* the sense of loss in a man whose penis is no longer able to stay hard and thrust and what do I mean *probably?!* Fortunately, gorgeous, show-offy thrusting isn't required for us to have a pleasurable sex life with a man but what *is* required is *him,* a man.

If an older woman doesn't have a husband, or possibly if she *does* but sex doesn't exist in the marriage and she still *wants* it, she has to go looking; sex mostly doesn't come looking for *her.* Says a realist friend, "Between fifty and sixty, sex is out there; if you want it, you can connect. After sixty, you have to supply the sled, the snow and the dog team."

I'm going to say something you may hate but my research tells me vast numbers of wives have affairs *whatever* they have to do to have them. In certain circles almost as many women as men indulge if they have the opportunity and I think 90 percent of men cheat at some time in their lives. Wives cheat, I think, not because they are unhappy in marriage—the standard reason given for female infidelity—but because these women simply like *sex* ... the act ... the accompanying play, fun and glamour. Sex is thrilling for them but what's offered at home just isn't scintillating anymore, as we said, so they reach *out.* Enjoying sex with someone not your husband is *no* reason to divorce, of course ... what a dopey idea!

Everyone who *could* participate sexually *doesn't,* of course. Someone recently came on to Jennifer, who reported, "My spirits lifted, my body said yes, but my brain said no. I'd had several affairs during marriage ... I'm still married. One lasted several years, but the lies, the complications ... I just felt I couldn't rev up and go through it again. No, sex is not going to get wonderful with Harvey [her husband] again. It takes somebody new to light sexual fires, but I'm going for the tranquillity."

Annabel, widowed in her fifties, says she "wouldn't even entertain the idea of sex for sex's sake. Friends of Phil's and *my* friends' husbands suggested in the beginning they would be willing—actually *pleased*—to take care of— well, you know—'certain things I must miss.' I knew exactly what they were talking about but it would be unthinkable for me to separate sex and love. I had a long, good marriage. I'm Catholic. I would wait *forever* for somebody to love again but I'd never settle for just casual sex!"

So why try to locate a man if it's so much trouble and you aren't *certain* you want one? One more round with my rationale: Sex is good for you. Physiologically it keeps your vagina from closing down (am I getting vulgar?). Psychologically it keeps you joined to the young ... a functioning female instead of a sexless old woman. Older men get neutered, *too*, of course, and I don't want any part of *them*, at least not *that* part (now I *know* I'm getting vulgar). The actual act of sex causes your body to be *used* (in a good way), renewed, regenerated, if not actually reignited (you may not have an orgasm). Welcoming a penis just seems more womanly to me than baking chocolate-chip cookies or doling out money for a grandchild's college tuition. Those things are admirable but cookies are the boonies; sex is New York City! You are to be very *proud* of yourself if you enjoy sex.

But don't most women, particularly older women, want love, companionship, intimacy much more than sex? Certainly. And if there's a man in your life at *all*, an older woman is more apt to *have* love, companionship, intimacy than sex! Some of us, once past puppyhood, have finally got it through our heads that a man frequently has other things on his mind than sex and that sex, after *his* puppyhood, is pretty heavy-duty stuff (huff-puff). He can't indulge sexually now like a guppy going for the food flake in the aquarium; he has to ration, and if he is sexually driven at *all*, he may want a younger woman (more in a minute). Yet you can have *love*, companionship, intimacy from a man, if you've got one, and from family, married friends, work friends, even platonic men friends if you don't. Nobody more caring in the world was ever invented than darling women pals.

Oh, I know *romance* is what you really want. Well, I'm going to let other (brave) people tell you how to get romance into your life. There aren't enough men to go around and the ones there are are spoiled senseless, so good luck! Romance is always more prevalent among the young anyway. Remember, Juliet Capulet, Scarlett O'Hara, Cathy of Wuthering Heights were in their teens when Heathcliff-hangingly (!) in love. And don't give me the Duke and Duchess of Windsor. The Prince of Wales fell in love with Wallis Simpson *after* she taught him about sex (he couldn't really *do* it before her, according to biographer Charles Higham). Anyway, that case was very kinky and special *and* both were forty, not sixty. If you've got a lover or a husband with whom sex is happening, I'm also not going to say how to try to make things better in bed with him ... you've heard it all before, some of it from *me* (we never let up on you!). I don't think I have a single new thing to say about rekindling the flame. But if you don't have a sex partner (you're married and sex has petered out, if you'll pardon the expression, or you're single with no man in your life), then I'm going to strongly *suggest* you not leave it at that, but that you try to have sex at least occasionally. The suggestions that follow are gleaned from sexually participating females who had to go out and *find* it, or at least encourage it; the sex did not arrive by Federal Express. But shouldn't the romance come first and *then* the sex? Ideally, yes, but romance is a pretty big-deal proposition; waiting for *it,* sex could *die.* The charms that get you sex may *also* get you the romance you crave so badly. It's *possible* and lots of good luck.

Okay, you've got a million excuses *not* to look for sex. The famous man-shortage, of course, but that shortage is more of men to be our steady beaux and marry us. ... We're talking sex here ... a challenge, to be sure, but he doesn't have to be your permanent mate, so statistics can be dispensed with for a minute. Okay, the very idea of *looking* for a man for sex is repugnant. You cannot believe that *you,* who once fought them off with fingernails, screams, hisses, elbows, insults, pleas of exhaustion, illness, insanity, virginity and "how *could* you think of me that way?!," could now be living in a world in which no man *ever* makes a pass at you! Of course, we didn't do all that fighting-them-off because we were Ava Gardner lookalikes—at least I wasn't and didn't. At that time, any breathing female was a prize. For so long "nice girls *didn't*" that men were needy all the time, and even after "nice girls *did*," we had only to decide on whom to bestow the treasure. We weren't always asked to *marry* any more than girls are now, but you would be asked to *bed* as surely as Franklin Roosevelt kept getting reelected and God made little green zucchini. "I don't know at what moment I stopped being insulted because somebody tried to get into my panties and began to be insulted because nobody tried but I sure switched aggravations in there somewhere!" says Mattie.

So now we come to the hard stuff: You are good and pissed because men don't *want* you. Still, being practical, you just *might* be willing to head on out to try to find a man except—here comes the big whammo except—*you* may have stopped wanting *them!* "My sex drive is so faint these days," says Caroline, "it's like a tiny vessel you sight off the deck of the *QE2* in the Indian Ocean and you put your hand up to your eyes and say, 'Sex, is that you out there, old friend? I can just barely make you out!' " A sex drive uncalled on does tend to get fainter. So, far from experiencing pulsating, pelvis-sweeping desire like you felt at nineteen, the thought of piling under a man to make love may hold all the appeal of being thrown into a garbage scow with your hands tied behind you. "I look at those hunks on television and imagine them kissing my breasts," says Ellen, "and think, oh, please, God, no, not all that nibbling!"

So the truth is that even if you were seriously propositioned by an okay person, you might rationalize your lack of enthusiasm this way: You haven't worn your good underwear. It's late and you need to get home to pack because you're going to Nassau in the morning. And the biggie: How can you possibly undress in front of a man who's never seen you naked . . . that cellulite, those folds, those pooches! First, you should *always* wear your good underwear on a date just in case. Second, you can pack at two instead of twelve and sleep on the plane. *At* the assignation you can wear *something* up to the last minute before getting into bed; turn off the lights if that makes you less nervous, and *back* out of the room when it's over if you think your front is better than your back. If you've been exercising like a good girl, your body will probably look okay—not sixteen but maybe forty, and you surely will be *limber.* Your vagina is something else. Because it's out of practice being thrust into, entry is not so glidingly easy for the enterer *or* for you but I have instructions in a minute.

Back to the biggest negative of all, however; forget underwear, packing and cellulite . . . it's the "I don't know, I'm just not in the mood!" syndrome. "Forget 'in the mood,' " says Ginny. "At sixty or sixty-five you probably won't be in the mood until it's over . . . *then* you'll feel *wonderful!"* You have to keep reciting to yourself, I am a sexual person. I want sex in my life. I deserve this (perfectly normal) activity. I refuse to be brainwashed out of it by myself or anybody else and the biggie: I do not have to be madly in love or even *in* love to have a sexual affair, so here goes!

I'll get arrested and shipped off to prison (at least attacked on *Donahue)* if I suggest big doses of estrogen to shore up a wimpy sex drive; estrogen supplements are said to be cancer-causing in some women. I'm *not* recommending—only a doctor can do that but yours can *test* your hormone level to see if, because you're postmenopausal, it's down in the dumps, give you the artificial stuff (Premarin, Enovid, Estrace) to get it up. I take *two* 1.25-milligram Premarin tablets seven days a week, twenty-five days a month. That's massive. Of course, having had a hysterectomy, I don't have to worry about cervical, uterine or ovarian cancer and I sure love feeling sexy. My breasts even got bigger. Do you shore up with estrogen before or *after* you find a man? Well, an active sex drive could motivate you to find one, definitely make you more responsive after he's found.

Carrie on the subject of sex in your sixties and beyond: "I am an old fighter, which may seem an odd description for a size four, one-hundred-ten-pound Linda Evans look-alike but battle is what I go into when I start out for the first assignation with a new man ... one more time, oh Lord, coupling, going stomach to stomach with an authentic other-sex person. I put on my mental armor ('I deserve this, I deserve this, it's *good* for me!') and march onto the field. Each time that first night or afternoon is over I am so grateful I had the nerve to do it. Each time I'm contemplating the procedure with someone new (affairs may not last or lead to marriage when you're sixty any more than when you were twenty), I say to myself, how long can I go on *doing* this ... who will have me, where will I get the energy? But, so far, both the 'love' object and the life-force have been provided me somehow and I'm able to participate. No, I don't think I'm a silly fool, trying pitiably to play at a game meant only for the young. Fuck 'em! I am participating in life rather than death. Coupling may happen only to the young but I'm young *enough!*"

Mallen de Santis sums up the challenge this way: "Women are reluctant to show overt interest in sex, let alone chase a man. After all, we are sensitive, scared, vulnerable—smarter than men, who don't seem to *know* they are not real bell ringers at sixty and plunge right ahead!" Older men do more about sex than *many* older women, despite thrust problems, partly from supreme confidence—they think they *deserve* it, by God—and partly because lots of women are available to them. (Forget older men having a stronger sex drive than older women—or younger men than *younger* women, for that matter—that silliness has been murdered at last: Past puberty, women are *stronger* sexually than men.)

But why, aside from sheer perversity, do men rarely seem to want somebody their own age? This is the biological explanation: By nature a man needs to get his genes into the gene pool—i.e., procreate. The need is programmed into him. Impregnation is done with his penis and *it* responds best to young, healthy women with whom he figures he can produce a healthy baby. Women need to procreate also but don't require a necessarily *attractive* man for the assignment. We are more apt to be drawn to somebody who will stick around the cave to provide for the child, fight tigers, bash in the heads of intruders—that sort of thing. Our vaginas will *accept* whoever will do that—ours is a passive role—though we might have *preferred* Peter Jennings. Though a man doesn't *now* wish to have a baby, his penis *still* performs better with an attractive young female. We have to let him *be* that way—it's in his brain and body's primordial memory bank, plus he also likes to *look* at her (we *all* like to look at pretty girls), show her off to his buddies and, hard as it is for us to comprehend, some men actually prefer talking to airheads than to intelligent us.

But how does an over-fifty (or -sixty) man *attract* somebody half his age or younger? First we have the famous man-shortage (you remember *that* ... more single women than men in later years), plus the over-fifty/sixty man is often smart enough to *pay*—restaurant tabs, tennis lessons, trips to Acapulco, jewelry, furs, the rent money— for his pleasure. Younger women are not necessarily *averse* to the "helping out." The men keep two sets of books, of course, rationalizing the woman loves *him*—and his penis—which she *may,* but only a moron would try to convince himself the mere presence of himself and the Great One would drive a twenty-five-years-younger-than-he female over the cliff with longing. He is practical and lets worldly goods (plus power, career help, attentiveness) make up for thrust.

Many older women, on the other hand, still think a man should lay down his life and his body just because we're in the same room. God forbid we should "pay" for sex ... our crowd can be so *irrational!* Even now, many of us have not quite relinquished the idea that a man, to be sexually viable, must offer protection, financial stability and be at least our age or older. Oh, dear, truths have to be unlearned! If you *insist,* maybe you can *have* an older

man who doesn't *have* many worldly goods to offer a
young woman, never mind his "need to get his genes into
the gene pool," so he'll accept solvent us. And, of course,
a few have beaten the gene-pool rap altogether and *appreciate* us.

Okay, you're going to "cooperate" and the search is
on. How do you attract a man sexually? Phyllis Diller
says, "I'm looking for a perfume to overpower them—I'm
sick of karate!" Perfume *might* not *do* it. My participating
friends say attraction starts with attitude. Psychiatrist Martha Friedman on the subject: "You have to like sex, even
if it's been dormant in your life for a little while. Then you
have to let people know of your interest by looks, intent,
friendliness. Not hysterical friendly like a Great Dane that
hasn't been fed for six days and sees a can of Gravy Train
being opened, but just receptive friendly. Your attitude
says to a man, 'I like you, I'm glad we're here together,
I'd like to hear what you've been doing, I have plenty of
time to listen.' "

"You keep your eyes open, your pores open, your
brain open," says *Cosmo*'s executive editor Roberta
Ashley, sixty-seven, who married a man eight years younger after being widowed for five years. "Don't close down
the shop. You are fun to be with. There's a fine line between coming on strong—a total turnoff—and seeming to
be available. This is hard for some women to bring off because, while *wanting* to be approached, they're shy, not to
mention prickly and suspicious!"

Frances Lear, owner/founder of *Lear*'s magazine,
speaks of "a charming woman who is almost everybody's
senior. When she wants a lover, she goes out and gets
one—and not just any man, but a good man. 'When you
want to go to bed with a man,' she advises, 'make him
know you admire and want him. Men are not into rejection.' She makes a man know that he is the center of her
universe. Women who 'blow up a man's balloon' without
resorting to empty flattery have in their possession an art,
a magic, that can turn casual interest into passion and ful-
fillment. The problem is that it is difficult for a 20th-
century woman to live in a single body with two equally

strong ideas that oppose each other. One is the freedom and license to argue her point of view with men. The other is the belief that many men simply are not attracted to a woman unless she behaves like a geisha. An artful woman is one who can place a man, without resorting to tricks, in the center of her universe. My friend meets a man, asks him what he does if she doesn't already know, and keeps the conversation going—about him. Interesting questions. Thoughtful remarks. Insightful observations. Strong, positive reactions to his accomplishments. She never stops talking about him; she never stops being interested in him. And the secret is that she really is interested. She hears every word he says because she wants to. She has forgotten herself. She is outside of the center. He is the center, and he is smashed with her. Seduction, when it gets past the perfect-bod state, demands more from us—more thought, more intelligence, more understanding of the nature of men, and more everyday simple, genuine interest in them. The desire to make someone else feel good, and the ability to be centered without being in the center of the conversation can go a long way."

Gladys Nederlander (about sixty—she won't tell), married for the third time to a man ten years younger than she, says, "Enthusiasm is a major asset—a zest for living. So many women have traveled, speak foreign languages, have money, clothes, houses. Nobody gets very excited by those things, but being seriously turned on by life is a big attraction. Any older woman can be good at *living*—fun to be with." That word again—fun. (Gladdy is a *little* irritating. She is terribly pretty and pretty women almost never mention looks as part of their arsenal but Gladdy says looks aren't a big number.) "Most older women are dour," says Gladdy, "so full of problems, complaints. They get out of a taxi and start kvetching . . . he drove too fast, he made a wrong turn, he was rude, or her *hairdresser* messed up again, the electrician didn't show and her son-in-law is out of a job. I make Robert [her husband] laugh. He has a good time with me."

Martha Friedman told me about a seminar she attended for older people at which a bosomy, somewhat

blowsy woman kept lighting up a man who came there
with his wife. "She was hysterical to watch," said Martha.
"The man kept sneaking away from his wife to take this
woman to lunch." What did she have? "The bosom," said
the doctor, "plus that look in her eye." The look in the
eye. We all know a woman like that . . . a little too fat,
drinking a little too much but she gives off the old vibes
and men are always there.

Kiki Olson, a youngish *Cosmo* writer who before her
marriage shared many of her sexual romantic adventures
with *Cosmo* readers (Kiki never left a foreign city without
somebody and *something* to write up in her diary), says,
"You have to be a player. Your attitude has to say, 'I'm in
the game.' Use your legs if you have good legs . . . show
them off. I think legs are actually better than bosoms if
you have to choose—legs are young, playful, they lead to
your sexiest part. Bosoms can belong to a dowager but let
me not knock bosoms—depends how you display them.
An older woman should be comfortable to approach . . .
friendly . . . he doesn't risk rejection as he does with a
younger woman." Kiki mentions her sixty-seven-year-old
mother, with whom she recently took a cruise. "Mother
had an escort the whole time," says Kiki, "a hunky, older
union organizer. He might have *preferred* a younger
woman but my mother is cute and she came on. 'I love the
way you dress,' she told him. 'The tie . . . the blazer . . .
and the *socks!* Do you know I was lying out by the swimming pool this morning and saw those socks go by and I
said to myself, those socks must belong to somebody really wonderful . . . and it turns out to be *you!*' She was
outrageous but my mother is cute, and let us not forget she
is good *company.*"

Park Avenue matron Lauren Veronis says her mother
was sixty-nine when she met her husband to be—again, on
a cruise. "She always traveled alone," says Lauren. "She
felt it was important not to hang out with the blue-haired,
over-permed ladies . . . a group makes you unapproach-
able. My mother was very feminine, always came on soft.
An older woman may feel she doesn't have that much
time, so she'd better get on with it, but she'll just scare

him off if she's pushy. Wiles and smiles. You need those especially when you are older." Did he marry your mother for her money? I asked. Lauren's mother is loaded. "No, he was just as rich as she," says her daughter.

According to my players, looks do not seem to be as important an asset as when we were young, thank God! Even the homecoming queen's looks dim down so behavior can finally come into its own. Three other women who write for *Cosmo*—all around fifty and just this side (but not much) of scruffy—blow me away with their first-person tales of love. Fiction writers make stuff up, of course, and nonfiction writers *could* but I believe these three. "I am a little tired of waking up in strange bedrooms, of leaving a (strange) man sleeping in mine," writes Wanda Mae of the lantern jaw and when they were passing out hair, she must have been in the loo. "I plan to concentrate on Cliff for at least the next three months." Another of my "scruffies" writes, "I longed to be at my office in pinstripes instead of looking for a taxi at 7:00 A.M. in green chiffon because I slept at Hal's and we made love all night." A writer who resembles a bloodhound just a little and is very skimped of bosom told me at a *Cosmo* Christmas party, "Helen, I don't see how anybody can think sex has quieted down in this country. It has only quieted down for women silly enough to let it." She had brought one man to the party, but was leaving him to spend the night with somebody she liked better. Age: fifty-four. Looking as good as you can doesn't *hurt*, of course. As one of my sexually active women puts it: "You wear makeup. You dye your hair. You can't go to beef—but looks aren't as important as liking sex and liking *men.*"

Do I hear you insisting yet again that a sexual act must be accompanied by love or you won't play? Please! Accompanied by *like*, yes. I doubt anybody would have at us sexually at our age unless he *did* like us and we wouldn't like "it" if we didn't like *him* but like is sufficient. At fifty-nine or whatever age you are, you are simply renewing womanliness. Perhaps you only need *him* for sex . . . husband or friends offer brighter hours *out* of bed. *Two* can tango. And I really doubt you have to worry about that silly conscience/morality business either. Is it right? Am I a slut? Will he call? Will he respect me in the morning? If you can get a man to bed to cherish your definitely not nubile body, I think you deserve as much respect as Joan of Arc, Queen Victoria, and Lassie all put together. Judy says care must be paid not to fall in love with the man who merely offers sex. Ah, yes, as Stephen Sondheim's countess warns in *A Little Night Music,* "Too many people muddle sex with mere desire and when emotion intervenes, the nets descend. It should on no account perplex or, worse, inspire ... it's but a pleasurable means to a measurable end."

What kind of advice is that? asks my romantic friend Patricia. "Do you suppose a girl gets any *better* at not being emotionally zonked when she is getting *sexually* zonked just because she is older? Your brains leave town just as they did at twenty when someone gets *to* you in bed. You find yourself wanting to call him, to cling, to be reassured ninety times a day. The only thing that keeps *me* from being a total idiot," says Pat, "is the vision of Glenn Close losing her grip over Michael Douglas in *Fatal Attraction* after one little sexual romp."

Wynona agrees. "I don't see how you can have sex without *any* kind of emotional connection because somebody is inside your *body,* for God's sake, it's just too intimate. Yes, massage, even a manicure, are sensuous ... somebody is holding your hand or kneading your fanny and you can manage to be impersonal with *them* but a man pumping himself into your vagina, you've got to be affected! No wonder from teenage to the present moment, we all go a little crazy when somebody is fucking us, succumb to the 'I love you's.' Anybody lucky enough to *have* a sexual relationship can expect a touch of the crazies ... we're *vulnerable.*" Alexandra says, "Two people are almost never obsessed with each other at the same time. One of them can *enjoy* the other but only one is a nut case." In her play *Tru,* Jay Presson Allen avers there is hope even for the nut cases as she quotes Truman Capote: "You can get anybody you want to love you ... you just wear them down!" Good to know it can happen even if it doesn't always, but sex is what we are after here . . . worthy, honorable sex even if you "suffer" a bit.

Rejection after an affair begins has to be the living *worst.* Liz Smith says, "Narcissistic mortification is something you feel because the affair has been ended not by you. Your main feeling is that of not being loved, of having your ego shattered, of not being worthy. It is not that you love the other person so much—later you will find that you hate him—but, for the moment, because you have been abandoned, your perception is that you are *mad* about him, more so even than before he left." If he's not rejecting you, you may still have to remind yourself that sex is possibly the main thing this man can give you and you may have to find companionship and other necessities somewhere else. You are *not* necessarily a sought-after sex object these days but this man likes you in bed so glory hallelujah, go for it. Yes, sex *can* unnerve but if you keep a full life going around you—which Glenn Close certainly didn't in the film—you can manage not to go toes up and become a monomaniacal nut case.

Whether success (he *finally* adores you) happens or not, I will guarantee you this: The one who loves more will wind up loving less; the one who loves less will love more. The obsessed lover finally just gets plain sick of his obsession and gets *out* . . . like the snake from his winter skin, while the obsessed-about one has now got *used* to massive fixes of unconditional love and wants them to continue. Astonishing . . . this person you worshiped you now think is an asshole. He, on the other hand, is possessive of you. You almost—*almost*—*miss* your erotic preoccupation.

Repeat: Sex *can* be separated from love, even from friendship, as you well know, so don't argue! God knows we've all been to bed with men we didn't like—or anyway hated on *occasion.* If you can masturbate—which we all can—you can have an *orgasm* with somebody you aren't in love with . . . why even point *out* such a banality? I agree, of course, that in your sixties, even if you can't have sex connected with love and marriage, you at least need a responsible and kind person . . . a friend . . . but I also agree with Chloe, who says, "You don't turn down too many offers or chances if you want to keep sexually alive." Let's just say that people who might hurt, steal, embarrass or blackmail you are out but perfectly nice, unspectacular men are *in,* so to speak.

If you *do* want to participate and I hope you do, how often is this fix necessary? Not too often if the activity doesn't really grab you but *occasionally,* one would think—a few times a year? If you have an ongoing relationship with a man, you would be more sexually active probably, but we are talking about what to do without a steady or sex-providing one. You may extrapolate sex from a *friendship.* Occasional sex. You could both be married to somebody else. I've already told you about *that* group of women.

So now let's start the search. Who is your partner going to *be?* "I'm big on fantasy," says Catherine. "I fantasize this wonderful man and I will be thrown together during a bombing or flood or other disaster. We get separated from the rest of the group or they're all dead. Maybe we're huddled under a tarmac with soldiers poking at us with bayonets. Of course we'll get out of it okay but for about forty-eight hours we'll be so intimate and close, clinging together for strength, he'll forget I'm sixty and he looks like Kevin Costner and wants me for sex." But of course! That's the daydream; now for *reality.* Who out there is *possible?* Here goes: A happily married man you can pretty much forget. Nobody is happy with his mate all the time, but certain men simply don't *cheat.* Angela circled one for about a year who seemed promising (for dalliance). "We saw each other socially, had lunch maybe once a month . . . we're in the same business. He was *interested* in me sexually—you can tell—but he has four sons he is nuts about; his wife is part of the package and I finally concluded that man and I would *never* be in bed."

Forget anybody even mildly in *love* with another woman. Other forgets: the handsome, aging idol, causing melt-down from TV or movie screen, the rock star in both kinds of beads (Indian and sweat), the young actor hunk in tight jeans. These men bed only the young. (*Anybody* who exclusively worships famous men is hiding *out* from sex, of course, and that *goes* for the young, give or take a few groupies who *do* bed down.) A group one would *think* possible for us who aren't are the womanizers ... sniffing everything female but their wife's poodle. ("He would fuck a garden hose if nothing else was handy," they say of a certain dynamo New York theatrical agent.) Ironic. Wanting to be confirmed female, we might *welcome* an approach from a professional appreciator—some are attractive—but their target is under forty, thirty or *twenty*—I know you're tired of hearing this! So who *is* the best possibility for sex? Consider the man who is mildly or seriously unhappy in his marriage or simply bored with it. His numbers are legion (can you count to about thirty million?!). Sure, a widowed or divorced man is fine if you can find one but they are heavily booked. Even a scruffy *old* bachelor has girlfriends if his money hasn't given out. So don't go moral on me. We're talking dalliance here, not a permanent husband snatch.

So how do you figure out who is a good prospect? You look for tiny signs of interest or accessibility ... just a little curiosity on the part of someone sitting next to you in a dental office waiting room, at a dinner party, on a plane, at a business meeting .... somebody who, glory be, seems to be appreciating you as a *woman*. Again, friendship romance could develop but I'm concentrating on sex for the moment. Now, an interested person may not be appropriate ... I mean, we don't have to deal with *flakes*. "A man seated near the door when I was getting off the bus tried to pick me up," says Carol. "Then later a cab driver asked what I was doing *later,* and someone very strange in the Plaza Hotel lobby started a conversation one day when I was waiting for my daughter for lunch. Naturally those men wouldn't do, but I feel," says Carol, *"whoever* perceives you as a woman is a blessing, don't you? For a little while you are cuntier, insouciant ... a throwback to your old sexual self ... more ready for somebody *suitable."*

Somebody suitable is usually from your own world, at least not somebody you'd feel peculiar about, but keeping your pores open for *all* signs of appreciation is appropriate behavior for an older woman. Says Carol, "If you are a prissy ninny and the light is always turned off except for Paul Newman, the night is going to stay very very dark." "People think you ought to have somebody like Warren Beatty, as fancied by Vivian Leigh in *The Roman Spring of Mrs. Stone,* if you're somewhat glamorous yourself," says my actress friend Veronica, "but that kind of person in the movie—gorgeous gigolo—is just money and trouble. I don't care much what he looks like—your friends aren't necessarily going to see him ... he isn't a trophy for the mantelpiece—as long as he appreciates *me* enough to sincerely want me in bed."

Briefest word here about AIDS. It is probably not really something to be worried about if your lover is not an intravenous drug user, a homosexual or bisexual. This proposition was well documented in a January 1988 *Cosmo* article by Dr. Robert Gould, which got us plenty of flak but the basis of which has never been proved wrong by subsequent events.

As Daniel Lynch wrote last year in *The Washington Journalism Review,* "Our [press] stories have failed to communicate to our audience that male victims such as Magic Johnson who say they could have contracted the disease only through heterosexual sex are but 3 percent of the total number of persons with AIDS (among both genders, it's 6 percent) and nobody knows how many of these men are telling the truth. We still live in a society in which people have good and sufficient reason to lie about homosexuality and IV drug use. The reality, painful though it may be to people concerned about discrimination against gays and poverty-stricken minorities who make up the bulk of IV drug users, is that AIDS in the United States remains overwhelmingly confined to members of those groups and their sexual partners. By featuring women as typical potential victims, the AIDS-prevention advertising has been designed to scare the hell out of everybody. And it has worked."

Nevertheless—big nevertheless—the AIDS conference convened in Amsterdam last year reported the fastest-growing number of AIDS cases to be among women—you *must* be careful. If you're starting a sexual relationship, *try* to ascertain his sexual history and whether or not he has or has *had* a drug habit (which would involve needles). Of course, he could not tell the truth or not tell the *whole* truth. A widower who seems to have had a long monogamous relationship with a wife is probably "safe," but the safest thing to do with *anyone* you haven't been to bed with—or *have*—is for him to have a blood test to ascertain whether he's HIV positive. You could do that too. If sex is spur of the moment with someone you don't know, he's *got* to use a condom. Have your own supply if necessary.

Now here, according to my advisers, are good things to do in the presence of a man in whom you hope to develop lust: Stay quiet. Don't chatter. You are animated but not nervous. Look in his eyes, smile. Laugh if he's funny. Laughter—of course he's really got to *be* funny—is lapped up like cream. A warm kiss on the cheek when you greet a male friend is de rigueur. A bear hug for a *longtime* friend puts you chest to chest, pelvis to pelvis for a moment . . . he might *be* a Possible. Kissing somebody good night when you've just met is sensible. He should feel lips. Touch the possible man during the evening if you've got a chance . . . your hand should rest lightly on his sleeve. As for securing an actual date which could *lead* to an assignation, everybody says you mustn't make the first move—not only the first *sexual* move (pulling his face toward you, moving in for the kiss), you can't even make the first heavy-duty *verbal* move. ("What are you doing later?") "You can't assume the reason a man doesn't ask you for a drink is because he doesn't know *how,*" says Frances Lear. "Even the shyest, most forlorn man knows how to ask. To get the invitation you simply use the same method you used at seventeen or twenty-seven. You let him know by attitude that you are interested." A *very* wise *Cosmo* articles editor says, "The 'hard sell'—'I find you so attractive . . . should we plan something later?'—makes your customer back right away. You have to have him thinking you're appetizing and available; *he* makes the decision to buy." Nellie adds, "Sales people do a lot of groundwork before they achieve success; the 'cold call' is a nightmare ... almost guarantees rejection. You need to be familiar with the buyer; he has to feel comfortable with you."

Maybe yes, maybe no. We don't want to miss a possible happening with a stranger just because we weren't briefed. Anyway, we can be a quick study. It *is* a little boring to have to let a man move first as though this were 1928 and "nice girls didn't," but some things don't change that *much*. Aggression on the part of a man *is* how sex works. Entering a woman's body *is* aggressive. When you see a man and woman on a date, having dinner or whatever they're doing, they are moving toward the time when *he* will hump *her*, not the other way around. And God deliver us all, Tiny Tim, from a man who only wants things to be done *to* him. . . . "I'm your slave this afternoon, do with me as you will." It's like positive and negative currents—you don't get toast from the toaster without both currents, but they can't switch roles! Okay, so you make it possible for a man to "aggress." A sexually active single man told me the other day you can tell whether a woman will be good in bed by how she dances ... uninhibited, full of rhythm, she's going to be that way making love. Okay, that's one signal you can give off if you're a good dancer.

"Work is an incredible incubator of sexual attraction," Carrie reminds us. "You don't have to say one sexy word to get yourself in a position where something *could* happen, when alone with the man is what you want. If you have to finish a project together, perhaps it could be at your apartment—'I'll cook, you write; I can make a quick omelet while you organize the summary.' Or maybe you'll volunteer to drop a report off at his hotel after *you* finish it. Who said anything about sex?! If he says fine, leave it with the doorman, he'll never know you had something else in mind." Carrie is right, of course. A hundred zillion affairs—conservative estimate—have started at the office—for older as well as younger women. There *is* no better culture to get the yeast to rise.

"If you should actually be having dinner with a targeted man [this sounds like Dick Tracy!], office mate or otherwise, try to make sure the evening ends at your place or his place or some place where you *might* go to bed," advises Diandra. "If the man gives you a ride home from a party, kiss in the taxi ... at least be ready though he must make the first move. If he's driving, your skirt could be slightly above your knees so he can see legs ... and *think* sex!" Same advice over and over from the players— you make it easy for a man to say yes, or rather for him to ask you and *you* say yes.

Example: On a cruise ship—another of *those!*— Millie sat next to the ship's doctor. She had been playing deck tennis and was hungry. "Dinner is so good when you are really hungry," she recalls saying. "Yes," he answered, "when you have an appetite." She looked at him very carefully. He was attractive and she decided "to go for it." "That's true of anything," she said to the doctor. "Making love, for example ... it's better when you're ravenous." (Not a word about him or *them* making love ... just simply giving *him* the chance to move things along.) He took the bait. "When you feel anticipation," he continued. "When it isn't just routine but something very special." They were in his stateroom by 9:30. "He could have *not* gone further with the conversation or the act," says Millie. "I just gave him the opportunity to make a move."

Gladys Rackmil had a business relationship with theatrical producer Robert Nederlander before *she* made a move. "I had worked in the organization for three months," says Gladdy, "when I told Robert I was going to Manchester to see a play, then up to London. Perhaps he'd like to come with me. 'Are you seducing me?' he asked. 'I certainly hope so!' I said. If he hadn't responded favorably, I had a perfectly legitimate reason to have suggested the trip because the company looks for plays in Europe to bring to Broadway. It was all so natural and easy," says Gladdy. "We had such a good time." They married three years later. Yes, sex can come before love.

The right attitude, open pores, judicious choice of target. Okay, you're prepared to do *your* part, but what about those crushing disappointments along the way? Yes, they happen. An attractive man offered Ginny a lift home from a party the other night, suggesting they stop by his flat "to see my Etruscan artifacts." Must be what they are calling etchings these days, thought Ginny, as she accepted with pleasure. "I expected to be in bed within the hour but, alas, he had merely found me an intelligent dinner companion—somebody, by God, who would probably appreciate his fucking Etruscan artifacts . . . some of the best stuff this side of the Metropolitan apparently. I was down on the street looking for a *cab* in fifteen *minutes!*"

Lydia seemed to get *further*. A "virgin" widow for one year, she asked a man over for a drink. He accepted and as they talked pleasantly and drank a bottle of Cristal she decided, *"This* isn't so hard to do," and suggested they go upstairs to her bedroom . . . "a nice silky place—where we both undressed and got into bed. So far so good but then nothing happened. Or what *did* happen wasn't what I had in mind. He went mushy. I kept trying to coax him back to life . . . I mean, I'd heard you could *do* that and I was going about it like artificial respiration when he finally removed my hand, and said, 'Honey, I don't think this is going to work.' No, he wasn't gay, he wasn't even drunk and wasn't temporarily impotent out of nerves with a new partner. He said he had a twenty-six-year-old girlfriend who frankly supplied all the sex he could manage—that is about all she did supply, however, and he had hoped he and I could be really good friends on another level. I appraised him in the dark with all the compassion of a lizard who has just had a small bird removed from its jaw. Sexual rejection is the pits!"

A famous friend (not an entertainer) tells me a couple of men love to take her to lunch. "They think I'm interesting, nice-looking, and it's fun to be with a celebrity. I don't know quite how to tell them that lunch dates for me are a dime a dozen . . . I could have two a day. I'm wildly busy and if the man isn't interested in me as a possible *sex* mate, I simply can't spare the two hours it takes to sit and gossip ... better for me to spend it on my business. *Sex,* which I need a little *more* of, I can spare the time for!" Oh, how things change from girlhood when all you ever wished was a man who *only* wanted to lunch!

Sometimes a man is thinking business while you are thinking romance or sex. A literary agent I know, having met a television host on a press junket to open a new hotel in Madrid, couldn't have been more pleased when he called to suggest dinner. "I think we have things to talk about," he said. "Do we *ever?!*" Arlene purred as she quickly accepted. "At dinner he told me he was forming a new production company and would need properties to make into miniseries, could I be on the lookout? I had to have dinner with this hunk in a sexy Beverly Hills boîte to hear about miniseries? I said I would put him in touch with our television department which I may or may *not* ever do, *screw* the commissions!"

And Doris tells of a Sunday morning walk along the Malibu beach with a friend (she married, he not) on whom she had had a major crush for about four years. Skies mutinous, winds howling, ocean roaring, "The two of us were one big walking bear hug for two hours," reports Doris, "while he talked about a girl he'd fallen in love with ... the Wrong Girl. The subject didn't bore me ... I've cheered up lovesick men before and am good at it, but it would have been so right to stop and kiss ... so easy to enjoy a nice friendly smooch that miserable day but he never seemed to realize I was physically *there* except to hold him up and keep us both from freezing or blowing out to sea ... and, of course, to *listen.* He and the girl were later married and I gave up on him." One would surely *hope* so!

But let's talk about *connecting,* not short-circuiting, and remember that people *do* connect. This might just be the time to put in a good word for younger men. Question: Why in God's name would one suggest younger for somebody older when she mostly turns off men her own age? Because she can *attract* younger, that's why—not all but some. She appeals to a junior by being competent, worldly, glamorous, fun, adoring, good in bed and having a little money! (Young women can't or don't offer most of those things.) He may be live-in and totally kept or she may only take care of some bills and give presents. She can help with his career if she's in a position to do *that*. But forget things you can *do* for him; some younger men actually prefer older women. Unresolved childhood crush on a teacher? Need for a "mommy" to nurture and protect him? We don't always know *why* they fall but not *all* juniors are looking for teachers or mommy.

Lillian Hellman had a sexual friendship with writer Peter Feibleman, twenty-five years her junior, for many years though he gave her such a bad time—she was in love with him—I don't know whether I should be mentioning her as a role model. Mallen de Santis says, "An older woman uses what a man does to interest somebody younger or even her own age: glamour, money, position, fame, family background. Anybody will fuck a Kennedy!"

But not *every* young man goes for older. "He may look through you like glass," says Carrie. "No, not glass . . . they would linger to see their reflection . . . but like *smoke* . . . you're not even *there.*" Brrrrr. "If someone only goes for tight ass, flat stomach, forget that person," says Gladdy Nederlander. "There are plenty of others." Frances Lear says, "You can't go to bed with a man who wants a twenty-three-year-old. Some men you can make interested in you, some you can't."

Roberta Ashley tells me about two young men who came to do some work at her house—"good looking, hunky. They kept rechecking stuff they'd already checked 'to be sure the second staircase wasn't going to get in the way of the pipes . . . to see if the stresses were adequate.' We'd get one thing settled, then they'd find something else to check. I think I could have made a date with either one of these men to come back later. [She didn't, Harold, she *didn't!*] Young men are so horny they have enough to give an older woman—not on a permanent basis but surely for a fling."

I know five wealthy women (ages fifty-five to sixty-five) who are keeping or have kept younger men. One, married, had a chalet in Gstaat and tended to *change* her younger (usually ski instructor) companions rather often. She's gone back home to Palm Beach to live quietly with her once-roving husband. . . . They seem to have both got it out of their systems. Another married friend kept a lover in Paris (yes, these are ritzy locations but money tends to bring *on* ritziness). Her adored one wasn't accepted in the circles in which she moved—*quel* embarrassment—but the problem was short-term as he left her for somebody even wealthier. (Listen, I never promised *all* happy endings.) A third friend—widowed—lives at the Waldorf Towers, is about as pretty as it gets and was happy for many years "helping out" a not-that-much-younger textile executive until *he* departed for a husband-collecting-and-gorgeous-movie star who left *him* six months later for a writer . . . it evens out. Friends four and five are still at it, successfully, the way it looks to me, paying for sex and companionship with younger men. One actress-philanthropist is in business with her selected one and, as another friend describes them, "He is attractive, isn't a dum-dum, defers to her. So what if she pays the bills? She couldn't give away all her money if she opened the window and threw out thousand-dollar bills every morning." (They're getting married.) Alana's (my fifth friend's) live-in, about twenty years younger, looks like one of the studs on daytime television but she is also drop-dead great-looking, so why should she pick a gargoyle?! I run into this couple at parties and love to be with them because they're lively and friendly. He is devoted to her and she can afford him.

Of course, these are heavy live-in commitments and what I more or less have been stressing is *occasional* sex—at *least* occasional—which may indeed be with somebody younger. Let me tell you about Ursula, who has had a nine-year liaison with a young mergers and acquisitions maven. It is friendship *and* sex. He is thirty-two; she is fifty-eight. "I met him on a plane coming back from the Republican Convention in 1980—he was with his wife," says Ursula. "Well, he was so cute and funny and something just told me he might be a Possible! Of course, you can feel that way about a dozen people before you actually connect. And, no, you aren't out there with a dragnet . . .

you just think 'what if' and quietly 'investigate' ... try to
make it happen. I knew where he worked and I called him.
'My husband had made a lot of money,' I said (not actually true though we are comfortable), 'and I need some
advice.' He invited me to lunch in his firm's executive
dining room. I wore my prettiest dress—and underwear—
for courage. As I plaintively asked whether he thought I
should try to get Otto to set up a separate little portfolio
for me so that I would feel more independent, he looked
at me very searchingly, said stocks weren't really his specialty, but he could introduce me to one of his partners if
I liked; meanwhile, why didn't I try to make sure a
'friendly will' was made out. Since I wasn't planning to
divorce—was I?—that would be as safe a bet as anything.
Lunch was very proper. I felt like a junior-grade nitwit but
only junior grade—at least I had been subtle.

"Six weeks went by—nothing—then one summer day
he telephoned. His wife was in Vermont, would I like to
have dinner. Just me or me and Otto? I asked. Whatever
you like, he said. Otto happened to be away also—how
fortuitous can things get?! And so it began. And so it continues. I ask nothing of him except a sexy evening occasionally ... usually at his apartment when his wife sees
her family, which is fairly often. Since Otto and I have not
slept together for years, though we are devoted, I don't
feel any guilt and I don't really need sex more often ...
just to stay in the game."

Let's say *you* have connected ... what might you do
with a lover once he is signed up? Same things you did
when you were younger, only now you may want to be
more pampering (change, change ... we have to accom-
modate ourselves to *change* ... the challenge and the sal-
vation of the older, but then, when was man-pleasing *not*
part of your repertoire?). I get criticized a *lot* for my pampering advice, but loving has always required as well as
created a desire to pamper—him of you as well as you of
him. If you were slogging your way through the back rubs,
his special French toast, hating every second, only to reach
a goal of his total enslavement, that might be naughty, but
girls in love instinctively pamper (he *does* become en-

slaved but that's merely a by-product). An older woman may plan a little more carefully the things she will do for him but he will surely be doing some back. *Surely!*

"I planned a great evening of love the first night we were together," said Ursula, "and I nearly drowned him—or at least waterlogged him. He came to my house, gray and exhausted from a heavy day on Wall Street. I gave him a terry robe and said I'd meet him in the guest wing in a moment and left. I had this sexy bath waiting for him—just him, not us—votive candles around the tub, hot water laced with Jean Naté, cold Dom Pérignon in a bucket and Carly Simon on the stereo. Great idea except he assumed the terry robe meant shower and took one in *his* bathroom before joining me. I plunked him in the tub *again* and the poor darling was turning into a prune before he confessed that perhaps he'd had enough soapy-water pleasures for the moment. Then he went to the library for shrimp and caviar and I planned to take Polaroids of him because he *is* endowed and had maybe never been photographed nude. God knows I'm not great with a camera—I borrowed this one—but he simply got terrified—I guess blackmail crossed his mind. I put the camera away and *then* we made love. Sometimes you have to adjust as you go along."

Natasha, fifty-eight and I doubt *ever* without a man, has been dressing up for *her* younger lover for several years. "I have worn everything from a genuine Japanese Kabuki kimono and no underwear to pink tights and a Hell's Angels black leather jacket with insignia all over the sleeves. You think I feel like an idiot? Right! One thousand percent going in; then I get into the scene and kind of *enjoy* it. I never knew in the beginning he cared the slightest thing about *what* I wore although God knows I always knocked myself out to be gorgeously dressed—or undressed—in whatever peignoir or lounge costume he hadn't seen the last time, but then one day as we're making a date—always the same place—my girlfriend's flat—he said, 'Wear a garter belt.' I started to say—like a goddamn mynah bird—wear a *what?* . . . . a garter belt seemed such a cliché, but obviously I heard him the first time and recovered enough to ask, 'Any particular color?' 'White,' he said. Odd choice I thought—black or red came to mind—but I scrounged one from the prop department (Natasha works for a television station), created stockings by cutting the panty part out of some white pantyhose, pinned a fake gardenia in my hair and *voilà*, a kind of South Sea Island, nurse-angel tramp-of-the universe combo he seemed to like! May I tell you that none of this time was I going on instinct. I don't *have* instincts about dressing for fantasy ... I'm rather straightforward and practical. You see magazine articles about what sexy things to wear to bed or sexy-lingerie fashion shows on Phil Donahue and you think, oh, those people are so cheap and vulgar. Well, just wait until you start having an affair and they don't seem so cheap and vulgar anymore!"

Some women are naturally *drawn* to dressing up, says author Nancy Friday (*Women on Top,* Simon & Schuster). Exhibitionism is part of their sexual nature ... they love to get into revealing clothes and call attention to themselves, turned on by their own sexuality. Do all women feel that way? Definitely not, says Nancy. For certain women, being noticed is absolute poison ... they wear ladylike, ankle-skimming peasant dresses, go absolutely berserk if a man says they look nice in turquoise or have good elbows (the only thing he can *see*). Women who pose for *Playboy* and *Penthouse* are carrying exhibitionism to the ultimate degree, says Nancy, but reminds us these women are *not* exploited by men; obviously they are proud of their sexuality, or at least their bodies, and want to show them off.

Does being a show-off mean you enjoy yourself more in bed than somebody projecting a quieter image? I really don't know ... don't you think it probably does? Anyway, for our purposes ... older woman luring somebody to bed ... a touch of showoffiness, particularly if she has a good body, couldn't hurt. When you're walking around the room and he's watching, this is a sexy look: pelvis pushed forward *slightly,* elbows close to sides and bosom also pushed forward. Oh, come on ... it *is* you! Speaking of how to walk and what to wear to bed, how about sprucing up the bedroom? Fresh flowers in a vase if there's a place to put them, spanking clean sheets, a Rigaud candle in their basic Cyprus scent ... nothing is any more haunting or sensuous-smelling in the world (expensive but lasts for hours, can be relit for next time—of *course* there is going to be a next time).

How you look undressed isn't a big deal, according to the players. If you've got him as far as bed, he's hardly going to bolt when you expose a midriff, a thigh. He's there because he is attracted to you ... again, it's that attitude of liking men, accepting them, liking *sex* that has placed him in your bed. "Of course, you can be going along doing pretty well in the confidence department," says Ginny, "figuring you look better than most girls your age, and one day catch a surprise glimpse of your upper arms in a mirror from behind ... you usually see them head-on ... and you freak! Somebody with *those* arms is thinking of men, thinking of sex ... are you crazy!? The horror doesn't last long though and here you are in bed." Says Ginny: "So get undressed in the dark if you like. Put twenty-watt bulbs in the lamps. Wear high heels to bed— they make your legs look longer. If you're planning sex, slip into and *stay* in something silky-pretty until the last moment and it's time to Get On With It, then get right back *in* your silky garment the moment *it* is over or at least when the lights go on."

Ursula says, "We usually lie in bed and talk after we've made love, he frequently *under* the covers, leaning on three or four pillows, me sitting cross-legged on the bed facing him—attentive, vivacious—and, though my body is still pretty good, right then I slip on a minislip or maybe a tiny nightie and we talk and *talk*. If I get tired of sitting cross-legged, I just change positions but I never lie down beside him under the covers. It just feels right to me—he's fifteen years younger than I—and I think it's charming for me to play the insouciant schoolgirl."

"My lover can't see the rug beneath him without glasses," says Chloe, "so cellulite doesn't exist for him! I didn't pick him for that reason but sometimes when we lie in bed after making love I know he would kind of like to have his glasses returned to him, and I tell him I don't want anything 'mechanical' to come between us and don't give them back until we get dressed."

As for the *act* of love, another practical note. The vagina does not lubricate as it did when we were young. Estrogen supplements help. That's up to you and your doctor. Premarin *cream* in the vagina every few days can certainly be a good substitute for actual estrogen production, again prescribed by your gynecologist. (Jesus, the stuff is expensive!) As noted earlier, you'll want to use Vaseline, K-Y jelly or Astro-Glide (check the labels for any possible warnings) *at* the assignation; it may be the last detail attended to before answering the doorbell or slipping out of your clothes in the john before getting into bed. And I know a girl who—now don't go disgusted on me—puts one of these products on a banana and carefully, gently inserts just the end—up about three inches—to stretch her vagina several nights before a rendezvous. Vaginas *do* contract if not entered very often. Tenderly stretching ahead of time instead of having a penis do all the work—and possibly *fail* because you're constricted—isn't such a dumb idea. (A gynecologist I checked this out with says he should have thought of it, it's fine and there are papier-mâché bananas out there that *last*). Joanna thinks older women are crazy if they don't keep a supply of Vaseline handy (hers is in a little silver pot on the night table), to use in stroking do I have to tell you *what?* Jo's lover has inquired, "What *is* this stuff?" and she tells him it's a special ointment she brought back from Nepal. Actually Jo's the same person who suggests the banana/Vaseline trick for stretching the vagina. Chesebrough Pond's ought to pay that girl *royalties.*

What about telling a man what you like? Everybody says to do that these days, but Caroline puts it another way. "I think we've earned the right to tell what we *don't* like . . . like you don't plan ever again in your life to perform fellatio more than just an ordinary number of times . . . maybe set quotas . . . like once a week or just on his birthday." Elisa says, "I rather enjoyed doing that when I was first in love with Sam . . . *he* worshiped his penis, *I* worshiped his penis and it didn't *take* long. He's older now and it's those interminable gagging sessions I dread— not from revulsion, don't misunderstand, but a penis down your throat *long* enough can block the oxygen supply and cause you to choke!" Laura tried to cut down with a lover of many years but "he was damned if he was going to withdraw from this particular ecstasy and his one fool-proof way to orgasm. . . . I waited too long to speak!" (It's been said of others but I'm sure Laura was the one about whom it was first said: "She could suck the chrome right off a Cadillac bumper.")

Sighs Irene, "I have screeched and said ouch to Stephen for about fourteen years now . . . well, actually only about eight of the fourteen because the first six I was so much in love I just winced and didn't let on when he was biting my breasts instead of caressing, so 'containing' is undoubtedly the problem. Since I didn't say anything for so long, he probably thinks *that* was the real me and this new ouching person is some kind of fraud . . . the complaint just doesn't ring true for him."

Brave Karen said to herself and then to the famous actor (her own age . . . she looks better than he at sixty) with whom she was starting an affair, "Look, we're just beginning this friendship, and I've decided never to lie anymore about whether I do or don't have an orgasm . . . I am simply not going to fake." He looked at her as though she were reciting the Koran backward in Swahili . . . total incomprehension, plus total lack of interest. "Was I crazy?" asks Karen. "You make those pronouncements to a man who might possibly be interested and with whom your views could possibly sink in. I didn't *have* to fake orgasm. . . . He didn't care whether I did or didn't as long as *he* reached a climax. I never do with him but it doesn't bother me particularly. I am there because I enjoy turning the man on . . . because I like the physical act of love . . . an orgasm I can always have later."

Masturbation. We don't really have to discuss that, do we? If you don't know how or don't indulge by now, surely you have a learning disability or priorities misplaced. Karen again: "What I like about the Big M, as I call it, is that I can *always* reach a climax and nobody cares how long it takes. It *does* take different amounts of time even if it's just me, but who's counting?" Psychiatrists, friend-interviewees, personal experience confirm that masturbation is one of life's *serious* blessings, one that doesn't diminish (they can't take *that* away from us!) with age. My friend Joan Bové says at eighty-seven masturbation is definitely what you do when there isn't a man, but "I try not to be in that position!" Elisa says she "starts feeling 'lovey' just about every time I lie in the sun, especially in the Hamptons where the air is so soft and caressing or in the tropics and don't leave out the desert! I call it creeping orgasm and can practically *think* myself to the finish." But we are talking about being with *men*— sometimes a little self-centered—in bed. To continue . . .

"You can't imagine how ignorant—I think it's more ignorance than selfishness—a man can be," says Carol, who tells of a disturbing visit to a once U.S. senator, age seventy-two, in his apartment at the United Nations Plaza. "Gorgeous apartment, wraparound view of New York City with the lights twinkling on. Utter glamour!" Thinking they both knew why they were there (both were married and "a kind of understanding" had been reached at lunch), Carol sank into the couch and began to unbutton her blouse. "Let's don't rush this along too much," said Mr. U.S. senator. Carol quit unbuttoning, whereupon Mr. senator took out his penis and brought it close to her face. Being rather an agreeable as well as a sexually experienced girl who *liked* to give men pleasure, Carol performed fellation . . . "didn't take too long" . . . after which he said magnanimously, " 'I hope that was good for you, too' . . . I mean he was *serious!*" End of sexual activity for the evening and of him altogether for Carol! You see, darlings, some relatively attractive, accomplished, even respected-by-their-peers men haven't a *clue* about what brings a woman sexual pleasure. Says author Shere Hite, "All too many men still seem to believe, in a rather naive and egocentric way, that what feels good to them is automatically what feels good to women." It's almost—but not quite— hard not to feel *sorry* for them!

Men, generally, are *kinkier* about sex than women, don't you think? Again, it may be because they have to perform and need stimuli, even if weird, to get going. We *don't* have to perform, as I keep pointing out, which makes our sex lives simpler. A woman I don't know well told a natural friend about "the things she does for love." This nice (under ordinary circumstances he is a New York pillar) man visits her apartment to be led around like a French poodle. She puts on his little collar and talks to him in doggie baby talk and puts Scotch and milk in his dish on the floor. For another man she has "boned up on" what went on in prison in the seventeenth century—"certain kinds of unpleasantness"—so she can describe the proceedings to him. Nobody gets hurt apparently—except in the French prison—"he just likes to *hear* about manacles and whips."

This woman is sixty and *attractive,* isn't even given presents by her friends. Why does she indulge these weird people? Her rationale: "I feel it gives me an edge to be the paramour of these megasuccessful if major-kinky men. I like being the one who gets them off . . . and it *is* a kind of power, no doubt about it, which a wife frequently doesn't have (or maybe *want!*). Anyway, I don't think you can denigrate people's sexual needs if they don't hurt anybody else. . . . What gets you to orgasm is as personal as fingerprints."

Well, I guess we don't need to dwell on kinkiness or the compassionate one's tolerance; let's get back to more traditional sex/romance stories. I want to tell you about Georgina, who does enjoy just about everything she does with a man and is never without one. Wish I could tell you her real name because she's famous and wonderful and sixty-five and you'd say, but of course, that's exactly what you'd expect of her, but I can't—it *is her* sex life.

Georgina is at a dinner party at my house—I don't give many—and I put her next to a Wall Street baron. I'm watching. He does not tip over for her but, after dinner, Georgina finds me and says, "Who *is* he?!" Head of a brokerage house, I explain, one of the best financial brains in the world. "Oh, I don't mean *that,*" Georgina says. "Is he

married? Does he have a girlfriend? How do I get to see
him again?" You'd think she might have found this stuff
out at dinner but her table pretty much talked as a group.
Even after I explained his stature—I mean, he is a Very
Big Deal in his world—she wasn't interested "in all that
business stuff" but said he was the sexiest man she had
ever seen (each to her own). I called him the next day to
present her case but he wasn't too enthusiastic. "Listen," I
pleaded, "she doesn't even know who you are. She doesn't
know about your money or your power or give a damn . . .
she just thinks *you* are a hunk. How long has it been since
a woman wasn't impressed by your money or your power
but responded overwhelmingly to your *bod?*" He said he
couldn't remember that far back and, though he sort of had
a girlfriend, agreed to call Georgina.

   He took her out, the romance "took," and they began
to date. He brought her to a big fund-raiser of which he
was the chair; she took him to the opera. He took her to
a party at his daughter's house (always a good sign when
they want you to meet the family); she invited him to the
country. After four dates, Georgina decided it was time for
the assignation and called her godmother, me, to discuss
details. Would they dine in the living room in front of the
fire or in the studio with all her busts? (She sculpts.) By
the fire, we decided. "We'll have Israeli melon, the best
chili in the world . . . Bessie makes it . . . Bibb and endive.
Cristal champagne. Apple tart." Wardrobe next. Would it
be her Valentino caftan or Armani pajamas with the
dragon pin? We decided Armani. I couldn't get my mind
on *Cosmo* one whole day anticipating her evening.

   Like a good goddaughter, the darling girl called the
next morning with gory (wonderful) details. "He knew tonight was the night and we went upstairs after dinner,"
said Georgina. "Fortunately I have this dressing room off
the bedroom and he could go there and undress. We met
in bed. He wore nothing. I had on this long-sleeve China-
silk sleep shirt." (Isn't that perfect? I might have known
she would pick the ultimate sexy-chic garment to wear to
bed.) Then the description of *it*—and I mean we are not
talking about twitty *young* people from whom you'd *ex-*

pect a night of wild sex and who wants to hear about it anyway but these are *grown*-ups. I held my breath. On arriving in bed they kissed passionately. He made love to her (he's sixty-three), was very pleased with himself and went right to sleep. "We were simply glued together all night long," said Georgina, "although I did get up once about four o'clock. He said that to me next morning—'We haven't been three inches apart all night.' I felt he was about to be aroused again but decided not to encourage him ... it would have been ... pressing. You know, we were a little inhibited, I think ... our first time and all that, so I couldn't really do all the things I'm able to do." (I know what *those* are. Georgina has told me she goes down on her restaurant-owner, married boyfriend by the *hour* and, "It just drives him *crazy*. He makes love and then he can start all over again ... he is simply *insatiable*. He gets a hard-on the minute we get in the cab.")

But back to Wall Street; after a few more assignations, all described to me on the phone, Georgina and her financier did not go on together. He was so caught up in his charity work, even more than trading, and Georgina was really in love with the restaurateur who made her feel "so successful," but who didn't, of course, ever leave his wife ... the man knew a captain's paradise when he *had* one. Georgina presently left *him* for a widowed, handsome art dealer who may or may not be a womanizer but I never worry about Georgina. She will *always* be involved with the "wrong man," the right man, *some* man, and will not just be having sex, which is very important to her, but in *love*. Dear Georgina.

And Irene. "I know other people's romances are yawnsville, but I'm so flabbergasted by what's happened to me I have to talk. I'm sixty-four; if a major romantic affair can happen to me, it can happen to anyone. I'd been hoping for years to find someone to have a sex life with (I've been married forever but there isn't any sex in our lives; Jim abandoned that years ago) and a romance with but had virtually given up. My girlfriends were awful. 'You *know* men want young p— — —y,' they would say or, 'Who needs the *aggravation?!*' I've had a lover or two in recent years but nobody to really enjoy making love to—if you could call it that. Then he just quietly came into my life . . . sixty-two . . . sat next to me at a charity luncheon. Quiet, not drop-dead gorgeous though very manly . . . solid, sturdy, gray . . . brilliant but not a great conversationalist—he talks better than he listens—but something clicked on . . . like maybe you don't start the motor the minute the ignition is turned on but you know it *will* start.

"We had five lunch dates . . . he's married, too . . . over a period of six months and I finally had to seduce him. He said he hadn't asked me to dinner before because he didn't want to be rejected . . . how undiscerning can somebody *be?!* When I finally got him to my apartment, we began to kiss like schoolkids . . . I think we were both starved—I know *I* was. Well, I simply went toes up . . . I haven't been so moved by anybody since high school. Sex when you're older is so often to make the *man* happy—you *have* to be good in bed or they won't be there with you—but this man is actually thinking about *me* . . . the best kisser I have *ever* known . . . the best *lover* . . . I get melted down just thinking about him and I have *orgasms.* I wish he cherished me . . . adored me . . . I'm not sure he does. I have some bad moments, even days, when I feel he might check in oftener, stay a little closer even though we can only see each other once a week. I'm in love, I'm afraid—not just in like—and in love always makes you vulnerable no matter what age you are. I have to accept the risks—we're going into our eighth month post-lunch dates now. I will just hold on tight and be grateful to the edge of my soul this could happen. I'm often blissed out. When it's over, if it has to be, I hope to have enough sexual confidence to find another lover."

Sexual confidence. How can a woman in her sixties, for God's sake, have sexual confidence? By taking somebody to bed—giving them both something to smile about in the morning. Occasional sex, as I keep saying, keeps the juices flowing, keeps you from drying up like an ancient apricot, keeps you thinking *female.* If romance accompanies, hallelujah. If it doesn't, you can do without. But you have to get in the game to play it. You can do the "what if's" forever, participate only in your head because you have less than luscious legs and arms *or* you can go into the icy water, swim around a bit and find it isn't *that* cold ... you *don't* get pneumonia ... actually it's *invigorating* ... and with sexual activity comes, inexorably, sexual confidence. If you can "do it" with one person, you can with another and sex is your registry of possible acts. Forever, or nearly forever, I hope. I don't know that you can dive in and start an affair if you never did earlier—or can you?

I give you Rex and Louise, both seventy-one, he married three times, she widowed twice, the mother of three daughters. They are lovers as well as friends and have a good sex life. ("I can't believe I'm telling you this," screams Louise as I skulldrag the details out of her. "You've got to camouflage me!") How did you two get together? I ask. "Three different sets of friends tried to fix us up," says Louise, "and we did meet but he was involved with a current flame. Ten months later we began to date and the relationship was sexual from the beginning. Nobody seduced anybody; we just both wanted it that way."

Why don't more older women go for sex? I ask. "I think a lot of people just can't wait to leap into old age," says Louise. "Women don't care if their backsides look like the back of a truck, flesh rotting away ... old age is comfortable and cozy. In my case, after Morris [her husband] died, I was in deep mourning, couldn't really eat for months and lost a ton of weight. What have we *here,* I asked myself one day as I observed this first-time-in-twenty-years slender body (my bust was always okay). Looking in the mirror sort of turned me on ... sex *is* narcissistic, you know. When you like the way your body looks, you somehow feel you want to *go* for it. Too bad Morris didn't have the fun of sleeping with a non-fattie but he just loved *me."* Will she and Rex marry? "That would be seven marriages between us," says Louise. "I don't think either of us really needs it but I surely do need this strong, wonderful friendship and physical relationship. I *know* I'm lucky."

A much-admired woman I know in her late eighties has been rendezvousing with a man fifteen years younger than she once a month for many years. They spend the evening together at her house. They have fun; they have sex. He is married. She couldn't care less. She doesn't want him for a mate; she wants him for "something special in my life, I don't think I could have made it without him . . . my special friend," she says. "I look forward to seeing him like a schoolgirl. We talk frequently on the phone but this night of love . . . well, it keeps me going."

"I've always been totally man-oriented," says a woman I met on a Roxbury, Connecticut, weekend, "started having sex at fifteen." Don't you miss it? I ask the cliché thing, assuming she doesn't have sex anymore now that she's seventy-two. "Who says I miss it?" asks my new acquaintance. "I have two men—one in Brussels, one in Los Angeles—I see several times a year. I never wanted to marry again . . . Sam was the best . . . but this is perfect. Older men get things wrong with them and need a nurse . . . as in Wife. These men give me what *I* need; their wives get to be the nurse." Isn't that a little heartless? I ask. "Their wives don't *want* them sexually," she explains. "They could even be grateful!"

To continue the "don't count me out sexually because I'm not young anymore" brigade, a gynecologist friend tells me of a patient, ninety-two years old, who, he assures me, has sex regularly. "She came in one day slightly worse for wear," he said "three different partners in one weekend, presumably people she paid, which caused a little havoc and we had to do a D and C." Is this somebody gaga? I ask. "No," says the doctor. "She is quite personable and definitely all there. She just overdid it."

Maxine, attractive, famous, divorced, sixty-nine, has "four men in my life I can call on . . . and I just started a new romance last month. Listen, your girlfriends are the greatest and you can go to the theater or the beach with a *group* of friends. I keep being with men because I like *sex!*" How did she meet the new man? "I picked him up on Fifty-seventh Street at Fifth Avenue. . . . I was on the Bergdorf side and locked eyes with a man coming toward me. I crossed to the other side and he crossed also. Later he said, 'Maxie, you picked me up.' 'I *didn't,*' I said. 'You crossed the street and came after me.' 'Maxie, I had to cross the street *anyway,*' he said. I think I'm going to see less of the other three men . . . this one's special."

It just makes me so happy to report on women our age and older who are sexually active and alive. These are *true* stores; let me repeat: I can't write fiction worth a damn and my pals have trustingly let me tell *their* stories. Sexual confidence for the over-sixty single *or* married woman . . . isn't that terrific?

I'll just remind us again that sex is one of the three best things there is and I'm not sure what the other two are. Women our age should *indulge.* It's free, give or take a few new outfits, hairdressing appointments and leg waxing to make you pretty for a lover. Sex is healthy . . . revitalizing, energizing, nurturing. God knows it *feels* good . . . the best *physical* feeling there is. A planned sexual rendezvous gives you something to get *up* for in the morning and to look forward to during the week. It is definitely youth preserving, mentally and physically, stimulating as well as relaxing. There! I just don't want you to feel one hour of guilt if you are enjoying sex or planning to—you are *exemplary;* a role model for all of us.

chapter four

Beauty

Are we older females utter nitwits to care so much *(still)* about beauty? Certainly we are, but the world rewards beauty so lavishly it's hard not to take it seriously even at this late date. Men—if you want to use *them* as a yardstick—still value beauty in a woman—and we are talking here about the outside stuff as in Diane Sawyer, Kim Basinger and Cindy Crawford, not inner as in Mother Teresa—more than any other asset, no matter *what* they say, and they say a lot of silly stuff like what they care about most is intelligence, pleasing personality and "she should be fun to be with." Don Johnson said in a *Cosmo* interview, "The most important ingredient for a woman is a good sense of humor. If she can make me laugh, the rest is workable." We should give him perhaps Phyllis Diller? Sylvia Miles? Reizl Bozyk as the divine matchmaking hag in *Crossing Delancey?* What they mean is that after the requisite *beautiful* is taken care of (Don has married beauteous Melanie Griffith *twice),* they can *then* start to appreciate other things.

Of course, after marriage they do start caring more about whether we can get the septic tank unclogged than whether our eyes are clear emerald pools of light, but going in, beauty zonks. I never knew a beautiful woman who couldn't find a man if she wanted one until she got to be about sixty; after that the going gets tougher. Brains, humor, charm—even goodness, in a pinch—are what some of us use to make *up* for not being gorgeous. Sometimes I, not a great beauty, make myself *sick* being so perky and sweet all the time with doormen, elevator men, gas-station attendants, flight attendants, bus drivers, receptionists, manicurists, hairdressers, masseuses, salesgirls, doctors' and dentists' nurses, hostesses, hostess's children, hostess's husband, hostess's mother, hostess's aunt visiting from Witchcraft, Wisconsin, the busboy who puts down the rolls and butter, the one who picks up the dishes ... you name it and I am nice to it! If I were gorgeouser, I know I would be less adorable!

If you want to let us *all* off the hook for our preoccupation with beauty, I will just reprise the primordial reason I mentioned in Chapter Three about why men respond to youth and beauty as they do. Men have to get their genes into the gene pool, i.e., reproduce. To do that their penis has to get all perked up. It does that *best* when its owner encounters young and beautiful. And our sex *wants* the other one to get its genes into our pool (give us a baby) so the race will continue, so we go around trying to be gorgeous and, if we can't make it all the way, we do the best we *can*. Striving to be beautiful to have babies may seem a little farfetched *now* (it's twenty years too late) but that's how the whole birdbrained thing got started and maybe what continues to fuel the scramble on a subliminal level. In addition to baby-production needs, beauty has always been such a *negotiable* asset; whether man *or* woman, if you're a smasher you get offered worship, dinner in Paris via the Concorde, roles in movies, *big* diamonds, blue chips—things like that!

Men like to be beautiful, too, of course, though their looks don't deliver quite as well as ours except in the gay world. A man married for his beauty who doesn't also *do* something in life will tend to be denigrated. (Did anyone ever really admire Joan Collins's Peter Holm other than for his looks and his chutzpah?) Still, a darling CEO I know sighs wistfully when he talks about the blond, sculptured looks of the actor who played Sebastian in the TV miniseries *Brideshead Revisited.* "It wouldn't hurt to look like that," he says. I'll bet nearly every man you know knows another man about whom he thinks, "It wouldn't hurt to look like that," though looks-envy in men is rarely revealed. (Thank *God!* We've got enough to cheer them up about!) Occasionally it slips out. The first words out of the mouth of a man I know who'd just read a major story about himself in *The Wall Street Journal*—flattering, almost idolatrous—were "Do I really look like that?" referring to a *not* flattering line drawing that accompanied the article.

I'm going to say this just once again, having said it so often I've really become a bore: Not being beautiful doesn't make any difference to one's friends, loved ones or employers most of the time. The friends figure our being plain makes *them* look better. Parents love you anyway even if you're a turnip . . . bone of my bone, flesh of my flesh, etc. Employers reason that average looks don't distract co-workers, plus maybe you won't be such a target for a rival-company "takeover," but few people don't line up with the idea you have to try to look as good as you *can,* even if you don't make it all the way to gorgeous. If we had the *choice* of beauty or brains, which we don't, brains are better—truth!—yet I always wonder what it must be *like* to be Catherine Deneuve, Michelle Pfeiffer, Claudia Schiffer. Beauties never tell you. Darling Candice Bergen, one of the prettiest and *best* women—a class act— absolutely hisses if you mention her looks. "Who, me?!" She is glaring over her shoulder to see whom you might be referring to. An early film star, Dolores del Rio, may have started that "beautiful on the inside is all that matters" crap. When reporters remarked her deep Latin beauty, she would always say it came from "drinking weak tea and spending a whole day a week in bed." On *Today,* when Gene Shalit asked Sophia Loren what it was like to be gorgeous, she said, "I have good friends and, finally, peace of mind," paying no attention whatever to what she'd been asked. I was recently chatting with my gorgeous friend Georgette Mosbacher on the subject of beauty and she said, "The most important thing a woman can do if she wants to be beautiful is exude a feeling of confidence." I am pounding my forehead. "Georgette," I scream. "Where are we *getting* this confidence if we aren't beautiful?!" Darling girl didn't *know.* Beauties are frequently well meaning on the subject of looks but full of shit! Great beauties are supposed to suffer *more* as they age and the looks they have so depended on fail. Forget it! We nongreat beauties suffer just as much.

The beauty preoccupation starts early. Richard Lacayo writes in *Vogue,* "Our sense of the matter is wrapped up in teenage traumas. There comes a point in adolescence when you start to imagine that some people are born with every molecule in place. Every high school boasts its elite squad of lookers: sparkling teeth, merciless anatomy, sunny filaments of hair—even their cuticles are kind of interesting. Between classes, they parade down the halls, trooping their supremacies like Clydesdales. Everybody else is supposed to feel like a waste of protoplasm. That sort of thing can complicate your feelings toward physical beauty for the rest of your life." Certainly confidence in your looks comes and goes . . . a shaky business indeed. On a particular day, for no special reason except you got enough sleep, you may just strike yourself as delicious. Another day, looking about the same, you think, Oh, my God, gargoyle! What else to do but *live* with this confidence inconsistency? Confident or not, this is what befalls *all* of us sooner or later.

Skin gets papery.

Spots appear on hands, arms, calves . . . we're no longer one smooth creamy surface.

Hair, moisture, bosom disappear.

We start looking a little neuter in photographs . . . you can't tell the girls from the boys.

A lot of that stuff can be *fixed,* thank God. A sure indicator that it *needs* fixing is when construction workers stop whistling. It was bad enough—well, many women thought it was bad, I never did—when you ran the gauntlet and they said things like "Hey, Big Momma, you lookin' great!" Much worse is walking past now when they say *nothing!* Some men you know do *try* to fill the void. Donald Trump told me the other night at a United Cerebral Palsy gala, "Baby, you look beautiful!" I felt all perked up until three hours later when I made the mistake of looking in the mirror and found I resembled Baby Jane (as in *Whatever Happened to?*) in her terminal stage. (We usually look great going in but I, for one, begin to disintegrate within about forty-five minutes.) Ryan O'Neal greeted me on an airplane: "Helen, you look so *young!*" You know *they* know you aren't and they know you know they know you aren't, so I'd just as soon they pick another compliment. (Is anybody telling Brooke Shields *she* hasn't aged?)

Many intelligent people declare that women should quit *worrying* about looks. Germaine Greer in a *Vogue* article: "You could fight matronliness. You could dye your hair. You could diet until you were as thin as a rail and then get your collapsed jowls hiked up and your crow's feet ironed out. You could get your empty bosom pumped up. And it would all be a dreadful waste of time, money and energy." She goes on. "The great privilege of the middle-aged is to make their own faces; gradually their personality obliterates their physical inheritance, the phenotype prevails over the genotype . . . now, at last, we can escape from the self-consciousness of glamour; we can really listen to what people are saying, without worrying whether we look pretty doing it." Oh, dear, I can listen like a maniac and *still* worry about pretty!

Other abstainers: The wife of a famous politician refuses to dye her hair, take off weight or follow fashion and is the role model for millions of women who also don't want to bother. She is one of the most admirable women who ever lived but not necessarily, in my opinion, for her stand on beauty. (It is said her husband had a mistress of some tenure at the time he last ran for office and the wife refused to help him campaign unless he gave the lady up. He did and she did. Threatening the loss of an election is *one* way to get a man home again but still doesn't convince me letting yourself go gray or portly is the *most* wonderful idea.)

Switching to the believers: A CBS cameraman told me that when Margaret Thatcher was interviewed by Diane Sawyer, she told Diane she wanted "exactly the same lighting and flattering angles they're giving *you.*" Smart! Even for us who care seriously about our looks and pay close attention, the giant breakthroughs are still to be made, of course. Wish I were going to *be* here for them, living to be two hundred wrinkle-free, but meanwhile, I think about Queen Elizabeth I in 1590, with that pocked skin and black teeth and the Marquise de Montespan in the seventeenth century, with those jowls the size of airplane flaps and tubs of baby fat, and think I am lucky to be living *now* with all the stuff we *can* do to look better. There is no comparison between *us* at our age having just come out of New York Hospital after a $15,000 face-lift and a twenty-five-year-old girl just getting out of *bed* in the morning doing *nothing* about her looks. But if we stop acting as though we *could* compete with a junior and stick with our own age group for comparisons, it's really quite gratifying to see how good we *can* look.

I see these nifty women in the streets, stores and restaurants of New York City with their sleek bodies, streaked hair, clothes so *Bazaar* and *Mirabella* and am in *awe*. Probably more beauty paragons exist here than any other place on earth but they *do* exist. Countess Aline de Romanones, an OSS agent in World War II, now in her late sixties, gives me a jump every time I see her. She is stunning and there are lots more like her. One day I was lunching with usually acerbic John Fairchild of *Women's Wear Daily* at La Grenouille, New York's posh French restaurant, and he said of Pauline Trigere (Pauline was born in 1912) across the room, "Look at Pauline . . . doesn't she look great?!" That's what I want them to say about me a few tiny years from now when I am Pauline's age or even right *now*. In a perfume ad Bill Blass declares, "Looking good is the best revenge." Bet your ass! You need self-discipline to keep up the looks grind and I guess you either have it or you don't. I find it relatively "easy" to do whatever you have to do to keep a job and look okay because the alternatives (unemployment and crone-hood) are unacceptable! *Fear* "self-disciplines" me!

It's good to start at least by your forties to preserve your looks, but if you didn't start then, *any* time is okay. I'm doing stuff now I couldn't be bothered with at thirty. Who tucked her tush against the back of the chair *every* time she sat down?! Or Scotch-taped her forehead lines every morning? I don't think it's smart to pretend to *be* younger. Somebody always has a sister who went to school with you who has a *brother* you can't shut up. ("Jessica couldn't have been born later than 1928 because she and Janice were roommates at Wellesley and Jessica was two years older than Janice who was born in 1930.) But looking sensational at *our* age, oh, yes! Of course, *deep* reality dawns some days . . . like nobody says skiddeldy-boo when you announce at the Delta Shuttle you'd like the senior-citizen rate to Washington ($60 as opposed to $142) and they write it right up without even a lifted *eyebrow?!* I glance carelessly into the floor-to-ceiling bathroom mirror as I am planting a kiss on David's shoulder as he gets out of the shower—he's so pink and cute and all steamed up like a Chinese dumpling—and confront this apparition with sort of fangy yellow teeth and dim eyes (me) and think, who *is* this? I don't recognize this person. The ghastly feeling doesn't last too long, however. It's back to the oatmeal scrub, the face exercises and picking out a pretty dress to erase the mirror image.

On the subject of mirrors, you have to treat them, even at home, like alligators: Don't *surprise* one. Whoever said, if you want to know how you'll look ten years from now, look down in a mirror, has to have been a masochist. It will take you three weeks to recover! The trick is not to be depressed by looking straight *into* a mirror. We've got a killer one just outside the ladies' room at *Cosmo* I ought to have yanked years ago, but the girls like it and I've got my own friendly one with pink lights elsewhere. The mirror by the door of my florist, Macres, at Seventh Avenue and Fifty-seventh Street, you need chloroform to get by (close your eyes and *grope* in and out!). Certain restaurant ladies' rooms are uplifters. At La Grenouille you look sixteen. Frankie and Johnny's steak house on West Forty-fifth Street is a surprise flatterer. Le Cirque, La Côte Basque, "21" are just okay. In some fitting rooms you could take your own life . . . how do they *sell* anything?! I got stuck with a monster three-way job at the Houston Grand Hyatt just before making a talk and nearly couldn't go *on.* Cellulite I couldn't see at home was clear as Lucite and never mind it didn't show during the speech. I was acutely depressed. You probably should have both types of mirror at home—friendly to stay cheerful with, brightly lit *magnifying* for putting on makeup; your audience won't be gazing at you through a silk screen so you need truth. After you finish with the magnifying mirror and look in an ordinary-size one, you look tiny and great! P.S. There are no nonvain people who never *look* in mirrors whatever their age. I see *everybody* gazing surreptitiously in the mirror-lined promenade in the Parker Meridien Hotel that goes all the way through from Fifty-sixth Street to Fifty-seventh. I just wish they hadn't put so many chairs in front of the mirrors.

So now could I tell you a few thoughts, I hope encouraging, about beauty and older?

MAKEUP

Back in the late-sixties, early-seventies hippie period, and again in the strong feminist early eighties, makeup got such a bad rap I thought we might actually quit wearing it. We didn't! (I never intended to.) Manufacturers keep making more and more wonderful products, their ad agencies presenting them ever more enticingly, and some of us will undoubtedly keep using them until our fingers numb. The addiction has certainly been *around* a long time. Cleopatra had those kohl-rimmed eyes, girls of ancient Greece, Kabuki-white faces with red circles painted on their cheeks, the sixteenth-century courts of Louis, the Henrys and Charles, fluffy powdered wigs, so we, with gold glitter for our shoulder blades and lash-thickening mascara, are just a continuation of history, right? I hope you're still experimenting. *I* am. Wish I looked a little more ravishing after the experiment, but it doesn't matter. The point is to look alive and so almost every day I hit the street running beneath something old *and* something new.

Everybody says use *less* makeup as you age. My darling friend Grace Mirabella (mid-sixties), the longtime editor of *Vogue* and now of her own *Mirabella,* is surprisingly pristine. "The less you do the 'younger' you look," says Grace. "Artificial 'fixing up' tends to be aging!" Well, okay, Grace, I'm not pushing lime-green blusher and fuchsia eye shadow, and of course you're marble-bare when nobody's around, but foundation, eyeliner, lip pencil and blush are almost as fundamental to me as *teeth*.

What about learning from a professional makeup artist exactly what he/she does and doing it yourself? Sounds sensible but for one thing: There *is* no ultimate, perfect, pull-all-the-stops-out look just right for you to be duplicated every day. Makeup artists all have different versions of you, and do different things. As for *learning* from them, your eyes are closed a lot while they work; also they go so *far*. There they are stroke-stroking away every little blemish with Pan-Stik, painting over lines like Tom Sawyer whitewashing the fence. After the camouflage comes contouring with cream rouge and blusher, six things on your eyelids, then liner, brow pencil, the Rita Hayworth mouth . . . are *you* going to do all that? It can actually take an *hour!* I remember fondly the late, great Way Bandy following me downstairs from the office to the curb where David was pacing—and roaring like a lion—as Way put on the last fake eyelash: He did them individually.

The point is, it's hard to learn from the pros and mostly they don't teach. I think you have finally got to figure it out for yourself. You're not going to spend more than five or ten minutes a day on your face anyway. For something special you start earlier and work harder *or* have a professional makeup job just for the night. We do many before and afters at *Cosmo* with models (who *don't* look all that great before the makeup, incidentally) *and* civilians, and none of them ever continues to do the "after" makeup on a regular basis. Too much work, too fakey and, if you've pulled all the stops out every day, where would be the joy and drama when you need to look really fabulous? So, what you do to your face is a work in progress *still* but, for God's sake, this is not the time to hang up our brushes, and look as bare as Mother H.'s cupboard, do you think?

Hair Health

"Hair is what life is all about," says my delicious friend Nancy Collins of *Prime Time Live*. Who could argue? I have learned not to wince (well, maybe one little wince) when I see somebody with a head of bushy beautiful hair—which is all the time. My own is ridiculous! Split ends, overbleaching, temporary loss from illness, childbirth—those can all be *fixed*. Baby-fine, not thick, the wispiness exacerbated by aging (aaaaagggghhhh!) hair is from genes and *cannot*, though you try *everything*. (According to an archaeological exhibit at the Israel Museum in Jerusalem, people in the ancient world rubbed their hair with the fat of lions, hippos and crocodiles to fend off baldness. Maybe I should give that a shot. I would gladly trade my twenty-two inch waist, pretty ears (what can you do with *ears*, for God's sake?!), ability to tango and three-karat ruby ring for Dyan Cannon's hair. I mean how *could* they have given that girl so much more than she needs when we're out there *starving?!* Being the world's living expert on crumby hair, I'm going to offer some thoughts about that kind. Girls with Alice-in-Wonderland hair can go shred a coconut (with their bare hands) for all I care.

Tips for Skimpy Hair

If your hair is *worse* than it used to be (let's start on a really high note—although actually everybody's *is* worse . . . age does that), you need to check with a doctor. He can't do a thing about genes but can monitor your estrogen level. It drops when you get older, causing hair follicles to give up hair more easily, and it may not make a comeback. New hair that comes *in* is skinnier and more fragile. Your doctor may prescribe Premarin or another estrogen supplement which at least helps you hold on to hair you now have. About estrogen supplements increasing your chance of getting cancer, doctors don't agree. My two—an internist and gynecologist who confer with each other— prescribed semi-lethal amounts of estrogen for me for twenty-six years (to stave off osteoporosis, prevent uterine shrinkage *and* help hair). The twenty-seventh year I had to have a hysterectomy, but neither doctor thinks the estrogen did it. Low thyroid can affect hair, and your doctor may prescribe thyroid (I'm up to three grains a day).

Minoxidil, the tincture for which everybody had such high hopes, has helped virtually nobody grow or hold on to hair, as far as I can glean. Twenty percent positive results would be a high estimate. My beloved dermatologist, Norman Orentreich, has been mixing minoxidil with progesterone with some success. My two droppersful a day over a two-year period have produced a *little* action in the temple area (small and fuzzy *counts!*). As for general good health, that won't improve crumby hair, though bad health could make it *worse*. Translation: Broccoli and oat bran are better for your hair than pecan waffles and hot dogs, and lay off the drugs, booze, caffeine, cigarettes, but you *know* all this stuff already. I take thirty vitamin and mineral supplements every day and haven't a clue whether they help my hair but I'm never sick and figure they're my friends.

Hair Care

To shampoo every day or not is still up for grabs. Noted trichologist Philip Kingsley says daily is fine, even for thin hair, but while using Philip's clean, elegant products, I shampoo just three times a week or never more than every other day. Seems to me that when there's a tiny buildup of debris, when you *do* shampoo, hair gets fluffier. Hair-thickening mousses and gels would seem to have been invented for us, but weren't necessarily. The first few hours you've got more body but then the hair gets kind of icky. Just plain hair seems best for us skinny hair people. No hair spray and no sleeping on rollers or even bobby pins. Rollers or pins go into *dry* hair only. Blow-drying makes hair look better than air-drying, and Philip says it doesn't hurt if you blow-dry just to the point of dry. Don't brush thin hair *ever.* Use wide-tooth combs. Don't ever back-comb or tease except for special occasions. What little hair you have needs to be made maximum with cutting so you need a good haircut every four to six weeks. *Very* important. Coloring isn't thrilling for wispy locks but some of us don't want white (we're too young!), so we color. I go to Gabriella at Donsuki every six weeks. A shade or two up from your original color is usually best.

Beauty salons are for people with *hair,* so I spend little time there. I'm too busy and the operators get frustrated with the "just one soaping, please, no spray, no teasing, no back-combing . . . stop! Those are not *leaves* you're raking!" For a big night, a hairdresser comes to my office or house. We go all the way and use gel, hot rollers (awful for fragile hair), hair spray, and we tease . . . we are *very* wicked! I do the same thing for television.

You would certainly think hairpieces helpful for skimpy hair, but I don't think they are. A friend who has virtually *no* hair (alopecia) has been wearing full wigs for thirty years and always looks nice, but hairpieces to augment *skinny* hair are not magic. You have to get your own hair brushed up over the join line of the fall in front and that requires back-combing—yikes! A full wig for everyday use is like wearing a close-fitting hat (not too comfortable), and without somebody to recomb you and straighten things up a bit as the day or night wears on, you may begin to look a bit "wiggy." A small curly hairpiece can be placed on the crown of your head to fill in *curly* hair but that doesn't work with straight hair. Genius wigmaker Nicholas Piazza made me a beautiful little real-hair wig recently—a Space Ball he calls it—with big holes you pull your own hair through—fake and real all mixed up— which sounded like heaven but it takes Nicholas to get it on. To get the real hair pulled through the holes, the hairpiece has to be left a bit loose, otherwise your hair is "hemmed in" and can't be pulled through. But if it's left loose and the hairpiece doesn't fit snugly against the scalp, by the time you've pulled the real hair *through,* you look like a Zulu.

I think I've discarded maybe twenty wigs and hairpieces by now, though that's not the case for everybody. I have a *couple* I like now. A glamorous (megafamous) television interviewer has a Nicholas Space Ball *and* full wig she plops on in civilian life and loves both. Joan Rivers has hair *extensions* for just a few straight locks on the left side of her hair so it can make a dramatic sweep across her brow. Listen, you probably have your own fake-hair solution. What seems to work best for me is a China-silk scarf, same color as hair, brought from underneath hair in back, up over tops of ears, tied over the forehead with two loose ends. You look perky. Tendrils are also nice. Set a pin curl on each side at temples close to your ears; unfurl just before going out. If you pile your hair (doesn't that sound lush? ... *pile* your hair!!!) on top of your head, unfurl tendrils and pop a taffeta one-and-a-half-inch-wide hair bow with ends sticking out beyond the sides of your head in back up near the crown, you also add the look of volume. Hair slicked back with a fake-hair chignon or braid added at the nape of the neck is fine if your face can take the severity; columnist Cindy Adams and Casey Ribicoff, the ex-senator's wife, look good that way.

Listen, mouse hair isn't the worst. We can talk, convince, persuade, flirt, do some decent things for society, get on with our work, our lives ... achieve ... and not a single soul gives a damn about our crumby hair except us (or so I *think* I've convinced myself).

SKIN

We have yards of skin, did you know that? It's our biggest organ. I find it fascinating you can do so many things to improve it, especially if you've got a killer dermatologist like Norman Orentreich. Norman injected tiny amounts of silicone into my face and hands every two months for years until the FDA made it illegal. They were wrong. In the hands of somebody gifted like Norman, if there *is* anybody gifted like him, it was wildly helpful and safe. I miss it and hope the decision gets reversed. Whatever Norman wants to do is just fine with me. You know better than to go to him in a low-cut dress because he will attack anything showing which reveals bumpiness, lumpiness, redness, roughness, pimpling or puffiness—I call it the Norman invasion! One morning I told him of an itchy back ... could he see it? he asked, and ten minutes later—he works like blue lightning—with needle, scalpel, laser, current, hyfrecator, aluminum chloride, lidocaine and gauze to mop up, we had taken care of tiny dots on chest, shoulders, throat, scar tissue behind ears from a face-lift and one tiny mole, the itchy back having merely been assigned a prescription. I would throw myself under a train if Norman told me to, and there has to be a *reason* his waiting room is wall-to-wall people, men *and* women. The reason is you look better, feel sunnier about your looks and life after seeing him. You might like to know about collagen for facial-line removal but I can't help. I've been getting silicone injections (now suspended because of the government edict) from Norman for twenty years and since he doesn't *like* collagen, I've never investigated. Some people who *have* think it's great.

Dr. Orentreich is onto something promising for skin cancer—Fluorouracil, an ointment that pulls incipient cancel cells up to the surface of the skin where they slough off—you don't have to dig the cancer out later. Having spent twenty-seven years in the California sun, I'm a good candidate for Fluorouracil. We've done my chest and nose so far (who cares that you look like chicken-pox city for three weeks while the cancer cells surface?!). Dr. O. is testing the product for faces now. Listen, this is experimental stuff. *Your* doctor has to decide what's safe and feasible for you.

Skin Home Care

Let's start with the soap or cream cleanser decision. Ninety percent of the "experts" (cosmetic companies, salons, beauty editors, *women)* vote cleanser. Dr. Orentreich votes soap (plus a Buf-Puf to exfoliate every night), so that's for me—*naturellement!* Having been plagued as a teenager with blotchy pus-filled acne spots that had to be opened twice a week—aaaagggghhhh!—I learned to cleanse religiously every night and would have to have just been hit by a train not to do that now.

Can spritzing with Evian help "moisturize" skin? Again, the experts say moisture can't be got or kept in this way, but considering the nice rose-petal skins of English girls in all that fog and the dried-leaf look of desert girls, I spritz away. The spray certainly *feels* good. (Special spritzing recipe in a moment.) What you put on your skin at bedtime or under makeup in the daytime is a wide wild choice! The Lauders, Lancômes, Revlons, Georgette Klinger, Elizabeth Arden and so many others offer a treasure trove of products, nearly all terrific. I'm hooked on a Retin-A formula from Orentreich for bedtime. According to literature in his office, "Older patients treated with Retinoic Acid are observed to have younger looking skin. The improved appearance is the result of: 1) exfoliation and increased epidermal turnover; 2) increased turgor fullness of the skin, reducing the appearance of fine wrinkling; 3) anti-tumor effects, with regression of precancerous lesions; 4) new blood vessel formation and increased blood flow (a more healthful color); 5) more uniform pigmentation; 6) increased collagen formation." Not bad for one little formula.

I'm sure your own dermatologist can prescribe something, but keep in mind some skins get an allergic reaction. Over-the-counter formulas contain only retinoids, a similar substance, not as strong or effective as Retin-A. Anybody's moisturizer is fine. Lubriderm from Warner-Lambert is the best all-around moisturizing product for *any* part of your body I have ever found.

COSMETIC SURGERY

So many books and articles have been written on cosmetic surgery you probably know a lot already. *More Than Just a Pretty Face: How Cosmetic Surgery Can Improve Your Looks and Your Life* by Thomas D. Rees, M.D. (Little, Brown) is a good one. New techniques are being perfected all the time, however, and you may want to skim through the newest books at your bookstore.

Not *everybody* thinks cosmetic surgery is a good idea.

On the *New York Times* Op-Ed page recently, New York lawyer Wendy Kaminer wrote: "I visited her [mother] the day after the operation. Her head was wrapped in bloody bandages, her face was bruised, her eyes were swollen shut and she moaned a lot. I managed not to say I told you so, and prayed I'd never care enough about looking young to let some doctor cut into my face."

Wendy dear, I have news. They don't just "cut into your face," they literally slit your throat, but, you see, you don't know a thing about it at the time—you're *out*—so who cares about all that mess if it's cleaned up before you open your baby blues?

Wendy goes on: "I don't think sex or femininity should demand sacrifices of women or undermine their self-esteem. Plastic surgery is a way of losing control, submitting to fears about aging or simply . . . risking your health to satisfy someone else's model of womanhood and the cruel equation of beauty with goodness." Heavens!

Naomi Wolf has the same idea. In *The Beauty Myth* (Morrow) she posits that now we women are achieving mightily in our careers, we are being "put back in our place" by the inexhaustible need to be beautiful, by the hours and effort *that* requires. Men insist on our being gorgeous, she says, and we go along; *they* get off totally free. "Beauty is a conspiracy of pain forced upon women," says Naomi. Well, darling, if penises could be enlarged by surgery, I daresay *our* sex wouldn't be able to book a hospital room—short of having a ruptured appendix—in less than a year—*they'd* be in all the beds . . . and if baldness could be eradicated by helpers in a salon, we wouldn't be able to get in *there* for a fresh perm until late October! Women are simply not the only insecure ones.

Ava Gardner once said, "Honey, there comes a time when you've got to face the fact that you're an old broad. I've had a hell of a good time, so my face looks, well, lived in. You won't find me standing in front of a mirror, weeping."

You won't find *me* in front of a mirror weeping *either* but I *will* be there checking to see if the silicone, face exercise, Retin-A, remembering not to frown *ever,* are doing any good and if it's time to do my eyes again. Ava gave up. I didn't have her life ... the fame, the gorgeousness, the men—Sinatra and George C. Scott for two—half insane over her, but I'm doing fine.

So Wendy, Naomi, Ava, your convictions aren't mine. It just seems silly to me *not* to have a lift (or two). The technology is superb; it gets better all the time; your looks *do* improve. Detractors say lifts aren't natural. You bet your ass! Natural at our age is droops and folds. Capped teeth, pacemakers, polio vaccine, hip-replacement surgery and blood transfusions are not natural either but do we want to do *without* those things? So far I've had dermabrasion, rhinoplasty (nose), blepharoplasty (eyes) and one complete lift. Time for another soon. If you get the right surgeon, your lift will *appear* very natural indeed. People will say things like "Eleanor, you look so rested ... have you been to a spa?" or "Who is your hairdresser? ... I want his name this *second!"*

Lifts don't last forever, true, and yes, sometimes mistakes are made. I have a friend right this minute who can't get her *eyes* closed—they removed too much skin—and another whose face is divine on the right side but cockeyed on the left, which brings me to a point. Will you promise me to go to the best surgeon in your city? Any big city has several bests—ask around. I don't think you can *get* a bargain with somebody good. Top surgeons don't cut prices even for magazine editors who might offer articles extolling their skills or for personal-friend patients. The top ones have more business than they can handle.

Just so we'd have a little *official* information, I asked Dr. Michael Hogan, my friend and surgeon—many say the reigning cosmetic surgeon in the country now—to answer a few questions. His response:

Q.   What is the ideal age for a face-lift?

A.   *Between forty and fifty-five.*

Q.   How do you know when it's time for you?

A.   *Throat is crepey, jowls have developed. Put three fin-*

gers (pads down) of each hand under your chin, pull the skin back toward your ears on each side and if the look is considerably improved, you might be ready. People differ. When you go to a class reunion and some people look great and others look terrible and you're all the same age, you have to know some faces just age better than others. Some people are having lifts in their late twenties, especially actresses.

Q. How long does a lift last?

A. From eight to twelve years, but many women are now having maintenance procedures—not the complete lift but a "pickup." So you might have a complete lift, two or three smaller maintenance procedures along the way and not have another complete total lift until perhaps fourteen years after the first one. There is no limit to the number of face-lifts you can have if they are done properly. However, as a practical matter, three or four would probably be all anyone would need if they started, say, in their early forties.

Q. Does the second one last the same amount of time?

A. No, it will usually last longer than the first because the surgery uses up more of the skin's elasticity.

Q. What about the third lift?

A. A third lift can be done, but you must be careful because there isn't that much elasticity left in the skin— you've used it up in the first and second lifts—and you don't want to stretch the skin too far or you get the mummy look or look like you're standing in a 100-mile-per-hour gale!

Q. The maintenance procedure you mention, what is it? And how many can you have?

A. The procedure is the upper face-lift. This is simply a repeat of the upper part of the original lift but with *virtually no bruising or swelling. Instant gratification. In-and-out same-day surgery. No limit. You might have five or six of these between regular face-lifts.*

Q. **What's the ideal age to have eyes done?**

A. *When you need it . . . eighteen to eight-five, average forty-five.*

Q. **What about noses?**

A. *Actually very young—around fifteen or sixteen—because by then most growth has finished. Oddly enough, though, many women are now having this surgery in their fifties. Their noses didn't change or drop or anything. It just took these women awhile to realize there was something dramatic they could do to change their look.*

Q. **How many men have face-lifts?**

A. *About eight to ten percent of our patients are men. It's not that men age better than women but people seem to accept the craggy look—deep lines and wrinkles—in a man better than in a woman. The men who have the surgery run the gamut from CEOs and actors to politicians and policemen.*

Q. **Are there any new procedures you're excited about?**

A. *Absolutely. We've vastly improved the technique for removal of fat on the neck. We're using liposuction surgery on neck muscles and facial fascia. It's been around many years now, but continues to be an important part of the face-lift. Operating on the forehead area for falling brows has become much more common.*

Q. **How far are you booked ahead with surgery dates?**

A. *I'm pretty much booked a year in advance.*

SPECIFIC THOUGHTS FROM FRIENDS ABOUT BEAUTY

I didn't do a cattle call but just asked a few friends who look great—all but two are over fifty—what they do to look that way. Here are their ideas.

Georgette Mosbacher

I tattoo my eyebrows. Mine are colorless and not too thick so I go to a tattoo artist. I read in *Playboy* magazine where the best tattoo people were and went to Gary, Indiana, to have this done. They can now reverse the procedure if you don't like it.

You should brush your teeth in salt and soda once a month. This whitens teeth, but don't do it oftener because it also takes off the enamel.

Alexandra Mayes *(travel-book editor)*

A good haircut is the one best thing you can do. If you have good hair to begin with, it will show it off. If you have bad hair, a good cut will improve it. Forget trying to do this yourself—you cannot do the layering and under-structure that can be handled by a haircutter—spend the fifty dollars.

I use lip gloss instead of lipstick. You don't need a mirror to put it on, don't need to match shades to your dress or blouse . . . it doesn't run into the corners of your mouth, can't be seen on cups and glasses . . . gloss is efficiency itself!

Shirley Lord (Vogue *beauty editor*)

When your hair turns gray around the hairline, it looks as though your hair is receding. It *isn't* . . . the pigment has just gone away . . . but you could scare yourself to death! I had remarkable strawberry-blond hair, always took it for granted, but when it went gray I had a totally different look . . . like flatheaded! Reinstate the color around the face and you get a big lift.

Retin-A is the biggest beauty news of the century.

Joan Collins

When I was twenty, newly arrived in Hollywood and a suntanning freak, a friend who had the world's most beautiful skin took me to the Beverly Hills Hotel pool to survey the crocodile-skinned forty-year-olds who were soaking up the sun.

No one was really aware then of long-term damage, but my friend was and she insisted I stay out of the seductive rays from then on. Well, she was right. Since then I have never let the sun fall directly on my face, although I admit that because I love it so much, I sunbathe my body.

Sun damage doesn't show up immediately—it takes years—and when you see it, it's too late to do anything about it. So my advice is—stay out of the sun or if you must go in it, PROTECT THAT FACE.

Lauren Hutton

Always sleep on your back. Wrinkles melt right down!

Go to a dermatologist and have every single brown spot you've collected from the sun burned off. The procedure is expensive and painful but makes a big difference. Sunspots can turn into cancer so you want them *off*. Your skin also gets to be creamy-smooth and all one color.

Phyllis McGuire

Put warm wet tea bags on top of your eyes for puffiness— not *cold* wet tea bags but warm ones. Leave a wake-up call fifteen minutes earlier than usual and have room service deliver the tea bags. You'll get rid of tired eyes and puffiness like you won't believe. [I assume, Phyllis, those of us minus room service can prepare the tea bags ourselves.]

Polly Bergen

My hair is just this side of Sahara Desert dry . . . always a dull, boring *mess*. It doesn't get dirty . . . it doesn't get *anything* . . . just fine, blowaway hair. Once a month I put on a lot of Best Foods whole-egg mayonnaise. Leave it on under a shower cap for at least three hours—overnight is better. Wash it out—takes two or three soapings. Hair is no longer brittle . . . it has sheen . . . there's something magic about the mayonnaise but it has to be whole-egg. Great treatment after hot rollers, teasing, any kind of hair abuse.

Barbaralee Diamonstein (*author; chairman, New York Landmarks Preservation Foundation*)

I think just plain clean hair is best, so I don't even condition. While the shampoo is still on, I comb my hair with a wide-tooth comb, then wash out all the soap. When you come out your hair will be very combable, without all those tangles.

Someone once said I had pretty lips and I took them seriously. I outline my lips with a pencil, fill in with gloss.

At least once a month slather baby oil all over your body, put on a terry robe and let the oil sink in. Best to do this in a hotel rather than at home as you will get oil all over the bedclothes!

Feet are never paid enough attention and should be babied. Wash them, put on gobs of oil or cream and tuck them into quilted electric booties. They'll be baby-soft and lovely!

Joan Rivers

I drink gallons of water every day. Great for the body, good for the skin.

Robin Chandler Duke (*activist for population control*)

I swim against the tide of aging every day—forty laps—breaststroke, backstroke, and the crawl. At fifty-five, I put myself in the hands of the best plastic surgeon I could find and he did a marvelous job on my sagging face. At sixty-six, I feel healthy and happy. I ski at least thirty days of every winter, and if permitted, would ski three days a week year-round and work four days. That is my ideal. No

sunbathing for me. My mother always wore hats and carried a parasol, and like Mother, I am hatted. No
smoking—it ages you terribly and also kills you very pain-
fully. My motto is keep working, keep swimming, and
keep hoping.

Cecile Zilkha *(socialite; board of Metropolitan Opera)*

In the Middle East—Iran, Egypt, Lebanon, Syria—men do
not like women to have *any* hair on their bodies, and they
take off pubic hair as well. On their wedding day, women
have a complete hair removal. This is done with sugar,
lemon and water, boiled until the mixture thickens. Spread
on legs with hands; pull out hair.

I tried this darling "recipe" without specific amounts
or instructions—just boiled up some sugar and water,
slapped it on skin and talk about *messes!* I had sticky
syrup all over my legs, the kitchen, the walls! Cecile
called Paris, where she has this work done, and got exact
instructions. Here they are:

RECIPE

> *1 cup sugar*
> *¼ cup water*
> *½ lemon*

Combine sugar and water in saucepan, boil over medium
flame until mixture just begins to thicken. Squeeze in half
lemon (keeps mixture from caramelizing). Cook some
more until mixture is thick like taffy. Let cool to room
temperature; start kneading with your hands like taffy.
Smooth on skin; let set for a minute and pull off. Hair will
come with it.

This formula doesn't open pores, so you don't get in-
grown hair, just soft-as-velvet skin.

Kitty D'Alessio *(former president, Chanel)*

I use a smudgy blue pencil to line the upper lid, also a charcoal-gray regular pencil. The blue gives your eyes, your whole face, a lift.

I figure you can't be all colors in the rainbow—you'd look like a Gypsy—so I concentrate on black, white and pink for my face—blusher for the cheeks, then a tiny touch of blusher on both eyelids.

I plucked my eyebrows when I was young and they never grew back. I now draw them in with a charcoal pencil.

Veronica Hearst *(wife of publisher Randolph A. Hearst)*

I curl my eyelashes every day and brush my eyebrows into an arch. My father, thank God, would never let me pluck them.

A few drops of apple-cider vinegar mixed with Mountain Valley bottled water is a wonderful facial spritzer. Spray it on first thing in the morning and clean your face that way. That's all you need. Spritz again possibly an hour later, then put moisturizer on top when you're ready for makeup.

Put fresh avocado puree or olive oil or castor oil on your hair and wear this mix an hour or two or even overnight before you shampoo. Hair comes out luxurious.

Betsy Bloomingdale *(socialite)*

My best beauty trick is to stand up straight. When I was young, I used to see tall girls trying to be the same height as their dancing partners and their fannies stuck out and looked awful.

The one cosmetic I couldn't do without is mascara. I definitely don't leave home without it.

Aline, Countess of Romanones *(author)*

My miracle medicine is to have fun working. Do something you love as work and do it intensely. Have lots of physical fun. I take aerobics classes regularly, dance strenuously at least once a week, preferably ballroom dancing, which is sexy and healthy. (I go to Café Society on the corner of Twenty-first Street and Broadway in New York which has a wonderfully wholesome atmosphere with a live band. Yes, you have to bring your own partner.)

Betty Furness

Nothing looks worse on an older woman than little lines of lipstick leaking into tiny lines around the mouth. There are two things to do: 1. Don't wear lipstick at all. That solution is too drastic and unbecoming to me. 2. Use Elizabeth Arden's Lip Fix both under lipstick and on top. This way it's possible to keep a clean lip line (which I do with a lip pencil) all day long. I reapply the Lip Fix after eating. Remarkable product without which I'd look as old as I am . . . not acceptable!

Charlotte Ford

I glue my hair. My sister Anne got the good hair . . . Mother and I both have baby-fine hair, I shampoo every other day or every three days, blow-dry or air-dry, roll up in hot curlers, comb out and spray . . . and *spray!* We are talking major spray here, but the spray makes your hair look and feel thick. I don't think it hurts my hair . . . I use Clinique hair spray that brushes right out.

Pat Bradshaw *(writer; widow of RCA chief Thornton Bradshaw)*

I love *really* red lipstick . . . go through about a tube a month. Pale lipstick is for people who want to look as though they have tuberculosis! In winter I wear only black and red so it matches my clothes but I like it in summer, too.

Lynn Revson *(widow of Charles Revson, founder of Revlon)*

People tell me I look natural and fresh. The "trick" is lots of blusher, transparent foundation in the darkest shade by Revlon—nothing else on the skin—mascara, liner and eyeshadow—no skimping there. I use cocoa butter (comes in a tube) night and day on my lips—no lipstick—plenty of lip gloss—Chanel—no color.

Gloria Vanderbilt

I drink Evian all day long—tap water would be just as good—it keeps your weight down. Not sure how this works but probably it takes your mind off eating actual food. I have had the same hairstyle all my life. Sometimes Kenneth, who's done my hair forever, tells me people compliment him on the cut. That's nice to hear but I think you really can only please yourself. If you do anything because "they" like it, it doesn't work.

Ali MacGraw

I have finally realized that no matter how well cut my hair is, or how well made up my face might be for "an occasion," it is all pretty much of a Band-Aid job if my insides are rattled. So what I really do when I want to look as terrific as I can is take even ten minutes (preferably thirty) to meditate in silence and solitude, with a masque of crushed green papaya on my face. (I get it at Laise Bianco in the Beverly Terrace on Wilshire Boulevard, where I get facials at least three times a month—since forever.) But for *me,* I have to be pretty centered and calm to have a prayer of looking good and these minutes of yoga meditation take down the worry and stress wrinkles and lines and restore me to my own sense of self. I tend then not to go through all that ghastly worry about How-Do-I-Look?—I spend my time being present for the actual event minus a whole lot of my giant ego. Deep and specific breathing and visualization are part of that process, and the whole method of stilling my craziness has totally changed my way of dealing with "occasions." And I look much better.

Dina Merrill

My beauty secret is—fall in love! When Ted [Hartley] came into my life, people began to say, "Gee, you're looking so great these days!" And the comment seems to continue!

I truly believe if you love someone and are happy in all aspects of your life—work, friends, health—you look and feel younger. [Dear Dina—another one who had the bones and skin to begin with and, of course, you have to forgive anybody in love this slightly cliché, old-fashioned, touching recommendation . . . love is love. Maybe Ted Hartley has brothers?]

Andrea Pomerantz Lynn (Cosmo's *beautiful beauty director*)

I never buy eye shadow that comes in thin pans—too limiting and delicate. These only work with their enclosed brushes, which are lousy. I prefer the single pots that give you a palette of color to work with.

Brush your lips when you brush your teeth to scrape away flakes. Nothing's less alluring than dry, cracked lips. If a toothbrush is too harsh, you can use a washcloth. Next, apply regular moisturizer to lips, then lipstick. blot with tissue, reapply, then powder through tissue. (Press tissue against lips, dip brush into powder, dust brush over lips.) This method guarantees smooth lips and keeps color on.

Yellow-based makeup works wonders if skin looks pale and tired. I use a gold foundation, banana-toned face powder and light-yellow eye shadow (dust the entire lid and brow area as a base before applying any other shadow). I learned this trick from makeup artists on location. Traditional powders and foundations are pink-based; these make skin appear red and tired. Yellow makeup also works if you tend to look too pink or foundation turns orangy. Prescriptives makes a slew of yellow-toned makeup.

This is the best way I know to add volume to hair. Once dry, you sort of style and crimp with your fingers. Spray hair with hair spray, wait one minute, then tease areas you want voluminized using a vent brush. (This has a row of space between each row of bristles.) Brush hair into place, then spritz again to "set" style.

When I go out at night and want *incredible,* even longer-lasting volume, I mist hair with beer or champagne before styling. I find this old trick works better than any mousse/gel/sculpting lotion.

Sounds disgusting, but Preparation H, mixed with moisturizer, plumps up wrinkles, makes skin look baby-fresh! Mix up a jar and apply daily.

Soak hands in milk for twenty minutes a day to fade age spots and reduce wrinkles. Milk contains alpha-hydroxy acids, which have the same effect as Retin-A but won't cause hyperpigmentation.

There's nothing like cold, thinly sliced cucumbers when you're tired or skin is irritated. They should be paper-thin; lie down and cover your face with the slices for ten minutes.

I absolutely avoid caffeine. Not even tea. I drink herbal ones and water. Caffeine makes skin look and feel dirty and old. Smoking is another no-no. There have been actual studies that show when a smoker quits, she looks ten years younger. It's the same with caffeine.

Give your hair and skin a break when possible. On Saturdays, you can dust on a dual-finish (powder combined with foundation) powder eye shadow base if you're going to see people—that's it. On vacations I never blow-dry—just slick my hair back with gel.

AND TINY TIPS FROM ME

Keep your pencils (eye, lip) *sharpened after every use.* You can't do precision work with dull pencils.

Don't forget the magic of powder to *set* makeup—eyes, cheeks, lips—and get rid of the shiny look. (Shiny is okay for love-making, playtime.)

Lipsticks make perfectly good rouge.

Fragrance was born to cheer up older ladies and those in the room with them. Inexpensive works fine. Wear a ton. For a really good base, rub over bare shoulders, legs, anyplace you can get to before you dress.

Perfect manicures separate elegant ladies from

scruffies—one area you can keep looking good as ever, maybe better. My nails have been elongated for years with no bad results. You can do the manicure yourself, though it isn't easy, especially if you have weak nails like mine (goes with the weak hair). A manicurist comes to my office every ten days. Develop 10, applied every other day over polish, keeps manicure fresh, nails from chipping.

Facial Massage

I learned this technique from a Dallas girl and can't begin to do it justice in a paragraph or two, but you can write for complete instructions if you like (Pyrrha Malouf, 6050 Ridge Crest #318, Dallas, Texas 75321).

Basic instructions: Cream face generously with Pond's cold cream. Using all fingers of both hands except thumbs, stroke forehead horizontally—light feathery little strokes—one hundred times. With little finger and fourth finger repeat procedure in space between eyes—fifty tiny strokes. Now using fourth finger of each hand, do another hundred strokes around eyes. Next, tiny circles (fifty) the size of a dime on upper cheekbones at lower outer corner of eyes (great for zapping laugh lines). Next, cheeks and chin: Using third and fourth fingers, another hundred circles the size of a quarter—move all around your face. Now, go all the way around your mouth with fourth finger—a hundred strokes. You can do different amounts of strokes and use different fingers—whatever pleases you. Wipe cream off totally with clean terry towel or washcloth, being careful not to stretch skin. Start again. Pyrrha repeats the procedure three times (takes about twenty minutes) but you can do less if you like. Your face will emerge more serene and relaxed (desirable for us) and little lines actually disappear after a few weeks. I find this procedure in conjunction with Retin-A cream at night absolute magic.

Flawless Complexion for a Party

This routine is from Jessica Crane. Put on a shower cap; grease your face with Vaseline, cold cream or something goopy. Fill the bathroom basin with cold water. Dump in two trays of ice cubes. Using a snorkel (a little rubber tube, one end of which you clamp between your teeth; the other end—open—sticks up out of the water so you can breathe. Any sporting-goods store has these), stick your face down just below water surface and stay as long as you can. Twenty minutes is ideal, though you may come up a few times to breathe normally. You never *saw* such skin . . . poreless, glowing. The only reason I don't do it more often is that water sometimes seeps under your shower cap and messes up your hair, but if that doesn't bother you, you're in business.

Baby Body Skin

This procedure bleaches hair on thighs and arms, and you get velvety at the same time. Particularly good for brunets who don't want to shave hair above the knee or bother with a bikini wax, which grows out soon anyway and is a stubby mess while doing so.

Procedure: Wear bikini pants or nothing and slather Andrea Extra Strength Creme Bleach—a nice thick paste—over thighs, calves, arms, your whole body if you like. Leave on ten minutes and don't mess with it. Now start rubbing with your hands . . . stroke stroke stroke rub rub rub. Dead skin will come off with the dried bleach—a most gratifying experience. Even if you shower or bathe daily you rarely go to the trouble to seriously rub off dead skin and this is like an exfoliation. Now, dead skin rolled away, hair on arms and thighs nicely bleached (I still shave legs below the knee), you are ready to silken your beautiful body with cream or lotion. I use Georgette Klinger's pale-peach Body Creme mixed with Johnson & Johnson's Purpose . . . that combo is pure heaven. Put tons on feet and ankles and wear socks around the house as long as possible.

A Dancer's Posture

Betsy Bloomingdale is right—good posture is the single most important thing you can do to look terrific, or let's just say, if you *don't* have good posture, nothing else you're doing will be all that noticeable. The boring thing about posture is that you have to have it all the time, not just for "special occasions." *Lucky* women started early. My Haitian secretary, Ramona, with those long dancer's legs and regal bearing—I think of her as the Girl from Ipanema though I know I've got my countries mixed— started as a tiny girl to stand and sit up straight. In the seven years we've been together I have never seen her slump *once,* hateful creature! Okay, you can start late like me but you can't remember posture just *occasionally* because it won't be the right times. You'll practice when you're alone and relaxed instead of at a party when you need *most* to look elegant and regal but you're too glassy to give posture a thought!

You know what to do: Buttocks tucked in, rib cage lifted up up up off your stomach, shoulders back, neck and head lifted and back, *breathe!* I go on remembering binges and then get so harassed, who can think *posture?!* What gets me started again is seeing a photograph of me in a slump looking one thousand years old ... *that* does it. What also helps is Cecile Zilkha's Scotch-tape trick (Cecile uses it to remember other things). I also have POS-TURE! signs posted all over my office and in the ladies' room. We discard the old and do new colors and type frequently so I won't get *used* to any of them and can be rejolted (do you suppose I am ever going to *beat* this rap?).

Scotch-Tape Trick

Put a tiny piece of Scotch tape across the inside of both wrists. It won't feel strange enough to annoy you but it's *there,* saying sit up, stand up *straight.* The nudging is very effective for about five days; then you get used to the tape being there and backslide again. Wait a few days and start over.

* * *

So, my darling, the words you've been reading here—the philosophy, tips—are, I suppose you could say, not nearly as important as some other things we should be worried about. The pursuit of beauty once in a while strikes even *me* as absurd. There was the day my hairpiece fell into the john at the Broadmoor Hotel in Colorado Springs—splash!—just as I was getting ready to put it on and go make a talk to the Magazine Distributors of America. On such an occasion you can either lock yourself in the room and let them send a posse to get you or you can say beauty *is* absurd and they're going to *love* me with a flat head. As I was complaining about my thin eyebrows one day to a beautiful friend (not Georgette Mosbacher) she said, "Get them tattooed—Big Joe Kaplan in Mount Vernon, New York, is the place to go." I went, liked huggy-bear Big Joe immediately and assessed him the total pro: Walls and scrapbooks of photographs bespoke his art; motorcycle groups and brassy young women were stacked up all over the place awaiting their turn. After coloring my eyebrows, Big Joe and I decided to go for a little camouflage at my receding hairline. Tattooing procedure for brows and temple took about three hours . . . mildly uncomfortable from the noise of the drill plus prick, prick, prick of the needle into your skin but nothing terrible. We glob on a tube of Bacitracin to prevent infection; I hotfoot it back to New York. That evening I realize the color is really *brown*, almost black . . . matches the color of my original hair which isn't that color anymore but dyed lighter. After you start coloring gray hair, you're supposed to lighten your original shade. Even powdered down, my new eyebrows look like two black crows in flight. . . . I am Vampira's sister!

People *warn* you about bad cosmetic surgery but *it* is often correctable, or the tight look you hate loosens up in time; tattoos are *forever* . . . they tell you that going in. Well, I have been *more* depressed but can't remember more than two times in my life and I did this to *myself* . . . the "accident" isn't a random mugging or being knocked down by a runaway Harley-Davidson. I'm too heartsick to call Big Joe immediately—what can he *say?!* I let the miserable weekend go by and telephone him Monday. "Come on back," says Joe. "I can do something." I went. He did. He injected some white dye into the areas and that took the color down. I'm back on the train ... choo-choo-choo—beauty doesn't seem absurd again.

Some lovely day perhaps we *will* all be judged strictly by what we are—not one *scrap* of attention paid to creamy thighs, goddess cheekbones, Mona Lisa lips, but that isn't the situation *now* and I'm not sure *we,* the getting-up-there group, are the ones to strike out and demand love and appreciation totally without artifice. Should we *really* plan to attend the next charity dinner—or even show up at the office—in a gunnysack, with faces scrubbed like an Irish potato? You can. I'm not going to. Yes, there is a lot more important stuff than thinking about your skin tone, I *know* that, but no apologies ... you can take the world seriously, do whatever you can to make it better *and* fit in exfoliation and lip gloss. Truth!

chapter five

Clothes

C lothes have long been a major pleasure for some of us and at least an innocent, available, if sometimes expensive, *cheer*-up, particularly for *older* (in the they-can't-take-*that*-away-from-us category) women. Mildred Hilson told me in her ninetieth year that clothes gave her more satisfaction than anything else and she had a ton of friends, helped the Hospital for Special Surgery for years and was hardly self-centered. Mildred went to Europe twice a year to order dresses from her friend Hubert Givenchy.

Alice Mason, the real-estate tycoon, who has "sixty or seventy, I'm not sure how many" Galanos gowns hanging in her closet ("I never give *any* of them away") lifts an eyebrow when I inquire about the "selfishness" of owning and loving clothes. "I figure I made it, I deserve to spend it . . . on *me!*" says Alice. "It's ridiculous to say you can't concentrate on 'important things' and also be well-dressed. Most well-dressed women in this town [New York] have their minds on a million other things, particularly if they are in business. I give to charity—I just gave $2,500 to Nelson Mandela—and I pitch in for political candidates I think will do the country some good." Many people say Alice, with her personal contributions and fund-raising, virtually put Jimmy Carter in the White House. And recently she was a heavy fund-raiser for Bill Clinton.

I have been hooked on clothes from the moment they first put them *on* me. In my baby picture I'm wearing a little off-the-shoulder knitted camisole you can *tell* I think I look adorable in. The Depression never deterred my mother from dressing Mary and me well. She made all my clothes until I was out of high school ... wish I still had some of those pure-silk little blouses she hand-smocked by the hour. Unfortunately, Cleo couldn't help me with chic or super-taste which I *still* haven't got but am still working on. Cleo's tended to pastel, ladylike concoctions with wide ribbon sashes, princess-line navy-blue coats ... how she would have adored Ralph Lauren and *Victoria* magazine, not that they aren't *tasteful.* Anyway, clothes love got into me like a tapeworm with my mother's encouragement and never left. I should have picked up chic from *somewhere* because I'm surrounded by it. The most fabulously dressed women in the world are in New York where I live, forget Paris, and not just the rich but *all* types of women. Editors are welcomed to the showrooms of Seventh Avenue's top designers.

I will *never* make it to the best-dressed list (sigh!) because of 1. Lack of *innate* good taste. 2. Won't spend the money. You *can* qualify without Christian Dior and Yves Saint Laurent in your closets but it's easier *with.* 3. My hair is scruffy unless I'm wearing a hairpiece which is too much trouble and too destructive of your own hair—what you've got left—just to have lunch at La Grenouille where some of the judging gets done. 4. The edict, "If you haven't worn it in over a year, throw it out," has eluded me. (Don't you have *friends* you haven't seen in over a year but don't want to get rid of?) I'm running around in clothes that never had any class from the day they were *born* because somebody gave them to me—I love *free*—or I bought the mess *myself.* Anal doesn't make you best-dressed.

Aside from all those other reasons, I don't look smashing; things slippy-slide off my body. Blouses ride up from inside skirts and try to make it all the way to the top. Shoulder pads shift. I'm always rushing, squirming, changing positions ... high anxiety doesn't do a thing for your clothes. Maybe three times in my life—three *times!*—I have felt so perfectly dressed I thought others might have noticed or even been *respectful!* Jealous would be going too far because what you get jealous of is not altogether somebody's *clothes* but how they look in them. Long legs, slender hips, nice bosom, lush hair can't hurt ... they actually *contribute*. Maybe *fifty* times I have asked somebody, Where did you get that dress (blouse, raincoat, swimsuit?), and subsequently bought it but on me the magic doesn't happen. David's California colleague Pamela Hedley came to New York one year without enough clothes so I loaned her a knit dress and a Rudi Gernreich suit. She looked better in them than I. ... I was glad when she went home! I went to a lot of trouble in London one year to get a Jasper Conran navy silk dress David Frost's new wife, Lady Carina, was wearing. A spectacular blond ex-model of twenty-nine with race-horse legs—did I expect I'd be she in that dress? Certainly not, but I've loved it for years.

Okay, I'm going to tell you the three times I thought I looked perfect ... three times in a lifetime!

1. At my *Cosmo* twenty-fifth anniversary party in the Rainbow Room at Rockefeller Center, I wore a Bill Blass short-short dress of pale pink feathers from the pelvis down, fitted bodice of pale pink glass sequins ... with short sleeves and jewel neckline. I looked like a Barbie doll (tons of fake hair and great makeup didn't *hurt*).

2. One deep rainy night in Milan I went to dinner in a long-sleeve beige silk shirt with French cuffs, soft, nonskimpy tie at the throat, black wool skirt, ankle-length black wool cape that had once belonged to a gondolier, now lined in silk, black boots. I don't know why I got it right that one night of my life.

3. For Malcolm Forbes's seventieth birthday party in Morocco, I know all the other ladies will be in Givenchy ballgowns. How to compete? I'm gazing in the window of Rita's Blue Tent at Sixty-fifth and Madison, thinking it over. Rita comes out, hauls me inside, picks out a white sequin tank dress with three big (two on the front, one in back) Mercedes-Benz insignia embroidered in navy sequins. A knockout! Even the Ford and Chrysler CEOs at the party thought so.

Conclusion: If you ever thought money and labels and even *desire* could get everything fixed and you'd henceforth look incredible, well, that may not happen. But *pleasure* in clothes . . . that's *there* for (us) older women. Ursula told me about the time she bought two Thea Porter dresses in London—a long mauve chiffon with matching stole and a red chiffon that "must have contained twelve yards of fabric with embroidery-encrusted jacket—another jewel. I'm euphoric," says Ursula. "Well, back in the Dorchester my husband gets word the director of his picture, a project he's worked on roughly eight years, has walked, taken along his two stars so the financing has fallen through. . . . Greg is suicidal. Five minutes later my mother calls from Santa Barbara . . . she's being kicked out of her senior-citizen facility because she has bitched too loudly once too often and actually bit another old lady. She plans to come live with Greg and me because 'you have all that room and I can help with your hydrangeas . . . they're buggy.' Within one hour my husband has turned into a doomed hero in a Verdi opera and I've got major Mom problems (hardly the first). Well, some people advise you to think of waterfalls or beautiful sunsets when you need peace of mind but for the next two nights I went to sleep thinking about my Thea Porter dresses . . . how beautiful they were . . . like pieces of art. Greg finally got refinancing, the senior-citizen place decided to keep Mom (they well *could* at those prices). So I figure as long as you haven't blown your grandchildren's college education *or* your mother's senior citizen's care, clothes love is okay."

I've got too *many* clothes. I know that. I don't enjoy trying them *on* much and prancing around to see how I look or even *wearing* them as much as I just like *having* them. Could that pleasure-in-owning have to do with being a Depression child when people could own so little? Maybe, but I think older women deserve this indulgence. *You* may prefer buying things for daughters and granddaughters, of course. My own mother always bought pretty things for me rather than for herself (what *is* it with you people?!) but since there are no daughters in *my* life to resent Mommy putting it all on *her* back, I'm in marshmallow city. I do get a little vexed sometimes that my closets—between visits from Jill Cassidy, my genius closet organizer—are a jungle. I tell myself I'm going to let loose a bunch of moths in there someday who will gobble everything up over Labor Day weekend.

Of course *nobody* has enough closet space except my friend Ann Siegel who says it doesn't help. You collect too *much* and can either never find anything or decide what to wear after you've found it because you have four of everything. Ann ruthlessly got rid of two thirds of her clothes last year and says it's the best decision she ever made (I've thought of asking if I could ship some of my things over to her closet for the season). Two of the most pleasant, almost euphoric, evenings of my life—once in spring and once in fall—are the ones that come after Jill and I have spent the day organizing my clothes and closets for the coming season. You'd think any fool could do that for herself and any fool might but *shouldn't* if she's got somebody as gifted as Jill to do it with her. I picked my helper up at the dark-glasses counter of Saks one day ... she looked so smashing I just told her so as is my wont sometimes when people look nice. They either appreciate the compliment or edge away from what they perceive as a dotty (old?) lady, oh, well. Jill gave me her card, said she was a fashion coordinator and would be happy to help with my wardrobe if I ever needed her. I needed.

Before she visits, I start shifting summer from winter or the other way around. You can't do everything in two swoops, summer and winter, because New York has four seasons and you have gradually to ease into the major new ones. I have a *small* storage room under the kitchen where off-season clothes hang out with the wine (probably all vinegar by now from the heat), so when summer is *about* to happen—through spring you wear your lightest winter stuff—or *winter* is about to happen—through September you wear the darkest summer stuff—I begin taking the *big* stuff—dresses, suits, coats—down two flights of stairs, one of them steep, to the storage room. This takes roughly nine round trips (as you bring the in-season stuff *up)* and the energy required to push a wheelbarrow full of rocks up Pikes Peak. It can't all be done in one afternoon; you gradually ease into the new season, keeping out a few things that are transitional. I mean it's *work*.

With Jill arrived, dozens of sweaters, which *never* wear out and rarely get given away, have to be brought down from a high dressing-room closet shelf where *they* have been resting off season to be put in shelves where they can now be reached. Whatever is *in* those shelves must be placed on the high off-season shelves. Murder! Jill shakes out every T-shirt, sweater, stole, folds it carefully over tissue paper, slips it into a vinyl Baggie to go to the top shelves for six months' layaway. She does the same thing with the crop she's getting *ready* for me to wear. She likes to file by style (cardigan, pullover, jewel-neck, turtle, evening wear, etc). I prefer color. She *weeds*. I can barely part with the first garment I ever owned and she tactfully (firmly) suggests the skinny red-silk blazer was better four years ago, particularly since I have two other red blazers; but we probably never go far *enough*. If there's *time*—we will have worked perhaps five hours by then—she will put little outfits together, suggesting shoe-bag-belt-stocking combos—but we don't always get around to that and I've got better at it myself in the fifteen years we've been together.

Sometimes she shops for me. After the current-season stuff is in the closets and my darling friend has organized it by categories—pants, shorts, jackets, suits, dresses, evening stuff—it looks so pretty, is so orderly, I just feel wonderful. It takes only about two weeks for me to louse it all up, but after she leaves I spend the evening just looking and looking at the order wrought and admiring the pretty things I own. Oh, God, I sound vapid but, as my shrink once said about dealing with "older," find out what pleases you and do a lot of it. Well, clothes please me, and I "do a lot of it!"

I think there is a little daydreaming and fantasizing even at our age about clothes, some "wait till they see me in my leopard jumpsuit, my baby peach cashmere sweater that makes me look like a schoolgirl." I think buying and wearing still has the tinge of sex in it. You are going to show *off* a bit, say please notice and admire me— otherwise you would garb yourself in fitless schmatas which some women *do*. That's their business, whatever pleases one, but the woman under the tent is often hiding out from sex—and from exercise and diet, of course—saying it's over for her and that isn't what some of us want to say. I am not married to a man who pays much attention to women's clothes except he *seriously* likes blondes in black skinny dresses. He rarely buys me anything to wear or asks that I buy something he has picked out. I feel lucky! Men who tell you how to dress are a burden, in my opinion, unless their taste is a lot better than yours, and *expensive* . . . buying things you can't take back because it will hurt their feelings while using up your clothes budget.

"I think one reason John has a girlfriend," says Marie (she and her husband have an "arrangement"), "is that he loves to buy her things to wear. This may sound swell to you but I'll bet even *she* doesn't like it. Unlike most men who delight in teddies and peignoirs for their special friends and nobody's going to see them, or, better still, fur coats, John's taste runs to severely tailored pantsuits, almost mannish. I'll bet the poor girl hasn't been out in a dress for a year! Well, that's *her* problem!" Every wife doesn't mind a beloved buying "inappropriate" stuff, of course, if it's *his* money. You have to whoop and holler over whatever you get. I prefer to pick it out and try it on. Do I pick out or buy my *husband's* clothes?!

So you don't think I'm the *only* clothes-crazy person, I decided to ask some women (many our age) their *favorite* dress. Veronica Hearst, Randy Hearst's exotic Venezuelan wife: A pink organza tulip dress Balenciaga made for me when I was a teenager . . . just one big pink petal in front and one in back. Angela Lansbury: A black-and-white number Bob Mackie whipped up for me to wear at the 1989 Tony Awards. I once owned and loved an original silver silk Fortuny sheath from Paris circa 1935—a gift. I lost it in the 1970 Malibu fire that destroyed our home. Evelyn Lauder: The Claire McCardle dress I was *engaged* in . . . navy-blue peau de soie with a fitted bodice, three-quarter sleeves, white collar and a pink rose. I wore it to a charity event at the Whitney Museum not long ago. Also my Pucci shirt. Someone took a picture of me in that shirt and it was converted into a painting. Park Ave-

nue elegant Kay Meehan: A floor-length ombré—twelve
shades of mauve—chiffon Adolfo made for me for a wedding. Skin-care maven Georgette Klinger: White silk-
organdy by Stravopolous ... every time I wear it I feel
like Cinderella. C. Z. Guest: An ankle-length, embroidered, gold dress by Mainbocher. It's twenty years old and
I've promised it to the Fashion Institute but keep wearing
it one more time.

Cecile Zilkha: A green faille Saint Laurent simple
A-line with little sleeves, embroidered bodice. It's going to
the Metropolitan Museum if they can ever get it away
from me. Hollywood press agent Pat Newcomb: A gold
lamé dress I had made for some Hollywood wingding I
just keep wearing and, of course, my Armani suits. Alice
Mason: Every single Galanos I own. My favorite right
now is a simple straight dress with pleated skirt and a
sailor collar—I have it in twelve different colors and fabrics ... great with jewelry. Ann Siegel: A silver metallic
knit dress and sweater Herbie bought for me in Italy the
year we were divorced (they remarried). I never wear
them, but they're the first thing I'd grab if the house was
burning down. Inger Elliot, wife of Oz Elliot, journalist
and Columbia University professor: The red/orange feather
boa which makes me feel sophisticated and chic. In my
boa I can do things I wouldn't ordinarily do.

Mine is an ivory chiffon crystal-beaded backless shift
from Fabrice that dances like Eleanor Powell and flatters
every *part* of me plus the Pucci I plan to be buried in and
three other Puccis with flirty fringe skirts. So, *isn't* it wonderful to feel that way about clothes? ... they are our
friends, maybe even our *jewels.*

Where does shopping fit into our lives? Between the
ages of nineteen and forty, I think I must have spent an ag-
gregate two years shopping. I would often cover Saks
Fifth Avenue and I. Magnin in Beverly Hills, I. Magnin
and Bullock's Wilshire further east on Wilshire Boulevard
in one Saturday afternoon ... try on, try on, try on—even
bathing suits which are supposed to be a chore—and never
buy a thing except occasionally an Anne Klein dress
$29.95 and $39.95 and delicious. Bless those stores and

those (indulgent) salesgirls. It was a way of associating with beautiful things I couldn't afford to buy. When Gucci was in its heyday (late sixties) I would camp in the Rome Via Veneto store from about 11:00 A.M. to 3:00 P.M. In the past twenty-six years at *Cosmo* I virtually haven't been in any stores except to buy shoes. I'm *busy*, plus magazine editors can buy direct from the manufacturer if you establish a rapport. . . . I often do it by phone.

I do think shopping is a *major* pastime for people all over the world, not just Americans. You don't want to get behind a Japanese lady or gentleman with a shopping list at the scarf counter at Hermès at Christmas and this is not said pejoratively. Tour buses *always* dump you out to shop. Recently in Shanghai where there wasn't that much to buy, we were dumped, and some people could hardly get back on the bus with their purchases. Tour buses stop to shop in Jerusalem, Istanbul, Tangiers, Manaus, *everywhere*. I've thought about this a lot and I believe the main reason we shop is that our purchases make us feel less puny. We are so naked, so vulnerable . . . we *know* how easily we can be snuffed out. I think of us—me anyway—as the rodent in Franz Kafka's *The Castle*. He's got this big pile of stuff he is very pleased with—dead spiders, flies, beetles—he just keeps moving from room to room as he senses the arrival of the Creature that will destroy his castle and crush *him!* We, too, are fragile, so we shop, fix ourselves up, add *to* ourselves and, when we get through with our bodies, we fix up our houses and offices, make them better and better in order to be admired and to feel less naked. You don't *need* all that stuff to have a super life but you need it for admiration.

Jesus and Buddha said get rid of all your possessions and follow them if you want to be a Good Person, but hardly anybody does that. We're willing to *visit* Marie Antoinette's ball gown and tiaras and Louis XVI's commodes at the Metropolitan Museum but we want the rattan furniture and duck pillows and the Norma Kamali jumpsuits and Adrienne Vittadini separates for *ourselves*—to make us more acceptable, to add luster to our lives, to shield us from pain and help us achieve a little self-expression on the side!

Yes, the shopping goes right on for many women *after* they are sixty, does it *ever!* Some women never met a twin-sweater set they didn't like—and buy—plus a whole lot of other stuff. Nina Blanchard, owner of the Nina Blanchard Model Agency in Los Angeles, says "compulsive shopping crept up on me and lasted for four years. I would go into a shoe store and buy the same shoe in three different heel heights—flat, medium, spike—and in several colors. You know you're in trouble when you buy twelve of the same thing. Sweaters were my specialty and everything that went *with* them—skirts, pants, shorts. One year I wanted to buy a divine little house in Montecito and, of course, I couldn't. I walked into my closets and said 'There is your *house!*' Four years of compulsive spending and it was over."

Sometimes it's tough getting away from salespeople, particularly in an uncrowded boutique. You take three things to the fitting room, reject two and say, "Oh, if only you had this in a ten but you don't . . . I've already looked." "Too bad," says the vendeuse. "We had it only yesterday." You dress, smile—one more narrow escape—you wouldn't have bought it if they *had* the suit in your size but they *don't,* so you can get out gracefully . . . *almost!* Just as you near the door, she comes racing to you. "Here it is, here it is," she cries. "It was in another fitting room!" Now you're into hard-core getting away without buying and there *is* no saving face. Inger Elliot "bought an expensive cocktail dress because I had dashed into a store to use the ladies' room and felt guilty about not buying *something.*"

Speaking of shopping *(heavy!)* some American women buy *their* clothes in Paris. France is still the fashion center of the world although American design is superb . . . and not *inexpensive.* The most successful couture houses now, according to Nicholas Coleridge in his book, *The Fashion Conspiracy,* are Saint Laurent, Dior, Chanel, Ungaro and Givenchy. Nicholas says, "The average American customer orders three pieces a year—the richest, of course, may order a dozen—which means that more than two thousand couture dresses, out of a world sale of three thousand, go to the United States. Average price: $9,000 per dress." Listen, I'm glad *somebody* is keeping up the standards, reaffirming that fashion is important, making the rest of us feel almost carefree about our clothes craziness. I love the fashion shows here, don't you?, though I only allow myself three per season (Calvin Klein, Donna Karan, Adolfo). The New York shows during market week are *almost* as glitzy as the Paris couture. At Calvin you see the *Cosmo* cover girls *live* on the runway, even more gorgeous in person. New York's fancy society ladies, some of the ones who also go to Paris, are in the front row along with celebrities. Photographers are jammed in, flashing and snapping; the music is hot. It's almost like a Broadway opening and once again the designers have come up with . . . magic! Along with watching the show, I also enjoy watching the girls from *Vogue* and *Harper's Bazaar.* They haven't changed in the forty years I have been attending shows . . . cozy and comfortable in those surroundings as you and I might be in a warm bath . . . faintly haughty and superior in their soft wools and accessories nobody else can find even though they are right there in front of you. "Barry [Kesseltein-Cord] made this belt specially for me," says a smashing seatmate. No wonder I didn't pick *that* one up . . . $975 at Bergdorf. Wherever they are they make me feel wrongly . . . not *badly,* just wrongly . . . dressed. If I am in pastel, they are in black; if I am in black, they are in red; if I am in red, they are in checks. They are great at putting old with new, the *old* Fendi bag with the perfectly cut *new* Valentino culottes. . . . Frankly, they give me a royal pain but I'm bewitched!

Can somebody our age *acquire* taste? (I haven't, but can *you?)* Louise Grunwald, the beautiful wife of Henry Grunwald, our ex-ambassador to Austria and former editor-in-chief of Time Inc., who *has* it, says, "I think good taste is innate. You are born with it and it doesn't have anything to do with money [Louise is wealthy] but you can learn it . . . just sit at the feet of somebody who always looks fabulous and do what she does!"

Ruth Manton, the CEO of Aries Design, which licenses and markets products of designers and celebrities, agrees. "You have innate taste or you don't, but it can get better if you are sensitive to the environment. At *Vogue* [Ruth was executive editor], we used to hire little mouse-secretaries and six months later they had been transformed. Perhaps you can't acquire taste, but you can acquire *style.*" Alice Mason says, "Many young women hit New York and are nowhere with clothes but through the years they grow and grow and get to be smashing." She mentions a friend: "Soignée and terrific *now* but she looked like a bran muffin when she arrived here from Minneapolis. If you aren't *around* people with taste, you can't get it . . . you have to let the good stuff sink *into* you." Alice sighs over S., a much-publicized Los Angeles divorcée. "She comes into Le Cirque with green stockings, green dress, pink shoes . . . taste will never happen to her or to V [a celebrity]. Her taste is better than it was when she was paying fifteen dollars for dresses but she still looks a little left out in the rain." Alice declares, "It's hard to weigh two hundred fifty pounds and qualify for chic. Nothing looks good even if it's museum quality."

Betty Kelly, *Cosmo*'s elegant, long-legged—the best knees in New York—book editor, says, "I think you have to have *some* artistic sensibility to begin with. I have a girlfriend who had it from the time we were in the sixth grade—she just always had it; then you have to be exposed to good things. People who live in Mistletoe, Montana, and never *see* anybody wonderful are not going to acquire taste. When I married John [John Sargent, former head of Doubleday, scion of a wealthy New York family], I had very little money and dressed conservatively. Maybe that was how you were supposed to dress in the publishing industry but I had no particular flair. Then I started looking at John's friends, New York society, if we can call them that, in their designer clothes and I got *better!* Weight matters, of course. There just isn't anybody whose taste you gasp about who is pudgy. Of course, weight con-

trol is within your grasp so that doesn't have to stop you."
Betty mentions Christy, another friend from Michigan,
"someone with millions whose family has even *more* millions, at a party the other night in turquoise Day-Glo
pants, a pink organdy ruffled blouse, turq shoes ... she
looked like a court jester! You know Angela [the mother
of Christy's beau] has more taste in her little finger than
the rest of us in our entire torso but obviously taste is not
what Johnny is looking for. Christy is a mess with *all* her
millions."

Kay Meehan describes some wealthily married
women we both know, "still out there in their red fox
bomber jackets and purple see-through pajamas. Of
course, if the girl changes her look *too* much, she may lose
the man," says Kay. "He obviously married her for other
things than her taste." Kay thinks good taste is "not to be
showy ... keep it simple."

"Elizabeth Taylor has terrible taste," says another
friend, who obviously doesn't want her name used. "She's
short, of course—five-two—and her weight goes up and
down but even at one hundred ten, it doesn't happen. Shirley MacLaine ditto. Shirley has a great body but whatever
she puts on never works." Elizabeth and Shirley both look
great whenever *I* see them but then there's the question of
my taste. My opinionated friend continues: "Geena Davis
everybody raves about in those dresses she wears to the
Academy Awards but who knows about her regular look,
young actresses are mostly in jeans and T-shirts in the daytime. Barbra Streisand has exquisite taste. She buys from
thrift shops, flea markets, boutiques, major houses. Her
furniture is great and she has the best jewelry in the world
though she doesn't flaunt it. I think you have taste in your
genes. French girls have it maybe because they're *surrounded* with clothes-conscious females to identify with
from *birth*." Alice Mason says, "You can't totally depend
on designers. Nearly all of them make some silly things.
Galanos is the exception—anybody can look good if she
wears only Galanos [and would only need to enter her
gelding in the Kentucky Derby every year and *win* to finance such a plan]."

I ask glitzy, smashing Diane Von Furstenberg if someone can acquire taste. I don't get a straight yes or no. Diane says, "To be well dressed you must seem not to have *worked* at it ... it should all look easy." This from a person (we are lunching at Cipriani), who is wearing long jawbreaker pearls but *small* pearl earrings, a nothing sweater but nothing-ever-*like*-it jacket made for her by Yves Saint Laurent, red hankie tucked in the pocket, numerous rings on both hands, a double charm bracelet, fairly subdued print silk skirt shorter than winter afternoons in Stockholm, long rectangular patterned silk scarf, black leather belt with silver buckle ... everything but the kitchen sink, my Aunt Gladys might have said, but it was all perfect, it did not look worked on, but I assure you if I were wearing all those things—if I even owned them—it would take me about two and a half days to get them together.

Novelist Judith Krantz (*Scruples, Princess Daisy, Mistral's Daughter*, etc.) says don't *bother!* "In all my life, I've met just four women with great instinctive personal style; each one of them has a career in fashion. They can put things together in innovative, daring ways. This kind of style sense is an artistic gift. If you don't have it, don't even think about it. You can't learn it. Stick to the basic rules of looking well." How *negative!* Can't somebody without, let's say, inherent taste dump all her belts, handbags and scarves on the floor and by putting them together dozens of different ways get to have *flair* at least? "You can get C to B or B-plus," says Betty Kelly. "You probably cannot ever get to an A."

Forget these defeatists! I think if you have the time and *desire,* you can surely benefit by trying on a lot of stuff with a lot of other stuff, then freeze the best looks. Our age group is certainly in a good position to try this as we probably now have a ton of accessories to work with. An article in *Cosmo* a few years ago said French girls have no shame about spending hours in front of their mirrors with every scarf, belt, brooch, blouse, bag, bagatelle they own, working out little looks. Pauline Trigère says you must look (coldly) at *yourself* in a three-way mirror and see yourself from all angles. "Do not turn away. Do not lie to yourself. Just know that your look can probably be improved but you have to see what you really look like before that can happen."

What about what it costs to dress well? Betty says, "You can't do it with *no* money. The women you faint over have spent a ton but if you haven't got the ton, the best thing to do—cliché but still true—is put what you've got into two good suits—tailoring shows—and a good simple black dress. You can do a lot with them. Yes, you need the good bag and the scarf ... probably the former from Chanel, the latter from Hermès, plus some big gold earrings. Fit is important. There is *young* chic like Mary Margaret in the art department ... she puts the gray flannel tights with white ruffled puritan blouse ... major earrings. You can only get away with young chic when you're *young.*" Candy Pratts, a young *Harper's Bazaar* editor, visits me at *Cosmo.* She has on a black wool wrap skirt short as Crisco, black silk cardigan sweater that reaches the hem of her skirt, canary yellow silk shell blouse, a Chinese *red* cashmere shawl (this *cost* her) over one shoulder, black patent shoes (in *February!*) with glass heels. She is to die ... another of the perfectly put-together young ones. I am in awe of these fashion mavens and *now* if you want to look like that, you have to wear your best clothes every day and not be scared to throw the schleps *out.*

Casey Ribicoff, on the best-dressed list for many years, thinks, "It's a good idea to buy fewer clothes and buy better. There is no way you can look as fantastic in a three-hundred dollar suit as you look in a three-thousand dollar one—sorry! You will *want* less if you buy good. Next year you will still love the expensive dress—you will hate the cheap one." Oh, Casey, that's right for you but it isn't right for *everybody.* If you work in an office five days a week, go out to dinner frequently, you may prefer a *lot* of clothes rather than wearing the same five good things constantly and boring yourself silly. The rule has always been, of course, to put the money into *basics*—blazer, coat, suit—*never* plunge for the orange organdy evening dress. Okay, but a sensible girl I know plunged for a moss-green velvet evening cape fifteen years ago she has worn eight months of every year ever since.

Maybe some things are basic for *you* that aren't for anybody else. I know expensive *conservative* things can double-cross you! I have had mistakes in my closet for years that just stare back reproachfully—"What's the matter with *us,* floozie?"—as you pass them by for something cheaper and more interesting. I never have the guts to discard a mistake immediately. Right this second I am living with a beautiful black wool Chanel mistake—a Chanel, for God's sake! The cut is wrong for me. It makes me look matronly ... a condition I would as soon be in as flat on my back in a swamp with water moccasins swimming around my ears. We shortened it ... I mean short ... added a white faille collar—sorry, Karl! I even practiced walking and standing better in case it might be *me* but that dress is a disaster!

The fashion *geniuses* make mistakes. Ruth Manton says it's always "ruffles and bows ... velvet with beads ... something hot at the moment but too fussy ... I'm not the fussy type." Evelyn Lauder says, "My mistake with windows are a lot more expensive than my mistakes with dresses but when I do go wrong, it's something too gussied up ... the print is too busy or two prints are not working together. Unfortunately, I do quite a lot of this!" Lois, a delicious redhead, says, "I never want anything to do ever again with a tuxedo, 'le smoking,' as they call those silly masculine outfits fashion magazines keep pushing which make me feel like the headwaiter at my son's wedding."

It wasn't exactly "a mistake," but Betty Kelly speaks ruefully of the day she "went to Bergdorf's on my lunch hour to get something for an important reception that night. I picked out a long black Oscar de la Renta dress with a bolero. The saleswoman said she would deliver them to my house later that day ... the dress needed a little fixing. She arrived at five with the outfit, departed; I got home at six, and started to dress. *Alors,* the big white plastic tag—the one that lets the store know if you are trying to get out of the store with stolen merchandise—was still on the jacket. I don't know how *she* got out of the store. Well, I put on the dress, carried the jacket, grabbed a butcher knife and pliers from the kitchen on the way out, got into the car. During the drive I tried sawing the tag loose. At stoplights the driver would take over because he had more strength. Just before we pulled up to the Plaza, we got the tag off. I was sitting next to Oscar so it's just as well."

I ask Judith Krantz, who always looks perfect, for some specific ideas on looking good. Judy writes me an eight-page single-spaced report. At her going page rate I could probably sell this report for enough money to spend the winter in Gstaat, but instead I'll extrapolate. Here are a few things Judy recommends:

No one of any age ever made a mistake in passing up the baggy, droopy, slouchy look. It's only for fashion models. The same is true for oversized jackets. Oversized should be confined to sports sweaters on thin women, best bought in a men's shop.

Ethnic looks are sloppy, cost too much money to put together and can't be worn often unless that's the way you always dress. CRISPNESS, an essential for being well dressed, demands a skirt at mid-knees, or slightly above or below, depending on your legs. "Crispness" is another way of saying "neatness," which comes next only to FIT.

Solid fabrics are always a better investment and more becoming than a print.

Stay away from all "Day-Glo" colors forever. Stay away from all "faded" colors like old rose or mossy or olive green or dusty blue. Stay far away from the muddy, chic, nameless colors that Giorgio Armani uses. Electric colors are not for *anyone*.

Most blues are good on all women but "electric blue"—never. "Jewel" tones, ruby, emerald, sapphire, in moderation, yes, but basically navy, gray, red (on some women), white, off-white, and camel are best. Navy is good on *everybody*. So is amethyst and eggplant and some purple if they're not too intense. Pastels aren't something you can generalize about. I love them when they are trimmed with black or navy so that the all-over-ice-cream-cone effect is tamed. Brown? Run a mile! [I don't agree.] Don't take those self-help books on "your colors" too seriously (it gets boring to always wear "redhead" or "blond" colors) but the books have something to offer.

I won't try to deny that being thin is the first and best aid to being well dressed, but most women aren't. Larger women must depend on uniforms too. Delta Burke, who was on *Designing Women,* looked fabulous in her uniform of intense or dark colors, busy necklines and large, distracting jewelry, with her dresses invariably covered by A-line coats or jackets. It costs far more and takes more effort to look well if you're overweight. However, if you put the major clothing emphasis around your face, use makeup brilliantly, have a becoming hairstyle and keep your hemlines even, with impeccable shoes and stockings, you will look your best.

Clothes must *fit.* Somewhere, somehow, you must find someone who can sew and alter your clothes. Proper fit takes fifteen years off your age no matter what you wear. Never buy anything one size too small thinking you can get it altered. Do not shop right after you've had your hair done and love it.

This all sounds sensible. Judy says some things I *don't* go along with, however, never *mind* she usually looks better than I do. Judy says, "Every woman must make some firm resolutions about how much to expose, *ever,* of her underarms, elbows, bosom, shoulders, back and legs. Anyone over fortysomething, no matter how fit, who wears skirts more than a little bit above her knees, except for sports, is making a mistake. Even if you have fantastic legs, it simply looks wrong. Bare arms over forty-five are almost always a mistake as well." [I don't agree!] Then she says, *"Separates* rather than dresses give every woman with a waistline the biggest chance to look her best. In my entire wardrobe, with the exception of a few long dresses for big parties, and a few simple basic cotton summer dresses that are years old, I own only one dress, which I bought for my older son's wedding. I've worn it rarely since. When my younger son gets married, I'll look for a great skirt and blouse."

Okay, this isn't a dress person—some of us *are*. Judy doesn't like color *either*. "This year the fashion world is touting magenta and yellow and orange and similar colors. None of them deserve to see the light of day on women young or not." How harsh! Some of us who bought one think our buttercup yellow blazer looks *terrific*. Judy is a delicate, Botticelli blonde, so maybe that's why bright colors bother her. She continues, "Scarves are the *best* way to vary your look and still stick to what looks best on you. I've never thrown away a scarf or left the house without one." I've never thrown away a scarf either (anal) but rarely leave the house *with* one—they make me nervous— slide off and get lost. Judy says she "won't wear any shoes that don't have low heels *ever.* Comfort is more important to me than a few inches of height." Well, I might not wear heels to get the luggage from the airplane to the parking lot but high heels *never?* I'm of the wear-anything-while-they're-looking-at-you-then-slip-out-of-it—shoes that is—under-the-table-at-the-first-possible-moment school.

Judy says, "It's impossible to be well dressed without black. I limit it to pants, skirts and trim unless it's covered with glitter for night or trimmed next to the face with another, flattering color. Unadorned black—magnificent black—next to the face? No. Not unless you're going to the guillotine." I'm not going to the guillotine (so far as I *know*) and wear unadorned black *constantly* . . . it's my best 'color'! Well-dressed people have varying convictions about clothes. Judy was wonderful to do this report but I'm not buying *everything.* You probably *should* . . . she's awfully smart.

How helpful are fashion magazines? Not dreadfully, in my opinion. You're going for the Christian La Croix dance dress it took three hundred Gypsies two years to embroider the sleeves of that cost $12,000? Lime-green leather short-shorts with tassels? Judy Krantz recalls, "About six years ago I had lunch with the then editor in chief of an important fashion magazine. We were both dressed in becoming but unexciting suits. I complained that the pages of her magazine were filled with clothes I could never wear. She looked at me in amazement and said, "Really, Judy, I thought you were more professional. You know we have to show unwearable clothes to get women to buy *anything* new."

Fashion magazine copy says ridiculous things like "A new attitude for day ... more easygoing, more polished, more of what's inherently attractive." What's *that* supposed to mean? Gianfranco Ferre is quoted in *Vogue:* "I wanted the glamour of winter sport clothes the way it used to be, a very elegant ski look for the city. Even the sunglasses continue the freezing glamour look." I'm attending business lunches in a parka and frozen-glamour dark glasses? Yet *Vogue, Harper's Bazaar, Elle,* do show us what's happening, what's (sometimes) gorgeous, what isn't weary and safe. *That* we already *know* how to do. I feel you'd have to have totally resigned from youth and maybe life not to enjoy looking through fashion magazines. They do show what's out there and perk us up. Occasionally you copy. *Vogue* used to have a feature called Mrs. Exeter, starring a gray-haired sixtyish lady who wore clothes "appropriate for her age." Thank God they saw fit to jettison Mrs. E. I'm happy to be folded in with the young.

Paula, my beautifully dressed friend, says, "A lot of self-delusion probably happens as we read fashion magazines. I never say, looking at Christy Turlington in a satin shift. 'Oh, this gorgeous woman ... who could hope to look like *her* in that dress!?' I just concentrate on the dress, maybe order it, never let 'truth' seep in to spoil my pleasure." I *like* the system. Show me the stuff on people *not* like me who can inspire me.

Are *designers* our friends? My pal, Faith Stewart-Gordon, a pretty woman who owns the Russian Tea Room, says, "I don't think designers are doing anything very beautiful just now ... they are doing retro stuff ... back to the sixties ... or just *anything* crazy and different that might get somebody into the store because she doesn't already own one. I especially hate short skirts and feel anybody over fifty looks ridiculous in them." Oh, Faith! She always looks nice but that hating-what's-happening in fashion, whatever the year, seems wrong to me. Were the seventies *my* finest hour with all those pantsuits? Short hippy girls look like *sausages* in pantsuits but I owned a couple not to feel left out and continued to wear skirts and blouses, even dresses. Everybody made a *few* ... my beloved Anne Klein, Calvin, Rudi Gernreich.

If you avoid expanding to houseboat proportions, I think you can always find something becoming in the new crop. Bill Blass and Adolfo—we're talking expensive but I'm trying to make a point—are kind to a *fault* to not-size-two ladies while making them pretty as toast. Right this minute slender *is* de rigueur for a lot of styles. *I'm* even too "fat" at 102 because my hips are too big for a Calvin Lurex tube. Okay, I have to settle for some of his "roomier" styles (he didn't make *many*). I think short-short skirts—miniskirts—are the best thing fashion-wise that ever happened to women—some women at least, maybe even *most* women—though by the time this book is published, skirts may have dipped and fashion followers will be dipping *with* them.

Nevertheless, this afternoon I'm on Fifth Avenue in this ecstasy-making first day of June and coming at me is a good-looking woman about forty-five in beige-linen double-breasted blazer, *short* slub-silk ivory skirt, silk shirt, good accessories, industrial-strength-I-would-kill for blunt-cut flax-colored hair ... and the worst knees and legs a girl could hope never to happen to her if we got to choose. She was wonderful! *It* was wonderful ... the fact that this woman without great legs was wearing a skirt *that* short ... could say screw what God gave me, I'm going to participate and look great! I've seen a ton of girls/women like that this spring and summer, some not young, and all of them *not* camouflaging bad legs by wearing mid-calf skirts—*going* with it—saying fuck you, world, short skirts are fun and young and I'm into it.

Somewhat the way I have been the last forty years about my bosom. I used to pad and pretend something was there that wasn't. I once made little falsies out of tiny balloons filled with water so the "breasts" would seem weighty and "real"—not like my usual cotton-stuffed bra.

Well, I quit that and just went with small and cute and fuck you, these are my tits, and I got used to going braless and weightless and it hasn't been a bit bad—kind of young and carefree, I've convinced myself. Periodically I go to a plastic surgeon to check the breast augmentation situation, but nobody has too much good to say about breast implants and plenty *bad* to say—so far I've decided against. Well, I think it is just great that we aren't assholes any longer and telling ourselves we can't do something we'd like to do because we haven't got the figure for it. I'm going bare-armed though I *know* the arms aren't what they were—very hard for arms to be what they were when you're over sixty-five—but I love strapless and my arms are good *enough*, thank you very much.

Colors! The garbage they used to tell you about what you couldn't wear with what. You may not be old enough to remember but definitely not pink and red together—people's eyes crossed and they threw salt over their shoulder if somebody tried *that*. Navy blue with brown or black? Kelly green with royal blue? Red and orange? People excused themselves, went to the bathroom and threw up if such combos were suggested. Magenta, crimson, poison green, acid green and gold in one print? Only for the criminally insane. Know what was okay? Beige and brown . . . together or separately. Pink and blue . . . *any* blue with any pink. They loved pink but not, God forbid, for redheads. A redhead in pink would have been thought to be *asking* for an escorted trip out of town. White had to be virginal from nose to toes, no foxing it up with a black patent belt. Stockings were supposed to look as much like skin as possible; black hose were for *nuns*. Do you realize there was no real stocking news until about ten years ago. It was such fun when stockings ran amok! So I've got three dozen pairs of black/brown/white/ivory/lavender and pink lace numbers, waiting in limbo . . . they'll make a comeback!

Can you dress *sexy* at our age? I don't see why *not*. You can never look as succulent as the young—let's be real—but you can at least not look as though a man would have to use a blowtorch to get *to* you. Projecting sexy has most to do with attitude, of course, but it also has to do with good posture, slenderness, firm flesh. The first two are attainable, the third *semi* within reach. *Exercise,* pussy-cat! If you aren't pudgy and stand up straight, I think you can wear just about anything you *please.* Backless (every-body's back holds up okay ... get the moles removed); décolletage, if you've got the bosom, plunge V-neck with chains or pearls if you don't; black or beige camisole or bra-lace peek-a-booing—these are all great possibilities for our age. I think there is nothing sexier right this minute than a woman *any* age in opaque black pantyhose, microshort black skirt, a skimpy little blouse or a sweater that comes to about the waist, sky-high heels or knee-length boots ... you can *forget* garter belts, see-through peignoirs and being sixteen. (If a new look has swept by the time this book is published, don't condemn me as be-ing too "out of it!")

I give you C. Z. Guest, early seventies, at the Adolfo show last week, looking great in a corn-colored linen dress too skinny to reach farther than about ten inches below her hips when she sat down. Tiny cap sleeves. Good, stock-inged summer legs. Everybody recommends against show-ing arms at seventy but C. Z. has obviously said to hell with it. She is simply sexy, that's all. One thinks she might get attacked in her garden—she writes gardening books—someday. Kay Meehan says, "A woman absolutely cannot go wrong in black chiffon. Ask *any* man ... he just loves her in it ... it is sexy, sensuous, moves with the body but is in elegant taste. In the olden days you could wear white fox—so flattering and beautiful—it was a Gloria Swanson specialty and she was always elegant. Now it looks a little el cheapo." We have to hope white fox makes a comeback but don't wait for it to if you want it now.

Casey Ribicoff brings up the old stuck-in-a-time-warp problem, saying that a woman to be chic has maybe got to cut her shoulder-length hair, come in out of her tight jersey toreador pants and get herself a grown-*up* sexy look. Pos-sibly, but it's hard to get people to give up something they feel truly is *them.* That goes for the conservative in her beige shirtwaist with double strand of pearls as well as the baby dolls. Casey and I discuss a retired actress who still favors ruffles, feathers, spangles and beads. Well, maybe it isn't appropriate, I say, but if it makes her happy, why fight time-warp? Of course, you might have a little more *fun* with a fresher look. I'm time-warped in *skinny* but since I'm little and look swallowed up in lots of fabric, surplice necks, major lapels, roomy jackets, why resist? (Though skinny girls actually look kind of cute in tent dresses—what's *under* all that material? people wonder).

A change of image might not hurt in my case but I'd rather be pushed into a trench and have sand shoveled over me than wear Laura Ashley lace collars and mid-calf sweetsie dresses, never mind that's *all* some people will wear and they look fine. So let them cluck and gossip about us and say, you'd think at her age she'd change her look blah blah blah. I'm perfectly happy to give them something to cluck and gossip about that doesn't really *hurt* unlike if I'd done something truly disgraceful—lying, cheating, stealing, not attending a class reunion as promised.

Jewelry. Real jewelry. Ah, to be Louise Grunwald or Celestina Wallis, whose mothers left them such great gems all they have to do is sort through when they get dressed. (Something blue to match this scarf? The sapphire brooch, I think. Green to perk up this old jade evening dress? Probably the emerald drops.) Maybe W. R. Hearst pressed diamond wristwatches into Marion Davies's baby palm before they'd even been introduced (she was fifteen and her autobiography *says* that) but I didn't know about real jewelry until I was *ancient*. Here was this forty-six-year-old person with a high-school gold watch and a wedding band *period* until one lunchtime Genevieve Gillaizeau, the twenty-one-year-old girlfriend of Darryl F. Zanuck, legendary producer, took me shopping. We hit Cartier's, Van Cleef, Harry Winston in one hour. Genevieve didn't buy anything but I gleaned a purchase was imminent and we are talking *rocks*.

That night I asked David how he felt about real jewelry. Not warmly, it seemed. "Jewelry is for getting you mugged or getting lost and breaking your heart," he declared, an observation not without prescience, it turned out. Nevertheless, he did crash through with a David Webb emerald ring and a brooch . . . beautiful! Probably we should have bought three of each they were so cheap at the time but who *knew?!*

A few years later I lost the brooch in a taxicab in San Francisco. It wasn't a mugging; I did this to *myself!* Zonked from a long plane trip, late at night, driving into town, I dumped the contents of my Vuitton tote out on the seat of the cab to be sure I still had the gold chains I'd tossed in. Chains there. The brooch, in a black-suede container, I dumped right out on the seat with everything else and, because it was dark in the cab and I was crazy-tired, I just didn't get it back in. After checking in at Campton Place and discovering what I'd done, I went totally mad. We called the police, checked taxi companies, placed an ad, offered a reward, hired a private detective . . . forget it! I wasn't insured. (I still think insurance is too expensive—I'd rather just take a chance.) Well, the pain has hardly subsided to this *day.*

What about saving yourself all that pain and going for fakes? Well, I think anyone who has any *mixes* real with fake. Surely Chanel costume jewelry—beginning to cost like the real stuff used to—is delicious and nobody is going to sniff at you and say hmmmm, those aren't real rubies. With pearls you *almost* can't tell by looking what is or isn't real. The way you tell, apparently, is that fake pearls are smooth and real pearls are grainy when you bite them with your front teeth, but who is going to remove her necklace and say, "Here, bite my pearls." I love the real pearls I bought with the money I made from a twenty-six-week television show but fakes are perfectly fine. Nobody would know Barbara Bush's pearls aren't real if she hadn't told. Kenneth J. Lane makes other lovely costume jewelry, bought by fashion mavens like Jackie Onassis, Joan Collins, Marcelle de Cuellar, wife of the ex–U.N. secretary general, and others, but I think real jewelry is a real cheer-up for somebody past sixty or seventy if she is lucky enough to have some. Before that "youth" makes up for all!

I don't know why I think it's tacky to have a fake-gold Rolex or Cartier love bracelet even though you can hardly tell it from real by looking. The people who could "get *away* with" fake signature pieces, because nobody would ever suspect *them* of faking, usually don't, and that would be true of real as well. Is anybody going to suspect Gloria Vanderbilt's or Elizabeth Taylor's diamonds of being *glass?!* (They aren't.) Some wealthy women do have their big real pieces duplicated in paste, leave real in the vault and wear the copy. Not everyone with great jewelry *flaunts* it. Barbra Streisand has one of the most beautiful jewelry collections in the world—she has the taste and the money to acquire—but she never talks about it. Maybe she doesn't want to get robbed.

Well, let's get just a few final thoughts from the knowledgeable about looking great. Sandra de Nicolais, *Cosmo*'s fashion director, one of those people who seems to have fashion in the genes: "You have to take a good look at yourself and decide what you look good (and bad) in. To some extent this has to do with what image you want to project—elegant ice-princess (Grace Kelly), casual and understated (Candice Bergen), brassy and hot (Cher). Whatever look you decide on for yourself, pick the items in each new fashion crop that work—there's always *something*. As for the budget, one great jacket or fabulous black skirt will go a long way. A Calvin Klein or Ralph Lauren jacket is expensive going in but lasts forever—they're classics that *stay* in fashion, just depends what you coordinate with them. A leather skirt is also expensive but can be worn for years and look terrific. Make changes on the garment. Change the buttons on a blazer or cardigan. Narrow the lapels. Shorten the skirt, nip in the jacket, turn up the collar, *eliminate* the belt or whatever will make the garment more interesting or becoming to *you*.

"What I'm saying is you have to care. We all know the Hermès scarf trick. Buy one and wear it to pieces. Every time it will make the thirty-dollar skirt or twenty-dollar sweater okay. When I lived six years in Paris I remember how hard French girls [*them* again!] worked to get their clothes together—they would stitch down the

pleats, wear a flat instead of high heel, add a pocket hand-
kerchief. They didn't have great jobs but they looked as
though they expected to. It still isn't a bad idea to have
one super handbag. It may be your only bag for a couple
of years. The problem is picking the right *one*—worth
working hard at closing in on. Catalogs are great for
pull-on pants, basic shirts, sweaters, but stay away from
the stuff that has to fit. You can always send things back
but who needs the hassle? Catalog merch is usually more
expensive—or at least *as* expensive as what you get in
stores."

Here's Ruth Manton's fashion plan. Ruth was executive editor of both *Vogue* and *Harper's Bazaar* before starting her own business. Her ideas are so sound anybody
who wanted to could copy ... she *always* looks sensational. Ruth says, "Women buy couture because they're insecure! It isn't necessary. To have people admire your
clothes, you have to take fashion seriously—not feel you
are 'caving in,' being a slave. Don't kid yourself that last
year's look will do just fine this year, that you don't need
to change a thing! Try it all on at the beginning of the season. Is the shoulder an inch too wide? Is the jacket too
short? If you can fix it—and everybody surely needs a
good alteration woman if you can't do it yourself—fine,
but are you really going to be all that pleased and proud
of yourself in the fixed-up garment?! Be ruthless about
discarding! I keep clothes two years max; then they go to
a charity thrift shop which gives me a percent of the designer stuff they sell. If three new things come in, three
old ones go out of the closet. No letting myself off the
hook. Yes, I would keep an expensive suit but not forever.
My basics are always a well-cut black suit and a well-cut
beige one—even *those* go out regularly. A pair of well-cut
pants and a white satin shirt."

I recall Ruth at a party last year, red from head to toe.
Anybody else would have looked tacky, I tell her. "Not
true," she says. "At that particular moment the look *was*
total color ... anybody could have done it ... lipstick red
dress, sheer red hose, red suede shoes ... that was *then;*
now it's a dark stocking with a light shoe. You have to

stay *tuned* to fashion, then count on some innate or learned sense to say what to *do* with what's out there. Your eye tells you those three shades of khaki *are* working together but the belt you'd hoped would cause magic between an old suede skirt and a new mohair sweater *isn't*."

I ask her about a costume she wore one Christmas years ago . . . tucked white-satin shirt, white gabardine pants, masses of pearls clasped with a red/blue/green Maltese cross. The Chanel look, only this was ten years before Chanel accessories came to the States. "Practice," says Ruth. "I fooled around with that stuff. Experiment. You tie the scarf around the shoulder or the fanny instead of the neck, put the brooch at the waist instead of on the lapel, pin a gardenia at your throat so the basic becomes something else, something better."

How does she have the guts to buy a bright purple coat when everybody else is in taupe or black? "A bright purple or red coat over a classic dark suit or dress can be more outstanding than sable—which I don't own," says Ruth. "Show a little spunk!" I've enjoyed seeing what she wears for two dozen years—she inspires me—though I tell myself about 80 percent of her smashing looks are her smashing looks—canary yellow, Dutch-boy-cut silk hair, serious bosom, sleek pelvis—but I know the stuff from nature probably isn't more than *30* percent of the fabulous look she *makes* happen. Ruth is sixty-eight.

May I say a word now about people like Ruth who are generous with themselves about clothes (and probably generous about everything else)? My good-looking friend Ellen Levine, editor of *Redbook,* and I sneak off to Washington, D.C., one day to see the Stately Homes of England at the Smithsonian. Ellen is in a black Chanel suit with gold buttons down the sleeves, a black, navy, gold Hermès scarf (another one of those), black Chanel bag (another *Chanel!*), burgundy and black Chanel spectator pumps . . . she is perfect. I am in a hundred-year-old oatmeal-wool chemise chosen for comfort on the plane and you also couldn't hurt it if you turned your box lunch and a glass of red wine over in your lap. So why would you wear a super suit and accessories on a shuttle to spend the day tramping around a museum? I ask Ellen—we're good friends. She says, "Well, it isn't my *only* good suit and maybe there should be *no* day when you don't feel happy and proud of yourself (in public anyway) in what you're wearing." I threw out the oatmeal dress when I got home, and am trying to get the hang of further purging.

So this is what I have gleaned about us and clothes:

- Some are born with taste in their genes.
- If you weren't, you can get better—maybe never quite incredible but better—and you can have a lot of fun doing it.
- You need to be with people who *have* taste, flair. Don't just observe, do what they do.
- Money helps but *lots* isn't required. Designer accessories, not designer clothes, will do it.
- Enjoying clothes is an honorable enterprise, a cheer-up for older women—nothing to get the guilts about as long as you give of yourself (and your worldly goods!) to others.

If trying to be fashionable and a preoccupation with clothes gives you a royal pain, however, then *don't* do it! Plenty of nifty women don't know Isaac Mizrahi's welded seams from Mary McFadden's *pleats* and they're doing just fine. Nobody really gives a damn except maybe people who take you to dinner and a few local stores. *I* sure can live with the decision if *you* can!

chapter six

Food

Can we all agree that food is one of the major pleasures of an older woman—possibly *the* top pleasure? Good. So, having been a good girl about so many things for such a long time (survived killer love affairs, dumb marriages, money woes, job disasters, family trials), can we now at long last at least stop worrying about diet and reward ourselves with fabulous things to eat? Certainly ... if you don't mind looking like two sailors inside a gunnysack coming at you down Balboa Boulevard or care that your body is operating with the efficiency of an outboard motor covered in tapioca. If you have a shred of vanity or want to *feel* good, you probably have to "watch it." You pretty much need to make the good, decent healthful choices so that sin-food doesn't get you all that often.

Anybody who sits around rationalizing that now that she's fifty-seven, sixty-seven, seventy-seven and by God, "I *deserve* this martini, these nice shelled pecans, lobster swimming in butter, the rum-raisin cake," I'm afraid I think is an asshole because she is not only blowing looks but, more important, health, the most important thing we've got, or if you haven't got it, nothing else matters. (If she should reach eighty-seven or ninety-seven, I guess she can relax a little.)

But who wants to live without the good stuff or, actually, put another way, can you call that living? (No more fried onion rings *ever*? No marble cheese cake chased with cappuccino?) Well, you don't have to live utterly without them but you probably will want to cut *down*. I've said for years I think renouncing bad food is like renouncing a bad (killer) lover. The pain finally outweighs the pleasure and you go cold turkey. You finally *do* learn to love somebody decent (veggies and brown rice) and when the old lover (Toll House cookies, chili dogs) comes around again to reclaim you, you just say no! Renouncing sin to get off the twenty pounds was bad enough the last time; why would you want to go through that *again?* One day the real-life lover actually *doesn't* appeal (that Colosseum-size ego, his tiny brain!) and you aren't even tempted. Alas, the comparison with food stops there because, though you may get *him* out of your system *forever,* chocolate-chip cookies *do* still appeal and you can go right off the wagon again. Many of us have found the temptation to eat bad (delicious!) food does get weaker, however. You get so used to making decent, healthful choices you almost don't even think about sin-food anymore. Some purists don't think about it *ever.* I'm not one of those. I think you can sin occasionally and still be a Good Person.

Most women probably "get religion" (knowledge about healthful eating) when they need to lose weight. At our age, we may have "got religion" several *times!* Finally you realize that to *keep* the weight off, you have to change your eating habits for the rest of your life—eeeek!—and that includes the awful business of having to eat *less* when you're older just to stay the *same* weight . . . more eeeks! That rationalizing "innocent" who slimmed down and then said to herself, Okay, I did it, now I can *eat* French-bread garlic toast with butter oozing out, coquilles St. Jacques, Mom's cherry cobbler—all the lovely things I was willing to give up *temporarily*—is going to find herself bigger than she was before the diet . . . reality is beastly! After losing weight, you can take in a *few* more calories, but they pretty much have to be of the "good stuff"—the "most bang for the buck" as diet doctor Stuart M. Berger calls it. Who can afford to blow a hunk of her 1,700 daily cals on crème brûlée or two gin and tonics? Paying the rent (eating the basic good stuff you need) doesn't leave too much room for frills. But life *isn't* dismal. We'll get to that in a minute.

Most of us are a *little* smarter in our fifties, sixties and seventies about eating. You know grapes are fruit and fruit is one of the *"good guys,"* but grapes are loaded with sugar, never mind it's *natural* sugar, and have not much food value compared to *other* fruit and are calorie-heavy. As for figuring *räisins* are good for you since they once *were* fruit, forget it . . . they're like grabbing a handful of candy. You know brown sugar is just as sugary as white sugar, never mind it *looks* "healthy." Honey, ditto . . . not any more "innocent" than white sugar. Tomato ketchup is laced with sugar and preservatives—things like that you know. As Monica puts it, "You get more selective about *friends* through the years . . . avoid the bores and takers, so you get more selective about food . . . bye-bye to the empty, greasy, sugary. Most of the time, if it gets into you, it's gotta *mean* something."

Aside from learning about nutrition from dieting, your real store of knowledge probably comes *gradually* through the years . . . sort of osmoses into you. Growing up, I never heard anything about good nutrition, did you? In my home-economics class in Pulaski Heights Junior High School in Little Rock in 1935, where we cooked baby meals, blancmange, a delicious, sugar-packed little vanilla pudding, was accorded all the gravity of meat loaf and string beans. Nobody said a *word* about empty calories, let alone the sinfulness of sugar. During the Depression years, my sister, Mary, and I were allowed to go into the kitchen whenever we liked and make fudge (two cups sugar, three tablespoons cocoa, one fourth cup milk). Our darling mother, what did *she* know about nutrition? Cleo grew up in a farm family were lard was a staple in all baked goods, where turnip greens were cooked six or seven hours and flavored with bacon grease.

I was in my twenties when two nutritionists came to see my boss in a Los Angeles advertising agency and, while waiting for their appointment, laid on me crazy things like "When you cook vegetables and pour the water into the sink, you are feeding the sink better than yourself." My eyes crossed . . . obviously these were nut cases. I didn't start thinking nutrition even a *little* until one summer day twelve years later when, age thirty-six, I'd been working at the Miss Universe pageant in Long Beach for two weeks and was feeling like the invisible woman from being around all that teenage pulchritude, totally ignored by anybody male over the age of seven. I decided to stop by Gladys Lindberg's Health Food Store on Crenshaw Boulevard on the drive back up to L.A. to see about vitamins ... maybe *vitamins* would make a girl visible again. Gladys was in residence and happy to prescribe for me the very same Varsity Vitamin Pack said to have revitalized the entire University of Southern California football team! She also began the more arduous task of separating me from a lifelong sugar addiction, a chore roughly as challenging as separating a tree from its bark with your fingernails (I'm not separated *yet!*) Dear Gladys. I'm almost glad she *isn't* still here to see what's happened to her beloved protein. Gladys said a girl who didn't have at least fifty-four grams a day would probably die. Current guidelines suggest forty-four and the figure is still dropping.

So, a Gladys or other nutritional influence may enter your life and get you switched to healthier eating. More likely you will gradually absorb nutritional wisdom from many sources. For his excellent book, *Win the Food Fight* (St. Martin's Press), California real-estate tycoon Sam Grossman sent questionnaires to a lot of successful dieters and concluded: "They were all types who had their antennae tuned and ready to pick up new ideas. They read a snippet in *The Wall Street Journal* that said oatmeal lowers serum cholesterol and would decide to eat oatmeal for breakfast; they'd see a news magazine item that broccoli contains anticarcinogens and decide to eat broccoli twice a week; a friend would explain they'd be better off eating less red meat and another would tell them potatoes and pasta don't make you fat, etc., etc." Eating is so *personal.* It's *your* body, *your* taste buds, but, oh God, all the proselytizing out there! Would there were one simple diet plan everybody agrees on but there *isn't.* I was in the big New York Doubleday store at Fifty-seventh and Fifth Avenue the other day and counted thirty-two diet books—everything from *Formula for Life: The Anti-Oxidant Free-Radical Detoxification Program* to *My Mother Made Me Do It.* (So handy, blaming mother.)

So who knows the most, who's right? You could quite literally go mad trying to sort it all out! Dr. Nathan Pritikin's regime allows only one *pound* of meat, fish, poultry for a *week;* H. L. Newbold, M.D., on the other hand, in his best-selling book *Mega-Nutrients: A Prescription for Total Health* (Body Press), says people need not fear a high-meat, high-animal-fat diet if their cholesterol count isn't high and they don't stay on the diet too long. I love to read *all* the diet books (except for the technical stuff about resting blood sugar and sucrose traveling straight to the brain ... you need a Ph.D. in blood chemistry to sort all *that* out). The recommended-food sections are delightful, however ... all those things you can do with seaweed, prunes and chicken breasts, how to pass Hubbard squash off as candied sweet potatoes, instant bliss with instant coffee milkshakes that miraculously contain no *milk.*

Reading about food is like reading about *sex,* however. ("Ask to have your tummy stroked during lovemaking, at the same time you tell him not to go *near* your toes.") Yes, yes, that sounds sensible and delightful, you say to yourself, but then you're only *reading* ... you have to get into bed to *do* it. You can read about food, *too,* quite delightedly—diet dinner number 7 calls for two whole-wheat matzohs, six shrimp and a teaspoon of mustard, half a cup of broccoli, eight large strawberries—without having to *eat* it. Still, with all that reading you actually *do* absorb information about nutrition and diet, pouring it all into a memory bank, and your plan develops. You *revise* the plan as you go along because they "discover" something new—and contradictory—about every five minutes. We'll get to a basic food plan in a moment but first let's decide how much you should *weigh.*

Recommendations vary a lot and some are wildly generous. If we weighed what the insurance charts say we *could* at our age, we could be a baby blimp! Very sweet, very reassuring those charts, but for some of us, they have nothing to do with reality. You probably know by now *exactly* what you think you ought to weigh, whether it's what you *do* weigh or not. If you want to consider a serious, tough, live-longer-through-diet recommendation, nutrition-ist Stuart Berger says in his book *Forever Young* (Morrow), "The single surest way to guaranteeing yourself a longer, *healthier* life span boils down to three letters: VLC and they stand for Very Low Calories." Dr. Berger says among the benefits of a VLC diet are these:

- Extends life spans in lab experiments
- Lowers blood pressure
- Reduces destructive antibodies that attack the brain
- Reduces the loss of certain brain cells
- Strengthens the immune system
- Slows the aging process
- Lowers cholesterol and heart-disease risk
- Reduces muscle oxygen loss, and improves muscle function
- Reduces free-radical damage to the body's tissues
- Helps stabilize the blood sugar in balance in diabetes
- Helps the body run at peak metabolic efficiency

"Most dramatic of all," he adds, "scores of studies show that animals on VLC diets live dramatically longer, without disease, with longevity increases of 50 percent, 65 percent, even 83 percent!"

Also espousing the skinny-is-better philosophy, David Klurfeld, a pathologist at Philadelphia's Wistar Institute of Anatomy and Biology, says, "Underfed rats, those getting less calories but the right amounts of protein, vitamins and minerals, live fifty percent longer. Nobody knows how much longer underfed humans would live but you don't see many fat ninety-year olds."

And from *Newsweek*:

For a tantalizing clue to near-eternal youth, consider the 18,000 to 30,000 mice and rats romping in cages at the National Toxicology Laboratory in Little Rock. Keepers give these lucky volunteers 40 percent fewer calories than they would eat if left to follow their appetites. As a result, animals that usually die at 30 months are going strong at 60. Also, as their healthy, useful life-span lengthens, their immune system responds more quickly, they repair broken genes better and they have less disease. "You can't help but be impressed," says lab director Ronald Hart.

While acknowledging that we are not laboratory mice, Berger reports, " 'The basic aging process of all mammals are similar ... nutritional manipulations that slow the aging process in rats will do the same in humans.' " As for figuring out how much to eat on VLC, he says, "For women, who normally need 2,000 calories per day, that would mean gradually dropping to 1,300.... Gulp!" These, he says, are the principles to remember:

1. In general, the fewer calories you eat, the more years you add to your life.

2. The less you eat, the more *efficient* your diet must be. Berger's Six VLC tips: 1. Make every calorie count! With so many fewer allowable calories, those you do eat must give the most "bang for the buck." (NO refined or highly processed foods, eighty grams of protein daily and make sure your protein and carbohydrate sources are as 'pure' and fat-free as possible. Keep fat to a bare-bones minimum.) 2. Go for bulk (include a lot of fiber and bulky foods which, ideally, pass through your system undigested, yet give you a feeling of having eaten). 3. Don't spare nutritional supplements (vitamins, minerals). 4. Ease into a VLC program gradually. 5. Prepare yourself for a change in appearance—you will lose excess fat in places you didn't even know you had it. And, finally, he says, "Metabolism will adapt to your new dietary levels, becoming ever more efficient, extracting maximum energy from every bit you eat." Nifty!

Okay, that is probably too stringent a plan for most people, but I think we're all getting closer to recognizing that eating *less* is better for older people who want max health.

Suppose you are now overweight. What's the best,

best, BEST way to *lose?* There isn't any best as far as I can determine but the winners have all faced two things: 1. You can't get the weight off with the speed of a BMW in heat if you have a *lot* of pounds to lose, or *keep* them off if you go back to your usual food plan. 2. The only way to lose weight is to eat less than you have been eating; it doesn't really matter *what* you lop out of your diet and don't eat so much of. Every single diet in the world will work if the calorie count is less than your body needs to maintain its present weight. In theory, even in practice, you could consign all your calories to Scotch and ice cream and never gain a pound—you might even lose weight—but you probably wouldn't last long on your diet because you'd be ravenous, dizzy and drunk. Your body wouldn't function right and you'd be far hungrier than on the same calorie count of good stuff. Alas, there probably isn't a diet in the world on which you can eat as much of *anything* you want, even the "good stuff." I feel safe in saying this as nobody has yet put forward a total 100 percent celery diet. (Celery is the milk of magnesia of food. Nobody likes it but you let it into your life for health reasons.) I suppose you *could* pig out on celery and nothing else and the pounds would vanish but nobody is going to.

The absolutely maddening thing about *any* diet is that after you have "gone straight" and eschewed the bad old things (runny Brie, Mallomars, buttermilk biscuits and honey) and have got so fond of the *good* things (crunchy potato skins, papaya doused with lime juice) you absolutely *adore* them, you can even gain weight with these *friends* as in a 3,000-calorie lunch of lump crabmeat, cottage cheese, bran muffins, strawberries, raspberries, peaches, bananas under a mountain of yogurt and a few slivered almonds. Pile up enough calories of *anything* and you can balloon right up. Sigh! The winning ticket seems to be "moderation"—ugh—just eating until you're full but never stuffed to the gums on the *good* things (we'll get to them). There is, as somebody brilliantly pointed out, no free lunch. I heard about a ninety-four-year-old woman who ate *only* Eight O'Clock after-dinner mints—no other food—for years and *seemed* to be having a "free lunch";

she died from being hit by a taxi which ran a red light. But for his carelessness, possibly she would still be here wolfing mints but I don't think she's a good role model.

So, listen, before we go a step further with our diet discussion, perhaps I ought to ask if you even *want* to discuss this with me. I weigh 102 pounds. Once when we were working out material for me to use on *The Tonight Show,* I suggested to my talent-coordinator buddy, Robert Dolce, we might try diet as a subject. "Do you want to get stoned?" he asked. "The audience will not only hiss, they'll ask for your blood—if you've got any. Who's going to listen to somebody whose ribs stick out?"

Never mind my ribs; I probably know more about dieting than anybody this side of an angel. If I may speak for my group—skinny—we are not this size because we don't know about food or how to eat, nor are we psychological freaks. Our taste buds have not left town. I could be Rosemary Clooney or Roseanne Arnold—in girth not in talent—in ten minutes if I didn't watch it. My sister is obese. And *I* am totally *preoccupied* with food. (You probably think that's because I am starving but that isn't true—I eat a *lot.*) I weighed 105 pounds for years, carefully maintained, but in the summer of '89 I went from 105 to 95 in just ten days. A sort of crisis made me just not hungry. What an easy way to lose weight . . . food simply doesn't appeal . . . if they put a pepperoni and sausage pizza before you, you'd ignore it and ask for iced tea.

The crisis passed but by then I'd begun to enjoy having a flat stomach for The First Time in My Life. (I had a little pot even in grammar school.) It was *heavenly* not pooching . . . being straight as a slide rule in profile. The tush shrank . . . I could get into *anything.* We started moving hooks and eyes and snaps over on the waistband by *inches.* Then my hair began to fall out . . . worse. It always fell out some but they thought *maybe* too little food to supply sufficient nourishment (you know whatever nourishment there *is* goes to the most vital places first—liver, muscles, bone) was making it worse so I had the "happy" assignment of gaining five pounds—wow! on purpose—

but it's confusing. A brain disciplined not to let one extra grapefruit section inside your mouth, let alone a lemon tart or blue-cheese salad dressing, suddenly trying to get itself to tell you to *go* for it . . . it just can't believe it's *supposed* to. I would add a dab of chicken salad or Fortnum and Mason shortbread to one of my little meals, then anxiously get on the scale next morning hoping it wouldn't show a single-ounce gain (it did). So inconsistent . . . *supposed* to gain but afraid you *will*.

So, there isn't any doubt I may have carried it "too far" (I finally got back to 102 and am still there)—a grown-up anorectic (unless Stuart Berger and the others are right and very low calorie intake *is* healthy and long-life encouraging), but this is how I feel about at least being *slender:* I can't speak for all the other skinnies about motivation but I'm *afraid* to be fat or plump or even "comfortable." I don't like the physical condition of being older, with things inside you going blooey a little, with looks fading a little no matter *what* you do, with men taking their eyes off of you *frequently,* but by God, slenderness is something I *can* control. Slender to me represents youth and health *and* being in charge of your life. As Dr. Berger said, you don't see many fat ninety-year-olds. University of South Florida researcher David Schapira, who surveyed thirty-five hundred men and women, said the vast majority of people who diet and exercise have as their prime motivation not better health but increased sex appeal and self-esteem. Only 30 percent of those studied listed improved health as a reason for changing poor eating and exercise habits.

Forgetting wanting to be in control, slightly nut-case me and the sex-appeal-desiring group, what do the dieters and nutritionists say is the *best* diet for *anybody* who wants to get off five to a hundred pounds? Repeat: There isn't any. *All* diets work if you stick. Sybil Ferguson, founder of Diet Centers, says, "Most dieters fail because they refuse to realize this is a change in life-style; they want a quick fix." Myrna Blyth, editor of the *Ladies' Home Journal,* says she lost weight simply because she had the kitchen redone. "Not that I cooked that much, but for a month we had no food in the house because there was no icebox. I quit snacking. Then we went to Bali for two weeks and it was so hot and steamy, who could *eat?* By then I'd lost six pounds and was on a roll ... I just kept going." In her case, there *wasn't* any "diet." For others, it isn't so simple.

To illustrate serious dieting with just *one* case history, I will tell you about somebody I have watched for fifteen years go up and down, mostly up, and who looks as though she has finally beaten the rap. *Cosmo's* art director, Linda Cox, is down from really large to fighting weight, now going for the final twenty. Linda has tried a smorgasbord of diet plans (and gurus) through the years—Diet Center, Weight Watchers, a nutritionist at New York Health and Racquet Club, Marilyn and Harvey Diamond's *Fit for Life Plan* (what counts is *when* you eat), liquid diets, "my own folder of food plans," etc., etc. What finally tipped her over? Something called a time-management workshop. "In one meeting we were supposed to write down ten lifetime goals in five minutes so you wouldn't dawdle and get intellectual," says Linda, "LOSE WEIGHT came out instantly at the top of my list. I was surprised because I didn't know how important it was to me. I thought I was happy as a fat person. I decided yet one more time to try to do it and, since I had so *much* weight to lose, went with a doctor-monitored liquid diet— five drinks a day of high-protein powder mixed in the blender with ice cubes, fruit and diet soda—yummy.

"I've lost sixty pounds so far and expect to get off another twenty—and stay there. The results are spectacular but the downside is that you have to learn a whole new way of reentry into the world of food and that takes more discipline than the weight-loss diet itself. You think you're almost done and can relax just a little and wham ... the pounds start coming back. Unless you relearn a workable way to eat, the liquid diets fail. I've maintained my weight for a year, which I guess is worth some applause. The main reason I've been successful is the support I get from Overeaters Anonymous, a twelve-step group based on the same principles as Alcoholics Anonymous. It helps me to be with people who share honestly about why they over-eat. The goal is abstinence, the freedom from obsession with food, one day at a time. In the beginning I attended daily meetings, but now, unless I run into trouble, I feel comfortable going three times a week, never less."

Good for Linda. Of course, some of us can't do *anything* in a crowd. As I mentioned in a previous book, my therapy group finally threw me out because I brought sewing and put up hems while everybody "confessed." One group participant was so irritated that I was doing my nails during his segment, he broke his hand banging it on the floor. Linda's story has nothing to do with *your* weight-loss intentions, of course. You go with what helps *you* and you go when it's "time"—stick when you're *able*. And there are people who will *never* take it off and keep it off—*never*—particularly at this age and that is their business. Brave . . . taking all that abuse from us puritans. The fattest people you never *see* eat, have you noticed? Fatties can be rather dainty in restaurants, eat like robins. Thin girls are showier. One day I watched dancer Ann Reinking at La Côte Basque put away three plates of potage Saint-Germain (thick, green, gelatinous stuff, about 200 cals per plate), a gravy boat full of buttered croutons (another 200 cals), ten or so petit fours . . . that's a 1,000-calorie snack for the nymph. I'm sure she danced it all off later that afternoon.

Having people tell you how they keep their weight down can be seriously irritating. It's like their saying how good they are in bed or that they made a killing in hog bellies or Kevin Costner kissed them . . . what good does that do *you?!* (Though I'm going to share a few diet tips in a moment.) Finding out what people did before they started to diet can be *pleasant*, however. *Cosmo*'s publisher, Seth Hoyt, told me that before going "straight" he consumed fifteen cups of coffee daily, half-and-half and four teaspoons of sugar in each, rolls and butter at all meals, numerous rum and tonics *before* the meal and, if available, Key-lime pie for dessert. He's so cute now . . . looks like Robert Redford but he looked like him even *before* the weight loss.

Having dieters tell you how they fell *off* the wagon is more gratifying. ("Jesus, I ate sixty-four snails in buttery white sauce, an entire Camembert cheese with a loaf of sourdough French bread, pâté by the pound followed by soft ice cream!") Attaboy! One thing's certain: Practically everybody backslides before Going Straight Forever. I was chatting with photographer Francesco Scavullo's stylist Sean Byrnes about Madonna whom they had recently photographed for a cover of *Cosmo*. As Sean showed her all the clothes he'd picked out, she said, "Sean, these are for the old me.... I've now got a roll around my hips and middle." How *could* she, I was tsk-tsk-ing, let herself get heavy like that and Sean instantly came to her defense. "Listen," he said, "she's happy right now ... she's in love with Warren Beatty ... things are going well for her career ... so she has a few extra french fries and the Italian food she loves. She's *human*. She'll get back to the old self-discipline pretty soon." She did—and to some *new* men. Finally though, hearing about someone slipping off the wagon doesn't help because there remains the business of *your* diet ... the one you have to get on and stay on.

Should you check with a doctor before you decide to diet? Everybody says do that but why? You probably know as much as *he* does if you've been reading magazines and newspapers. Doctors even acknowledge nutrition isn't usually their area of expertise. I suppose if you are about to try for sixty or seventy pounds and are contemplating one of the liquid diets, you ought to run that by a doctor—or get the formula from him—and there are now some bona fide nutritionists in New York and Los Angeles at least. I just don't see how you could get into too much trouble shucking off ten or fifteen pounds on your own just by giving up dessert, sauces, bread, butter, cocktails, wine ... the ordinary stuff any dieter knows to do.

After you lose the weight comes that tedious business of not gaining it back. (If you want to stay the weight you are, multiply that weight by fifteen and you'll get the number of calories you need to sustain. If you *exercise*, you can take in a few more cals without gaining.) Alas, "maintaining" is not that different from dieting unless you were on one of the liquids. In a way you are still "diet-ing"; *maintaining* just has a less pejorative sound. Perhaps it's better to think of what you do now as "My Personal Eating Plan" (Lifetime Eating Plan sounds daunting!). We know you can't go back to your old buddies too often without puffing up again. In the simplest terms, staying on an eating plan is just a matter of *deciding* time after time after time in favor of something "healthy" and low-calorie (Evian, broiled swordfish, asparagus and melon) instead of gin and tonic, duck à l'orange, creamed spinach and pro-fiterole. After making the "good decision" about a million times, it gets to be so ingrained you don't even feel the need to hug yourself in a self-congratulatory fit every time you do it. You don't even have to lie to yourself weighing in. My skinny friend Betty says, "I had a friendly scale for years that registered approximately two pounds low even when 'adjusted correctly' and it was very cheering. Then you get on a true-weight scale at your doctor's office or the gym and consider slitting your throat. It's just simpler to have an honest one."

Does binging show up the next day on the scale or not until the day after? I have never quite decided. Occa-sionally it doesn't show up at *all* though you're dreading the worst and that's because you've compensated so hard with walking or swimming or dancing. Then occasionally you feel you really didn't do a thing bad—honest!—and you're up two pounds. You have to live with this craziness and cut back whenever the scale—always sickeningly true—says you're up a pound or two.

Many diet advisers suggest weighing just once a week. That must be for the really overweight. I'd gain ten pounds if I looked that infrequently. I need the (bad or good) news every single morning to stay honest. You may want to decide what you won't have to keep your weight down and don't have it *ever.* Don't pick something you adore and maybe it's just a particular *time* you don't have it, but what I don't have *ever* is hors d'oeuvres. They seem such skimpy innocent little things . . . veggies with dip, a tiny shrimp or two, but no calories whatever are always better than *some*. I have used this plan for years (unless it's Beluga caviar), and God knows bacon-wrapped pine-apple and shredded crab on toast are more delicious than lots of main dishes, but going hors d'oeuvre-less is just a foodproof way to save up calories for what's ahead: first course, main course and dessert.

For my friend Ellen the permanent reject is candy . . . "not a single piece *ever* because I'm not that crazy about candy anyway . . . cookies are something else!" If you keep an "unfriendly" food out of your life long enough, it *almost* doesn't exist. The hors d'oeuvres float past me; I go through the years ignoring them, simply getting on with Perrier and a squeeze of lime. (God, I missed Perrier when they took it off the shelves from a scare. I'd even con-vinced myself it tasted good—all that sodium, of course!—and those dear little kamikaze bubbles, always giving their *all*. It came *back* in six months, thank heaven.) The *good* news is that after you "stabilize" your weight and stay at that particular place for a while, you will prob-ably be able to stay more or less *permanently*—you really don't gain unless you're into the crazies.

How do you *avoid* the crazies? We've all heard all the maintaining tips, like put tiny portions on a *tiny* plate so they will look bigger (do people who suggest that think we are *morons?*), don't prowl the supermarket when hun-gry, don't order an ice-cream float when all you may be is *thirsty,* put your fork down between bites. I love hearing everything any dieter ever said about maintaining, whether it's the go-to-the-movie-during-a-hunger fit, hang the bi-kini on the fridge door or take bubble baths every half hour. Angie Dickinson once said she brushed her teeth and used a mouthwash a *lot* because she would never louse up her nice fresh mouth with food by eating afterward. Sweet.

I can eat if I've just had a *tooth* extracted. So it's never easy. Sometimes the self-discipline doesn't take and you're sinning again. As I have got older I have become such a nut-case maintainer, however, it's not a problem anymore. I love too much being slender (even if others say the look is *skeletal*). I am too healthy, too smug, too well

fed and like what I eat too much (I get dewy-eyed about
brown-rice pudding!) to go very far off the wagon. The
things that get *me* by I will share with you in a minute;
meanwhile, I guess we'd better have a small discussion
about what *basically* you should eat. You couldn't have
been alive the last ten years without being bombarded with
nutritional lore, but for purposes of a little review here of
what we older (aaawwpp!) people should be eating for
max health and efficiency, I thought I ought to study a bit.
So I began to read. Well, the deeper in you get the gum-
mier the going—especially if you're determined to *understand* things like glucose, fructose, lactose, blood sugar,
insulin, etc. From *Jane Brody's Nutrition Book* (Bantam
Books) (and she's supposed to be the *bible):*

"All carbohydrates are made up of one or more molecules of sugar. The *sugars,* or simple carbohydrates, may
be single molecules—*mono*saccharides, such as glucose,
fructose, and galactose—or double molecules—
*di*saccharides. The disaccharides are sucrose, a combination of glucose and fructose; maltose, a combination of
two glucose molecules; and lactose, a combination of glucose and galactose." (Do *you* understand that?)

I decided to call on my old friend Dr. Robert C. Atkins, who, nineteen years ago, had all of us dieting (rather
effectively if controversially) on high fat and protein/low
carbs (he was *very* tiny on carbs) to define some basic
stuff. We talked for an hour. I took a shorthand book full
of notes. Result: I can't make any sense out of them
whatever—not because Dr. Atkins isn't articulate and possibly even brilliant but it's like you don't ask the head of
the Federal Reserve Board to explain how to balance a
checkbook—he's *beyond* that. Hearing what happens
"when a load of sugar hits the bloodstream and causes 'insulin resistance' " didn't really help me since I'm not
clear, you see, on what insulin *is*. Never mind whether I've
got all the terms clearly defined—and it was good of Dr.
Atkins to see me—I think the best thing I can do is syn-
opsize what *most* nutritionists are recommending, give or
take a few oat-bran extremists who'd rather have you

break your ankle than not have oatmeal for breakfast. Unless you're one of those lucky metabolic cases who can polish off a buffalo steak chased with cherries jubilee and not gain an ounce, this is what they think will keep our weight down *and* provide maximum health—ready? Low-fat dairy products, fish, skinless chicken and turkey, lean meats, beans, fruits, vegetables and grain foods—best to select food from each of these groups each day. To be even more specific, I've appropriated a page from Sam Grossman's book *Win the Food Fight*, which lists the whole collection:

Fresh fruits: grapefruit, oranges, lemons, peaches, pears, plums, cantaloupe, apples, grapes, strawberries, blueberries, kiwifruit, apricots, figs, bananas, raisins, papayas, watermelon, honeydew, limes, cherries

Whole-grain cereals and breads: oatmeal, oat bran, pasta, rice, wheat, barley, corn, kasha, popcorn, couscous, bulgar, quinoa, rye

Fresh vegetables: avocados, lima beans, green beans, snow peas, beets, cabbage, broccoli, brussels sprouts, potatoes, green peppers, red peppers, carrots, cauliflower, celery, chard, onions, artichokes, kale, leeks, lettuce, spinach, mushrooms, okra, parsley, parsnips, peas, pumpkin, radishes, rhubarb, turnips, bok choy, zucchini, tomatoes, acorn squash, butternut squash, sweet potatoes, eggplants, watercress, jicama, green onions

Lean poultry and fish: chicken, turkey, salmon, halibut, mackerel, trout, swordfish, tuna, pickerel, cod, flounder, snapper, grouper, wild game

Dried beans: lima, black, kidney, garbanzo, great northern, navy, pinto, soy, lentil, split pea

Very-low- or non-fat dairy products: skim milk, low- or non-fat yogurt, very-low- or non-fat cottage cheese, hoop cheese, string cheese

As for breaking our dietary needs down into categories, okay, let me have a go at it—just a little synopsis of basic nutritional information. (Right, this is going to be really *boring!*)

PROTEIN

Important, but recommendations of how much we need have *changed* in recent years and it wasn't just Dr. Atkins for whom protein was belle of the ball in the fifties and sixties; everybody thought you couldn't be too rich or too thin or eat too much protein. Well, since cholesterol and carbohydrates got to be the new girls in town, they've actually been *hissing* protein and the current agreed-upon amount we need is 44 grams. Catherine Houck, *Cosmo*'s sensible—and well-informed—nutrition writer, says, "I think people who are told to 'watch it' are those having *massive* amounts—like eighteen-ounce steaks seven days a week. We shouldn't be put off this very necessary element." Robert E. Kowalski, in *The 8-Week Cholesterol Cure* (Harper & Row), says, "Throughout our lives we need protein to maintain and build body tissues, which are constantly being replaced; to make hemoglobin in the blood to carry oxygen to the body's cells; to form antibodies in the process of immunity which protects our bodies from infection; and to produce enzymes and hormones that regulate bodily functions." There! *Newsweek* describes proteins as "the beams and girders of the body's tissues." What our bodies really need, says Kowalski (and all others), are the eight or nine *essential amino acids,* which are the "building blocks of protein." It seems you can *get* the amino acids from rice and beans "in the right combination" but that's pretty complicated to figure out and why bother (unless you're a vegetarian) when fish, chicken, red meat, eggs, milk, cheese, yogurt are the big protein suppliers.

I would just like to sneak in a little personal testimonial for protein: Regardless of everybody's love affair with carbohydrates, it's easier to diet or stay on a maintenance program if you build each of your little meals *around* protein. That's because protein is digested much more slowly than carbs. (I've absorbed *this* much technical nutritional lore.) The blood sugar rises slowly and steadily, remains sustained for a longer period of time, falls slowly ... you stay *satisfied* for a few hours. I start with chicken or tuna salad, lean hamburger or egg-salad on skinny toast and any calories *left* you can give to those prissy vegetables and fruits; those alone don't leave you satisfied. This plan is the total opposite of everybody else's pushing veggies, fruit, carbs, and *protein* can just go take a hot bath *alone* on Saturday night—but it works for *me*.

CARBOHYDRATES

Carbs are the other big category, along with protein and fat (just a little), that we need, but *complex* carbohydrates, if you please ... don't even answer the *phone* if you think simple carbs are on the other end. The "simples" are found in scads of products in stores, such as refined sugar (both brown and white), anything that *contains* sugar (or fructose, sucrose—whatever *they* are), honey, syrup, ice cream, candy, pies, cakes, cookies, just about anything from the bakery that smells so good it makes your toes curl. There is a lot of sugar in processed food, as we know, of which there are miles and miles on shelves in a supermarket. Sugar, it seems, is the *worst*—I mean *nobody* doesn't agree on that. Exercise guru Jack LaLanne says, "You could be addicted to sex, dope, booze, but nothing—nothing—is worse than sugar. And once you're addicted, just try doing without it. Nothing is tougher." All those sugary products just mentioned contain practically *no* nutrients—only calories—so that's why they are called *empty* calories and we have to try to stay away from them *most* of the time. On the other hand, complex carbs (the good kind) are also all over the place—found in starchy foods like bread, cereal, grains (including rice and barley), vegetables (including potatoes, carrots and broccoli), beans and fruit. After you eat complex carbohydrates, they break down into glucose (the body's main energy source) just as simple sugar does but at a much slower rate so as not to trigger the excessive release of insulin (apparently we don't want excessive insulin released). Complex carbohydrates give you long-*lasting* energy without significantly altering your blood sugar level.

Listen, I already told you I don't understand all this worth skiddeldy-boo. I've been reading like a maniac and am trying to distill what everybody keeps *saying*—you need oodles of complex carbs!

FAT
(AND ITS BUDDY CHOLESTEROL!)

You need a *little* fat or you would *rust* but you can't mention fat without addressing cholesterol. According to Robert Kowalski, "Cholesterol ... is an organic chemical compound [that] looks and feels like soft wax [and] is just one of a whole group of compounds in the body known as sterols, all of which are essential to life. Cholesterol enters the body through the foods, specifically the animal foods, we eat. It is also manufactured by the body in the liver. . . . If the body doesn't have enough cholesterol to form vital hormones and metabolic products, we would not be able to survive. . . . If the body has too much cholesterol, the excess begins to line the arteries, leading to atherosclerosis."

There! But, you see, there are two *kinds*. From an Abbott Laboratories report: "HDL [high density lipids], known as the 'good' cholesterol (the kind you make yourself) scavenges cholesterol from the walls of arteries and carries it back to the liver, to be removed from the body." Kowalski says the same thing: "HDL actually acts to draw cholesterol away from the linings of the arteries. The higher the HDL level, the more protection against heart disease." Now for the *bad* cholesterol. Abbott again: "The LDL 'bad' kind of cholesterol (that *may* come from what you eat or may *not*) is the kind that builds up on the walls of the arteries and won't let the blood get through." Kowalski again: "LDL carries cholesterol through the

blood and deposits it in the arteries in a concretion of calcium, fibers, and other substances collectively referred to
as plaque. The formation of such plaque is called atheroma
and the disease is atherosclerosis." Abbott once more:
"Research indicates that, in some cases, heart disease can
be attributed to a shortage of HDL cholesterol (the kind
you make yourself) rather than the much-publicized excess
of LDL 'bad' cholesterol (that you may get from the outside)." Kowalski: "There is far more LDL trying to line
the arteries than there is HDL trying to keep the cholesterol away from the arteries." Yipes!

So how much should you and I *worry?* After reading
a collection of books, papers and opinions roughly the
height of Pikes Peak on the subject and feeling, toward the
end, I was up to my navel in a vat of soft, yellow, gummy,
waxy cholesterol, I concluded it may not be the problem
it's cracked up to be.

Cosmo's wise, possibly iconoclastic, former health
editor Mallen de Santis has *this* to say: "I think one has to
be rather skeptical about *anything* the medical establishment espouses wholeheartedly. Remember, one hundred
years ago all the eminent doctors believed in bloodletting
as the cure for every ailment (most patients died of
exsanguination!!!). The whole cholesterol scare thing is
kind of trumped-up . . . some people think it was dreamed
up by the food industry to create an outlet for their corn
oil products, which they'd never been able to sell much of
before creating the cholesterol scare. So anyway I pay little attention to all the fuss about eggs and animal fats. . . .
The jury is still really out on all of this (and nutritional
fashions will keep on changing as time goes on)." Catherine Houck says *she* has been "eating two eggs for breakfast every day for the past two decades and my cholesterol
level is fine."

I never had mine checked before last week when I
felt I *ought* to so I could join in the "fun." It seems to be
minuscule, with eggs, whole milk, cheese and beef having
never been off *my* reservation, though I don't eat pounds
and pounds. Before Mallen, Catherine and I get you felled
from ignoring cholesterol, let me mention an item in *Good*

Housekeeping. "According to the American Heart Association, more than half of all women age fifty-five to seventy-four have blood cholesterol levels above 240, the level at which heart disease risk increases dramatically." But *Vogue* counters, "If you believe the hype, we're all walking around with time bombs in our rib cages. But cholesterol is not a code word for heart disease. Things aren't as bleak as they seem—especially for women. Women have built-in defenses against the buildup of fatty deposits in their arteries. Compared with men, they tend to have higher levels of 'good' cholesterol." The Abbott Laboratories report says, "Certain people do have a definite genetic predisposition to elevated lipid levels (LDL) of all sorts . . . i.e., a genetic metabolic disability to handle dietary fats and cholesterol," plus they say, "Coronary heart disease afflicts more than 5.4 million Americans and is the nation's No. 1 killer, responsible for 550,000 deaths each year, [*but*] cholesterol is one of the *many* culprits—along with smoking and high blood pressure—behind the disease."

What we *don't* know, of course, is how much diet *affects* cholesterol—we really *don't.* From the *Harvard Medical School Health Letter:* "Some people are blessed with genes permitting them to eat almost anything and keep their cholesterol levels near 200." An article by Toni Tipton in the *Los Angeles Times* says that people who discount the cholesterol scare "claim a prudent diet has little or no effect on the system . . . there is only a small percentage of the population that can benefit from restrictive diets because the body will maintain its [cholesterol] balance even during periods of excess or, after a time of marked elevation, it will eventually return to its genetically determined level." In the same vein, the article reports that Thomas J. Moore, author of *Heart Failure* (Random House), "claims there are some people for whom restriction of dietary cholesterol [the kind you *ingest*] will be ineffective against decreasing blood cholesterol levels, so diet isn't that significant. He said the dangers of high blood cholesterol levels have 'frequently been exaggerated.' "

One more denial of danger: Frederick J. Stare, Robert E. Olson and Elizabeth M. Whelan write in their book *Balanced Nutrition: Beyond the Cholesterol Scare* (Bob Adams Publishers): "If you're a physiologically normal individual, your body constantly monitors what comes in and alters its own production of cholesterol in order to keep body stores constant and guarantee essential functions. And even in those people who exhibit modest short-term serum [blood] cholesterol increases or decreases due to diet, there is a general tendency in most of the serum cholesterol—over a period of years—to return to genetically determined levels." The Tipton article also points out: "Some species of animals have a very high threshold of tolerance. Carnivorous birds, rats and gophers, for example, survive on a diet of raw flesh, so they are genetically adapted to a meat diet. Although they eat a high cholesterol, high saturated fat diet, they have an inherited high HDL cholesterol level—the type that carries excesses out of the body and has been named the 'good' cholesterol." Maybe we're more like *them* than "rabbits and chickens who are genetically adapted to a vegetarian diet and a high cholesterol, high saturated fat diet is unhealthy for them." Whatever, I've about had it with the cholesterol hullabaloo, have *you?* (Does it rain the day you wear your new strappy sandals? . . . Why do I *ask?!*)

Let's finish off the "essential nutrients" discussion with fat, which you *do* need in your body. Jane Brody says, "Fat helps support and cushion vital organs, protecting them from injury [and] the layer of fat under your skin provides insulation against extremes of heat and cold. . . . Fat deposits in muscles are a source of energy for the muscle, including the heart muscle. . . . Oils in your skin and hair follicles prevent dryness and give your complexion a healthy glow. Fats also provide the construction material for hormonelike regulatory substances called prostaglandins. Prostaglandins are essential constituents of cell membranes throughout the body and help to regulate the body's use of cholesterol [oh God!]. And without some body fat, a woman's sex-hormone balance and menstrual cycle may be disrupted." Your body can make fat from two other ingredients, according to Brody—proteins and carbohydrates—*if* your diet contains more calories than you need for energy on a daily basis but you don't want that to happen because that is how you get *fat*. Your daily need for good nutrition and to keep body fat from "escalating," says Brody, is just one tablespoon per day. (I'm relieved we need *that* much. A New York hairdresser says he can tell his clients who have totally eliminated fat from their diets because "their skin resembles that of a crocodile!")

There are two *kinds* of fat: unsaturated (liquid at room temperature) as in safflower oil, sunflower oil, corn oil, cottonseed oil, which is okay, and *maybe* best of all, olive oil (though there is some question now whether it's *that* much better than the others), and *saturated* fat (solid at room temperature) as in butter, cheese, chocolate, and lard—a demon if you are watching cholesterol (well, you *might* be ... I may not totally have destroyed your will). Palm and coconut oils are the *most* saturated, even if liquid at room temperature, and are to be shunned (according to the cholesterol "pushers"). Okay, even for those of us who may *not* be watching the old C—fat is still something not to think of as friendly.

Reasons: The famous Framingham (Massachusetts) Heart Study suggests a high-fat diet increases the risk of colon cancer by 70 percent and more. Closer to home: Fat is loaded with calories—nine calories per gram as opposed to only four in protein or carbohydrates. In other words, you get fatter on the same number of *ounces* of fat. I am not paying too much attention myself to which is the bad kind and which is the good kind (saturated and unsaturated) of fat and far exceed a tablespoon a day. Would *this* be the place—probably not a minute too soon—to point out that everybody's body and nutritional needs are different? I would think you'd be experimenting, possibly with the help of a nutritionist at some point, continuously with which foods you like that also supply energy and weight control though what you decide now may not be forever.

DAIRY PRODUCTS

Cheese, butter, cream we are told to keep to a minimum because of their fat content—what about milk? Terrible warnings are sounded about grown-ups drinking milk, as though it would *kill* us. *Cosmo*'s Mallen de Santis has this to say: "The people who are against whole milk (but okay skim) are afraid of the fat and cholesterol. A few say adults don't need milk at *all* on the theory that animals don't drink milk after infancy. Some people have lactose *intolerance*—dairy products give them indigestion. Most experts *do* approve of milk for the calcium and protein content. I think milk is important and would even go so far as to say unless you're overweight, whole milk is better than skim. Seems to me the *natural* state of foods is best and there may be something in whole milk that we need." Recent news items about children put on low-fat diets (by their middle-class, nutrition-conscious parents), whose growth is stunted and who suffer from "failure to thrive," spurred pediatricians to say children should have whole milk at least until they're two years old. Again, I think you have to follow your instincts and use your own judgment. I read the obituary the other day of a prominent cardiologist who died of a heart attack at age fifty-five. I'm sure he was doing everything he thought was good for his heart—no fat or cholesterol, etc., etc., but obviously he was wrong! The fact is, we really don't *know* what's best to eat to stay healthy (except for the obvious things). Milk is fortified with vitamin D—another reason to drink it. Calcium plus vitamin D seems to prevent colon cancer. So there!

FIBER

Fiber is one of the good guys apparently (I'm only *semi*dizzy trying to keep track), though Jane Brody says, "Fiber is not considered an essential nutrient. Human beings can survive without any fiber in their diets and insufficient fiber does not produce a classic deficiency disease."

She pushes it for diet purposes. However, many nutritionists state unequivocally that fiber 1. Helps lower cholesterol (that word is as hard to stamp out as crab grass). Robert Kowalski: "Oat bran is the fiber of choice for those who want to keep their cholesterol levels out of the risk zone." Sam Grossman: "Eating foods, like oatmeal, that are high in soluble fiber cleans bile from your system that otherwise would linger and act as an agent for the manufacture of more cholesterol." Those folks are *crazy* for oat bran. 2. Prevents colon cancer. Grossman: "Quick and frequent passage of wastes cleans your system, allowing carcinogens less chance to linger in contact with your intestinal walls [and] reduces the risk of colon cancer." 3. Helps with weight control. Brody: "The more fiber your diet contains, the fewer calories you're likely to consume. Fiber itself yields few, if any, calories, and many fibrous foods, especially fruits and vegetables, are themselves low in calories." Great! 4. Helps with elimination. Kowalski: "Wheat fiber is excellent for speeding up the 'transit time' it takes for food to move through the digestive tract. Such fiber is the ultimate natural laxative." Mallen reminds us: "The colon is a *storage* container and the bowels move when the storage tank is full, so if you eat just a little real food, you need to add something like fiber (or Metamucil or psyllium seed, another bulker) to fill up the tank (the colon) and stimulate it to empty itself."

All fiber comes from plants; whole-grain cereals contain the *most*. Listed in order of highest content: All-Bran, shredded wheat, bulgur (cracked wheat), Grape-Nuts, grits, rolled oats. Veggies and fruits are good sources, too. In order of importance: parsnips, peas, carrots, potatoes, celery, summer squash, apples, pears, strawberries. Fiber is soluble or *insoluble*. From the University of California *Wellness Letter:* "The grains are mostly *insoluble* and move food quickly through the digestive tract, increase stool volume and may protect against colon cancer. *Soluble* fiber is found primarily in veggies and fruits and *may* lower blood cholesterol and help control blood sugar levels in diabetics. Chopping or cooking foods does not have any significant effect on fiber content."

Since fiber is so delicious, one doesn't have any problem getting oneself to eat it, right? Maybe we can't any longer rationalize that all those oat-bran muffins the size of Kansas City were absolutely required to keep us "regular," but we can still enjoy this healthful, satisfying "treat."

About our food intake generally, can you eschew the bad and embrace the good all the time? Does Yasir Arafat have long blond hair? On your own—especially totally alone—you go for the good a *lot*. You have no excuse that "the hostess made me do it" or the buffet table groaned and I groaned back. Catherine Houck thinks there doesn't need to *be* any binging because the naughty food you adore (heated croissant with cream cheese and jelly, fettucine Alfredo) should be *in* your diet occasionally. "Maybe you'll have the courage just to have a small portion or have it rarely." That seems a sophisticated, realistic way to look at things.

Would you like to know the favorite binge foods of some people you know? Diane Sawyer: "arrested-in-adolescence" food—hamburgers, potato chips, malteds. Raquel Welch: Belgian waffles, loaded with syrup and whipped cream and strawberries on top, served along with scrambled eggs, bacon and sausage. Ivana Trump: palacinky (Czech crepes), any kind of pâté or terrine, duck or goose with German dumplings, sauerkraut and gravy. Ali MacGraw: bittersweet chocolate, "any form I can get my hands on and there is *never* enough!" Dinah Shore: chicken-fried steak, chicken-fried chicken, cream gravies, cornbread, biscuits, potatoes, fresh breads—all with butter—pasta, hamburgers, hot dogs, chili, corn on the cob—in *quantity*. Walter Cronkite: "bread—hot bread—any hot bread!" Martha Stewart: "a Papaya King hot dog with mustard and sauerkraut, sometimes a hot fudge sundae, mostly for the hot fudge." Frances Lear: "chocolate and butter." Nora Ephron: "Le Petit Beurre cookies, lima beans with butter, Wise potato chips and cottage cheese, blanched salted almonds toasted in the toaster and then cooled and corn on the cob." Peter Jennings: "no particular 'sin food'; I will eat anything anytime, from caviar to cattle. In Paris the other day someone offered me a liqueur from Vietnam which tasted fine until I noticed the dead iguana in the bottle. Then someone else said it would contribute to sexual prowess. I'm off to Vietnam." On a visit to *Cosmo,* Henry Kissinger said he had lost a lot of weight, gained some of it back, that his favorite sin foods were *"everything* fattening!" Joan Rivers: "I am constantly dieting. I'm so concerned about my weight I'm often afraid I might eat in my sleep! But when I do indulge in something, it's fruitcake. Definitely, fruitcake . . . or carrot cake . . . or brownies. Actually, anything with icing. Let me put it this way: If shoes came with icing on them, I'd be barefoot."

Even if binging is wicked, I don't think we have to eat anything we hate. Example: Everybody out there now says you need two servings of vegetables and two servings of fruit per day *minimum.* Sybil Ferguson says a dieter (which we all are in a way . . . we're on some kind of life-long maintenance plan) "should eat five to *seven* vegetables daily, an apple every day and a good variety of other fruits." Jesus! I only have one of each of those categories on a good day, frankly, and I'm still here and healthy. You see you can *defy* the gurus.

Reading all this stuff on nutrition to get this chapter written and being *inundated* with pro-veggie propaganda, I did have a go at a veggie-binge the other day. I asked Julian at New York's four-star Four Seasons if they could fix a vegetable plate. Julian gave me his this-customer-must-be-deranged-but-I-will-go-along-as-this-is-a-first-class-place-and-this-woman-pays-her-bills-on-time look and ordered the nonprotein mess. Veggies gorgeous—deeply green string beans, broccoli, snow peas, regular peas, artichoke hearts, asparagus, plus orange as in carrots. Realizing rather soon I wasn't going to be able to hack through the forest without *help,* I sent out for hollandaise and wild rice plus a tiny whole-wheat roll with butter. I figure I had about a 2,000-calorie lunch and *still* felt deprived. I think it's better not to *force* yourself to eat things you don't like, just *don't* eat too much of things that are bad for you. People are pushing fish fish fish like we can't live without it, but any nonshell fish (all the boring, low-cholesterol, low-calorie ones) turn my friend Judith ashen. Red *meat* isn't recommended so she makes do with *chicken* (I'd rather live on roots and berries). Well, *nobody* can brainwash our tastebuds (tastewash them?) so you "adjust."

I think you do finally get the better of serious bad-girl binging . . . it's too crazy at our age. I misbehaved so badly so often with sweets a few years back: two pounds of shortbread cookies in an hour and a half—nibble, nibble—all gone. A whole box of 100 Percent Natural Quaker Oats in one sitting when it first came out, then the shame-and-guilt-twenty-four-hour pure-pain total fast to atone. I finally couldn't stand the binge-purge routine any longer and went straight, not one grain of sugar for five years; then I quietly let it back in my life. I haven't begun binging again and don't *think* I will. It's just too important to me to be slender, agile . . . to feel young and sexy even if I don't quite look like that. Yes, I know men joyfully go to bed with plump ladies so let me not be ridiculous, but you have to perceive *yourself* as sexy which I absolutely can't do if not at greyhound weight.

I *sin* . . . but nothing much wrestles me to the ground I hadn't figured on. I know I'm going to have rice pudding at Manhattan's "21" Club after our weekly Thursday advertising lunch but I will bring my Reeboks and jog back to the office. Monica says she knows she will have chocolate cake with whipped cream at our city's sinful Des Artistes after a movie if she's walked *enough* that day or week. I had the "cake of the day" for one whole week at Claridge's in London recently (what are you going to order from room service—crudités and hard-boiled eggs?), but then I don't use escalators or moving walks in airports; I schlep fifteen pounds of junk in my Vuitton and *that* burns the cals. Laura says, "Dinner at La Grenouille doesn't happen for me without a Kir Royale, quenelle in champagne sauce and *all* the petit fours, but I've had a light little lunch and maybe walked in a snowstorm to get to the restaurant." Weather is a big diet helper in New York. Instead of getting into a car, you bundle up, put on your sneakers, mush mush mush, then change to satin pumps at the coat-

check ... these things can be *managed!* Walking is maybe
the easiest and most available of *all* exercise to neutralize
a planned or already consummated food binge. You can
walk to and from meetings, lunch, dinner, parties. Walk
home. If they don't want to go with you, meet them later.
New York City is one of the walkingest in the world,
thank God ... nobody even thinks you are *weird.*

I do sometimes *daydream* about food, do you? What
I am *going* to eat later in the day and, after a sumptuous
meal and lying in bed at night, about what I *had.* Can't see
any harm in that. Once when David and I flew in a single-
engine Cessna from a game preserve in Botswana back to
Johannesburg, strapped in with just enough room for knee-
sies in front but not another inch, flight too choppy and
everybody too dizzy to read but not sick enough to throw
up, I "put together" little meals for four straight hours—
lethal chili con carne with a *cup* of chopped onion on top,
shepherd's pie in a feathery pastry crust, prosciutto, Swiss
cheese, mayonnaise and mustard on chewy French bread,
crab cakes with coleslaw. Then I did restaurant pets: fish
pâté and stuffed vine leaves from the White Tower in London, bouillabaisse to die for from Tetou in Golfe-Juan in
France, Risotto con Filetto di Sogliola from Harry's Bar in
London, Black Forest fudge cake smothered in whipped
cream from Des Artistes in New York. At home I try to
confine my dreaming to things that are going to be *possible* later that day at dinner (Sunset Salad with Lorenzo
Dressing at "21," Salmon Pajorsky from the Russian Tea
Room) and not drive myself crazy with longing for the old
untouchables.

Changing food plans through the years isn't flighty or
inconsistent but realistic and even smart. Along with the
sugar expunging, I have been "good" to the point of paranoia about fat (anybody plunking down a plate of fried
zucchini in front of me would be considered trying to *poison* me!) all the way to my present "everything in moderation." Of course you need to be knowledgeable about
cals. Alison puts it this way: "Once you've worked out
some little meals you adore that don't destroy you with
cals, it's tempting to have them every day until you die!

Surely taste buds are something we don't have to bludgeon to be creative. Sure you may be missing a thrill or two with the same monotonous 'good foods' but you'll run into food thrills at parties where somebody *else* plans the food." As Alison says, "You *know* the calorie count of your best-pal foods ... start messing with strangers and you can blow it." Still, you can get burned *out* on your "perfect foods." (I've *almost* had it with tuna salad, having been its love-slave all my life.) Dr. Robert C. Atkins, who really knows nutrition, though he is controversial, says, "You should keep your body guessing. It gets used to a certain metabolic pathway and gets lazy. You should give it some surprises so you can say to it 'gotcha!' Go from red meat to seafood to vegetables and different *kinds* of seafood and red meat ... vary your pitches."

TIMING

When should you *eat* your daily allotment of calories? Five small meals a day versus three regular meals is up for grabs. Shirley MacLaine has long been an advocate of five smalls. I never have fewer than four or five. Catherine Houck comes down firmly for three regulars. "There is just something satisfying about a piece of chicken, brown rice, veggies *and* fruit—a complete meal," says Catherine. "You really fill up and feel satisfied, not to mention not having to bother preparing all those little snippets." Dr. Newbold, in *Mega-Nutrients* (over 400,000 copies sold!), says, "Doctors tell patients to have frequent small meals. That's nonsense—unless the patient's eating things he's allergic to and trying to prevent withdrawal reactions. The truth is, if you're eating a proper diet, one that does not contain things to which you're allergic, you should do perfectly well on three meals a day. Many people do well on two meals—if they're staying away from foods to which they're allergic." Sybil Ferguson, founder of Diet Centers, recommends having *six* small meals a day!

Obviously it's *totally* up to you. Though it's not supposed to be good for you, if you *should* happen to be so revved up someday with work or love or so totally preoccupied you totally *forget* about food and are not hungry, what the hell, go for it! Usually you "make up for" the skipped meal by eating twice as much at the next one, so I'm just talking about a *really* skipped meal. It has to be a "natural" occurrence—either disaster or joy trip—you just forget to eat because other things are so much more important. It's happened to me about twice so far in a lifetime! Conversely, one should never be *without* food for a fix if you need one. Funny rule for somebody trying to stay skinny but it's important to be comfortable, not starving. My staple is mozzarella cheese—good old protein plus a little fat; a few slices are easy to carry in your purse in foil or a Baggie. This fix always goes with me to airports or wherever a meal isn't scheduled for six hours. It's also a good one-hundred-calorie breakfast in a taxi.

We should not ever eat just because *they* are eating or *they* are nagging. Bonnie, a slender *Harper's Bazaar* assistant, says, "My roommate and I virtually never have dinner, lunch or breakfast at the same time at home. Our 'hunger' schedules are different. I visit while she eats but probably eat later when I'm really hungry." Carol of the iron will says, "It is totally *possible* to sit in a restaurant and consume not one calorie—no, not even a breadstick—if, for some reason, you've recently eaten and it's too soon for another meal." *I* know it's *possible* to take "Eat, *eat!*" abuse from friends—the creeps!—and *still* not eat. Discipline gets to be easy—it *does*—if you care a lot and get nutrition on your brain.

What about eating breakfast like a king, lunch like a prince, dinner like a pauper and nothing between (early) dinner and bedtime, as recommended by so many? "That late-night calories are more fattening is a *myth,*" says Artemis Simonopoulos, M.D., director of the Center for Genetics, Nutrition, and Health of the American Association for World Health in Washington, D.C. "What's important is still the total number of calories consumed per day versus the amount expended."

Is *breakfast* necessary? Nutritionists all say yes. Sam

Grossman: "Morning is the time your body is coming out of its rest cycle and starting its active cycle ... your body's core temperature is down as much as two degrees. Your pulse is often ten beats or so lower than during the height of your active phase ... hormonal production is also down. The evidence is conclusive that what you need in the morning more than anything is energy to get your body out of its rest cycle.... Studies at Rockefeller University have shown that eating a light breakfast or skipping breakfast altogether throws your brain's neurotransmitters out of balance." I feel terrible breaking the news to Sam if he hasn't already heard that a recent Gallup poll says one third of all people in the United States *skip* breakfast on a typical workday and, well, you don't see nearly *all* of them dropping in the streets.

Polling my friends over sixty, I find they eat everything from bananas and peanut butter to leftover corned beef hash for breakfast; some skip breakfast altogether but mostly they now go for bran cereal or grapefruit and protein toast. I have vegetable stew. In a big pot of water, throw in a ton of carrots, broccoli, celery, string beans, cauliflower—whatever is handy. Add a beef or chicken bouillon cube, a few scraps of ham, chicken, beef or fish if you have any left over, and herbs. Boil the night before or as long as you have time for in the morning. *Drink* the broth—which is where all the vitamins went—and *eat* the veggies. If you feel about vegetables as I do—I *loathe* them!—this is an *almost* painless way to get them in you.

After the breakfast veggie soup (alternated sometimes with two soft-boiled eggs and a piece of seven-grain toast buttered or occasionally Opti-fast in a blender), lunch at my desk, brought from home in brown paper bag, is homemade tuna or chicken salad or sometimes cottage cheese with apple and part-skim-milk mozzarella cheese diced in. Restaurant lunch is broiled fish and a veggie, no first course or dessert except that once a week, after selling advertising at "21" Club, I have rice pudding as a reward. Six P.M. daily office snack: five thin slices part-skim-mozzarella cheese and half a sliced apple. Dinner at a restaurant—same deal as lunch—fish, veggie, no first course unless I'm making people nervous; then I have consommé or green salad without dressing. At home David gets a grown-up dinner but I don't have anything until bedtime; then it's a bowl of equal parts shredded wheat, Shredded Wheat'n Bran, Nutri-Grain (wheat), Kellogg's All-Bran with two packets of Equal and skim milk, plus a big dash of whipping cream (talk about inconsistent!). Reading in bed just before turning off the light I have a dish of sugar-free Jell-O (one package makes one gooey-gummy dish—forty-two calories) and a few grapes.

On weekends David squeezes a big glass of fresh grapefruit juice for my breakfast—the one food chore he *acknowledges* knowing how to do—which tides me over until 2:00, 3:00 or 4:00 P.M.—whenever I stop work. Saturday and Sunday are big workdays; during the week I flit around a lot and talk and visit. Weekend lunch is HGB salad and skinny rice pudding (recipes in a minute). Dinner around midnight is the rest of the salad, bran-cereal mix, Jell-O and grapes. Yes, darling David is cooked (by his bride) a decent dinner.

My food plan sounds grim, right? Well, don't cry for me, Argentina. At parties I eat sumptuously and sometimes in New York Italian restaurants (Cipriani, Patsy's, Bellini), I have clams and linguine or risotto. I know *how* to eat—skinny people *do*, you see. We just have got so used to not ever putting anything junky or too *much* (even the good stuff) of *anything* down our throats more than a few times a year it's kind of ingrained in us. Anybody who wanted to—and I hear a lot of people say they would love to weigh twenty or thirty pounds less—could get the skinny-eating habit, but food brings them too much pleasure. I love food like a normal person but love being skinny more.

Drinking doesn't seem to go with slender *or* healthy, although some heavy drinkers *do* stay wraithlike. Certain medical savants have even debunked the popular (very! especially with my husband) idea that a couple of belts a day stave off heart attacks. One drink or a glass of wine a day couldn't *hurt*, I suppose, but we prissy ones would rather put the ninety calories into something delicious *and* even good for you in the way of *food,* like a baked apple, tossed green salad, plain yogurt, but *you* may prefer the wine—fine. One of the friends I wrote about in the sex chapter drinks champagne only with her *lover* ... not a drop between times (and it may be weeks between visits) but they kill *two* bottles of Perrier Jouet at a rendezvous. Sweet. I'll just add this unsolicited, *totally* empirical opinion about alcohol (and my sister is a recovering alcoholic—twenty-six *years* in A.A.!). Seems to me the men or women who have drunk for a long time don't look as good as they used to (well, who *does?!*) but they don't look as good as people their age who *don't* drink. Around forty, and surely by fifty, their faces get a little shabby or slipped ... not fresh and glowy. The word *blotchy* comes to mind ... the color is too pale *or* too florid. If they drink and also don't exercise, the body *and* face look just plain wasted. Exercise makes up for a lot of sins, of course. ... We'll hit that in the next chapter. A heavy drinker I know says he sweats it all out on his daily three-mile jog. Maybe. My darling husband will have a drink or two plus wine if we're out for the evening and no snippy remark from me will *ever* restrain him. He says I am a totally insincere person—that when we were courting, I gave him double Scotches and melt-the-asbestos-strength bloody Marys but I tell him that was *then* ... I *got* him and things *change!* Others are just as enthusiastic about liquor. Angela says, "I'd rather give up Roger than my perfect Manhattan every night."

VITAMINS

Do vitamins work? Up for grabs. Robert Kowalski says, "Traditional nutritionists and dietitians state rather unequivocally that diet alone provides all the nutrients we need ... supplementation simply results in expensive urine. On the other side of the argument are those who say supplementation is more important than the foods we eat. The truth probably lies somewhere in between." My own doctor, New York internist Eugene Cohen, possibly a *ge-*

nius diagnostician, thinks nutritional supplements are nonsense. I pay no attention whatsoever to him and take thirty a day! I've only missed seven working days because of *illness* in the past twenty-five years at *Cosmo*. Who knows what part vitamins had to do with this wellness? Maybe it's the hour and a half of exercise every day, eight hours of sleep a night or catnaps next day, no caffeine, virtually no booze, cigarettes, or drugs, and the fact that I adore my work that are responsible but I'm afraid to go cold turkey and stop taking vitamins *now*. For me, eating as little as I do, they *may* supply some stuff I would ordinarily get from food.

Lots of studies are being done now with vitamins. A recent Centers for Disease Control study has found women who are taking multivitamin pills at the time of conception are 60 percent less likely to have a baby with a serious neurological defect than women who are not. Okay, that's not too fascinating at our age but how about this: Smokers with potentially precancerous lesions in their lungs showed significant improvement after taking megadoses of vitamin B_{12} and folic acid for four months, according to a report in *The Journal of the American Medical Association*. And twenty-six women with cervical dysplasia (precancerous lesions) were given large doses of folic acid; an equal number received a placebo. The condition of one of those who took the vitamin worsened, seven improved, eighteen remained the same. In the placebo group, five got cancer, nine worsened and twelve showed no change. A *Finnish* medical journal reports that women with lower vitamin E and selenium levels have a risk of developing breast cancer that is ten times greater than that of supplement takers with the highest levels of these two substances. That would be reason enough for taking them.

Who figures out what vitamins you should take? After my initial indoctrination by Gladys Lindberg in Los Angeles, we moved to New York where Sam Brown at Brownie's Health Food Store worked out a new mix for me. (Most doctors then wouldn't go *near* vitamins and it isn't so different now.) Later the list was revised by a doctor who does go near vitamins, Dr. Robert C. Atkins, and recently Dr. Ronald L. Hoffman, who helped me get over shingles (aftermath of surgery), revised it further still.

You *can* read and study and work out a vitamin regime for *yourself*, of course—many do—or perhaps there's a nutritionist in your town or, yes, a knowledgeable owner of a store. Remember, doctors usually aren't enthusiastic *or* knowledgeable about vitamins—not part of their curriculum in medical school. My thirty vitamins a day (half at two separate times) include C, E, massive B, folic acid, biotin, L-cysteine, acidophilus and some other things, plus two teaspoons of flaxseed oil and a package of Greenmagma (dried juice from barley plants) dissolved in water. Do I have a clue what all these things are supposed to do for you? Absolutely not! I've read but the study of vitamins and supplements seems to me very complex. The doctors who practice alternative medicine and worked out a vitamin regime for me I trust. I'm healthy . . . what more do I need to know?

RESTAURANTS

How can you diet or eat healthfully in a restaurant? If they aren't lacing your food with butter, they are embalming it with salt or dumping it in the blender with *both* salt and butter and a little half-and-half as in pureed spinach. . . . No *wonder* theirs tastes so much better than what you cook at home (if you're cooking healthy). When *they* dress a salad, oil swims in the plate. *Your* salads are dressed with lemon or wine vinegar. Restaurants push desserts (who can *blame* them, that's how they make money).

Well, never mind what they're pushing; anybody who can't diet in a restaurant just doesn't *want* to. The food is there, yes, but that's got nothing to do with *you*. They only bring what you order. In any restaurant in the world, they'll give you melon instead of marzipan in phyllo pastry, saccharine for your coffee instead of sugar. There is incredible food all over town (in bakeries and delis) that is *also* none of your business (unlike the food in your own home which can actually reach out from the shelves and put its arms around you).

I learned about restaurant abstinence a few years ago when David and I used to take our then daughter-in-law to New York's upper-crust Lutèce, the Four Seasons, wherever, and while we *ate,* she moved around a few lettuce leaves, drank gallons of tea and smiled. Nobody *hit* her although the thought crossed one's mind. I didn't know it at the time but she was on a macrobiotic diet and ate only little loaves of brown bread she baked herself—later she fattened up. You can diet *anywhere* if you *want* to. Every country has fresh fish; ask the captain to broil the fish and make you a salad ... dressing on the side—or ask for a wedge of lemon. I've learned to eat salad *without* dressing and I like to use my fingers. ... I know, disgusting! You can skip the first course *altogether* or have consommé or jellied madrilene (*no* calories) or asparagus and lemon juice while others eat something decent. I can get through a first course having *nothing* while they eat because I know food is coming *later.* Oh, God, that does sound prissy, but if you blow all the cals on shiitake mushrooms sautéed in butter on toast going *in,* you've got the task of trying to be good all evening.

As for dessert, well, even fruit has cals. While your mates have dessert, ask them to bring tea, decaffeinated coffee or coffee and that's what *you* do with your hands and mouth. If you must have dessert, melon or strawberries—dry—are the most pristine. The restaurant doesn't care how skimpy the portion as long as they are charging you $8.75 for *something.* You can *leave* food on your plate though I have never got the hang of *that*—if it's there, it's mine and I *eat* it!

THE SEARCH AND DESTROY CROWD

Three people I adore are close to sumo-wrestler condition but I know they *can't* diet so I leave them alone. My compassion comes from my frequently being badgered ... to gain. Sometimes people come up to me on the street and say things like "We've seen you on television, Ms. Brown, and admire you so much ... blah, blah, blah ... could we just tell you something [here it comes]? We think you would look better if you would put on ten pounds!" Do I explain the ten pounds would all go to my stomach, not to my face and bosom, that copious research indicates older people should weigh about a third less than they do to prolong life or that it's *my* body and bug off? I don't say nothin'. Mostly the pushers are your "friends." "For God's sake, have a roll and butter, have dessert ... you can *afford* it!" Listen, if you "afforded" it, you would be fat like they are ... the reason you are skinny is you resisted. But I'm probably not getting much sympathy here. ... If you saw me, *you'd* think I was too skinny *too* and start pushing something.

The things people *do* to cause you to sin ... and not just hostesses selling the luscious food at their buffet table but office pals plunking a piece of Larry's birthday cake on your desk at 4:00 P.M. when you are ravenous. They give you chocolate and homemade cookies for your birthday. They mock, scorn and say rotten things in restaurants (when you're taking *them* to dinner), like "I suppose she's going to order dry sole and plain broccoli once again," making sure to speak loud enough so everybody else at the table notes your prissiness. Once when the late gifted comedian Danny Kaye cooked dinner for David and me— cooking for friends was his pleasure—and I refused even a bite of his Grand Marnier soufflé (this was a month after I'd gone cold turkey with sugar and knew not even a grain could pass my lips), he tried to pry my jaws open with his hands for five minutes ... dear Danny (I won—I bit him).

Claudia reports an atrocity perpetrated by a close friend acting from blind stupidity. "Coffee?" her hostess asked after a perfect lunch at her country house. "Decaf if you have it," Claudia says, "Sanka, Brim, anything." Caffeine affects Claudia like a charge of dynamite, she says, lights up the skies, then leaves shards and splinters when the high wears off. "Coming up," said the hostess and returns in a few minutes with steaming cups of *something*. "I drank four cups of 'decaf,'" says Claudia, "as we talked of old beaux, rivals, jobs, ecology. I found myself getting maniacally articulate, brilliant as Capote, close to passionate on every subject and very very jumpy! Too bad I'm not as wonderful as this in everyday life, I thought to myself; why am I wasting this brilliance on my old dear friend? Finally, now in overdrive, thrillingly witty—it occurred to me to ask, 'Winnie, was that by any chance real coffee I had for lunch?' 'Yes,' she said. 'I didn't have any decaf and figured you wouldn't know the difference.' Not know the difference?! Did John the Baptist not know he was getting beheaded?! I excused myself and went for a swim. Twenty laps later in a forty-degree November pool the old heart was still racing like a greyhound. I forgave the darling girl (though I was a total slug at dinner and talked in monosyllables ... highs wear *off*), but now I don't even have decaf in restaurants late at night. It's cute to ask the waiter to give you his phone number because you want to call him at 3:00 A.M. when you are thrashing about in bed wide awake because he gave you the real-stuff coffee instead of decaf but that won't really get you back to sleep. I just order boring old camomile tea and save myself any aggravation."

Repeat: How big you are, what you do or don't want to eat, is *your* business. Saboteurs should get stomach cramps in twenty-foot waves and try to swim for shore.

COOKING HEALTHY

You've probably read plenty already about healthful cooking so we don't need to dwell. Just a few highlights:

Raw is best of all for veggies, al dente next best. You want to *steam* veggies so all the nutrients don't go into the water or into the air.

Let restaurants peel the carrots so they are smooth and glamorous. *We* should leave skins *on* carrots, turnips, apples, pears, potatoes. We weight watchers are happy to get our chompers on a few skins. I've found scrubbing carrots and parsnips with Chore Boy takes off just the lightest amount of skin (it's my one kitchen trick).

Pam spray allows sautéing without sin. Most of us can't remember when we melted a tablespoon of butter or margarine or poured cooking oil into a skillet.

If you're coating with flour or using it to thicken sauces or in baking, whole wheat, not bleached or even "enriched," or soy is what you want. Can't imagine you'd be using much of *any* kind of flour if you're cooking skinny.

Let congeal in the fridge whatever comes out of a chicken while cooking, then take the congealed layer of fat *off*. What's left is *stock* to use in soups or sauces (oh—you know this already? I just discovered it last year!).

We *are* cooking without salt, right? *Dashes* of naughty things—Parmesan cheese, real crumbled bacon bits, plain yogurt (instead of sour cream) in a baked potato, a few raisins—are okay.

Some nutritionists say that even though aspartame (as in Equal) has no harmful side affects like cyclamates, we should still stay away because artificial sweeteners simply cater to our need for sweets and you *could* be weaning yourself away if you lived without. Fie on them! I use at least two packs of Equal a day minimum, usually four or five; they are de rigueur to sweeten plain yogurt, Sanka, Brim, oatmeal, bran cereal, berries, etc.

I'm so grateful there's something really sweet that tastes like sugar and has no aftertaste and only four calories that I don't want to *know* from weaning. Equal disappears in cooking so you use Sweet'n Low or Sweet One. Butter Buds, Molly McButter are both great butter substitutes. No, you can't butter toast with them but they're fine in oatmeal, veggies, baked potatoes, my beloved rice pudding. I use *liquid* Butter Buds on waffles and pancakes (made with soy flour, of course).

The protein isn't destroyed if you "overcook" meat, fish or chicken and I find glutinous, bright-orange-on-the-inside salmon as revolting as beef dripping with blood, though rare anything may be your preference. Some of us southern girls ruined in childhood with overcooked never reformed.

The quicker you drink orange or grapefruit juice once

squeezed, or eat the fruit, the better. Vitamin C goes away
with exposure to air.

FRESH, FROZEN, CANNED AND READ LABELS!

Fresh stuff is best—does everybody agree on that except for the food processors? Frozen is next best, then
canned. (Sybil Ferguson says, "Shop the outside edge of
the supermarket for fruits, vegetables, meat, milk and
cheese. . . . Leave the cans and prepackaged foods on the
shelves.") Whatever you're taking *off* the shelves, you
ought to read labels, though you may not understand what
you *read.* (What *is* calcium chloride? *And* diglycerides?)
Ingredients are listed according to amounts contained in
the product; the more there is, the closer to the top of the
list. Joseph J. Percivalle, Jr., writes in *Reader's Digest:*
"The interesting thing about reading labels is that you realize you are washing dishes with detergent made with real
lemon juice and drinking lemonade made with artificial
flavorings." Preservatives we have to forgive—they're
necessary if we don't want stuff to collapse and die on the
shelves. Sugar is something else. Sugar is bad, agreed?
You can find a lot of that in *everything* from canned peas
to tomato soup. Sodium is another "enemy." Sodium is
salt. Doesn't mean you don't buy these things but you no
longer have to wonder why they taste so good, possibly
better than what *you* are cooking pristinely *without* salt
and sugar.

Here are the ingredients in a wildly popular, absolutely *delicious* spinach soufflé (a nice "vegetable" dish,
right?): spinach, eggs, margarine, partially hydrogenated
soybean oil, skim milk, salt, vegetable lecithin, vegetable
mono & diglycerides, sodium benzoate, citric acid, artifi-
cially flavored with beta carotene, vitamin A palmiate
added, food starch, modified enriched bleached flour, soybean oil, sugar, salt, monosodium glutamate, spice. Really!

Check the calorie counts of canned and packaged
food, bearing in mind that what they say "serves three"
will probably not tide your pet hamster over to the next

meal. You probably need to *double* one of their "servings" for humans.

COOKING HEALTHY

Recipes should be *straightforward,* the ingredients right out there, nothing tucked away in two-point type to come back and destroy you later because you didn't *know. But* many are naughty, no help whatever with weight watching. I noticed a delicious-sounding Swedish Meat Bake in the recipe section of *Reader's Digest*—two cups uncooked macaroni (that's 420 cals cooked), one *can* cream of mushroom soup (200 cals), one *cup* of sour cream (416 cals) not to mention a pound of ground beef (1,000 cals) and some other stuff. It wasn't even supposed to feed the neighborhood, just four to six people and, as we said, recipes don't usually "feed" as many people as they purport to. In the same issue a recipe (with a photo that makes you want to eat the page) calls for eight ounces of cream cheese, one *cup* powdered sugar, one half pint whipping cream . . . lethal calorie-wise and not much food value. Well, you're a big girl now and can admire recipes without cooking them. You can also smile at the advertising claims ("Natural goodness . . . nothing artificial for *my* family . . . Tetley Tea," as though caffeine, as in tea, has to be "artificial" to be bad for you!).

Okay, that's my whole healthy cooking repertoire. I'm a little nervous about giving cooking advice anyway. If you weren't good at something young, you don't necessarily get better. I conveniently blame my no-cooking talent on my mom. "Cleo was not a great cook" doesn't begin to *describe* what went on at my house when I was growing up; we just simply never *had* company for dinner. (Just *once* we did and all of us were puddles of nerves and anxiety.)

Well, when you grow up, you either "retaliate" by learning to cook well yourself or you stay traumatized and retarded, as far away as possible from the preparation of food. I chose the latter except for the thrown-together stuff

I give David when we're at home alone. Never mind one's *food* not coming out well; I have probably destroyed more kitchen *equipment* than Macy's sells in December. Saucepans are my specialty. Basic formula: Never put any *real* liquid in the pan because you know you are not supposed to boil veggies and have all their goodness ooze out into the water (which gets thrown out), so, of course, whatever minimal water you put *in* gets "used up" in about three minutes and the pan burns; even though you've checked four times, you wait too long for the fifth check and pppssshffftt, black happens.

I burn up about a pan a month with David's favorite food, Brussels sprouts (isn't that weird thing to be crazy about?), and don't tell me about *steaming* ... steaming Brussels sprouts takes approximately the same amount of time as crocheting an afghan, and water disappears from the bottom of a steam pot *anyway* if you leave it alone long enough. David says he *likes* scorched veggies—what else can he say if he wants to eat? Plastic tops on teakettles I can finish off in minutes. Recipe: Boil water. Pour scalding water into glass dish with diet Jell-O. In order to have water still boiling as you pour (so Jell-O will dissolve easily), do not pause to turn off fire or place plastic teakettle top far away from it. Squizzelllebbfft! In *seconds* half of teakettle top eaten away.

I haven't done in a Waring Blender recently because I learned to put in the ice cubes for my breakfast drink one at a time. I used to put all nine in the blender *with* the Opti-fast, vanilla, diet soda, Equal and turn on the motor. The machine would grind its little heart out—you could hear it making terrible death-rattle noises—then smoke would rise, things would begin to smell terrible and the blender would die. Someone I was telling this to said if I would put the cubes in one at a time they would be assimilable ... turned out to be *true*. I still lose a few chopsticks to the blender. If something seems not to be liquefying properly, I poke a chopstick down into the glop while the machine is running to try to get the mess unstuck. Takes too much time to stop the machine ... you might have to stop it three or four times to poke about if something is really clogged up in there. I try to keep chopsticks *away* from the blade close to the glass side but sometimes it doesn't work out that way and you get—what else?!— splintered chopstick. Listen, not *everybody* is an engineer. I don't *have* a microwave. What's going on in there is too dangerous and spooky.

So I once had a memorable cooking experience on television. Actor Robert Morley and I teamed up on a cable show called *Celebrity Chefs* to cook a memorable *dessert.* "Don't worry about not being a cook," they said, "we'll supply the recipe and tell you what to do." They certainly *did.* Their selection: chocolate tortillas with whipped cream and fudge sauce smothered in fruit. Only four component parts, right? Forget component parts . . . the twenty-two separate *ingredients* are what did us in. First we made fudge sauce: corn syrup, water, heavy cream, butter, sugar, salt, cocoa, unsweetened chocolate plus Grand Marnier. That went relatively well. Then the batter—eggs, egg yolks, whole milk, melted butter, salt, flour and Grand Marnier (they were *very* big on Grand Marnier). So far, so good. We were supposed to make a chocolate tortilla, which was what killed the act. The skillet wasn't hot enough to cook a drop of water, let alone a tortilla and we are mashing around these three tablespoons of chocolate batter from which a tortilla flapjack is *not* happening. Dear Morley . . . "Well now, it's coming right along," the consummate actor would murmur, gazing at the blob. I wanted to scream for the show food stylist to ask what the fuck she expected us to do with this chocolate liquid mess in a cold skillet, but we pretended there really was a grown-up tortilla in there and moved on to the next challenge: loading the tortilla (gooey mess) with fudge sauce, whipped cream, raspberries and oranges, after which we were supposed to *eat*—on camera—but who could *eat?!* And then they announced we would have to do the whole thing over! (P.S. They never ran our segment—we did just as badly the second time.)

That tortilla mess wasn't my fault but I can undo people who come to work *for* me. We once had a *filet de boeuf* for fourteen that was totally *gray* from my suggest-

ing to the caterers we "leave it in the oven just a touch
longer to be *sure*," and one whole batch of sorrel soup
was *sour*—the half-and-half curdled (let's not bring up that
old myth about cream curdling around witches). Well, you
don't want to hear any more. Age hasn't improved me,
only hardened my resolve to let *others* do the cooking.
Good cooks need *appreciators,* right?

I have digressed. Let's do some *skinny* recipes.

FAVORITE THINGS TO EAT

What is the best thing in the world? Gardenias? A
baby's smile? Sunrise at Waikiki? For me it's rice, especially in rice pudding. Here's my recipe for one that doesn't
contain much sin:

REASONABLY SKINNY RICE PUDDING

Put cooked brown rice in a no-stick or Pam-coated
saucepan—you decide how much rice, I use a *lot*. Throw
in raisins—I use twenty-four. Heat slowly or quickly if,
like me, you don't care whether you burn up a pan. In separate pan or skillet heat milk—enough milk to cover the
rice or you can use more. I use half skim, half homoge-
nized to give pudding a little oomph. Put heated rice and
raisins in a nice little bowl, stir in two packets of Equal,
dust on a *lot* of Butter Buds or Molly McButter, pour on
milk.

I don't know how many calories are in this rather innocent dessert—plenty perhaps, but if you've just had a
big salad with rice-vinegar dressing, you can *afford* a few
healthy cals at a Saturday lunch.

My housekeeper Anna's tuna salad keeps me alive
during the week—it may be the best tuna salad in the
world. It's my office lunch and I use just a tablespoon or
two in the Saturday salad.

ANNA'S TUNA SALAD

½ small onion, grated
2 medium-size dill pickles, chopped fine
2 medium (or one big) stalks celery, chopped fine
2 fairly heaping tablespoons mayonnaise
2 fairly heaping tablespoons plain yogurt
1 7-ounce can tuna (nondietietic, dump in the oil)
1 hard-boiled egg, grated

Add onion, pickles and celery to mayonnaise and yogurt. Let stand ten minutes. Shred tuna very fine and add to yogurt/mayonnaise mixture. Add grated egg last. On top of the salad I always pile more chopped onion, sliced green or red pepper, cucumber, undercooked green beans cut in pieces, cherry tomatoes and sliced mushrooms. Very satisfying.

Here's my Saturday Salad recipe:

HGB SATURDAY SALAD

Use as many of these ingredients as you like in the amounts you like—you certainly don't have to have them all:

Iceberg lettuce
Raw spinach leaves
Finely chopped cabbage
Green beans (cooked al dente)
Fresh parsley (a lot)
Cherry tomatoes (cut in thirds)
1 tablespoon or so tuna salad
Diced breast of chicken or turkey; couple of tablespoons
Grated Parmesan cheese
Sliced mushrooms
Crumbled bacon (from a can)
Cooked shrimp (very optional since so pricey)
Skillet-toasted sunflower seeds sprinkled on top

Chop everything rather fine. I use a scissors for the lettuce, spinach, beans, parsley, turkey/chicken breast and tomatoes. Toss with one tablespoon only Paul Newman's Own Salad Dressing or any other dressing, not to exceed one hundred calories, or just use rice-vinegar. One tablespoon of dressing will cover everything nicely if you keep tossing. I eat a big plateful of this for Saturday lunch, have the rest for dinner. It doesn't get that soggy.

Some of us are gummy and gooey lovers—gumdrops, chewy-chewy caramels and chocolate, gluey bears and fish candy. They're out, of course, unless you don't *care* about your teeth and insides (talk about empty calories), so here's my personal innocent gooey treat, *virtually* sinless.

Gummy Jell-O

Dissolve one packet of sugar-free Jell-O (strawberry, cherry, raspberry, lemon, lime or orange) in one half cup of boiling water, stir hard, chill. Package directions say one packet, dissolved in two cups of water, makes four servings, but that is *very* watery Jell-O. I make just one nice chewy serving with a whole packet of Jell-O in a quarter that much water. Top with a dollop of Equal-sweetened plain yogurt—fourteen calories—fifty-six calories total.

Warm Fruit Dessert
(110 calories)

Core and slice but don't peel a small apple or pear. Cook slowly in heavy saucepan without water, lid on. Peek often and stir fruit around so it doesn't stick or burn; pretty soon it will get quite mushy. Turn off heat. Mash fruit with a packet of Equal, a squeeze of lemon juice. Serve with a dollop of Equal-sweetened plain yogurt; top with nutmeg.

You can use an orange, though the calorie count is higher, *and* you can add a dash of cognac or Grand Marnier from one of those little bottles you take off the airplane: half a teaspoon for a little bounce.

HOT GINGERBREAD AND "WHIPPED CREAM" (130 CALORIES)

Mix three tablespoons gingerbread mix with two tablespoons water, eight or so raisins, two tablespoons Kellogg's All-Bran, packet of Sweet One or Sweet'n Low. Pour into small baking dish—bake twenty minutes at 350°F. Top with dollop of Equal-sweetened yogurt. Dust on cinnamon or nutmeg.

Have you *any* strength or desire to move on . . . to *exercise?!!* (Aawwpppp!) But it *does* sort of go with food if we're playing it smart at our age.

chapter seven

Exercise

This chapter which you are *maybe*—are you?— beginning to read took a thousand years to write because I kept stopping and saying, oh, no, nobody is going to *read* this ... exercise is *boring!* Everybody who wants to exercise already *is;* anybody who doesn't want to isn't and doesn't want to hear another word about it.

Well, the reason to bring *up* the subject is that you just can't age very well *without* exercise, never mind that only 10 percent of the American population *does*. Barbara Bush and Rosie Clooney are underexercised people's heroines: "If these *terrific women* don't care about their hips, why should *I?!*" (Actually, Barbara Bush swims.) Frances Lear, founder and publisher of *Lear's,* says, "I go in and out. . . . I can't do aerobics at my age!" Norma Dana, angel in charge of the flower program (they put flowers in every room) at Memorial Sloan-Kettering and maxi-involved in other charities, says, "Three things are more important than exercise: husband, charity, friends ... if I have any time left, I *might* do something for myself." *Cosmo*'s exec editor, Bobbie Ashley, says, "I once went to an exclusive little gym run by a seventy-year-old martinet. One day I was doing something wrong on one of the machines and Katarina *hit* me—I never went back." Penny says, "It just isn't safe for me to be near a machine. I can manage to unhinge it, both my shoulders and throw my back out in five minutes. . . . I just have so much *strength!*" Carol's excuse: "I enjoy gardening, horseback riding and maybe a little swimming but I am a secure person ... my children actually *like* me, I have a good job, my husband isn't going to leave me ... what's my motivation to do something so unpleasant?"

Paula goes even further: "Next to moldy cottage cheese and that orange drink you have to force down three pints of for a G. I. series of X rays, nothing in the world is more loathsome than exercise. Why would I do it?" Virginia Graham, whose successful television show *Girl Talk* ran for years on ABC in the sixties, says, "In thirty-nine years I raised 200 million for charity. You name it, I raised money for it ... the U. J. A., U. C. P., the local strawberry festival. For ten years I drove an ambulance for the Red Cross, lifted stretchers, pushed gurneys; I got *plenty* of exercise ... I *gave* already." What about now? "Travel is one long exercise binge," says Virginia. "Getting through L. A. International Airport with your luggage is the equivalent of three sessions with Jane Fonda, plus I am a compulsive housekeeper. ... I *sort* the garbage. I catch the dust before it falls. I'm *busy!*"

Jacqueline Bisset, who, according to *Harper's Bazaar,* does a little stretching, says, "I think this obsession with achieving the perfect body is a bit sick," adding, "The teeth-gritting and brow-furrowing that come with overextension produce unflattering facial lines." There!

Beverly Sills says, "Peter and I bought an Exercycle and proudly set it up in the bedroom but we kept falling over it ... it just took up so much room. Also the seat was too high ... we could never get it adjusted."

Lauren Veronis told her husband-to-be, investment banker John Veronis, when he asked whether she skied, "John, I don't do anything I can't do in high heels!"

Very creative, those reasons not to exercise, and we could also add these:

1. We don't like the way other people look in exercise clothes ... seeing Cheryl Tiegs in leotards makes us want never to get undressed.
2. The gym is too far from home.
3. We're afraid of jogging out of doors in heavy traffic and polluted air; also we could get mugged.

4. Not enough time. (Translation: Not enough time for something we don't want to do in the first place.)

5. We are lazy.

My friend Jackie Lehman says early demoralizing experiences in life can discourage exercise. "You were a klutz in school and you're sure you'll go on klutzing forever." Sean Byrnes, photographer Francesco Scavullo's stylist and a devoted exerciser, says, "Why don't people do a *lot* of things they should or do things they shouldn't? Fat people eat, smokers smoke, people with heart conditions have cheese and baconburgers . . . it's life!"

Lori Pollan of Pollan-Austen Fitness Center says, "Women make elaborate *plans* to exercise . . . they buy super jogging duds, one-hundred-dollar shoes, but the clothes can't do it *for* you. And they're ashamed of their bodies. I've heard twenty-year-olds say, 'I'm so out of shape . . . I should have started at fourteen!' Some people call up four or five times *checking* before finally coming in. Then, of course, you get the bingers . . . incredibly enthusiastic in the beginning—you have to shoo them out of the place—then the going gets tough and you never see them again . . . very similar to dieters who go all out in the beginning, then stop."

My hero, Jack LaLanne, the seventy-five-year-old exercise maven who invented most of the exercise equipment now used in gyms and who works out about three hours a day, says, "You want to know the biggest reason people still don't exercise? I'll sum it up in one word: Habit. You have to get into the *habit* of exercising thirty minutes a day."

It's funny. People used to think that exercise would *kill* an older woman. When I was twelve, my friend Elizabeth gave a swimming party for her pals at the local Y and Elizabeth's mother announced she would be going with us. Jaws dropped. Eyes rolled. It wasn't so much that a Parent would be in the pool—Elizabeth's mother was a peach—but we thought she would probably die or at least get pneumonia and slow things down for everybody.

"Older women" didn't go swimming in Little Rock in 1934; neither did older *men*.

That was then, this is now. Let's get serious. The reasons somebody our age—fifties, sixties, seventies—*ought* to exercise are these:

Your body *looks* better. You don't get so many of those "Who wants to talk to *her?*" reactions from people who judge us by our hips rather than our brains. Of course, if you keep your weight down, nobody can *see* under your clothes that your hips have gone to custard, but it's hard to keep the weight down *without* exercise. With your clothes off, people can see that exercise has made your body smooth and muscular instead of pocked and flabby. Sorry!

Exercise makes you *feel* fetter. Heart, lungs function at max, and you are just healthier. *The New York Times* reports on findings of Dr. Carl Casperson of the federal Centers for Disease Control in Atlanta: "Even modest amounts of exercise can substantially reduce a person's chance of dying of heart disease, cancer or other causes. The most striking finding is that the biggest health gain comes from just getting out of the most sedentary category rather than seeking the fitness achieved by dedicated athletes. Going from being sedentary to walking briskly for half an hour several days a week can drop our risk (of disease) dramatically."

Gary Yanker and Kathy Burton say in their book *Walking Medicine* (McGraw-Hill): "Researchers believe that half the decline generally associated with aging is due to inactivity. By exercising, a person may retain as much as 80 percent of his physical abilities between ages thirty and seventy." From an article in *USA Today:* "Recent research indicates that exercise strengthens heart, lungs, may lower blood pressure and prevent adult diabetes, can strengthen bones and slow bone-mineral loss during aging." (Older women's bones are always getting broken, as you know.) In another *New York Times* article, "The Trick of Growing Older," William Stockton says, "Exercise is now routinely prescribed for arthritis sufferers, asthmatics and people with high blood pressure. Even heart attack victims are encouraged, indeed ordered, to work out."

Backs are a consideration. Dr. Neil Kahanovitz, executive director of the National Spine Center at Arlington, Virginia, writes: "Today 195 million Americans have had some back problems and fully three in ten have a severe chronic back ailment. To continue to enjoy the free and easy movement of youth during your whole lifetime you have to avoid this most common crippling malady." He then maps out a series of exercises and tips used at the Hospital for Joint Diseases Orthopaedic Institute in New York and says, "These exercises are your best insurance against forfeiting youthful mobility to an aching back." (Less and less spinal disc surgery is being performed now although some is still necessary.)

Exercise helps keep weight down. This is bloody important since, "from age twenty-five on, the average American woman gains almost a pound and a half of fat each year," according to Jack Wilmore, Ph.D., in an article in *Vogue*. A *Cosmo* editor, who swims passionately, says she picked up four pounds in two weeks, with no change in eating habits, when the pool she goes to was closed for renovations. It's not just that exercise uses up *calories* but, according to Wilmore, "it burns *fat* while conserving lean tissue. Maintaining lean tissue while dieting is essential for long-term weight control since a body with lots of metabolically active muscle burns more calories in its day-to-day functioning than a body that carries more fat." Do you understand that? I'm not sure I absolutely do but I surely understand we want our metabolism to be *speedy*. (*Metabolism*, according to *Webster's New World Dictionary*, is the "chemical and physical process by which assimilated food is built up into protoplasm, the protoplasm then broken down into waste matter with the release of energy for all vital processes." There!) Well, metabolism slows *down* as we age. "This decline in metabolism is one of the main reasons for weight gain between ages twenty and sixty," says psychologist Allan Geliebeter, Ph.D., co-director of the Weight Control Counseling Center in New York. In a *Cosmo* article titled "Diet Deadlocks and How to Beat

Them," Richard Trubo says, "If your metabolism is sluggish, exercise is your best weapon to get it moving. Vigorous physical activity can not only speed up your body's inner mechanism *while* you're active, but it will probably keep your metabolic rate at a higher speed for several hours *after* you've stopped jogging, walking or swimming. Some weight-loss experts believe that in the initial hour or two after exercising, your metabolism will continue to work at a rate as high as 25 percent greater than its resting level, and then will start to gradually slow down after that."

May I continue the benefits? **Exercise is a spirit lifter.** It's hard to stay gloomy *during* the workout and you don't go back to the blues when you're finished unless it's very black indeed out there. Even so, you feel more able to cope. This from a dyed-in-the-wrap *frequently* depressed person—*moi*. Psychiatrists confirm that actual chemical changes take place in your body as you exercise.

Maybe the biggest reason to have at it is that **exerciser gives you a feeling of control over your life.** That's *my* biggest reason anyway. So many things you *can't* fix—trouble with a man, job, children . . . trouble with *yourself* . . . you aren't as beautiful as you'd like or as young. The world—the economy, ecology, our leaders are out there being awful—but by God, here is this thing—your body—that responds like a beanbag when you push it, comes *through* for you. As Paula says, "Exercise doesn't cost anything except energy; you don't have to get permission to do it and you can start right *away!*" A terrific-looking actress friend of seventy-four says, "I wouldn't want to look or feel any *worse* than I do at my age . . . exercise keeps back the jungle."

And here's the clincher: **Exercise separates the women who have given *up*—sexually and emotionally—from the ones who *haven't*.** A lot of aging in men *or* women is just atrophy and that particularly goes for sex. With a slender, well-muscled body you *look* like you're ready for sex and you *feel* more that way. A slobby body is a pretty sure signal to a man that you aren't interested in him *or* sex even if that isn't the case.

* * *

As for exercise giving you big, ugly muscles, forget it. From *Harper's Bazaar:* "Muscles are beautiful and feminine because they convey a sense of personal strength, of self-assuredness. You can be well-toned and strong and at the same time soft and sensual." Pam Haering, an account executive at the J. Walter Thompson advertising agency, says, "There is nothing wonderful about being a weak woman. Exercise makes you attractive *and* strong." And Arnold Schwarzenegger on the subject: "You aren't likely to feel fantastic until you accept exercise as a way of life."

Yet nearly everything I *read* about exercise I find a turnoff, don't you? You're supposed to get heartbeat up to a certain level with aerobics, then keep it there for a specific time, so many heartbeats a minute, to get out all the good, but I've never consciously done that in the twenty-five years I've been exercising. Articles talk about short-term and long-term goals. I guess those make sense to get yourself started, but for me it's like reading about sex . . . you still have to get in there and *do* it to reap the benefits. Does *anybody* tear pages out of women's magazines, including *Cosmo,* that show little exercise routines you're supposed to do and then *do* them? Not *me;* not *many,* I'll bet.

I just know exercise is there to help if you let it. All my life I've been trying to take advantage of whatever might improve an ordinary little life. I surely didn't start exercising early—forties somewhere—and I'm so average at it (huff, puff, puff, huff, lift that barge, tote that bale, huff, puff), anybody looking at me would think, poor *thing!*—but a day doesn't go by without an hour and a half of this struggle and "too busy" doesn't get you off the hook. Until my recent hysterectomy I'd only missed three days in the past twenty years . . . the day my mother died and I started *that* day—I knew she'd want me to—but couldn't go on . . . and twice after cosmetic surgery. You're supposed not to exercise for *many* days after facial surgery but I figured some mild stuff with legs and arms couldn't hurt, and it didn't seem to. The Big H grounded me for six weeks and then I jumped right back in. I've thrashed around in hotel rooms so small I had to stack furniture and put my head under the desk to make room, on boats fighting seasickness, in a DC-10 (just the standing-up stuff) ... in airports. On a trip to the Soviet Union during a stopover in Frankfurt, I found a stone bench in the Lufthansa terminal and went right at it. Nobody paid any attention. I don't even *expect* a flatter stomach or nicer thighs from the torture, though these things do happen. I also think ordinary people doing whatever works for them are better experts than the experts.

At the height of the hoohah about my book *Sex and the Single Girl* I had lunch with a Los Angeles doctor I had known since teenage, had had an affair with, gave the reception for when he got married, fixed up with girls after his divorce ... we were *pals*. Well, in the middle of Cobb salad at Hollywood's Brown Derby, he said, "Helen, why didn't you check with some authorities before you wrote that book? That really was irresponsible to just throw out advice based on your own experience without getting some real medical opinion." I looked at him hard, put down my fork, left the restaurant and we have never talked since. He wasn't thinking about the welfare of the single women of America or, as it turned out, a lot of the rest of the world (the book was published in twenty-eight countries), he was angry that his little playmate had succeeded in cheering up a lot of women with a personal story, and medical authority was the *last* thing we needed. Though exercise isn't as interesting to read about as sex, I guess I'm doing the same thing now ... giving a personal account of what exercise means to me and friends my age with only tidbits from the authorities.

My problem as a devout exerciser, if I may be so frank, is that I tend to get a little irritated hearing how dedicated *other* people are, and I don't just mean celebrities and fifteen-year-old gymnasts. You like to think *you* are so special ... brave, gutsy little person, getting it up for your leg-lifts every day while the sloths sleep, and then you find that Kitty D'Alessio, once CEO at Chanel, whom you've known professionally for years, has a trainer;

Ginny Salomon, a seventy-four-year-old New York society belle, swims forty laps a day; Jeane Kirkpatrick, ex-U. S. ambassador to the United Nations, does yoga, for God's sake. But are you going to be reasonable or *what?!* I just have to *forgive* other people's exercise achievements and find something else to feel "superior" about! (I can sleep standing up . . . does that count?) Meanwhile I hope *you* are exercising . . . why let your enemies reap the rewards?

To what age can you exercise? My idol Jack LaLanne says, "Day laborers in China are still doing what they did all their lives at age one hundred because they have never stopped. That's where the danger comes in. When you stop, you atrophy!" All retirement homes have exercise facilities, though that isn't where you and I plan to hang out. Apparently you can exercise *forever* without doing harm. Chinese movie tycoon Run-Run Shaw shadowboxes daily in his early nineties.

Does exercise make you live longer? Probably not. Genes program us to last a certain number of years and we can't extend the time by good behavior, but you could speed *up* death by abusing the old bod. Exercise, plus not eating, drinking or drugging like a maniac, sort of guarantees we'll at least *get* to our allotted age and feel alive while we're alive.

Okay, though I never knew which was which until I started to research this chapter, it probably wouldn't hurt to officially enumerate the three goals of exercise: flexibility, strength, cardiovascular conditioning. You might want to work up a little routine incorporating all three. Actually, a lot of routines that build muscle are also heart-pumping, and aerobics, which works the heart, also strengthens muscle, though a girl could go *nuts* trying to figure which category a deep knee bend fits into and is her butt being flexed or *strengthened*.

Cosmo's beauty director, Andrea Pomerantz Lynn, who looks like a baby doe but does killer exercises, delineated the three exercise goals for me:

Flexibility: Refers to the amount of give you have in your tendons and ligaments. You get flexible by stretching—important to do before *and* after exercise. Although you're born with a certain amount of natural flexibility, you become more flexible each time you stretch. If you don't stretch, you can 1. get injured during the workout and 2. build muscles that are short and bulky—not long and sensuous. Current thought on stretching is that you should do "static stretches"—hold the stretch for twenty seconds, no bouncing.

Strength: Strength is gained by doing muscle-specific exercises, usually against some kind of resistance. Nautilus machines and free weights build strength, as do calisthenic-type exercises. Aerobics contributes too, if you are specifically working one major muscle group. (For example, stationary cycling or stair climbing strengthens thighs and butt as well as your heart; rowing machines strengthen upper-body muscles plus heart—you get an aerobic and muscle-building workout in *one* routine, hence the popularity of these machines.)

Reasons to build muscle strength: You get better body composition—a higher muscle-to-fat ratio looks better. A more muscular body burns more calories than one of equal weight with more fat/flab. This fuel consumption happens even while you sleep. Muscle tissue uses more energy just to maintain itself. Muscle strength helps you avoid injuries (for example, strong calf muscles prevent buckling during aerobics).

Cardiovascular Conditioning: Your heart is a muscle. Aerobics builds heart as weights build biceps; the stronger your heart, the more endurance you'll have. Aerobics begins to burn fat after the first fifteen minutes, so if you're trying to lose weight you should do at least thirty minutes of aerobics three or more times a week.

"To be totally fit," Andrea says, "you need all three component parts of exercise. That doesn't mean you need to devote as much time to each activity, just that you should do some of each. Here's how many experts allocate an hour of exercise: ten minutes of stretching (five to warm up, five to cool down), thirty-five minutes of aerobics, fifteen minutes of strength-training. This time allotment will vary with your exercise goals: To lose fat, you'd spend more time on aerobics; to tone up (you aren't fat), spend more time on strengthening. The StairMaster machines, which simulate the motions of climbing stairs, are today's mechanical darlings. They give computerized feedback—how many stairs you've climbed, how many miles that's equivalent to, how many calories you've burned—very satisfying! Supposedly you burn twice as many calories for a half hour of stair climbing as you would running. The nontech way to stair-climb is featured in the new step-aerobics classes, where you hold weights and step on and off a bench to music. These classes are hot right now; intense but fun." Darling Jack LaLanne says the 640 muscles in your body don't care about the apparatus used on them; resistance is resistance, and the best form is still dumbbells. (Weight lifting is the fastest growing women's sport.)

I don't think we even want to start to discuss what exercises help a particular part of your body . . . "spot" reducing it used to be called. Let's just say flab gets reduced *whatever* exercise you are doing and you can specialize if you *want* to. The only specializing I ever tried was for my stomach and it's only *mildly* effective. Can anybody over the age of sixty *have* a flat stomach? All exercise gurus say with exercise you can. God knows I've been trying to prove them right, but I think genes have everything to do with whether you can ever be concave instead of convex. A gynecologist finally convinced me—I *longed* for convincing—that if you've had a pooch since age five and your mother was pretty much pear-shaped like you—or vice versa—probably you'll always curve *out*. I asked my internist about the never-flat-stomach also. Doctors are usually not for consulting on exercise, but I just ran this by him . . . stood in his examining room without my sheet and showed him my stomach—doctors so rarely freak about anything these days. Lie *down* on your stomach, he said. I did. He then heavy-kneaded my shoulders and back and said stand up. Funny little miracle—stomach no longer protruding. Doctor explained that one's muscles give out toward the end of the day and let the stomach sag. They sag even before noon if one isn't careful about posture. Dr. David Lehrman, M. D., chief of orthopedics at St. Francis Hospital in Miami, says, "When you slouch, your shoulders are rounded and your abdominal muscles are loose. You're letting it all hang out, which makes your stomach protrude."

Well, *few* of us have live-in angels who will heavy-knead our back and shoulders every day so our stomach will stay in. (If they do *that,* they probably fall down somewhere else like telling you about their miserable day while you're trying to get your mascara on for a party.) But posture—to keep tummy muscles from sagging—you can surely do something about. Elaine LaLanne, Jack's wife, a professional in the field herself, suggests "checking your posture in store windows as you go by. If you see yourself slumped over, imagine a walnut between your shoulder blades. Then crack that walnut!" There are lots of tummy-flattening exercises to *do,* of course, and anyone who doesn't want a stomach like a sumo wrestler should try them, heredity or no. This is mine: Lie on floor with legs up over the seat of a chair, hands on shoulder blades, eyes to ceiling. Lift shoulders and back up off the floor forty times. That keeps things *pretty* flat, though weight watching does the most. (Yes, weight does come off your stomach when you diet, not just bosom, throat and face.)

So how are we going to get in the *habit* of this semi-gruesomeness? "Anybody can exercise and have a great body with just two words," says Jack LaLanne, "Pride and discipline. Actually they're the secret of success for *anything.*" (Yes, we know that.) Elaine says, "You just have to decide to make exercising a daily way of life, like brushing your teeth. If you don't do it today, you won't do it tomorrow. And the only person who can do it is *you.* A trainer may be doing it *with* you but he sure can't do it *for* you." Elaine encouragingly points out that a muscle never loses its ability to respond to training. "It's just there waiting for you to give it orders."

Does exercise ever get easy? Is the Princess of Wales

Japanese? Jack LaLanne asks a visiting journalist watching him bench-press 100- and 150-pound weights, "Does it look like I'm enjoying myself? I go to the gym every morning and it's cold and lonely and everybody else is asleep. ... I *hate* exercise ... but I say, 'Kiddo, you've got to do it again,' and I do—one more time—and you become happy for that moment." His feats, in case you're interested, include: Swimming the length of San Francisco's Golden Gate Bridge underwater wearing 140 pounds of scuba equipment; swimming from Alcatraz to Fisherman's Wharf wearing handcuffs; swimming the length of the Golden Gate Bridge again, this time handcuffed, shackled and towing a 2,000-pound boat; towing from dockside *thirteen* boats (representing the original colonies), carrying seventy-six people one mile through Long Beach Harbor, California; towing sixty-five boats filled with 6,500 pounds of wood pulp, in honor of his sixty-fifth birthday, through Japan's Lake Ashino while handcuffed and shackled, and a few other little achievements along that line. If exercise doesn't get easy for *him,* how could it for *us?*

Almost *anyone* you ask whether they enjoy exercise will tell you all the things they get *out* of it ... pride, weight control, energy, health ... euphoria when it's over! Jill says, "My mind gets my body to do it, the body complaining every second; then it's over and my body says, 'Thank you!' " (I suppose it also says, "I *needed* that!") "Dancing with a partner is fun," says Alicia. "The music and the sexiness and showing off your new Donna Karan and God knows, it's using calories, but is doing forty crunches in three minutes, attacking a rowing machine, fun? What am I, a masochist?!" "You are proud of your body and know it couldn't look that way without exercise," says Pamela, "but if, by some miracle, you could just sit by the pool sipping cranberry juice and reading *Vanity Fair* and that was as good for you as swimming twenty laps, would you really be out there mermaiding? Do bats crave *sunshine?* ... Pull-eeze!"

So how do you *start* a routine? Elaine LaLanne and many other experts suggest walking as a great way to begin. "You have to walk *anyway* so you just do it a bit faster and farther than you ordinarily would. Start with a quarter of a mile (five city blocks) three times a week, then work up to a fifteen-minute walk every day. Swing your arms and move briskly . . . a leisurely windowshop or slow-and-gossipy-with-a-friend walk won't do it." She enumerates these benefits of walking: gets the heart pumping and sends oxygen through the body, helps prevent bone loss (osteoporosis), helps with weight reduction, diabetes control, relieves arthritis pain, aids digestion and sleep, soothes tension and anxiety, relieves depression, lowers chance of developing high blood pressure and just makes you feel better." There, for God's sake! Gary Yanker and Kathy Burton declare in *Walking Medicine*, "A sensible walking program can make *dramatic* improvements in physical and emotional well-being." If, like me, you prefer doing something at home, start tiny and build—ten push-ups, ten sit-ups, ten leg lifts. If you want to follow a leader (Jane Fonda must have shaped up a dozen million women by now), here's a list of exercise tapes and brief comments about them from *Newsday* and the *Chicago Tribune:*

Jane Fonda's Complete Workout
(1989, Warner Home Video, $29.98)
    The No. 1 fitness star for a reason. Fonda tapes are among the best researched and most professionally produced. Designed for people at all levels, her latest is the best yet.

Rita Moreno: Now You Can!
(1989, Wood Knapp, $19.95)
    For women of all ages who get discouraged by more difficult workouts.

The Firm Workout with Weights, Vol. 2
(1988, Meridian Films, $49.95)
    Once you get over being jealous about how great host

Janet Jones (wife of hockey's Wayne Gretzky) looks, you'll realize this workout is one of the most invigorating you can buy.

Kathy Smith's Starting Out
(1988, Fox Hills Video, $19.95)
Beginners in aerobics exercise won't find a more encouraging instructor than this fitness superstar. All her tapes are excellent.

Callanetics
(1986, MCA Home Video, $24.95)
If your doctor lets you try this controversial tape, you'll find it highly motivating and a refreshing change from aerobics. Callan Pinckney claims that her "deep muscle" exercises give you the same results in one hour that aerobics gives you in twenty-four. She measures results by the "bottom line"—how low your behind sags. Fergie, Duchess of York, is said to use a Callametric routine.

A Week with Raquel
(1987, HBO Video, $19.99)
Raquel's relaxing, yoga-based video is another good one for the sick-of-aerobics crowd. More active Welch fans should try her latest, *Lose 10 pounds in 3 Weeks*.

Angela Lansbury's Positive Moves: A Personal Plan for Fitness and Well-Being at Any Age
(1989, Wood Knapp, $29.95)
We wouldn't call this an exercise video in the typical sense. The exercises shown are more like relaxation or meditation techniques.

Couples Do It Debbie's Way
(1988, Vidamerica, $29.98)
> A good choice for middle-aged (Debbie Reynolds is fifty-seven) or senior fitness buffs, particularly couples who would like to work out together.

Cosmo's New Tapes:

Tonetics: Tummy Toning Workout
(1990, Goodtimes Home Video, $9.95)

Tonetics: Beginners Workout
(1990, Goodtimes Home Video, $9.95)

I haven't looked at any of these tapes except *Cosmo's* because I don't have a VHS or VCR in the room where I exercise (talk about your rationalizing!), plus watching somebody *else* do routines I'm supposed to follow is just anathema to me. We exercisers get as sticky as mangos about what routines we will or won't do, but it doesn't matter as long as *something* appeals, or let's say you hate one thing less than the others enough to do it. I just do stuff picked up from friends through the years and from Mike Abrums, a seventy-year-old exercise genius in Beverly Hills I've seen only a few times. Obviously, any physical activity—swimming, dancing, tennis—is desirable, but you're apt to do those things sporadically . . . we're talking *regular.*

Would you like to know what "they" are doing, they being movie stars, entertainers, models who have more *time* than we (except the ones with daily television shows) *and* were possibly nicer-looking to start with? Gleaned from magazine articles and personal research, here's a little smattering of their routines (seventeen ladies and one man), and one must just point out that the Most Beautiful People don't even *try* to live without exercise, so why let them corner the rewards? Some of these people are younger than we and some may have changed routines by the time we go to press.

Cher: *Age 44*

"My bad areas are the top of my legs and my butt. I've got a strict regimen I've developed over the years to take care of them: lots of calisthenics and also ballet. I'm a big believer in walking. I walk between four and a half and five miles per hour, which is a jogging pace. I've got a computerized treadmill, and I'll walk in front of my TV for three miles and not feel worn down."

Jacqueline Onassis: *Age 61*

Fast-walks around the Central Park reservoir in disguises. Each night at six, a yoga teacher comes to her apartment, and for the next hour she's incommunicado.

Farrah Fawcett: *Age 43*

Rigorous weight-training two or three times a week at a gym with a trainer; also gets in a few games of racquetball each week at her own court at home.

Brooke Shields: *Age 25*

"I try to exercise at least one hour, six days a week. . . . I cycle, run and swim, but I prefer to go to jazz class."

Maria Shriver: *Age 33*

"Either we [Arnold Schwarzenegger] go to the gym, where I work out on the Lifecycle [stationary bike] or we horseback ride."

Katharine Hepburn: *Age 81*

Still plays tennis regularly, swims, gardens, rides her bicycle.

Mary McFadden: *Age 53*

Plays tennis, plus two hours at the gym in her office building, usually late afternoon.

Dinah Shore: *Age 69*

"I walk just about every day and I work out two or three times a week in a special routine set by a fine group of experts from the Sports Trak group here in Palm Springs. Stretching, stomach crunches, some weights, tennis and, of course, golf—my addiction."

Alice Faye: *Age 74*

Keeps her weight around 120 by striding daily with her poodles around the golf club that rings her Rancho Mirage home; also swims in her pool four or more times a day, for ten or fifteen minutes.

Oprah Winfrey: *Age 36*

"I have to get up at five in order to run six miles, six days a week." Oprah also goes to the gym, uses the StairMaster . . . but "running is the most consistent thing I do."

Linda Evans: *Age 49*

Three-times-a-week regimen involves lifting free weights to strengthen and tone muscles, riding an electronic stationary bicycle for aerobic conditioning.

Sophia Loren: *Age 57*

When she is not working, her daily morning routine includes forty-five minutes of exercise while watching TV.

Sherry Lansing: *Age 47*

Does a hundred sit-ups and works on her treadmill fifty minutes four times a week, plays tennis twice a week. One day lets herself off. "I think people overachieve in exercise as they 'overachieve' in life—you see very few fat successful people. You may do it to make up for not being well thought of at some time in your life. Maybe you had a mother who only liked you if you got good grades. They are crazy about you but also critical."

Grace Mirabella: *Age 61*

Goes to a gym at the Regency Hotel to use their machines. "I like them much better than working with a human-being trainer—the machines just feel good—they make you work hard." Grace also plays tennis.

Mario Buatta: *Age 55*

While holding on to a bar, jumps up and down in a tub filled with six to eight inches of water with the overhead shower turned on. "If you jump five hundred times—twice a day—you can eat an elephant and it won't show. Sometimes I bog down and only get up to 120 jumps, but if you go the distance, it's the *only* exercise you need and you can *eat.*" (Be careful not to slip in the tub.)

Madonna: *Age 31*

Works out at least two and a half hours daily. For the first hour she runs or bikes, then does a thirty-minute stint on either a stationary cycle or mountain-climbing machine. Next, a workout with ten- and twenty-pound weights. Madonna is a vegetarian.

Denise Thyssen: *Forties*

Jumps rope 1,000 times every night!

Ali MacGraw: *Age 53*

Exercises *more* than two hours a day . . . "strenuous yoga but I wouldn't run if you had a gun to my head even though I live in Malibu."

Many celebrities go to a gym or health club. Among them Sally Field, Teri Garr, Lesley-Anne Down, Susan Anton, Shirley MacLaine, Jill St. John, Aline, Countess of

Romanones, Jennifer Grey, Phoebe Cates, Mary Tyler Moore, Jane Powell, Linda Gray, Connie Selleca, along with Robin Williams, Michael J. Fox, Sam Waterston—to let in a few men. Tom Brokaw jogs *and* works out in a gym with free weights. George Bush runs two miles at least three times a week, plays tennis and horseshoes, uses an indoor bicycle and treadmill. Ronald Reagan—Nancy too—are clients of exercise mogul Mike Abrums who created a gym for them at the White House. Ronald Reagan now lifts weights in his own gym, swims in a heated pool, chain-saws firewood at the Santa Barbara area ranch. Kirk Douglas has worked with Mike Abrums for over twenty years, fifteen minutes a day. His son Michael runs and works out, "determined to guard his remaining years as a lead actor." Geraldo Rivera trains six days a week. Three days he and his wife, C.C., run seven-minute miles. "We don't futz around."

These people have trainers (somebody comes to *them):* Steven Spielberg, Harrison Ford, Bette Midler, Morgan Fairchild, Priscilla Presley, Martha Stewart (she also walks the dogs and uses her StairMaster), Donna Karan, Evelyn Lauder, Calvin Klein (Kelly prefers workouts at a gym), Kathleen Sullivan, Nora Ephron, Faye Dunaway, Francesco Scavullo, and Princess Michael of Kent, whose instructor comes to the palace in Kensington.

Well . . . everybody's *very* busy! Including these people who don't officially exercise but say they burn up calories "unofficially": Socialite Anne Bass has gone to ballet class five times a week "since I was thirteen years old," Diane Von Furstenburg walks between fifty and sixty blocks a day. Diane Sawyer "races for airplanes, panting and swearing each time I'll get in better shape!"

Trainers don't seem to last too long: They open a pet store, move to Albuquerque or marry a rich client. *We* jump ship, too, wishing to try the latest state-of-the-art person. It seems to me trainers and people who run gyms are often *dedicated* encouragers, and that's why we need them. It's their livelihood but they also like to help. Lori Pollan of Pollan-Austen Fitness Center says, "It's wonderful to see a woman who is totally out of touch with her body—can't run for a bus, can't lift a suitcase, can't touch her toes, has to put the shopping bag she's carrying down five times to get it home—get into exercise, get control and become youthful and strong. There are lots of different *kinds* of gyms," she says, "from spartan and serious to frilly and feminine. Prices vary. Workouts vary. Some feature instructors who think of themselves as stars, who show off and entertain; others could get a Nobel Prize in discipline." The gym I went to for a while was one of the latter, really fabulous, but I just couldn't get myself into and out of a taxi, up the stairs, undressed, into workout clothes, showered, dressed again, off to the office, huff puff, so now I do things at home.

Can you get hurt exercising, particularly since we are "older"? The University of California *Wellness Letter* reports: "From runners' ankle and biker's knee to tennis elbow and swimmer's shoulder, there's hardly a sport or exercise that doesn't have an injury associated with it." Oh, my God! They describe tendinitis—" 'itis' means inflammation (characterized by pain, swelling, warmth, and redness). . . . People who exercise regularly are especially at risk because of the strong forces produced by their well-conditioned muscles. These increase tension on the tendons, which can then rub against bones, ligaments, and other tendons, causing irritation. . . ." You want sprains? "Sprains damage ligaments (the bands connecting bones) and joint capsules. They are most often the result of a sudden force, typically a twisting motion, that the surrounding muscles aren't strong enough to control. As a result, the ligaments, which usually wrap around a joint, get stretched or torn. Sprains can range from minor tears to complete ruptures." The *Wellness Letter* says the five most common exercise injury culprits are "overdoing it; inadequate footwear and equipment; poor conditioning; improper technique and training; and ignoring aches and pains." They *strongly* advise not "running through the pain." But I think (strongly) we should stay as far away from the *warnings*—not the exercise—as possible! A few meaty warnings are all nonexercisers and ready-to-lapse-ers need not to do it or to stop. Exercise *machines* . . . now there is something you might be a little tentative with. Evelyn once failed to get out of a leg pully she thought she was out of and was hobbling for days. But as for exercise generally being dangerous, rubbish! My role model Jack LaLanne says, "The fact that you get hurt when you exercise is an old wives' tale. The only way you can hurt your heart and body is *not* to exercise. It is impossible to overwork your body *or* the human heart. The people you hear of keeling over from exercise probably would have died sooner if they hadn't exercised." As for checking with a doctor before you begin, if any of my four—gynecologist, internist, dermatologist, nutritionist—was consulted about exercise, I would be gazed at halibut-eyed. Brilliant as they all are, exercise isn't what they *do*. Anybody who wants to can surely figure out a little exercise packet for herself or ask a friend, gym or trainer and assume she is not going to do anything really damaging. P.S. I also wouldn't read myself to pieces before beginning.

You can have many starts—and stops—before exercise "takes." In my twenties I dived in with a friend who later introduced David and me. Ruth and I used charts from a little kit and lasted five days. In my thirties I attended ballet class. Everybody around me was a budding Gelsey Kirkland, and I folded. The year David and I moved from Los Angeles to New York—by now I'm forty—a book called *The Royal Canadian Exercise Guide* (ten minutes a day, they said, could revitalize and reorganize you) swept the country. I swept right along—for three weeks. But sometime in those mid-forties I just started doing a few routines and haven't stopped. At some point in your life, exercise *takes* . . . it's just time, that's all.

May I tell you about *one* late-getting-started-to-exercise friend who never thought she would and is now "doing it"? Elizabeth Bixon (sixties), manager of the Adolfo salon, hardworking, man-loving, food-appreciating, cute, was chubby. Her lover tells her, "You're perfect . . . your body is the result of good living and good loving . . . I like it!" Her boss, the gifted Adolfo, says tactfully, "You have a tiny problem, Elizbeth, but nothing to worry about." Her daughter Harriet is less tactful: "Mom, you are fat. We lost Daddy from a heart attack, you lost George [her good friend in widowhood] the same way. Do you want to go out like both of them? Couldn't you think about the family if you won't think about yourself?!" Message delivered but not registering. One night Elizabeth is trying on clothes for a party. "I look worse in one thing than the other," says Elizabeth, "and, for God's sake, these are Adolfo's! The next morning I am checking in at the Cardiac Fitness Center and I'm hooked. You're supposed to go three days a week; I go five. I would go seven if they were open seven. I do stretches, stationary bike, rowing machines and leg lifts—about forty minutes. Of the twenty-five people there, I only say good morning to about two. Some of the men are husbands of clients I'm not thrilled to have see me exercising but what the heck— that's what they're doing, too. I've lost nine pounds— mostly from the exercise and just a little less eating. I could *die* I'm so pleased with myself."

How much exercise do you need? Fifteen minutes a day will do *something;* half an hour will do *more.* Enough exercise to Make a Difference (in your looks) takes a one-hour session at least four times a week for six months to a year. Sorry! If it's weight loss you're after, a University of Wisconsin at Madison study followed two groups of women as they went through programs that included a twelve-hundred calorie diet and either short sessions of high-intensity exercise or longer sessions of low-intensity exercise. They found both groups lost the same amounts of weight and fat. I'll repeat: When working out *your* routine, I think it's important not to worry much about what *they* (celebrities *or* friends) are doing or you may feel jealous and inadequate. Fortunately—*big* fortunately—anything/ everything helps; it doesn't matter a great deal *what* you do.

I'm also of the school—if there isn't one, we could start one—it's okay to do it "badly." Your sit-ups may be lie-downs in the grace department and your push-ups pitiable, but "badly" is better than sitting on your duff and you *improve.* Thank God, people aren't as hard on exercisers as they are on dieters. In the restaurant they *watch* you bypass the banana-cream pie in favor of melon, sniffing at you as *they* eat out the store. For exercising you're tucked away at home, in a gym with other exercisers or hitting the trail by yourself . . . semisafe. We aren't *totally* free of ridicule, of course. I read recently that people who do a lot of exercising "are addicted as surely as those who drink and do drugs"! We may be "addicted" all right but it isn't *we* who are filling up the rooms at the Betty Ford Clinic. . . . What we do is good old self-discipline (and it hurts, and it's boring, and nobody but a nut case could *like* it but the results make the torture worthwhile).

Jack LaLanne says it's important to change your program every few *days*. "Even in the pool sometimes you swim slow and deliberately, other times you go as hard and fast as you can. Change the number of *laps* you do so your muscles are always being challenged . . . make them go beyond what they are comfortable doing. When exercise gets to be easy, it's not doing you any good anymore." He also says, "Change your nutrition, change your lovemaking, do not let your body get used to *anything.*" Oh, God! I don't follow that advice. My exercise routine is challenging *enough,* thank you, for me not to have to make new friends! It's actually, as I mentioned, a mishmash collected from friends and gurus through the years. Sometimes I add or subtract a routine. Fresh *(fresh?!)* out of bed in the morning—*nothing* gets in the way—I do forty-five minutes of mat work and stand-up routines, another fifteen minutes on the face, then later in the day or night a mini-version of the morning stuff.

Routine: Sit on toilet seat, pull tummy in, bring knees to chest, blow on knees forty times. Fingertips on shoulders, forty deep knee bends, twenty lunges each leg on step machine, twenty lifts, knees to chest, hanging from bar, twenty high kicks to side with each leg, twenty each to back. With three- and five-pound barbells, ten-minute workout, then to the mat: Kneel, fingertips on shoulders, lean back toward ankles and come back up forty times; forty sit-ups, forty push-ups. Sit on fanny, tummy pulled in, fling arms *(way* back) and legs out at same time (try not to fall over), forty times. Lie down, throw legs over seat of chair, fingertips on shoulders, lift back off floor forty times, knees to chest, roll over on each side clear to floor forty times. Finish with headstand. Stay up twenty seconds if possible; I usually just get up and crash back down again.

Okay, into the stretch. We do tend to snap and crackle a bit in our sixties even *with* exercise ... we're just *crisper* now. Stretches, lifts, twists will all cause little snapping noises but the tiny pops and joint creaks are rather satisfying, don't you think? You have liberated a kink, prevented atrophy.

People our age *are* in better shape now ... much, much, much! Do you remember girdles in the forties and fifties—the only thing a woman whose backside had gone to Cincinnati could presumably do to get it back home again? A Playtex rubber girdle could take four inches off your bottom. It could also make your eyes bug out (Where do you suppose that flesh *went?* ... Probably up into our rib cage.) Any girdle was what you got out of, gasping with relief, when you got home. Of course, I shouldn't pass myself off as the Great Girdle Expert; modeling in career-girl fashion shows at the Broadway Store in Los Angeles, I was referred to as "that girl with the size five top and size nine bottom who refuses to wear a girdle." I wasn't *fat*, just a little pear-shaped, like *now*, though now I'm more "contained." Girdles *went*, thank God.

Sometimes, no matter *how* much you exercise, you look at your body and figure they've switched on you. You never were Marie McDonald but you were once smooth and cute and one color all over ... now it's pooches, puckers and multicolors. Looking south as you do push-ups, there is this spongy little balloon where a tender tummy used to be. Your calves have baby crackles and honeycombs despite *gallons* of Lubriderm committed to the area. I once made the mistake of looking at my back-side with a mirror way up between the buttocks trying to see where a mole had been removed. May I suggest you *never* do that unless elephant folds are on your wish list. With exercise, good posture, copious creaming, you'll look good enough from all easily *visible* angles. Truth.

I want to say again that I *understand* how pleasant it would be to "give up on" exercise and diet—haven't we earned the right to relax and enjoy life?! Of course we have, but that isn't how life works. You need diet and exercise more now than ever and, to do any good, they have almost to be a preoccupation . . . part of the fabric of life. Skinny exercised people tend to irritate their friends . . . *disgust* would be more accurate. Well, I can take the disgust . . . I just don't understand anybody our age *not* using diet and exercise to help fight the night.

I want you exercising, kiddo. It's your sacred *right*.

chapter eight

Health

When you've got health—even at our age—you don't pay too much attention. There's just so much else to worry about. (*Are* they ever going to send the chairs back? ... How big a deal can it *be* to put three measly scraps of fabric on three little chairs? Why didn't Gretchen call back? You didn't want to talk to her in the first place, for God's sake, but since you made the effort ... Which bathing suit is your stomach not going to stick out of *most* at the beach next week? ... *Important* things like that.) But then, when health *goes,* nothing in the world—nothing—makes any difference.

How healthy can we be at our age? Actually plenty. From a report in *Self* magazine, "After around twenty-four, an amazing amount of 'oldness' is up to you. In fact, almost half of 'aging' isn't aging at all. It's muscle underuse, sun abuse, fat buildup and bone-thin-down—all are preventable and, more and more, reversible." Nutritionist Dr. Robert Atkins says, "Aging is a disease. It should be *treated* as a disease that can be prevented." Dr. Mark Williams, medical director of the Geriatric Evaluation Clinic at North Carolina Memorial Hospital says, "Sure, limitations of reserve capability in various organ systems happen as we age, but the loss is remarkably benign; we lose only ten to twenty percent of our capability over time. People's systems age at different rates. While three out of four people will show a decline in organ function—heart, lungs, kidney—over the years, about fifteen percent show an improvement. We also have a lot of say-so about our condition. How we eat, exercise, live our lives has a tremendous amount to do with what our old age will be like. It's key for us to accept that we continue to grow and evolve as we get older. It's just not accurate to assume we all decline and fall apart. America is on the threshold of redefining what it means and doesn't mean to be old in our society."

Periodontist Dr. Bernard Wasserman told me this story. A friend of his became interested in the communities or regions of the world in which many people lived to a very old age—well over 100, some up to 113 or 120 years old. The friend, being wealthy, could afford to support research and sent a team into several regions to try to discover the secret of the longevity. The team worked in three different countries: Soviet Georgia, China and Colombia. The centenarians were studied carefully in terms of diet, physical activity, work patterns, life-style, genealogy, psychological outlook. The diets in the three places were utterly disparate—some ate lots of yogurt and grains, presumably healthy fare, but the Latin American contingent ate typically Latin food (starchy carbohydrates, etc.). The Chinese diet had nothing in common with the other two. The researchers concluded that the three groups were totally different from one another in all categories except one: attitude. All the old people *expected* to live indefinitely. Their ancestors had; their parents had; old people in the community had; so why shouldn't they? Conclusion: These people didn't know they *couldn't* make it past one hundred; nobody told them their chances were slim, so they kept living life pretty much as they had in their earlier years. One man who the research team thought would expire because he had a heart condition and was dancing up a storm one night at a local festival was very much alive when the research team left town.

We do *age*, of course. In a comprehensive study on aging, *Newsweek* says: "Theories of aging fall into two camps: call them wear-and-tear versus planned obsolescence. The first holds that the changes that accompany aging are the inevitable result of life itself. DNA, the molecule of heredity, occasionally makes a mistake as it goes about its business of synthesizing proteins; metabolism produces toxic avengers that turn lipids in our cells rancid and proteins rusty. This damage accumulates until the organism falls apart like an old jalopy. The other theory argues that aging is genetic, programmed into the organism like puberty. There is evidence for both ideas. Different species have characteristic life-spans—in the wild, an elephant lives 35 to 60 years, a mouse maybe two—and identical twins (who have exactly the same genes) have similar life expectancies. Both observations suggest that the rate of aging is determined by genes. But since individuals of the same species can have vastly different life-spans, exogenous influences must also play a role. Now the hunt is on to discover how environment and genes interact to make us age."

Well, however it's done, we *do* it ... age, that is ... and God *knows* things break *down. Newsweek* says one culprit may be glucose (blood sugar), "which makes proteins in and between our cells stick together like gummy linguine. It's a reaction called cross-linking, after the latticelike connections the proteins form. Since proteins are the beams and girders of the body's tissues, when they stick together they can cloud the eye lens, clog arteries, gum up kidney function and damage lungs enough to make breathing labored. Cross-links, then, explain much of the deterioration associated with normal, healthy aging: diabetics, who have a higher glucose level than nondiabetics, actually age more quickly and live about one-third shorter lives. 'There is probably no single thing that explains aging,' says Anthony Cerami of Rockefeller University, 'but cross-linking plays an important role.' "

Newsweek continues, "The body already comes equipped with a posse of cross-link scavengers. Immune-system cells called macrophages naturally recognize aging, cross-linked proteins and dispose of them. Working with Cerami, Rockefeller's Dr. Helen Vlassara is trying to find schemes to speed up these search-and-destroy operatives, which for unknown reasons become less efficient as we age."

Listen, we can't wait for a decision on whether genes or environment contribute more to aging, can we? or how this cold-as-mercury twosome works together to do it? We can't even wait for the cross-link-scavenger posse to destroy the cross-linked proteins. . . . I mean how much time and patience have we *got?* We just have to keep our bodies as healthy and un-age-ravaged as we can, right? It helps to live a long time if you pick long-lived *parents,* of course, since genes have more to do with longevity than anything else. How can we at least get what we've got to hold up? Doctor Williams and other cheerleaders notwithstanding, it *is* a little dicey out there some days, what with memory sags, failing grades on sex appeal and six new liver spots, even if nothing major is coming down. My friend Heloise says, "After sixty, *something* is not functioning as well as it used to, on any given day, maybe *several* somethings. Usually it does not make a comeback." Aside from malfunctioning regular body parts, some of us get stuck with extra stuff. Marguerite has tinnitus—buzzing, tinkling, humming, popping and clanging in her ears—I would go *mad!* Another friend has lupus, a degenerative disease of connective tissue that can be serious. And another, scleraderma, which gives you elephant-hide skin with itching and scaling; the only helpful drug—cortisone—makes her swell up . . . the *pits.* My lovely Japanese shiatsu practitioner, Yuki Irwin, who keeps the rest of us frisky, suffers from chronic intestinal problems brought on by malnutrition during World War II. A widowed friend who lives in my apartment building says, "I can't remember when everything was all working! At any one moment I live with respiratory problems, ocular hypertension and my back is out (I don't pay too much attention to it!). I have skin problems from sun damage—little basal-cell carcinomas that have to be removed plus high blood pressure (I do nothing about *that*) and hiatal hernia!" Philanthropist Norma Dana, who looks like a chorus girl, says, "At all times I've got allergies and respiratory disease that make it impossible for me ever to drink a glass of wine or get near oregano. Sometimes I have headaches and, oh yes, arthritis . . . we *all* have arthritis, don't we?" Camilla has "to pee every hour because a fibroid tumor is pushing against the bladder. A hysterectomy would take care of the fibroid but, since there's no bleeding, the peeing doesn't seem serious enough to justify surgery. Meanwhile I know the location of every ladies' room in every restaurant and hotel in New York and several other cities. Bore-ing!"

That's *that* crowd . . . with certain things chronically wrong and not afraid to say so. But there's also the camp that swears nothing's wrong or, if it is, they won't *admit* it. Beverly Sills declares, "At sixty-one I'm jumping around and have too *much* energy—I nearly drive Peter crazy." Margaret Thalken (sixty-six), longtime publisher's rep of *House and Garden,* says, "My eyes are a little dim so I get reading glasses from the drugstore. They're cheap and work just fine. Everything else is okay." Brooke Astor (ninety) says, "Nothing is really wrong. I can't write, of course, because a jealous dog bit my finger off but I love my dogs anyway!" I got a little weary waiting for my Latvian housekeeper, Anna Freimanis (eighty), to decide if anything was the matter with *her.* "Well," she finally declared, "there were my teeth six years ago—you remember them [I remember . . . we sweated out the fit and bite for *weeks*] and last year that mole on my leg didn't look too good but it wasn't malignant, and oh, yes, the Christmas I fell off the ladder, you remember *that?*" (I certainly do . . . any other helper would have sued the socks off me.) Conclusion: I honestly think we're doing pretty *well* in our sixties, seventies, even eighties, surely better than people used to do in their forties. Given a few things that fall on you or leave town on you, if we exercise, eat right, don't smoke, drink or drug much, we have a chance of living as long (and healthfully) as Dr. Wasserman's natives in Soviet Georgia, China and Colombia. Dr. Walter M. Bortz II, in his best-selling *We Live Too Short and Die Too Young* (Bantam), says, "The millions of Americans who die in their sixties and seventies do so prematurely. Your sixties and seventies should be your middle age."

One thing to be cheerful about: *Menopause* isn't the goblin it used to be. According to the *Los Angeles Times,* a five-year study conducted among 2,300 middle-aged Massachusetts women found that less than 17 percent expressed any strongly negative feelings toward menopause.

Gail Sheehy's book on the subject was a best-seller,

but menopause doesn't seem like a big *deal* to me. I *don't* think all the fine gynecologists in the country—and there are *plenty*—are *not* taking the condition seriously and recommending every intelligent thing they know to help us through it. Menopause is one of those things in a woman's *package,* you see, like menstruation and childbearing. Wouldn't you rather cope with menopause than with an enlarged prostate, which hits *most* men after fifty, causing urination problems, and can lead to urinary tract infections, even kidney damage? *I* would. According to Dr. E. Darracott Vaughan, Jr., professor and chairman of the Division of Urology at New York Hospital-Cornell Medical Center, one in five men (that's *all* men!) will at some point need a surgical procedure to relieve blockage of the bladder by the prostate. Prostate cancer, the most common cancer in men, occurs in one in *eleven* men. I prefer *our* "blight." Actually, I never went *through* menopause. In 1963 at age forty-one, after a few hot flashes—not terrible but not wonderful—I began taking the pill—1.25-milligram Premarin tablet—twenty-five days a month, with eight concurrent days of Provera, which produced a monthly mini-period for twenty-eight *years!* Did that seem odd in somebody my age? Not to me it didn't. It was only a baby period and I felt confirmed femaleness and sensuality just like earlier "authentic" periods. This past fall I had to have a hysterectomy but neither of my longtime trusted doctors—gynecologist and internist—felt estrogen supplements were the cause inasmuch as the Provera had produced a regular menstrual period all those twenty-eight years. The surgery didn't really undo me ... truth! ... only the shingles I got two weeks into recovery—which were *ghastly* but finally disappeared. Three months after surgery I felt terrific. Truth again ... I'm not being funny. Recovery is supposed to take a year but mine *didn't.* Probably all the years of reasonably healthful living before the operation helped with a quick rebound. I'm exercising an hour and a half a day again and I feel *frisky.*

The Harvard Medical School *Health Letter* says, "Use of the female hormone estrogen during and after menopause is becoming more common, because the benefits are believed to outweigh the risks. As the ovaries cease producing estrogen, replacement minimizes the uncomfortable symptoms of menopause (hot flashes and vaginal drying); it also diminishes the rapid loss of bone that leads to osteoporosis. The principal hazard of estrogen replacement is a somewhat increased probability of developing cancer of the endometrium (the lining of the uterus); this risk is thought to be diminished if another hormone, progestin, is given along with the estrogen." (Totally empirical opinion: I've always felt the doctors who were most vociferous against the Pill were somewhat antiwomen's sexuality. The estrogen-replacement pill is similar to the birth-control pill, both of which contribute to freer sex— one because you stand less chance of getting pregnant, the other because your vagina stays more enterable.) Increased vulnerability to heart attacks was once believed to be another adverse effect of estrogen replacement, but recent evidence has indicated that the reverse may be the case— that estrogen diminishes cardiovascular risk. A new study, based on research at the University of Southern California Medical School, Los Angeles, finds: On average, 20 percent fewer deaths annually among women who had used estrogen. The longer women stay on hormones, the greater the life-span edge—30 percent fewer deaths for those on estrogen for fifteen years or more. No greater risk of breast cancer, no matter how long women take estrogen. Not only is menopause not a big deal, you can even have a baby if you want to by having a fertilized-in-vitro egg from a young donor implanted in your uterus (would you *want* to?!).

Let's get very serious now because we have to deal with the big two: heart disease and cancer. *Fortune* magazine reports that 765,000 deaths in 1986 were the result of heart disease. "Cardiovascular disease kills virtually half the people in the United States: if it doesn't get the guy (girl) at the next desk, it will get you. This year 1.5 million Americans will suffer a heart attack and 500,000 will die—300,000 before reaching a hospital. Some forty-five percent of the coronaries will hit people under sixty-five. Strokes will kill another 150,000. Most are preventable."

The three major risk factors in heart disease are: high blood pressure, elevated levels of cholesterol in the blood, cigarette smoking. Diabetes, overweight, lack of exercise and family history of heart disease can also contribute. Why else are we susceptible to heart problems? "Just when antibiotics were wiping out infectious diseases," says *Fortune*, "prosperity allowed the masses rich food and sedentary lifestyles. No one is immune." Okay, we know what to *do*—cut out the rich food and get off our butts. *Fortune* doesn't say how many of the heart victims are men, how many women, but we know heart disease for women is on the rise (whether or *not I* want to acknowledge it's our problem).

About the other scourge: Why so much more cancer now than when we were growing up? Charles Dana, one of the founders of the Dana Foundation, which has contributed heavily to the Dana Farber Cancer Institute in Boston, says, "The reason more people have cancer now is that we are *living* longer. You get cancer because your immune system breaks down as you age and can't continue to fight off disease anymore. More people would have succumbed in earlier times if they'd lived long enough. People don't die of AIDS, for example, but because their immune system is shot and can't fight other illnesses— pneumonia or whatever—and that is what takes them off." *Fortune* reports: "Lung cancer is the most common overall, with about 155,000 new cases diagnosed annually, and death results in eighty-five percent of them. Colorectal cancer rivals lung in frequency but is easier to detect and treat, so average survival rates are more than twice as high and six times better if it's discovered early. Breast cancer is the most common cancer among women and prostate among men." They go on: "While the statistics are gruesome, the outlook isn't necessarily. Cigarette smoking accounts for eighty-three percent of lung cancer, according to the American Cancer Society [that you can stop, right?] and nearly half of all cancer deaths can be prevented with early detection and treatment."

Could we say a *bit* more about the smoking/cancer connection, as if you hadn't heard it all already? *Fortune* states: "It is numbingly clear that you should give up cigarettes, but since nicotine rivals heroin and cocaine as an addictive substance, that is easier said than done. In case you forgot: Smoking is the leading avoidable cause of death and morbidity and the biggest culprit in heart disease *and* cancer. . . . Two cigarettes a day doubles your risk of contracting lung cancer over the thirty years, three triples it and so on up to twenty. According to some studies, two years after you stop smoking, your chances of a heart attack return to normal, and ten years later the added risk of lung cancer virtually disappears but stopping earlier is better."

I had dinner with Yul Brynner the year he died and, though he'd stopped his four-pack-a-day habit, he hadn't stopped soon enough and now had cancer in both lungs. The cancer was in remission and he was appearing in *The King and I* on Broadway, more mesmerizing than ever, but still waging war. He showed me his orange-tinted hands and feet, the result of drinking two quarts of carrot juice a day as part of nontraditional therapy (he'd already had many rounds of chemo). Alas, he was gone within the year; his television "commercial" condemning smoking was shown a year after that. Dr. William Cahan, Emeritus Attending Surgeon at Memorial Sloan-Kettering Cancer Center and tireless antismoking advocate, says, "It's not just the lungs where smoking gets you . . . it's the larynx, the esophagus, the bladder, oral cancer, cancer of the cervix. I'm a pretty good surgeon but I tell people I've saved more lives at the dinner table (haranguing them to stop smoking) than I have on the operating table." Tony Schwartz, author and journalist who became a "fanatic on the subject" of smoking when his best friend died of lung cancer at the age of forty-seven, reminds us of other famous people who have succumbed from smoking-induced lung cancer: Sarah Vaughan, Lucille Ball, Desi Arnaz, Nat "King" Cole, John Wayne, Humphrey Bogart, Arthur Godfrey, Sammy Davis, Jr., Edward R. Murrow, Jackie Gleason, Lillian Hellman, Harry Reasoner, to name a few.

Five of my best friends smoke. One of them quit for a whole year—I used to leave a present at her office door every Friday morning to celebrate another abstemious week—then the day her husband died, she started again. I know she's *planning* to stop. Beverly (not her name) quit totally when *her* husband was told to stop or he'd die and she didn't want him tempted by her smoking. Clean for a year, she's started again. Carol had an abscess on her tongue caused by smoking, the removal of which she says has to have been as painful as having the tongue removed. She has been commanded to quit but hasn't. I could kill all of them. I love them and need them but I won't need to kill them because the smoking probably *will*. Two other buddies, beauties both, chain-smoke. I could kill them, *too*.

Other kinds of cancer, even with all the research and *some* breakthroughs, still carry too many of us away. A young *Cosmo* editor fought ovarian cancer for three years with both traditional and, some of us thought, off-the-wall therapy and died this year. A close male friend, not yet fifty, is battling leukemia. Both these people smoked for a long time, incidentally, though he has stopped. You can't always get an early cancer diagnosis . . . no opening things up just to see if anything's wrong in there. By the time you've got symptoms, the cancer may have metastacized. Pelvic exams can't *hurt*, of course, and breast exams are crucial. My internist bludgeoned me to get a mammogram though I don't believe in lots of tests and also had convinced myself (mistakenly) that people with small breasts weren't at risk. (Friends who have had one or both breasts removed all have or had ample bosoms, so I thought that was *one* thing a small-bosomed person might possibly console herself with—I was wrong.) I also sort of sensed the exam would be embarrassing. There I was right. We could hardly get my breasts up on the metal platform to be pressed into position to be X-rayed. Humiliating! We surely must do our *own* breast exam, quick and easy if you *are* small-bosomed and especially if you're used to exercising in front of a mirror without many clothes.

What about alcohol and drugs as troublemakers?

From an article in *The New York Times:* "One of every three truck drivers whose bodies were examined after they died in highway accidents had recently used drugs or alcohol." The captain of the *Exxon Valdez,* which ran aground and spilled all that oil in Prince William Sound, Alaska, was drunk. So have been the operators of school buses that went off roads thereby killing children, the pilots and conductors of planes, trains and subways that crashed, drivers of thousands of automobiles that caused sudden death on highways. According to the National Council on Alcoholism and Drug Dependence, 5 percent of women drink heavily ... that's millions of us; 35 percent of the members of Alcoholics Anonymous are women, and our numbers are rising. Because my sister (now a twenty-six-year member of A.A.) drank when we were young and smoked when it was ruinous for her polio-impaired lungs (she's given that up, too), alcohol and cigarettes so turned me off I never took them up. Judging by people who have kicked alcohol through A.A. or other means, that seems to be "easier" than giving up smoking. I can't report on anybody who's kicked a drug habit, because that doesn't seem prevalent in our age group. A younger friend who used coke but doesn't anymore never acknowledged she did in the first place so I can't say how she stopped. Narcotics Anonymous, a group founded on A.A. principles, has apparently helped lots of people.

Overeating may be harder to kick than any other blight. The off-coke friend is still fat, for example. My darling invalid sister who has beat the smoking and drinking rap even in her wheelchair (without the benefit of exercise, career or mind-diverting social activities) hasn't kicked overweight. When you kick the other two, she says you need *something* to do ... like *eat!* A friend of mine's brilliant husband weighs 280 pounds, has had a series of heart attacks and still puts away a chocolate cake at a time. After the last heart attack, he lost fifty pounds. Today, however, he's back to 280, 100 pounds over his "ideal" for six feet. He doesn't acknowledge the heart attacks. If anybody, knowing he had one, says, "I've got these pains; do you think I could be having a heart attack?," he says, "I have no idea." His wife, an elegant creature of fifty, tells me they haven't had sex in several years because he isn't interested. They are *affectionate* and he seems genuinely to care for her and to think she is funny—a very good sign. Men who hate their wives never think they are funny. He buys her jewelry—another good sign. Teri said recently— getting back to fat and sex or lack of it—he rolled over on her by mistake in bed one night and crushed her so badly they thought her back was broken. "I have introduced the subject of diet every day in every way—books, articles, endless discussions—if you call me doing all the talking a discussion. His response is invariably, 'I don't want to talk about it.'" Divine arrogance . . . and fear and dread, of course. People don't stop smoking, drinking or eating be- cause it *hurts* . . . a lot of pain is involved, but when you have been told not just that people kick off but that you *specifically* are probably going to be *one* of them, it seems to me you could try giving up a shot. It's very hard for practical, good-little-girl people like me to understand doing in your own body. Doing yourself in with a *man* is something else . . . I understand that totally though it's been years since I did it, but that madness involves another person whom you can't necessarily (and what do I mean necessarily?) get to behave. Your body is *yours*. I'm con- vinced people who do give up "bad things" are no more blessed with character than the ones who don't; we simply want to stick around for a while and feel as good as we can.

So these then are the health guidelines (all of which you've heard about a million times already): breast exams, gynecological checks every year or so, stop smoking, heavy drinking (mild intakes of alcohol and wine would seem to be one of life's pleasures at our age), doing drugs and dopey eating. Exercise we've dealt with in Chapter Seven. You need to do it daily. Office, woods, houses, streets, bars, parks, trees and treehouses are jammed with people who started and *stopped* exercising—too much trouble, too uncomfortable, so much else to do in that time slot. Damn right! So shall we get on with it?

If you dutifully do all the good things, and don't do

the bad, how *specifically* good can you feel every day at sixty or seventy? *Daily News* columnist Nancy McIntyre says, "After sixty-five, pulling yourself together in the morning is like knitting up an unraveled sweater. It can't be rushed. Getting out of bed is a serious decision. The first step is sitting on the edge of your bed until your head clears.... This is a crucial moment. Many elect to crawl back in the sack and say to heck with the complexities of life.... Nobody rises and shines. They stand up in slow motion.... Now you're on your feet gingerly putting one foot in front of another ... it's essential to shuffle into the day." Is this woman serious? Maybe just out of bed isn't our peak moment but one doesn't *shuffle.* After about a creak and a half to get your back straightened out, you move right ahead. If you think seriously about whether you *have* energy when you get up, you *don't* and you'll go right back to bed as Nancy McIntyre suggests. You can't *do* that, of course, so you move your tail and pay virtually no attention to aches, pains, lethargy. Betty Furness (seventy-three), formerly a consumer reporter for NBC, says, "I have tons of energy but it isn't physical ... it's *emotional.* I'm not strong physically. You are energized by needing to *do* something."

I actually feel quite *sparky* after an hour of exercise— not to push *that* again—but what mostly gets me going is I have *work* to do (even if sometimes it's *drudgery*). Energy, from wherever you dredge it up, *is* beautiful and we all gets bursts of it. When it runs out, nobody needs to *know.* You think if you don't get away from this meeting, this lunch, this party, these *people,* you will expire but you can't leave. Just shut *up!* Nobody is looking at you, thinking old, tired, collapse-city ... they can't see *inside* you. You just somehow manage (guts! discipline!) to get through the next hour and get away as soon as you can. An eighty-year-old famous New York society belle who goes to *everything* and is perceived as energetic and a dynamo, and *is* up to a point, stays only a couple of hours at each function, then quietly slips away.

Perhaps the major reason people have no energy is unhappiness. *Very* hard to get it up to work or play with a serious case of the blues (or "mean reds," as Truman Capote called them). Well, I couldn't understand more about *that* condition. If you are chronically depressed or have a serious current problem to get through, I think you go to a shrink. Otherwise, you get perked up with daily exercise. Your *job*, where they need you to be and be good at, helps with depression *and* "no energy." It *does*. Energy, real or "pushing it," makes up for not being a beauty, not being young. Energy is sexy, of course, and sexy—yes, even at our age—can make up for not being beautiful. . . . I know I'm sounding like a Chinese puzzle, but I don't think "no energy" is a legitimate complaint.

What about the Chronic Fatigue Syndrome we hear so much about? Sorry, darling, you may be *very* tired occasionally but you probably don't have C.F.S. A *Newsweek* checklist says: "Eight of the following symptoms must persist or recur over six months for a person to qualify: chills or low-grade fever, sore throat, tender lymph nodes, muscle pain, muscle weakness, extreme fatigue, headaches, joint pain (without swelling), neurological problems (confusion, memory loss, visual disturbances), sleep disorders, sudden onset of symptoms." See, you don't have it!

What about stress? Everybody has *that* and, if you live in a big city or have the job I'm always pushing, age surely doesn't eradicate it. Stress experts tell us we're still giving each stressful situation the old "fight or flight" response. As June Heimlich says in her book *What Your Doctor Won't Tell You* (HarperCollins), that reaction "was a lifesaver for the caveman confronted with a saber-toothed tiger; but today, when danger takes the form of a near dented fender, a deadline, or a conversation with an irate spouse, we respond to these emotional stresses the same way the caveman reacted to physical stress. What is so injurious to our health is that we react in this inappropriate manner—our entire system on alert—numerous times a day." She then quotes Dr. L. John Mason, author of *Guide to Stress Reduction:* " 'If a stress response is chronic, the constant presence of stress hormones begins to wear down the body's immunological systems.' "

I don't think stress is really about being "too busy"; it's about not being able to control a situation—job, man, money, parents, kids, cat—and another biggie: anger. *Fortune* magazine says, "The real problem [with stress] is chronic anger. The person who finds himself constantly fuming and yelling at the dunces surrounding him or at the cheats who try to cut ahead in line faces heart trouble." They quote Duke University's stress specialist Redford Williams: " 'The rushing around workaholic is not at risk [of heart trouble] as long as the stress is not a stimulus for anger.' " Okay, the rushing-around-workaholic-heart-attack-candidate angry person probably isn't *us* (I'm the former, not the two latter), but *whatever* is causing the stress, I don't think you want it out of your life altogether or you'd be limp asparagus. You want enough stress to keep your brain working, your world interesting. Parties, the job climb, going to bed with a new man . . . all stressful. We must just remember that automobiles never driven are "stress-free" but their batteries go dead.

Still, you do need to come off it sometimes. How? A relaxation therapist for major league sports teams, Dr. Saul Miller, suggests in his book *A Little Relaxation* that you chant hypnotic verses that relieve tense muscles and "promote spiritual serenity and positive self image." Example: "Feel a sense of spring in the pads of the soles of your feet, and your toes." I doubt chanting Dr. Miller's verses would do it for me. My recipe for getting off the stress track is not to leave town or leave the job or leave life but to curl up in a ball and *sleep* for a day, or anyway several hours. Don't talk to anybody, drink hot chocolate and do crossword puzzles before you drop off. And may I suggest for a stressed back—nothing out of place but just tight— you roll around on a tennis ball for five minutes. I do that every morning. It's hard to get the tennis ball to stay under your neck, easy under your hips and at the small of your back. You can feel and *hear* everything snapping, crunching, realigning . . . it's great!

How much sleep does somebody our age need? Everybody says it's up to the individual. I am *terminally* envious of people who say they need only five hours and have tried again and again but might as well not get *up* in the morning. Audrey Hepburn and other such okay people say they need eight, thank God, so I've even stopped *trying* to economize. If you sleep yourself to pieces, that is supposed to be a sign of depression; I guess you could investigate. I nap. My two assistants just say I'm *out*— which is certainly true. Sleep that falls on you like a sack of cement is surely one of life's most voluptuous experiences, say after an all-night flight to Europe and you only dozed on the plane, then you're in your hotel at 6:00 A.M., crawling in between these real linen sheets and SPHLONNKKK! You can get the cement-sleep feeling a little when you get up to go to the john in the middle of the night, find it's only 4:00 A.M., and you've got four more sleep hours to go.

These are the word games I use to drop off: Pick a letter, let's say *S*. Then go through the alphabet and think of somebody well known whose first name begins with each letter you come to and whose last name starts with S—*A*rnold Schwarzenegger, *B*arbra Streisand, *C*aroline Kennedy Schlossberg, *D*ean Stockwell, *E*unice Shriver, *F*rank Sinatra, etc. You have to decide whether you'll allow dead people or civilians (not household names); I rule out both categories. The other game is using a root sound like *ame;* then go through the alphabet thinking of words that rhyme with *ame*—*b*lame, *c*ame, *c*laim, *d*ame, *f*ame, *f*lame, etc. I've used up all the root sounds through the years and am now on to categories like clothing—again through the alphabet—*a*pron, *b*ikini, *c*oat (there are *lots* of *b* and *c* clothing items) *d*ress, *e*spadrilles, etc. Forget the *X*'s, *Q*'s and *Y*'s in these games. No need keeping yourself awake all night with frustration. Irene Copeland gave me a new alphabet game last week I think is the most fun of all: Go through and think of a disease and *city* for each letter (*a*ppendicitis in Albuquerque, *b*ursitis in Bangkok, *c*olitis in Cincinnati, *d*iphtheria in Denver, etc.

So you get sick sometimes, right? *You* get sick ... I *don't*. Okay, I had the flu twenty-four years ago. David and I had rented a house with friends in Puerta Vallarta and I simply sent him off without me. You don't want David under foot when you're sick. (Some men are married to their mommies and sick isn't what mommies *do*.) And one afternoon *five* years ago I was *dizzy* and went home. It was sweet ... crawling into a bed with virgin sheets, hugging a heating pad, reading something *slow* for a change. When I got to feeling better—about six hours later—I had waffles and applesauce and chicken croquettes. Listen, I have been such a total pain in the ass about illness I always suspected one day Something Big would get me and most of the people I know would say "Thank God!" I've been so unsympathetic with friends and employees, some one-*third* my age, who've had their third cold this year, the word *unreasonable* comes to mind.

Well, the bout of shingles that followed surgery should have satisfied all the bad-wishers though I never heard actual cheering. How such a blight (shingles—the surgery was nothing) could have befallen Prissy-About-Her-Health-to-the-Point-of-Craziness *me* was a bafflement; doctors say shingles have to do with immune system being weakened by surgery. I'll just suggest you wouldn't want Saddam *Hussein* to have shingles more than a week. Messy blisters pop out around your midriff (or wherever they hit), underneath which "electrical shocks" prod you intermittently, sometimes *continuously*, the pain grinding away like a drill. Traditional medical establishment virtually won't go *near* you because all they can tell you is "no cure, tough it out!" By the third week, I was going totally nuts-crazy and, figuring I had nothing to lose, checked in with a holistic doctor, Ronald L. Hoffman, who gave me massive B_1, B_{12}, adenosine shots six days in a row, which made me feel better. Maybe I was ready to get well anyway ... I surely appreciated his not taking the whole thing *casually* and trying to do a little *something*.

David doesn't *get* sick because he knows he would be maltreated by an unsympathetic mate if he did. Yes, I *know* innocent people get hit with illness, especially when older, but I mostly think you are *all* doing something to bring it on or not keep it away—like smoking or eating potato chips, bologna and Danish instead of veggies, fruit and real protein; you aren't *exercising;* you don't rest between orgies; and you don't care enough about your work and Being There to ignore a few scuzzies.

You *may* be gratified to know that denigrating illness as I do, *Cosmo* got into terrible trouble last year with an article recommending "chic" diseases to have and out-of-fashion ones *not* to have. (I was only *half* kidding.) On the former list, writer Junius Adams suggested Lyme disease as one of the "ins"—"an illness certain to put you on center stage because, although it has received enormous publicity, very few people actually *have* it" (the ones who have say one sufferer is too many). He went on to explain the infection is caused by the "deer tick, a minute creature about the size of a pencil dot (*not* one of those big ticks that buzz all over the countryside). He also recommended mononucleosis: "This old-timer has remained in the top echelons of sickroom chic for over forty years because it's close to the ideal malady: restful, non-fatal, ladylike, yet with the drama of potential serious complications." Candida albicans (chronic yeast syndrome) made the list, although "doctors who don't believe in hypoglycemia, PMS or vitamin therapy do not accept Candida either. So you must seek out an open-minded M.D. and while undergoing treatment, make the most of your ailment on the conversational circuit." Malaria was included in Junius's list ... "one of the grand old ailments of the 1930's and earlier, caused by the bite of a parasite-infected mosquito. The disease offers a resplendent alibi for avoiding undesirable obligations. You can just say, 'Sorry I can't (come to dinner tonight, attend your meeting, spend the weekend in Aruba), my malaria is flaring up.' "

What didn't get picked: *shingles*—too painful, *unusual or mysterious headaches*—ditto, *PMS*—boring and repetitive, *hypoglycemia*—ditto, *high cholesterol*—pull-eeze! Don't join every nerd in the United States, *thyroid problems*—interesting only to the sufferer, *lower back pain*—strictly pedestrian!

The howls we got, particularly from the Lyme disease group! I guess if you've ever had LD, it isn't funny and the disease can linger for years. But there *do* seem to be trends in illnesses. Of course, you *may* get sick because you've had it (life) up to your root-canal work for the moment and need to retreat; the old immune system "agrees to" break down and let you *get* a cold. Dr. Stuart Berger's definition of the immune system: "your body's network of blood cells, antibodies and chemicals which are your body's protection against disease. It fights germs, from common bacteria to exotic parasites to the deadliest viruses. It is also your sole guardian against the malignant, often deadly, growth of cancer. Your immune system is all that stands between you and disease that can sap your energy, threaten your life, and make your body weak and infirm many years too soon. Unaided your immune system will lose about ninety percent of its strength between the ages of twenty and seventy. Women live longer because they have a stronger immune system."

Okay, these are things Dr. Berger says we can do to strengthen the system and fight off, among other plagues, cancer: Eat more fiber, eat less fat, eat more mineral-and-vitamin-rich vegetables, stop smoking, keep alcohol consumption to a reasonable level. Lowering fat is *crucial.* Surely it's all worth a shot. Some of us are doing this stuff anyway; we just didn't know we were doing it on behalf of the immune system. (If green veggies, without hollandaise, were just not so disgusting, I'd do even *more!*)

Now, illness aside, things do go wrong with your body parts. They take a lot of tear and wear when they've been used so long; also accidents happen. This past year I had a broken toe (from sliding downstairs into an iron rail ... so embarrassing!) and a bump under my eyelid—mascara got up there somehow ... eyelid had to be rolled back and *puss* came out ... a mess! My gums are usually fluffy *somewhere.* I spend half my life at the dentist, or zonked from tetracycline, and I have to pee often. I'm just saying, along with the accidents and things wearing down, we don't have to help create illness by letting the old immune system get any scruffier than it needs to. I *would* like to put in a good word for diarrhea, often a component part of illness. I was felled twice, once in Cairo and once in Israel, from not drinking bottled water, and, as you know, the pounds *melt* away (euphemistically speaking ...

actually they are *flushed* away). Alas, they all come back when your appetite returns and maybe a few more. Big *bruises* are kind of pleasant, if you didn't get struck getting them. So pretty, going from black to purple to lavender to greenish-yellow and, finally, back to pink again. Somebody stepped on my foot in junior high school in football shoes yet and I remember all those pretty colors. Then last year when I broke my toe, the bruising was magnificent . . . my instep looked like a lavender quenelle. The show only lasts a few days.

Do vitamins help? As noted, you sure can't get the *medical* establishment to say so. If the doctor is over fifty, he wasn't trained in nutrition. According to June Heimlich, orthomolecular medicine, a term coined by Nobel Prize winner Linus Pauling, *does* correct "the body's metabolism by prescribing the right combination of nutrients—vitamins, minerals, amino acids, enzymes, and others. All of these nutrients, about forty in all, are normally present in the human body [and are] nature's biological weapons. These . . . constitute a defense system that has been successful for millions of years in the battle against all forms of disease. . . . In contrast to orthomolecular medicine, standard medicine uses drugs that are not normally found in the body. Orthomolecular doctors regard these drugs as 'alien chemicals,' which have no connection with the disease process."

Heimlich states that RDAs (Recommended Dietary Allowances), as set out by the U.S. Food and Drug Administration, are appallingly low—enough to keep you from getting scurvy, but it takes *very* little vitamin C to do *that.* Senator William Proxmire once declared, "It is in the narrow economic interest of the [food] industry to establish low official RDA because the lower the RDAs, the more nutritional their food products appear." He said the National Research Council's Food and Nutrition Board was heavily financed by the food industry! Possible. Heimlich warns that the nutrition industry can rip you off with simplistic claims but that doesn't gainsay the real good of vitamin supplements prescribed by knowledgeable people.

I'm a believer; I have taken megadoses of vitamins for twenty years and think they are part of what keeps me healthy. Never mind that some doctors who prescribe them *sell* vitamins and your bill can be bigger than the rent. You have to decide for yourself, then find someone who knows enough about vitamins to prescribe.

So, addressing again what is *possible* health-wise for us at our age, I'll quote from a letter from my friend Yvonne Black (seventy-one), an executive secretary with a Los Angeles law firm, bringing me up to date on her life. Yvonne and I were single girls in Los Angeles fifty years ago and I would have known *then* (if younger ever thought about older) that she would turn out this way. Says Yvonne, "I like to play tennis, bowl, roller skate, hike up the Mount Wilson toll road, work out on my bench press, use my weights, my twist platform, pay bills, wear jumpsuits, and go barefoot. I actually believe there isn't anything I can't do. When a rug was delivered (9 x 12) from India that I had made to go under my dining room table and I was alone, I folded it up and put it close to the legs of the table, got under the table, and lifted it up (it's 104 feet long) with my back and managed to get the rug under the table, perfectly smooth, with no help—except from my guardian angel who always takes care of me. After my last divorce (my husband left in 1979 and we were divorced, I believe, in early 1980), I needed to prove something, apparently, and got involved with Outward Bound in an expedition to northern Peru. There, with seven men, I managed to climb to the top of Mt. Pisco, 19,646 feet, using crampons and ice axes, four on a rope. It was a great experience, difficult, exhausting, and at the same time gave me a feeling of accomplishment. This was in 1980, when I was already sixty. I've done many trips with them and think they can give anybody self-confidence and a feeling of competence, not to mention some terrific workouts!" She's my role model. They gave her a seventieth birthday party and the town turned out. She's getting married this summer.

Now, shall we talk about doctors just for a moment?

chapter nine

Doctors

Where do doctors fit in our lives? There isn't anything better in the world than a great doctor, don't you agree?—even now when they are getting sued all over the place. While considering them geniuses, I also think you should stay away from them as much as possible. You can only stay away if you take care of yourself as I have been tirelessly pointing out. If you *don't*, no doctor can fix it anyway, so don't look to *them* for getting your body to be feisty and twenty-five again after you've screwed up. In my opinion, doctors are for going to when something is wrong and not too much checking in between times. My sister Mary and I were doctor-phobes from earliest childhood—hid in closets or under the bed on learning old Dr. Judd (he was probably fifty) had been summoned (you do remember doctors once made house calls?). She or I would be running a fever or have the blotchies; Ira or Cleo would surreptitiously make the call and soon this jolly, white-haired giant would appear in our doorway, we having been fished from our hiding places, with his horrible little black bag. A visit from the doctor was icky and embarrassing! *Cosmo's* long-time health director, Mallen de Santis, a pretty good doctor-phobe herself, says, "Trying to *prevent* illness by going for a checkup isn't how you prevent illness. Tests can't really reveal very much ahead of time. You prevent illness by living properly and taking care of yourself. You go to a doctor when you're sick. If you have cystitis, you'll have a burning sensation when you urinate. A yearly checkup isn't going to prevent your getting cystitis, or a cold or the flu. If something hurts or aches or you see blood, go!"

Doctors don't necessarily encourage you to stay away. Coretta says, "They don't get paid for your not coming to them. The finest and most gifted still want to see you oftener rather than less often." Sandra says, "The more you go the more you go. I barely make it to the gynecologist once a year—every two is more like it—though I'm taking estrogen that ought to be checked. The internist I really respect I see about every two years. Arrogance? I don't think so. I do every possible thing to stay healthy and I don't need doctors to tell me to do those things."

I don't go often either. One of my doctors can diagnose by phone. A couple of years ago the room was spinning when I lay down; I figured brain tumor. "Are you as thin as ever?" he asks me on the phone. "Yes." "Have you cut salt completely out of your diet?" "Of course!" "Eat some salt for a few days and call me." I did and the room stopped spinning. (I have low thyroid and get to eat salt all the time . . . it's heaven!)

As I mentioned earlier, what doctors don't know about nutrition would fill Grand Canyon *and* Regine's on New Year's Eve. Catherine Houck says, "In my twenties I was sometimes sick for two months at a time and no doctor *ever* asked what I ate. Breakfast was black coffee and a Tiger's Milk candy bar." A doctor I once talked to about my sweet tooth had this advice: "Visualize a hot fudge sundae, then pretend you are eating it, spoonful by spoonful . . . slowly, deliciously. When you have 'eaten' it all, you will feel satisfied!" Is this person ready for a brain scan or *what??*

Many people share Mallen's view about staying away from doctors. Leonora Hornblow (seventy-two) says she doesn't see them because "my late husband [film producer Arthur Hornblow] was a hypochondriac. He and Leland Hayward would talk on the phone every day, so worried about each other's health. . . . 'How'd you sleep?' Leland would ask Arthur. 'Dreadful,' my husband would say. 'I don't think I got more than forty minutes.' How would he *know?*. . . He was too busy snoring!" Leonora had one of the great marriages.

Betsy Cronkite remembers, "My family were on the Christian Science path and also cheap so we fell back on homespun remedies. You may remember from Arkansas horehound drops and camomile tea. I never met an aspirin until I met Walter. Now, aside from obligatory checkups, I don't often meet doctors except a couple of sailing medics [Walter sails] and an occasional tennis player."

Magnificent specimens Raquel Welch and Ali MacGraw both think doctors prescribe too many drugs too casually. Ali says, "They tend to be mad about antibiotics, which make me feel all muggy." Raquel agrees. "They may get rid of the flu or cold but your system is wrecked. Nobody tells you to take yogurt or acidophilus to undo the bad effects of the antibiotics." She also says, "Doctors can't tell until you're half dead of the disease that something is the matter with you . . . it has to show up on a test before they can help you. You need people before that to keep your system running smoothly." Ali says her doctors tend to be homeopathic. Designer Mollie Parnis said shortly before her death last year, "I haven't had much luck with doctors . . . they don't listen, don't take enough notes . . . too busy . . . sloppy." Agnes says, "My sons push me but I'd have to be bleeding from every orifice and turning blue before I'd go voluntarily. Tests, tests, tests and the *bills* they send!"

But let's get to some doctor *defenders*. My friend Ann Siegel, who, as a civilian, knows a great deal about the medical world, says, "You need a regular doctor—an internist probably—who knows your body and can spot *changes*—in blood pressure, weight, heartbeat, urine . . . the changes can be significant." Michael Castleman, author of four consumer health books, says in *Reader's Digest,* "Find a generalist you trust, preferably when you're healthy. A doctor familiar with the healthy you is in the best position to notice when something goes wrong. A new doctor has no basis for comparison. Even if a generalist can't solve your mystery, let him refer you to specialists and guide the rest of your work-up. It's a mistake to wander from specialist to specialist." Louise Grunwald, married to Henry Grunwald, long-time editor in chief of

Time and U.S. ambassador to Austria, says, "Because both my parents died young, I am a nut about doctors and go for a checkup once a year. An internist at New York Hospital orchestrates everything. If you need somebody for bones, breasts, hemorrhoids, feet, Dr. [Reese] Pritchett will track him down. You have a kind of *team* of doctors—frequently they know each other or at least know *of* each other but you have one central headquarters." Author Charlotte Salisbury (seventy-six), married to *New York Times* correspondent Harrison Salisbury, doesn't have a headquarters but says, "I go to millions of doctors—eye, ear, back, gynecologist, internist, dermatologist—oh, yes, and a foot doctor once a year. I don't know whether I'm just lucky—I go to the same ones everybody else goes to but I like all of them." Ann Ford Johnson has "an internist, gynecologist, dentist, radiologist and oncologist . . . I check in regularly. Dean didn't know when he married me he was going to be living with a medical groupie."

Another believer, film producer Sherry Lansing *(Fatal Attraction, School Ties),* says she wouldn't *be* here but for a bloodhound dermatologist. "I had a small bump on my face, went to a dermatologist who took a biopsy but found nothing. My own doctor still didn't like the look of things and sent the slide to *another* doctor, who diagnosed it as something different from the first doctor but still it wasn't serious; he suggested I might have it removed in six months. A *third* dermatologist—I didn't let up—sent the slide to a third *pathologist,* who found it was a melanoma. You die from melanoma. If I hadn't got it off in a few weeks, it would have sunk into the bloodstream." Sherry also blesses the doctors who saved her life—and got her walking again after a horrible car accident.

Lauren Bacall credits bone specialist Dr. James Nicholas with keeping her in the hit show *Applause* and out of surgery when her leg buckled and she crumpled during a high-kick dance number. "All I could think of was that my brief moment of glory was over—I might be incapacitated for weeks—but he kept me from even missing a performance . . . I could never be grateful enough." We all know Sophia Loren finally got *pregnant* with the help, forget the husband, of a wonder doctor in Switzerland. "Nine months in bed, no activity at all, not even talking on the telephone. The doctor said, 'We're going to produce this baby, you and I,' and we did!"

Phyllis Cerf Wagner (early seventies), vice-president of Wells, Rich, Green Advertising, had quit going to doctors altogether but her husband, ex-New York City mayor Bob Wagner, kept nagging, "So I decided to look around. One of my good friend's daughters had become a doctor I kept hearing good things about. I wasn't sure how I felt about a female doctor but decided to give her a try. That first visit she began to ask questions all about *me* . . . I felt this was a physician truly concerned with her *patient* . . . it was a wonderful feeling . . . I'm her *slave!*" The doctor's mother, incidentally, is Kitty Carlisle Hart, who says she goes to all the regular doctors and has no complaints. Travel-book editor Alex Mayes blesses the doctor who did skin grafts after cancer was dug out of her face and wouldn't show her "before" pictures immediately after the excavation or let her look in the mirror until the work was completed. "He knew I couldn't have handled it and saved me from total shock." Screenwriter Nora Ephron says, "I hate the scar that an extremely famous thyroid person left me with, but on the other hand I turned out not to have cancer so I really don't want to seem as if my priorities are all wrong."

Playwright Jay Presson Allen (*The Prime of Miss Jean Brodie, Tru*) says, "I call up with a *hangnail* . . . any occasion to get to see him. Dr. Rossman is *totally* dedicated to the practice of medicine . . . he isn't trying to be a demigod. I once asked him, 'Why do you *do* this . . . you could have been a rich man!' He said, 'I do it for Mozart . . . you live up to the highest standard you can possibly create for yourself.' " Beverly Sills (she with all that energy) says she has had only wonderful experiences with doctors. "Of course I'm biased. My oldest brother is a doctor married to a nurse. His two children are doctors. My other brother's *son* is a radiologist. I know where to go for a second opinion!"

Alison talks about her "very special internist . . . in

his seventies ... who treats half the wealthy matrons in Beverly Hills. He is about as un-Beverly Hills as you can get—he'd seem more at home in Vienna—but this wise and gifted person always gives me a bear hug when I see him—and sometimes he just lets me rub up against him but not to the point of orgasm—just scrunching against him because he's a man and it feels good ... something I used to do when I had lovers. Occasionally he kisses me lightly—*very* lightly—dry lips—and if I rub too much and he gets an erection, he stops instantly. I have no doubt he performs this 'service' for other of his older women patients. Moralists would be horrified, I'm sure, and there *are* creepy doctors who take advantage of silly women patients, but I never doubt this hugging is for *me*. He could surely have a girlfriend if he wanted sex—I think he is happily married. He is a doctor in the finest sense, understands the loss of sex and sexual attraction for older women. He used to say to me, 'Honey, don't ever give *that* up,' and I'd say, 'I don't have any choice ... find me a lover!' Then, after I had been his patient for ten years, I started an affair with someone that has been absolutely terrific, but I would say this darling doctor got me through the bad years by just being there and affectionate and healing and making me understand I was still attractive and female."

So are there some "bad" doctors out there ready to do careless, possibly hurtful things? Is Alaska north of the Equator? Anne C. Roark, reporting on a *Los Angeles Times* poll of 2,046 people, says it starts with the waiting room. What people most dislike about physicians are the *delays*. "One in 10 says doctors rush through visits. A handful complain that doctors are either too impersonal or fail to listen to their complaints. And some people even believe their doctors are unable to figure out what is wrong with them. ... Only one in five thinks a doctor orders the right number of tests. About 20% think doctors order too *few* tests and nearly half believe their doctors order too *many*. The vast majority of people ... think their doctors get some kind of financial benefit from the tests they order." (They don't. That would be wildly illegal.

They don't profit from prescriptions they order either, though drug companies surely romance doctors and leave samples.)

An oncologist kept Alex waiting for a couple of hours one day and she let him have it. "I gave him absolute hell when I got in. I explained that anybody with cancer (mine was skin cancer with subsequent grafts) is half dead with anxiety anyway, and to be kept waiting an unconscionable amount of time means that he is some kind of jerk or sadist or both. He took it and never kept me waiting again. Don't know whether this screaming would work for everybody." "My bad experience lasted for years," says Pamela. "My adorable regular doctor died and passed his practice on to a person identified as 'his' doctor, the head of a department in a first-class hospital. Off I went. As I left the new doctor's office after my first visit, I realized I knew a great deal about him. While he looked at my records and examined me, he kept up a constant dialogue about himself. The pattern never changed. On subsequent visits I heard lectures about his children, his wife, the food he liked and didn't; he took other patients' calls while I sat. After five years, I decided it was a waste of time to go to him. He never called to give me reports on how my tests came out. Once I called his nurse and asked if the doctor had found anything wrong. 'I'm certain he would have called you if he had,' she said. After that I stopped going to him, though I still thought of him as 'my doctor.' Then one day I didn't feel well. Very unusual for me. I called him. I told him my symptoms. He told me to come in. I went in. He told me he had the exact same symptoms. He prescribed some pills—and sent me for an X ray. He never told me what was wrong with us. I never went back. I hope he's feeling better. I am. I have a new doctor."

Ex-model film developer Mary Lazar went to a "hideously high-priced doctor in Los Angeles who, after the examination, asked me to step into his office. Another woman was already seated when I got there and I was about not to enter but the doctor said, 'Come on in, sit over there.' He then talked to both of us. 'Mary, you need a prescription and make an appointment in two weeks.

Carol, that disk is definitely nonaligned. We'll have to see what we can do without surgery.' He should have halved the bill . . . we're probably lucky he didn't try simultaneous examinations.''

A "bad doctor" caused a friend and her husband wild embarrassment *plus* major anxiety. *Ladies' Home Journal* editor Myrna Blyth says, "I was planning to leave *Family Circle* to become editor of *Ladies' Home Journal* but the deal was not yet closed. While I still had medical coverage with my present company, my husband decided to have a polyp removed at an important New York hospital. The head of the proctology department said probably Jeffrey would have to have major surgery—a colostomy— terrifying news in itself, but the doctor was so worried whether *I* was still covered by my company and whether my *husband* was that, without telling us, he called up the medical benefits department of *Family Circle* to *check.* Yes, we were covered, but the benefits department told my boss—this nice man who didn't know I was leaving—and that's how he found out. Jeffrey had the operation—it turned out to be minor—but he was so terrified by the warning, he has never felt comfortable about his health ever since, and I haven't felt the same about some doctors' *priorities.* "

Pat Saylor, dean of continuing education at New York University and sister of New York ex-mayor Ed Koch, reports "no bad experience with a doctor except the one who failed to find a fibroid tumor which, by the time another doctor discovered it, was as big as a grapefruit and causing a real mess." My friend Evelyn reports, "a prominent San Francisco gynecologist who told a friend she had syphilis, 'probably given to her by her husband.' It was bad enough being diagnosed with a venereal disease," says Evelyn, "let alone facing serious infidelity in your mate. Turned out she *didn't* have syphilis and the doctor was simply making a move—as he did with many of his patients . . . and with some success. You think this kind of thing only happens with a small-town doctor and silly naive females, but it can happen with prominent doctors and (otherwise) 'smart' women."

Inger Elliott, owner of the fabric ship China Seas, says, "I hate going to the gynecologist. Virginia Graham probably has the right idea. Virginia says hers has to be under five feet so she can't see him down there at the end of the table doing whatever he's doing. Anyway, this gynecologist was new to me and kept saying we had met someplace. I said I didn't think so, that I would surely remember him. Well, he is actually in the middle of the pelvic exam when he cries, 'I've got it! Phi Beta Kappa initiation!' You don't want somebody remembering you from *anywhere* from that particular angle!" Claire hates "all X-ray technicians and receptionists. I swear they all trained in Nazi boot camp . . . icy, slate-gray and cold, just like their equipment, exactly when you could use a little human warmth!"

Doctors are *not* always genius diagnosticians. Janice recalls an afternoon when "the doctor explored *everything* . . . taking stuff out of me and putting other stuff in and graphing it up because I'd come in feeling just awful but didn't know what it was. At the end of the probe, he said, 'Now just *when* did you lift that sewing machine?'—I'd told him that in the beginning. I felt better in a few days and I think it *was* the sewing machine . . . one of those ancient kind that weighed fifty pounds I shouldn't have lifted. I'd probably still be being tested if they'd had more sophisticated tests at the time."

Marguerite says, "One thing I don't do anymore is *wait*. I think many doctors are better these days about working women's schedules, especially if you establish a good rapport with the nurse. Tell them to call you when they're running late. Keeping in mind they all have emergencies, I just don't go to anybody anymore who keeps me in the reception room longer than twenty minutes."

One thing that's definitely improved: their talking things *over* with you . . . doctors have come a long way, baby, from their Hippocratic Oath. Hippocrates admonished physicians to "perform [these duties] calmly and adroitly, concealing most things from the patient while you are attending to him. Give necessary orders with cheerfulness and serenity, turning his attention away from what is being done to him; sometimes reprove sharply and emphatically, and sometimes comfort with solicitude and attention, revealing *nothing* of the patient's future or present condition."

I find doctors, for the most part, come off like pussycats compared to people's perception of dentists. I think the problem, when there is one, is that we tend to trust dentists . . . at least in the early stages. After all, it's only our teeth, not livers or lungs they are dealing with, so we let them have their way, no arguments or second opinions. Only our *teeth*, for God's sake! Our teeth are connected to our gums (if we're lucky) and gums are where all hell breaks loose if we aren't. The whole area is right next to our *brain*, which surely gets pounded when they drill. Somebody just returned from the dentist should be treated like a victim of shellshock, don't you agree? It's a trauma we all forget to acknowledge in others because you can't *see* what a sufferer has just been through. Some lucky people's teeth and gums never do bad things even with *minimum* care; others of us spend our days at the dentist, our nights waiting it out to call in for an appointment the next morning because something's flared up again no matter how careful we've been. Frequently I've got off an airplane and gone straight to the dentist with yet one more puffy gum. Age doesn't help, though the whole thing started for me at seventeen when I totaled my sled running into a stone bench which killed two front teeth, mercifully, instead of *me*. We were so poor I pitifully asked the dentists who did the subsequent root canal and capping if they would work for less if I hung in without novocaine. They thought I was a little saint but declined the offer. As recently as last week, we snipped off part of an inflamed gum that couldn't recover even though four times a year we deep-clean all the way to China. I'm convinced I'm so healthy that anything bad trying to express itself goes right straight to my gums . . . you know how they say stress has to go *somewhere*. I totally trust Lenny and, unlike other people who hate going to the dentist, actually feel quite *cozy* when I get into his big leather chair. I know whatever it is is going to get *fixed*—for a while anyway.

Lenny also tells me stories. There was this housewife who was being helped to her car with a load of groceries by a hunky teenager and, observing his elegant muscle mass, she says, "You know I have an itchy pussy," and he says, "Lady, those foreign cars all look alike to me; could you just point to it when we get there?" And my *favorite* about the three dogs at the veterinarian who are being put to sleep and one explains he's going bye-bye because his folks are redecorating and he has a weak bladder and they're afraid he'll pee on the carpets, and the second says he was like a beloved child to his owners, even slept on the bed, but now they're having a human baby and are afraid he'll be jealous and hurt the child. The third animal, a handsome German shepherd, says *he* got there because his mistress, a very sexy woman, was always running around in babydoll nightgowns and one morning when she leaned over to pick up a newspaper he jumped her. The others are horrified and try to comfort him ... so you're being put down this week also—what day? He says, "Don't be ridiculous. I'm just here to get my nails clipped!" Dear Lenny.

Others are not so happy with their dentists, even those they see often. "Why is it my lot in life to have to cheer this man up or at least listen to his agonizing?" asks Ellen. "I hear him say things like 'These are two weak teeth and I don't want to put too much strain on them' or 'The X ray isn't definite yet so should we *wait* to see if it's infected?' If he's having trouble making a decision or suffering an anxiety attack, couldn't he talk it over with the *nurse?!*" Pauline says, "I would have done *anything* Dr. K. told me ... divorce Allen, give up sex, move to Cincinnati. Recently I asked him about orthodontia ... even at my age. I have crooked lower teeth and their crowdedness had caused some of them to jut up beyond the others. He gazed into my mouth as though the New York State lottery winners were printed there ... then he said, 'I could fix that for you right here in the office, right now ... I'll just file down the teeth that are jutting up ...

the impression will be a nice even smile.' Didn't sound like anything horrendous, right? We went right ahead ... file, file, file, and though the teeth were still crowded down below, sure enough, the line across the top was straight and smooth. Well, a mere few *days* later the upper teeth started missing their jutting-up old companions and several of them decided to regroup. Dr. K. hadn't mentioned that possibility. I flew back to him; he had me scrunch carbon paper between uppers and lowers to see what wasn't hitting, after which we did a bit more filing— 'fine-tuning,' he called it, so things would match up better. *Alors,* after a few more weeks—this all happened gradually—upper teeth have stopped moving around but two of them by now have relocated to a whole new neighborhood! Having always had even, close-together upper teeth, my two *frontest* ones now had parted company and have a gap between them. I didn't go to Dr. K. again— figured he would feel really bad and what he did last time hadn't *helped* so I went to my regular dentist. After he stopped trying to convince me to leave the upper spacy front teeth *alone* ("I have a gap between my front teeth ... see?... and isn't Lauren Hutton's gap attractive?"), Dr. J. gave me a tiny rubber band to put around two upper teeth overnight to encourage togetherness. Sensational! As miraculously as the bottom teeth had been filed down to make a smooth smile line, the two upper teeth *did* join together again in just one night of rubber band wearing. I tore down to the doctor's office at eight the next morning and he cemented things so the teeth would stay together forever." So this is a bad- *and* good-guy story.

Some of my friends have experienced *super* bad. Playwright Jay Presson Allen went to a "substitute" dentist "who *destroyed* a tooth. My regular dentist was out of town, the referral dentist didn't return phone calls but when he finally did, referred me to still *another* dentist. The new referral was glassy-eyed when he arrived for the appointment. I knew better—he was totally spaced out— and yet I sat there like a ninny and let this person drill a tooth. A couple of days later the tooth exploded. On leaving his office they'd suggested I book another appointment and, glancing at the appointment book, I saw there was no-body there—just blank pages—I was probably the first and last patient he had that particular year ... don't *ask* where he was getting the money for drugs ... maybe he was sell-ing office equipment." Joy Philbin, the wife of TV host Regis Philbin, went in for "a simple crown and the doctor just couldn't get anything right—the more he tried, the more everything happened. First the lab sent back some-body else's crown, which the doctor kept trying to fit into my jaw. Then the assistant dropped the crown in the sink and broke it. Then once *he* broke it trying to get it on him-self. Every day Regis would talk about my latest dental drama on the air and of course hearing his story on syndi-cated television didn't do the cause any good. After eleven visits, the crown was finally in place."

Lenny Hirschfield, my wonderful orthodontist, told me about another dentist who made a crown for a patient and, as he was fitting it in her mouth, she swallowed it. He told her it would come out with a stool in a day or two—to eat lots of potatoes, rice, and beans and then look through the feces. She did, finally found the crown and brought it to the doctor to be sterilized. He was fitting it in her mouth once more and she swallowed it *again.* She said, "Doctor, this time I'm going to bring the feces to the office and *you* can find the crown." (She let him off the hook and they got the crown installed on the third try.)

Root-canal work is wildly effective in saving teeth, as you know. Grind down the dead tooth and replace the rot-ten nerve, but you need a winner-specialist for the work. "I was having root-canal work and the dentist who did it wasn't competent," says Carol. "It would be like your gynecologist doing a face-lift. Legally he's allowed to but it's not what he *does.* This doctor dug the canal too deep and there wasn't enough root to keep the tooth together. It shattered one night while I was having a chef salad at Elaine's. The poor thing was dead but seemed to be say-ing, 'Mother, I want to show you I can still do *something* on my own' ... shatter, shatter ... into tiny white pieces like goldfish-bowl pebbles. A dental surgeon pulled the tooth and I have a gaping hole where it used to be. Nobody recommended putting another tooth there ... it's way in the back. The root-canal doctor's bill arrived—I'd already paid a lot of it—and I just didn't pay the rest. The doctor said he couldn't see the connection between my not paying the bill and the collapsed tooth—after all, he'd already done the work. I told him, when a patient dies, maybe the family has to pay the bill, but when a tooth dies—and didn't need to—you don't. There wasn't a lot he could *do!*"

"I think you go into mourning for a lost tooth," says Sandra. "I still miss a big molar I lost several years ago like you'd mourn the loss of a friend—only new friends you can make and new teeth you *can't!*" And *this* is the worst dentist atrocity story I ever heard. My glamorous wealthy friend Marcia went to a Park Avenue dentist who said she needed a tremendous amount of "preventive dentistry." If she moved a couple of teeth around she would never have any more trouble. He said this would take a long time and be expensive and painful but it was the only way to save her mouth—reconstructive work. After she had suffered enormous pain and endless hours in the chair, he told her the work needed to be done *again*—everything but pulling the teeth since they weren't there to pull twice. Do you *believe* this?! How do you get into these situations? This man was recommended to her by one of the most respected dental surgeons in the city. She later found out the "preventive dentistry" person had a heavy drug habit which he needed to pay for. Maybe he got into drugs later and the referring dentist didn't know.

There are some politics in referrals. Your original doctor may not want to *treat* you if you don't go to the specialist that *he* recommends. You are a bit at their mercy. I guess I could mention here that dentists and doctors put up with stuff from *us,* particularly *older* us, particularly doctors. Do you ever wonder why anyone would want to *be* a doctor? It isn't as wonderful for them as it was. Even with our going broke paying the tab, they do have restrictions about fees plus other headaches. My gynecologist, Thomas E. Steadman, who delivered Caroline Kennedy

Schlossberg's baby and other spiffy kids, recently got out of the OB business because "the insurance is just too high and, if the baby isn't Venus de Milo (*with* arms), the doctor gets blamed for *that*. Everyone deserves a perfect baby, but if it isn't, the parents have to blame *somebody*. It couldn't be their *genes* or some unexplainable screwup of nature, so it's the doctor!"

There are medical incompetents, of course . . . to put it *very* mildly, but what can the percentages *be?* A doctor goes to medical school for four years, then interns for two, and then goes on to be a resident. And medical schools ruthlessly eliminate dodos. Repairing body parts that go wrong or that never were right to begin with is a *very* tricky business. You're dealing with living tissue that can sustain varying amounts of trauma, depending on the individual. Procedures don't come out the same with all of us and especially not if we've waited too long to get started. As for our daily misbehavior, Illene Springer writes in a *Cosmo* article that some patients "bark at the receptionist, elbow other patients out of the way and screw up everyone else's schedules by abusing their time with the doctor. One will come in," Illene says, "say, to check out a mole. But just as she's leaving, she'll comment, 'By the way, Doctor, I've been having bad chest pains for the past three months and difficulty breathing.' Unwittingly, the doctor then spends all this extra time with her, keeping other patients waiting. Other 'warrior patients' turn the office into an arena, challenging the M.D.'s every move."

"No matter what the doctor does, it's not good enough," says Barbara Henry, an internist in Boulder, Colorado. "And if the doctor does manage to help the combative patient, she can forget about gratitude. I once treated a patient in the emergency room who didn't have her own doctor. After, when I sent a bill, she called me up and said, 'I never asked you to be my doctor. I don't have to pay you.' And there is the 'patient pro'—the one who sits on the subway reading her own copy of the *Physician's Desk Reference*—from which she'll gladly quote to her physician. Another giveaway: the patient who comes in wanting a CAT scan before the doctor has even examined her or taken her history—which happen to be the most important elements in making a diagnosis. It's like an amateur pilot walking up to the cabin of a 727 and telling the captain how to fly the plane. One of the most frustrating of all know-it-all patients is the individual who majors in medication—the *antibiotic junkie*. Doctors complain that you can tell these patients over and over again that viral infections don't respond to antibiotics. And yet they'll come in with a simple cold and insist on amoxicillin."

"Some patients deny that their lifestyle interferes with their health," continues Illene. "They won't believe that being forty pounds overweight wreaks havoc on their back muscles. Or that marathoning is destroying their knees. Other patients refuse to take their medication because they just don't want to be bothered. We *deny*. Internist Dana Raymond told a patient—for the fifth time—that his smoking two packs a day was the cause of his breathing problems. Still her patient protested, 'But, Doctor, I've been smoking for twenty years and I never had this wheezing before.' "

"If I were a doctor, I wouldn't want *me* in one of the treatment rooms screaming my lungs out scaring other patients right out the door when I'm having collagen injections," says Letitia. And would you believe some patients are light-*fingered?!* "I hate checkups," says Inger Elliott, "all the needles and bloodletting and too many disgusting new tests so I compensate by occasionally stealing things . . . those very thin rubber gloves are great for housework. I once took a wonderfully cut white cotton gown from the X-ray department and sent it to people in Indonesia to make into a batik pattern for my store. Alas, it's been two and a half years and I never got it back."

A friend's daughter was furious with her doctor because she found her IUD floating in the bathtub one day—tore down to his office, handing him the gadget and yelling, "How sloppy can you *be?*" He said the answer was probably *plenty* but, in this case, what she handed him was part of a child's toy which must have been floating in the tub.

Okay, *we're* sometimes bad, but back to them. Perhaps our biggest doctor-horror is the missed or incorrect diagnosis. Marilyn Quayle, Ms. Vice-President, elected to have a complete hysterectomy rather than a more simple procedure because when her mother, a pediatrician in Indiana, found a lump in her breast, her own physician told her not to worry, he had seen many lumps in the past, was fairly certain this one was benign. Within six months the lump had grown and the cancer had spread to the lymphatic system. After breast surgery and chemotherapy, Marilyn's mother died at age fifty-six.

Nina Hyde, fashion editor of *The Washington Post,* also died of breast cancer at fifty-seven because of a missed diagnosis. Her first mammogram at age forty-nine was misread; she put off another until eight years later, by which time she had had cancer for at least three years ... biopsies revealed involvement in nineteen lymph nodes. Said Nina, "I'll tell you what's really shocking. If the cancer had been picked up, I would have had a ninety percent chance of living twenty years normally. Because it was missed, I was given a ten percent chance of living five years. It's my own fault that I didn't go back for another mammogram during the eight years."

Gene Wilder says of his wife, Gilda Radner, who died of cancer at age forty-two, "Gilda was afraid of cancer all her life [her mother died in her early sixties of stomach cancer]. Even with wonderful doctors, no one caught it soon enough because they weren't looking for it." Jim Henson, the beloved creator of the Muppets, died because the first doctor who saw him failed to diagnose his "flu-like symptoms" as pneumonia and gave him only aspirin. By the time Henson checked into the emergency room of New York Hospital, the infection had become "abrupt and potentially overwhelming," according to the doctor who treated him. "The outcome might have been different if Mr. Henson had been hospitalized only eight hours earlier."

Then there are the "too free with drugs" doctors. In his book *Head First* (Dutton), the late Norman Cousins talks about a woman who took three or four full-strength Valium a day for seven to eight years, the drug given to her by a doctor when she complained of dizziness, fainting spells, tremors in her head and hands and depression. "The pharmacist would telephone the doctor who always authorized a refill," says Cousins. "The woman said she thought Valium was something like vitamins ... so easy to renew the prescription, it didn't seem like medicine."

Years ago there was the famous "Dr. Feel Good," Max Jacobson of New York, who supplied vitamin shots containing addictive drugs to the likes of Truman Capote, Alan Jay Lerner, Eddie Fisher, Anthony Quinn, Tennessee Williams, Representative Claude Pepper of Florida, among others, his most famous patients being President and Mrs. John F. Kennedy. During Kennedy's term, Jacobson was a frequent visitor to the White House and accompanied the president on his first summit meeting to Vienna. Incredible! My own baby experience with a drug pusher came when my therapist (no medical degree but gifted) became fascinated with LSD at the time Cary Grant and other celebrities were reporting good results with it in conjunction with psychoanalysis. They didn't know until later that LSD scrambled people's brains and caused irreparable damage. Well, dear Lionel, whom I trusted *totally*, said a few sessions with LSD would speed up my "recovery." The only reason I escaped this "help" was that the sessions were 1. wildly expensive, 2. took a whole day, including the recovery, and 3. you needed a babysitter to fetch you from the doctor and sit with you until you got sane again, or as sane as you usually were. (Okay, the whole idea turned me off but sometimes you just get lucky and escape something that could ruin your life.)

And then there is the famous Elizabeth Taylor drug-prescription case. Elizabeth's personal physician and two other doctors who treated her have been accused of gross negligence for giving the actress potentially fatal doses of narcotics over a ten-year period. According to a Los Angeles deputy attorney, during one five-year period, the doctors wrote more than one thousand prescriptions for twenty controlled substances including sleeping pills, pain killers and tranquilizers. "With the kind of situation that's been created, the patient could just as easily have killed herself." (The Los Angeles District Attorney's office referred the case to the Board of Medical Assurance in the Attorney General's office. I haven't been able to glean the final outcome.)

On a less dramatic level, Dr. Mark Williams of North Carolina Memorial Hospital says, "In our geriatric clinic, I'm disappointed to have to say that probably the single most important thing I do is undo medical care: Stop medications, rearrange diagnostic tests, offer second opinions for various kinds of procedures. For example, the medications to treat hypertension can cause tremendous difficulties, sexual dysfunction, for one, fatigue, etc. Which would you prefer? Reduction of cardiovascular risk to maybe one chance in whatever or loss of sexual activity and energy and feeling good in the morning? You have to weigh carefully what the medicine is supposed to do and what would happen if the medicine wasn't there." Jennifer, a civilian, declares, "It's okay to throw out some prescriptions or not have them filled in the first place . . . you won't die of it! Doctors are too free—to put it mildly—with prescriptions, especially when you have the 'vagues,' especially when patients all *beg* for them." That noise you hear is probably Ali and Raquel applauding.

Researching for this chapter I figured I ought to check out holistic medicine and so I got hold of *What Your Doctor Won't Tell You: The Complete Guide to the Latest in Alternative Medicine* (HarperCollins) by June Heimlich, wife of the doctor who created the famous Heimlich maneuver to save victims who are choking. It's maddening if fascinating reading, not to mention confusing, because just about everything we are doing with a traditional doctor, according to Heimlich, is the wrong way to tango. From the book jacket: "For all its up-to-date technology, mainstream treatment is still based on the same violent approach to illness that called for bloodletting and poisonous drugs in centuries past. This book assesses the weapons in modern medicine's arsenal, presenting scientific evidence that many are simply ineffective and that many more— from chemotherapy to arthritis drugs—often do far more harm than good." Wow! Heimlich says: "In case you think incompetence and unnecessary surgery are a thing of the past, a recent *New York Times* story describes the current 'glut of surgeons [who] may perform too few operations to maintain peak skills.' " Yes, we've heard that.

In explaining how holistic medicine began, she says that "fueled by dissatisfaction with the impersonality of medical care and its reliance on drugs and surgery, the holistic revolution called for treating the patient as a whole person, not just a diseased gallbladder or bad heart." These new doctors, it seems, " 'stumbled' on nutritional medicine and ... set forth to train themselves in the complex subject of nutrition—no mean feat considering that nutrition is a stepchild in medical schools and nonexistent in continuing medical education courses (many of which are sponsored by pharmaceutical companies)." These doctors, Heimlich says, "encouraged their patients to take responsibility for their own health by practicing a healthy lifestyle." Aha! She predicts that in the future we'll have a "Mayo *Clinic* of Alternative Medicine."

Sounds good to *me*. Right now some kind of compromise is probably in order. There is nothing like an establishment doctor for a broken, bleeding, hurting, punctured or diseased body part—I mean they have done a *little* studying and had some experience—but to keep these things from happening, the philosophy of holistic medicine has to be sound: Keep the body healthy so you don't have to *rely* on doctors. Of course I like the *concept* of holistic medicine because it stresses *nutrition*. So, even though 98 percent of us are under the care of "regular" traditional doctors, it probably wouldn't hurt you to read this book—or others—on the subject. Heimlich, incidentally, looks great. She's sixty-five.

What *about* tests? Well, you need them, of course. *Fortune* magazine, in a comprehensive report, says the ones for blood pressure and cholesterol, pap smears and mammograms, are invaluable, but it also says, "A massive study of 169 diagnostic tests sponsored by the U.S. Department of Health and Human Services found many of the most common ones didn't tell doctors anything." It quoted Dr. Steven Woolf, editor of the *Guide to Clinical*

Preventive Services: " 'The average healthy man or woman having a physical is better off getting information on personal behavior at home and work than undergoing a battery of tests.' " *Fortune* says, "Among the most common useless tests routinely performed on people without a history of problems: chest X rays, electrocardiograms and a lung-function test called spirometry that requires you to blow air into a tube," and get this: "There is little evidence that chest X rays provide enough warning to reduce lung cancer deaths. Electrocardiograms in people without symptoms of heart trouble, such as shortness of breath or chest pain, don't predict much. A normal EKG doesn't mean you're okay, and by the time the test spots what's abnormal, your coronary arteries are often badly clogged." Whew! Dr. Woolf says women over forty should be examined for breast cancer annually and have a mammogram at age fifty. As for getting the results back, we know labs are overworked, tests sometimes misinterpreted. (Don't *you* make mistakes?) I guess we should go for the tests when a doctor recommends them but screech to a halt before we have any kind of surgery based on the findings. A great doctor will help you decide whether to "go for it" or postpone.

Three years ago I had the big three—a CAT scan, magnetic resonating imaging (M.R.I.), *and* a sonogram within a month ... I was *busy.* An endocrinologist I went to for my *hair* (I was willing to go to *any*thing to make it thicker and healthier), decided, based on blood tests, I had an excess of androgen, the male hormone that causes male baldness. Eureka! Maybe we're onto something. To see *why* excess androgen was being produced and if it might be symptomatic of a tumor, doctor went for the current belle-of-the-ball big-three tests. Darlings, if you've had them, you *know* the hours and days they take, the anxiety produced, not to mention the *(big)* bucks you or somebody pays and insurance never covers *everything.* These ran about $1,750 and *quelle* fun! I'm going to describe them whether you're hanging out the window to *hear* or not!

For the sonogram you drink six glasses of water an hour before checking into the hospital (Mt. Sinai in my case) and then hold *on*. For me to drink *one* glass of water automatically ensures having to go to the bathroom in twenty minutes. Six glasses inside of you for over an hour is like filling a rubber glove with a quart of milk (is this too vulgar?). It can be done, of course, but the result is a *very* bloated rubber glove which appears to be close to bursting—and *is*. I lie on my back and then on my side in my little white nightie in a darkened tiny room on a not uncomfortable table while Dr. Yeh, the tiny brilliant Taiwanese radiologist and his associate at Mt. Sinai, also Oriental but tall as Mount Rushmore, prod my tummy, look at me on the silvery green screen and mutter about what they are seeing. I can't catch a word, which is just as well. I am so uncomfortable I begin to cry. Finally I am released. My photographs will be studied by Dr. Yeh and the endocrinologist who sent me there. Three weeks go by with the film yet unstudied because one doctor or another is out of the country. Finally they look and think they see a tumor . . . at least they see a shadow which *might* be a growth but it's hard to tell, it might just be a shadow. Dr. X says I'd better have an M.R.I.

Off again to Mt. Sinai radiology, this time without having eaten or drunk anything so you go in clean. Into your little gown, then please could I go to the john, and they aren't cross because they are used to ladies who have to pee before *anything*. Now it's lie-down time on the gurney (incidentally, I've left out a few details like waiting for an hour to get in and their asking for the $1,200 up front). The technician wants to know are you claustrophobic. You don't think you are . . . as a little girl, you and Roberta Parker used to hide on *one* closet shelf the size of a microwave, *outdoors* is what makes you anxious. Technician explains they will be talking to you during tests, that you have a mike and can talk back. Good.

Deep breath and into the woods . . . you're slid into a white finger-shaped metal tube about as wide as *you* are but there seems to be space up beyond your head . . . reassuring since you're packed in like a camera in its carrying case down below. You notice something that looks like a coffee splatter on the wall just above your left ear, contemplate telling Mt. Sinai people about it but figure the only way it can be cleaned off is by you coming out and somebody else going into your white cave on a gurney with a sponge and they probably wouldn't be in the mood to do that. Decide to forget splatter. (I asked the man who tucked me in if *he* was ever "inside" the M.R.I. and he said yes, when they first got the machine he would be a guinea pig. Hmmmm.) So now, like a little bullet contained in its chamber, I have decided to be a Good Obedient Person. Technician has allowed me *not* to have arms strapped down to my sides underneath skinny rubber sheet. Victory meant a lot to me so I have no intention of betraying him with arm flailing. They have warned me about noise; they didn't warn me about *clanking*. It seems the only time anything is going on with an M.R.I. is when clanking happens; X-ray photography is causing the clanks. They sound exactly like the radiators in our apartment when the winter heat first comes up in the pipes, but this clanking is in my baby ear while apartment clanks are far away. Clank clank clank—at first, short sessions, then longer ones, and the last series lasts about fifteen minutes. I run through "Now I lay me down to sleep," then the 23rd Psalm, then the Lord's Prayer. Easy but over so *soon*. Next I do my alphabet game with *B's*. I told you about that already—Ann Bancroft, *B*eau Bridges, *C*andice Bergen, *D*avid Brinkley, etc. I've been playing the *B's* for a couple of months and already have twenty-three *B.B.'s* in addition to Beau Bridges, (Bruce Beresford, Brigitte Bardot, Barbara Bush, Boris Becker, Benazir Bhutto, etc.) and will probably come up with four or five more before this day is over. I even have five *K.B.'s*—*K* is a very challenging letter—Karen Black, Kim Bassinger, Kevin Bacon, Klaus Barbie, Kaye Ballard. It is rough going with the game in the M.R.I., however; your brain is crawling on its hands and knees on *nails,* what with the clanking all around your head, and you can't move a thing but your toes and your fingers . . . the old self-discipline is coming apart.

After an hour and a half, they have me out to walk around a bit and I am so soggy with gratitude I would do *anything* for them. The anything calls for returning to the tube for another hour, broken into fifteen-minute segments of picture taking. This time I use my *Cosmo* advertising presentation for something to think about and that is easier because I know it by rote and don't have to think. Finally I am sprung from the slender white tunnel and am out on Fifth Avenue. Daylight time is just in on this fine spring day and the city is still sparkly at 6:00 P.M. As I walk from Ninety-fourth Street down Fifth to Seventy-ninth to get the crosstown bus, the city is beautiful and gay and I think again that New York is magic and by some miracle I belong; I am *almost* giddy. Next day my own internist and gynecologist get into the act (they gave up on my hair years ago, which is what I'm doing with a "stranger," but I figured they ought to know about all the testing), have talked to the radiology people at Mt. Sinai and can't get a clear answer about what has been seen. On the other hand, the referring endocrinologist, the hair person, has got a clear-enough answer from Mt. Sinai radiology to suit *him.* "There's something there and you will need surgery," he informs me.

No, I am *not* relieved all the testing is not in vain. I am horrified! We now go for the third test: CAT scan. Such a cute name ... like a smart, perky old feline is going to scan your tummy through special feline glasses and report on what she sees but, alas, this test isn't cute. You drink three containers of orange-flavored, cold-cream consistency *glop* (revolting!), each container a bit more than a pint so it takes awhile to consume. I push mine right down, however, and they are very complimentary but you still have to wait half an hour for it to get distributed. You chat with the other victims. I am struck again, as I nearly always am in a laboratory, at how wildly impersonal everything is. I think you could be Queen Noor or Madonna and not get any special bedside charm as you wait. I call David to tell him I am at a Ralph Lauren fashion show. He is a *wild* worrier and I didn't want the aggravation!

My name is finally called and the technician is actually rather sweet (they *ought* to be at these prices—$450 for the CAT scan, payable in advance). They give me a suppository to put in my vagina, part of which stays in,

other part comes out. I have trouble getting the out part
out, leaving the in part *in* but I've coped with worse. I
managed to catheterize myself one day in a doctor's office,
getting a simple pap smear ... the hell with it, you don't
need to hear this. I finally manage. On the gurney I insist
on taking off pantyhose, not just sliding them down below
the knees as has been suggested—uncomfortable that
way—and shoes, though they have tried to get me to keep
shoes on. Technicians probably not thrilled to get intimate
with a lot of new strange bare feet every day. Doctor ar-
rives, introduces himself, asks why I am there. I start to
explain hair-loss problems. He encourages me to do short
version—can't blame him—which I do. I've signed a form
saying they can inject blue dye into the veins so they can
read the pictures. Ingesting dye through a tube in your
vein doesn't exactly hurt, just makes you nervous. X-ray
procedure itself is a piece of cake—you simply breathe in
and out on demand about fifty times—that I can manage.
X rays finished, comes the fun ... gas and cramps. We are
talking pain. They have warned me the dye may make me
feel "warm or even nauseous." Have these jokers actually
had *experience* with these dyes? Warm and nauseous
doesn't happen—hives and gas *do* ... big fat itchy hives
and enough gas to ... well, let's not get vulgar. You wonder if you will survive. You survive. Cramps and gas stop
in about five hours.

In a few days adorable gynecologist calls to say they
didn't find any new stuff with the CAT scan. My internist,
Dr. Eugene Cohen, calls too. Sonogram, M.R.I., the CAT
have really revealed nothing except that one original
shadow. There is still the business of the original blood
count indicating high androgen so we send me out for new
blood tests, "my doctors" acknowledging that the lab and
endocrinologist in charge of the first ones are both honorable (they *never* bad-mouth these people). New blood tests
do not reveal unusual level of androgen (testosterone) so
everybody quiets down. There *are* no more tests to take.
My hair continues to fall out. I live with it. I would just
as soon not have had those days of thinking I was facing

surgery. I *did* have a hysterectomy three years later after having *three* sonograms and a D and C.

My friend Alex Mayes had a lifesaving experience at Lenox Hill Hospital. She went in covered in spots and with 103 degrees of fever which quickly rose to 105 and they *froze* her ... a very good thing to do apparently because the fever came down. While she had such a high fever, her husband did a lot of research and determined she had Coxsackie fever—so named because it is transmitted by a bug first identified in Coxsackie, New York, but the doctor said no, she didn't have anything that came from Coxsackie, her problem was toxic-shock syndrome. His diagnosis was correct. I can't say enough good things about New York Hospital, where I had the hysterectomy. San Francisco socialite Clarissa Dyer has had *four* operations in the last few years—a hysterectomy, gallbladder removal, calcified ankle clot removed and breast surgery. "I'm fine. The doctors were all sensational." Surgery isn't all demoralizing.

Friends who've had considerable experience with hospitals offer this advice: In addition to reasons already given for having a regular doctor, even if you don't see him often, this person can get you into an emergency room in a hurry if you're dying or doing something a *bit* less drastic. Alex Mayes, who has been in both conditions, says, "Yuppies don't have regular doctors and they come to an emergency room with anything from tennis elbow to hives. The hospital has to take them in—they can't turn anyone down. You need a regular doctor to get you admitted fast." Russian Tea Room owner Faith Stewart-Gordon says, "They aren't just whistling 'Moon over Miami' when they tell you to get booked for surgery first thing in the morning—the first or second to be operated on. It's not just that the surgeon is probably fresher, it's the agony of waiting. When I needed surgery, the surgeon was going on vacation for a month and I could either take the last slot of the day or wait for him to come back. I chose surgery. Well, all prepped and ready to go, you wait in your room with nothing to think about but what's ahead. At least there you can walk around, but then they take you to the surgical waiting area on a gurney and *that* wait can be several hours. By the time your turn comes, you're ready to hurl yourself under somebody's gurney and let it run *over* you." Jennifer says it's okay to be a pain in the A. at the hospital to get what you need for a loved one. They will despise you but probably come through.

Of course, there *are* cases of doctors and hospital being really careless and negligent. Actress Peggy Cass woke up from a knee operation at Lenox Hill Hospital to find that the doctor had operated on the wrong *knee.* She was wheeled back into surgery and the correct procedure was performed (she later won $460,000 in a lawsuit against the doctor and the hospital).

Pat Bradshaw, the widow of Thornton Bradshaw, chairman and CEO of RCA, wrote me a nine-page single-spaced report of a ghoulish twelve-hour day spent in a New York hospital where she arrived for emergency treatment for a kidney stone, was never ensconced in the private room booked for her, was shuttled to many different parts of the hospital including ice-cold corridors without a blanket, totally ignored, then insulted when she tried to flag down an attendant, mistaken for another patient, refused help when her IV post fell to the floor with needle still in arm, denied morphine to ease the pain when it got unbearable (morphine had been standard procedure for a kidney stone, used for her on a previous visit to the hospital and was in her records), never taken to the john, not released after kidney stone passed by *itself* midafternoon but kept five more hours for a series of X rays her doctor hadn't ordered, unable to telephone the doctor who was supposed to meet her at the hospital but didn't (what happened to *him?!*), not allowed to phone a friend—a Kafka-esque scenario for this most intelligent, (usually) good-natured, wealthy, well-connected person.

Apparently most victims don't sue hospitals. Medical writer Jane Brody reports in *The New York Times* that in a comprehensive study by Harvard University of 31,000 patients hospitalized in New York State, 3.7 percent suffered an injury as a result of medical care. For about 1 percent of the patients, the injury was caused by medical negligence and sometimes resulted in permanent disability or death. Yet only one suit was filed for every 9.6 cases of negligence determined by experts who reviewed the hospital records. The reasons: People are too distraught to think of lawsuits, families may not be aware that an egregious error was responsible for the outcome, it is hard to prove that malpractice compromised the chances for a cancer cure, or people are just forgiving, feeling everyone makes mistakes.

I doubt that I would ever sue. I think you just get the most competent, high-powered if possible (that means on the teaching staff of a hospital) doctors you can and pray the hospital staff is competent, too. Then I think we stay *away* from the pros as much as we can and take care of ourselves, though *sometimes* we need professional help.

Surgery. Could I just say this as somebody who's had it but thinks much could be avoided? People who *don't* take care of themselves like to blame the fates, their genealogy (Dad had two gallbladder operations before he was forty), their city (all that stress, dirt and smog), bosses and companies (I haven't had a real vacation in two years), let alone *age* for having to have things removed or rearranged, but *some* of it is surely up to us. Common sense would surely indicate you aren't so likely to have to go through surgery if you don't smoke, drink, do drugs, overeat, eat the wrong things ... if you sleep, exercise and have work that engages you. Of course, if you don't go to a doctor when something *is* wrong (you ache, see blood in the stool or urine, can hardly drag yourself to work, etc., etc.), then you are Asking For It. By the time you go, something really could be wrong, surgery the only option. After everybody with an IUD was urged a few years ago to have it checked or removed, a friend of mine *didn't* ... peritonitis set in, then pneumonia, then kidney trouble; it looked as though she'd *never* get out of the hospital. Some people perhaps *need* to be sick, even to the point of an operation. The illness and surgery bring attention, punish despised "loved ones," excuse one from work or life's challenges, but I will acknowledge that most conditions requiring surgery, give or take a little body battering just mentioned, aren't the sufferer's fault.

Some problems don't get solved, of course. I mentioned *Cosmo*'s gifted editor, Barbara Creaturo, who fought ovarian cancer for three years—five bouts of surgery and untold other procedures—and died this year at forty-nine. My late brother-in-law lived with chronic pain for thirty years, twenty-five of them married to my sister. An accident in an Oklahoma grain elevator had crushed his shoulder, and doctors at the time had not sorted out the nerves and put them back together satisfactorily. He had numerous unsuccessful operations in Oklahoma to reorganize the nerves. None worked and I brought him to New York for surgery with a noted neurologist at New York University Hospital. That didn't help either. Disconnecting some of the nerves came close to rendering him incontinent. George next went to a hypnotist who used many kinds of gadgets to help distract patients from the pain— worth a shot but didn't work. Acupuncture arrived after President Richard Nixon's visit to mainland China and, though it wasn't legal in the United States, with the help of Robert Evans, then production chief at Paramount Pictures and a heavyweight Las Vegas attorney pal of *his*, we got George fixed up with a Chinese acupuncturist in Santa Monica, California. The pain didn't go away. Finally, my psychiatrist, Herbert Walker, called the head of the psychiatric department at the University of Oklahoma and set up an appointment for George, Mary and me. I flew back to Shawnee, where my sister lives, collected her and my brother-in-law and early one Friday morning we were on our way to the city. The psychiatrist assigned George to a medical doctor who gave him injections to try to kill the nerves (and the pain) and maybe it did finally kill the original pain—hard to tell—but that pain was replaced by *new* pain . . . so-called chronic pain which, even if "phantom," hurts just as much. So I know second*hand* anyway about serious (unsolvable) medical problems and, no, there *isn't* anything worse, is there? Mental problems perhaps, but somehow physical ravage and pain seem worse to me. So, we bless everything if we are reasonably clear of them and try surely to keep it that way.

What about psychiatry for somebody as old as us? If you haven't figured yourself out by now, should you bother? I think so. How can it possibly hurt to try to get a little relief from emotional pain when it gets bad? I don't go regularly now, just a check-in occasionally when things are a little woolly, but I doubt I would ever have got married *or* achieved whatever I have without shrinkage. And I never want to be without this particular help if needed. A shrink can so quickly help you figure out who's exploiting you (it may be *you!*), who the good guys and bad guys are. He/she positively will not let you go on bad-mouthing somebody who isn't very bad or good-mouthing somebody who is a schmuck.

David tells me I am crazier than ever, so why bother with a shrink since I *did* that already (starting about forty-five years ago). I explain craziness is not the point. You may not get any un-*crazier* but you do feel more comfortable and can get a few things sorted out even in one session. Shrinks go a lot faster than they used to . . . the ones I know tell me old formal Freudian heavy analysis isn't so usual now because nobody has the time or money. My friend Charlotte Veal's psychiatrist tells her it is his duty to correct her *distortions* (about herself and life). Carin Burrows, whose gifted husband, Pulitzer Prize winner Abe Burrows, died after a long siege with Alzheimer's, said her life was immeasurably benefited by seeing a therapist.

I have never had a bad experience with a psychiatrist except possibly with the Pasadena doctor I consulted with end-of-the-world personal and financial problems, who wanted to know if my mother was "putting out," as he called it. I didn't even know what that meant. Translation: He didn't approve of my single-girl sex life and wondered if I had possibly learned it from Mom. (Cleo slept with a total of two men her whole life, both of whom she married first.)

As for regular doctors, though I don't go often, I *trust* doctors and go meek and childlike in their offices, do you? And one has been known to *cry*. Some of us may tend to overdo *that* a bit because we feel so "safe" there and wouldn't do it any other place. They can't throw you *out,* though I came close when I had my nose done and wept so hysterically right on the table presurgery the doctor said he was going to ship me back to my room if I didn't shut up. I couldn't see going through *that* again ... revving up, getting druggy and finally shipped *up* to surgery so I quit. He'd already given shipping instructions ... it was *close.* My other crying spectacular was in the office of oral surgeon Dr. Stanley Berman who removed a lower right molar. This *not* unimpressive display of nonstop crying lasted from 2:45 to 4:15 P.M. when surgery took place. Having a tooth removed doesn't hurt, of course. The weeps had to do with aging and not being able to save your hair or your teeth or other things you used to think were *permanent.*

I'll just say again, it seems to me, if you get the top of the line, there is *nothing* in the world like a great doctor. You certainly want to go to the best in your city. In a big city, it probably doesn't hurt to find out where the rich people go if you can and sign up. These doctors aren't hard to *find;* getting an appointment is something else. Helps to get referred by another doctor but you might get in by mentioning another *patient.* Not all "society doctors" or cream-of-the-city are that welcoming, but doctors are usually doctors first—they want to heal—and they like nice patients (like you) who appreciate their wisdom and listen to them and who don't give them a bad time. As you do with other people, you can probably charm your way into this person's care.

You won't be dealing with him but with his nurse on prices. That is something else. Barbara Ehrenreich, in a *Time* essay, says, "The U.S. health system may be one of the few instances of social pathology that truly deserves to be compared to cancer. It grows uncontrollably—in terms of dollars—but seems to become more dysfunctional with every metastatic leap. . . . For the uninsured and the underinsured—who amount to twenty-eight percent of the population—a diagnostic workup can mean a missed car payment; a child's sore throat, an empty dinner table. Even among those fortunate enough to be insured, the leading side effect of illness is often financial doom. . . . Even with Medicare, older Americans are forced to spend more than fifteen percent of their income for medical care annually." That's a tough statement—and tough reality. I know about catastrophic medical expenses. My widowed mother was cleaned *out* paying for my sister Mary's care after polio struck, this before any kind of affordable medical insurance existed, and we didn't have that much to clean *out*. March of Dimes paid for one operation; everything else was on us. There isn't much question that worry about money grew me up fast and was the main motivation for any success I've had. The Hearst Corporation which I work for has a wonderful medical plan so I'm blessed. It covers David, too. I hope you are managing okay with *your* insurance.

On the good side, there have been fantastic breakthroughs in medicine and surgery. Cataract surgery is almost 100 percent effective now after modern extraction with intraocular lens implant (I.O.L.). Hearing-aid equipment is getting smaller and smaller . . . so small, in fact, it's almost a problem for some people to *see* the 3/16 of an inch hearing aid *battery* that has to be *installed*. People who have never been helped with amplification now can be, and in five years they expect a sensational breakthrough with a small computer in every hearing aid. My doctors also mentioned these medical breakthroughs: Nonsteroidal drugs to treat arthritis pain. These include Indocin, Naprosyn, Clinoril, Orudis and others. The treatments are so simple, and many doctors say the results are remarkable. Add gallbladder surgery to the list. With certain procedures you can now enter the hospital on Wednesday, be operated on on Thursday and released to go home on Friday. And we all know the shorter the stay in the hospital, the quicker you probably are going to recover.

But let's stay *out* of the hospital. I will if *you* will. *Promise* me you will do *some* of those things I've been pushing.

chapter ten

Work

About every ten days David says to me after a battering day, "Why are we *doing* this . . . knocking ourselves senseless . . . we don't need the money!" I get so bored with his question and *he* must get tired of the same old answer. A. *I* need the money—there will never be enough to make me feel secure, though my paycheck goes directly to David's office and I haven't seen it in years. B. People like us—like me anyway—don't work for money. Work is our chloroform . . . our *life* . . . our freedom from pain . . . supplier of esteem . . . our beloved, dependable friend who *almost* never lets us down. Unlike personal relationships—or *some* personal relationships anyway—if I give everything to my work, I get it back; the more I give, the more I get. The harder I work, the better I become and the more I get paid and the bigger fuss people make over me.

I don't put anything else in the same league satisfaction-wise, including love of a man. I don't think work is *more* important than man/woman love but I think it is just *as:* this wonderful thing that occupies your brain and your soul and gets you out of the house and out of yourself and keeps you out of (too much) *trouble.* Yes, I have what might be called a big job but I felt that way *pretty* much when I was making thirty-five dollars a week as a secretary . . . even though in 1942 every woman was supposed not to want to work any longer than necessary.

Work can make you beautiful. Or at least make people forget you *aren't.* I was at the Music Box Theatre for the memorial service for Irving Berlin and assembled on stage were possibly some of the worst sets of legs and ankles I have ever seen, and I could really see because their owners were seated on straight-backed chairs on stage right in front of me. I won't mention names; most were singers, all famous and, God *knows*, talented. One had on a gray flannel dress so voluminous it *sort* of shaded feet, legs, ankles and definitely camouflaged girth (close to battleship proportions). Another wore a shapeless schmata and boots so her ankles were not all that visible but as for overall impression of lower extremities: solid enough to hold up the World Trade Center. Two participants were over eighty, so whatever their ankles were looking like is okay with me—nothing physical holds up the way it might have earlier. Yet, these singers (and one actress who spoke) were so divine, gifted, pleasure-giving, I actually wept as they sang Irving Berlin's incredible music and I thought to myself, schmuck, you are thinking legs and ankles and it can't matter *less*. These people's *work* has made them beautiful.

You already knew that about work? I know it, too. I was permanently impacted early by the knowledge that I wasn't beautiful and would need to fall back on other things (if we could figure out what the other things *were*). My mother said frequently that pretty girls get all the spoils, failing to mention *ever* that I could possibly be *one* of them. I probably looked *okay,* just not thrilling, but since *nobody*—other little children, their parents, teachers, aunts, uncles—ever said anything to contradict Cleo's assessment, I *felt* not pretty.

Not being able to hack it with looks, I finally came to hack it with work. Work not only makes *them* forget pretty, *you* forget and can go long stretches without even looking in a mirror. Work makes you *smart*, not the other way around. An office was my math and algebra, history, economics, financial, political, social and charm school. I learned some things (not much) about decorating and food there, quite a lot about fashion (you work with girls with taste). What I really learned was survival. Give or take a few firings, I survived from age eighteen (when I began working for an announcer at radio station KHJ in Los Angeles for six dollars a week) to age seventy, which I am now, with only four weeks away between jobs when I was fired. I don't know too much about how to *play!* Eating, making love, cultural stuff and talking with friends are my play—forget parties, picnics, banquets and barbecues. I feel anyone can do what I have done who starts *early* enough and hangs on, doggedly, even *without* great talent, and works her butt off, isn't a pain in the ass, doesn't ask for too much money, says yes to every possible thing that could make her more valuable to her bosses (short of going to bed with any you don't want to or saddle-soaping the conference-room chairs), who changes jobs occasionally to get something better, tries to be good enough so she won't get dumped for somebody better or have her job eliminated altogether.

I've written in *Having It All* about getting fired several times as I journeyed through those seventeen secretarial jobs, and you can withstand *that* if you just pitch in and get a new job. Need surely motivates—in my case *no* money so I hit the deck running after high school with a little time out to learn shorthand and typing (now it would be computer and word processing). I lived with a widowed, seriously depressed mother, a wheelchair-bound sister, had terminal acne, love affairs with unmarriageable (already married or Don Juans) men, but all that boring, squirrelly work (which I wasn't very good at until my seventeenth secretarial job!) finally got me there/here. I began to blossom around age thirty-one—quite a trek from the teenage beginning.

I've often mentioned that I think one is blessed to have grown up in the Depression when you needed to take almost any job after you got out of school to support yourself. No soul searching or deciding this scruffy little thing they are offering simply isn't *me!* So much harder when you have the option of *not* working, are the child of indulgent parents who will subsidize you while you are "finding yourself" or pay the bills when you are "between assignments."

I had hoped to marry somebody wealthy and solve all my family's and my financial problems. Alas, I didn't have the credentials—looks, family background, emotional stability (I *did* have the youth ... we all get *that*). But then, living through a man is a hard way to make a living. I think I *always* knew that and was mercifully "spared." Now I think of those wealthy married women who don't work ... and them you can't envy (and *I* can envy just about anything if I put my mind to it). Maybe when the woman is about thirty-two and the mother of two golden children, all of them featured regularly in *Town & Country*, you could get a twinge of I-want-to-be-her, but depending on *his* money and approval instead of your own accomplishments is tricky. Later these women get to be really vulnerable ... trade-ins (of them for somebody younger) are a constant threat, though it will *cost* him. If he's rich, famous and *attractive*, trouble in River City! Even if he's not famous or attractive, just rich, you're at risk. Never mind rich, and forgive me for mentioning it, marriage and children do not guarantee happiness for a woman just as being without a man or child does not ensure misery. This is the conclusion of Grace Baruch, Rosalind Barnett and Caryl Rivers after interviewing hundreds of women for their book, *Lifeprints: New Patterns of Love and Work for Today's Woman* (McGraw-Hill). "Most women find career satisfaction to be the most rewarding aspect of their lives," the authors report.

So, okay, never mind that most of us aren't representing our country at a Geneva arms-treaty conference or closing in on a cancer cure, work is for getting respect ... feeling useful ... wanted ... for contributing somehow to the world's business. Work is also about *structure*. Throw a lot of stems, hands, pistons on a counter and you have a mess; put together they're a Rolex. Work holds you together like a Rolex.

What David is talking about when he asks why we are working like this (as I write, he is running a movie company, Island World, producing movies—*A Few Good Men, The Player, The Midnight Club, The Cemetery Club, Watch It*—through his own company, The Manhattan Project, has had two plays—*Tru* and *A Few Good Men*—succeed on Broadway, produced a television series for HBO—*Women and Men*—has written two books, has a

contract for another, has just received—with his former
partner Richard D. Zanuck—the Irving G. Thalberg Memorial Award, the Motion Picture Academy of Arts and
Sciences' highest award) is that some days frustrations are
fierce. I won't try to tell you what a movie producer does
but I have observed they mostly wait for somebody (star,
director, writer, distributor, banker) to say no (*yes* would
have been preferred) and are rarely "disappointed"; fur-
thermore, these people never say it nicely or promptly.
Movie people are the absolute *worst* about returning calls.
So on days of super pique he says he only works because
I won't let him stay home in his brown bathrobe.

He is, of course, full of baloney. He works, as I do,
because the alternative—lack of focus, challenge, recogni-
tion, applause (not money in his case)—would be too
painful to bear. Your mind gets soggy, plus you don't get
asked many places. Your friends love you anyway but the
others—those whose brains and achievements have quick-
ened your life up to now—don't come around much after
you quit. Who can blame them? We can all fit just so
much in and they haven't got time to spend with merely
nice folk who don't do anything official. They simply
won't talk to you at parties (I'm very big on who won't
talk to you at parties!). Women discriminate against non-
workers just as men do. Edward R. Downe, founder of
Downe Communications, which published *American
Home, Ladies' Home Journal* and other properties, and
now a private investor, told me he was asked what he did
by the elegant Park Avenue ladies seated on both his left
and right at a dinner party recently. When he said "nothing," that was the last he heard from either for an hour and
a half though they remained seated together.

Afraid I'm running on like a freight train here. Writing about work—even narrowing it to *women* who work or
older women who work, which ought to be the point—is
probably like trying to cram the history of the Peloponne-
sian Wars, the fluctuation of the Japanese yen since 1980
and the creation of the universe into one tiny little address
book: The subject is just too big for cramming. A work

treatise isn't necessarily fascinating reading. In every issue
of *Cosmo* we include career articles but never mention
them in a cover blurb because "Improve Your Management Skills in Three Weeks" or "How to Get Your Boss to
Stop Embarrassing Everybody in Meetings" isn't how you
attract readers. And yet work can be a miracle . . . can get
you from there to here. Pablo Picasso once said, "The pas-
sions that motivate you may change, but it is your work in
life that is the ultimate seduction." Neil Simon, author of
twenty-five plays, many of them smash hits *(The Odd
Couple, Barefoot in the Park, Plaza Suite, Jake's Women),*
Pulitzer Prize winner for *Lost in Yonkers,* said recently, "I
had one analyst tell me she thought . . . I didn't allow myself to enjoy my success long enough. I asked her what the
out-date was. One month? Three months? I don't want to
be like the woman who wrote *Abie's Irish Rose* and then
traipsed around the country with it for fifteen years. This
year's play is this year's play and I'm happy if it's a hit,
but it's on to the next one. I feel empty without something
to work on." On and off the richest man in the United
States, John Warner Kluge, seventy-seven, says, "The
thing I like best is not the score—that means nothing—it's
the game, seeking new challenges. I have hated weekends
all my life and I still do."

For me work surely is the ultimate seduction. Even
now I can't believe I've piloted a successful magazine so
long or am what is called . . . an *executive?? Moi?!* Okay,
it's not General Motors but about fifty people report to me
and considering where I *started*—being screamed at daily
on my first little job when I synopsized listener letters for
my announcer-boss at radio station KHJ in Los Angeles so
he could say on the air where a birthday child was supposed to look for his present and I had the kid look out in
the toolshed instead of searching under the divan and boy
did we hear from the mamas—to where I am *now*—we'd
have to call it *progress,* I suppose. A lot of days I feel that
this is finally the day they will realize I am a fraud. Yet
Cosmo has been the sixth top newsstand seller among all
magazines for twenty-six years, number one among all
women's magazines, the top seller on college campuses

for thirteen years. We publish in twenty-seven foreign countries . . . not *too* shabby a track record.

If I'd been born in post-feminist years, I would surely have wanted to own the magazine and keep all the money accruing from such a successful product but I have never really wanted that for one *hour.* I like doing what *I* do well—the creative stuff—and am happy to let the Hearst Corporation who own *Cosmo* deal with print orders, press runs, distribution, capital investments. We have been the perfect team all these years, me behaving like a dutiful daughter, always eager to please, them the appreciative parents. I have two bosses—Hearst's president and CEO and the president of the magazine division. You can't even call them bosses in terms of their *ever* telling me what or what not to put in the magazine but they can *fire* me and they control the budget—what I can spend on product, salaries and raises. I also enjoy a close personal relationship with the Hearst family. Gloria Steinem has chided me for not being on the Hearst board of directors, considering the dollars *Cosmo* brings in. I don't need it. It's been a wonderful—massive understatement—arrangement for *me.* I get stroked nearly hourly. I make a lot of money. They treat me like a princess. I *know* I'm blessed.

I always have, always *will* run scared. Don Hewitt, the brilliant creator and producer of *60 Minutes,* CBS's long-top-rated television news show, told me recently when we were discussing people out of work, "The first step to getting fired is complacency. The minute you feel comfortable, you're asking for it! You always have to see if life, the competition, are gaining on you and do it *better* than you did it before." Don is seventy. The show has been running twenty-four years. When Mike Wallace, one of his stars, collapsed at the San Francisco airport last year, Don said, "Oh, shit, Mike's gone, now we'll never pass *Cheers* [in the ratings]." I'm not in the Hewitt/ Wallace league, to put it mildly, but I surely identify with the dissatisfaction with one's achievements.

My husband advises me to "be happy with what you have achieved . . . no one can take that away from you." Is that ridiculous? Of *course* they can't take it away, but

like the most exquisite lobster quenelle you ever tasted (in
Antibes fifteen years ago) or dancing under the stars in
Waikiki when you were thirty . . . what good does that do
you *now?!* I don't know anything about the offices of tycoons and moguls with De Koonings and Chagalls on the
walls, leather couches soft as baby skin, Cordon-Bleu-
trained chefs in private dining rooms, conference rooms
with state-of-the-art electronics better than the Pentagon's.
I just know about small busy squares or rectangles with
computers, word processors, files and telephones, gray,
beige or brown really nothingburger desks. For so many
years I shared offices with other secretaries. Now I have
my own but *Architectural Digest* doesn't send scouts.
When we moved from the fourth floor of the Argonaut
Building eight years ago to the eighth floor, I just had
them take the office upstairs exactly as it had been four
floors below—didn't even take *that* opportunity to trade
up. My office has flowered-cloth walls, an armoire, fake
Queen Anne desk, a love seat with lots of pillows, two of
which are needlepointed I LOVE CHAMPAGNE, CAVIAR AND
CASH and GOOD GIRLS GO TO HEAVEN, BAD GIRLS GO EVERY-
WHERE, and two sets of dumbbells. Never mind its appointments, offices give girls like me a culture in which to
sprout, become a philodendron.

Ratty stuff does not quit *happening* to you in any job.
This isn't exactly typical of a trying day, but at the launch
of Spanish *Cosmo* recently, I'm in a great European city,
Madrid, in one of the best and most expensive hotels in
the world, the Ritz. Generous good people, executives at
Gruner & Jahr, our partners in this venture, are hosts—it
should have been spectacular. The day begins with my
husband waking me at 7:10, like maids used to do,
clanking around opening doors, "just checking." Jet-
lagged to smithereens, I planned to sleep until 8:00 but am
so mad at David I can't go back to sleep so I aardvark
around in a fog in our sumptuous suite, exercise for an
hour (talk about self-abuse), work at my hair and makeup
(sunken raccoon eyes require fifteen minutes apiece), arrive in Ritz lobby at 9:15 for first appointment. First appointment never shows. I eat sweet rolls, doze on the

couch, curse. Next three appointments—people from various newspapers—arrive *reasonably* on time—nobody more than half an hour late (this is *Spain!*). After giving it the old hard sell through an interpreter, and smiling up a storm for three different sets of photographers for the next three hours, I'm pooped. Suggest to PR person we cancel appointment right after lunch so I can conk out at hotel for a nap before first TV show. Interview canceled but PR person doesn't understand *why* and substitutes reporter who didn't show in the morning. *Try,* without stupendous success, to be civil . . . don't want to alienate new partners by having giant temper tantrum in classy Spanish restaurant.

Soon after, television interview takes place. First four questions: What, in your opinion, is the biggest problem of a transsexual? Tell us about your first lovemaking session (e.g., how old were you and how did you lose your virginity). How old are you *now?* What fantasy would you recommend a girl enact to get an impotent man to perform? These people obviously not real interested in merits of new magazine. Next stop radio station where Spanish *Cosmo* editor (a terrific girl) suggests I read a message about new magazine *in* Spanish, hands me a double-spaced typed page in my new language. I practice. I sound like somebody who has swallowed a word processor and is trying to cough up letters eight or nine at a time. Moronic! I can't even pronounce *buenas tardes* correctly. They decide typing words *phonetically* might help. Nóon-kah ah ah-bée-doe óo-nah pu-blee-káh-sea-own kó-mo és-tah én és-tay pie-eés. (Literally: Never has there been a publication like this in this country.) Lah chée-kah *Cosmo* es-pah-nyó-lah ah es-tá-doe es-pay-rhón-doe cone pó-kah pah-sea-én-sea-ah és-tay ah-cone-táy-sea-mee-en-toe. (Literally: The Spanish *Cosmo* girl has been waiting, with little patience, for this event.) Humiliating to be so really bad with people I want to *impress.* Zombied my way through the rest of the afternoon interviews, then dinner with business community (advertisers!) to close down shop around 2:00 A.M. Sleeplessness apparently a serious problem for Spanish executives . . . no problem for *me.* I wasn't really conscious during the last two hours of dinner.

You'll be relieved to know the launch was a big success and the first issue sold out in less than a week and we went back to press.

Most of one's tough days are not so exotic. You get rotten phone calls. A rival editor-friend is stealing one of your key people for twice the money, an advertiser is livid about his positioning, lighting for the fashion shots looks like participants were inside a cave. The article you thought would blow them away will cement them in place—at somebody else's magazine (it came in, was terrible, you said they could sell it elsewhere). Rejections are de rigueur. Tom Cruise not only won't release a Herb Ritts picture of himself in blue jeans but is calling his attorney to see if we can be stopped from using *any* picture of him in a poster with other famous men. (Is this child taking himself a *little* seriously or *what?!*) You survive. Model agency tycoon Eileen Ford says the cruddy stuff is *life* . . . it's on the agenda every week and some weeks every *day*.

So let's get to *you*. How many older women *are* working? According to the Bureau of Labor Statistics, four out of ten workers in 1990 were women over the age of fifty-five and in the three traditional "female" classifications (clerical, sales and service), women over forty-five represent 56.9 percent of those workers. (Don't you hate statistics? But I have to use official ones occasionally so you don't think I'm making up my own.) Still, lots of women over fifty don't have jobs and that might include *you*. How possible is it to *get* a job if you're, say, sixty and have been out of the work force a long time, were never *in* it or were in it until recently but have been fired?

Challenging. Very challenging. Virginia M. Hall and Joyce A. Wessel cite, in the Atlanta *Journal-Constitution,* a *Modern Maturity* story that found "all across the country an insidious and sometimes illegal age discrimination being practiced against older job seekers." They quote a job-hunting kindergarten teacher in Sheboygan, Wisconsin, in her fifties. " 'If you're an older person, you can't get anywhere in this town.' " Another woman talked of calling about a job and, as soon as she gave her age (fifty-nine), they hung up. Andrew Grove, author of *High Output Man-*

agement, also quoted in *Modern Maturity,* says part of the problem for older people is that " 'many hiring supervisors in today's workplaces are themselves comparatively young. A 30-year-old manager may feel awkward about supervising someone who could be his father or mother and may want to avoid such a situation by ignoring the résumé.' " Age discrimination against women isn't any worse than against men, incidentally.

God knows older people are good *workers.* A study by the National Commission on Working Women of Wider Opportunities for Women, as reported in *The Washington Post,* concludes that "it's cost-effective for an employer to hire an older woman." Its reasons: " ▪ The median job tenure of women fifty-five to sixty-four years is 10.3 years, three times that of women twenty-five to thirty-four years. ▪ Research shows that workers in their fifties and sixties function intellectually as well or better than workers in their twenties and thirties. ▪ Corporate studies show older workers are more dependable, have better attendance and do as much work as younger workers."

Okay, how do you get a job if you need one and work isn't what you have been doing in recent years or maybe ever? You sign up with employment agencies, of course, though nobody is real friendly to older women, especially those not equipped with skills. My friend Berna Linden, sixty-six, long-time successful Beverly Hills real-estate agent, who went back to work at age forty-four after being widowed, says, "I think anybody at any age can get a job if she really wants to and has a skill. If I were a never-employed or not recently-employed older woman looking for a job, I would learn to type, use a word processor, go to computer school, learn *something* so you're armed when you hunt. Being in your sixties isn't the point . . . having something to offer *is.*"

Of *course,* there are other kinds of jobs than those in offices and you want to figure out what you're *good* at, so you can match talent with what's out there. Maybe you can do research, cater, grow or arrange flowers, sew, shop, teach, style, sell. Selling sounds scary but takes only *quiet* guts. Most of the *Cosmo* sales staff is female, and these women are anything but brash, just persevering. Selling surely produces *bucks*.

Along with registering with agencies to get a job, you answer newspaper ads. Most won't fit your needs and vice versa but give it a shot. Networking is probably the best job opener for an older woman: Hit on friends, *their* friends, husbands of friends—especially husbands of friends—sons-in-law, neighbors. Bother everybody short of being such a pest they don't give you a job just because you are so irritating! Ask your doctors and dentists if they need office help—big turnover in that category. Ask owners or managers where you shop—boutique, florist, beauty salon, restaurant. Offer to work cheap, work hard and you *could* work for nothing during a break-in period, say one month, while both of you see if the merger is going to be satisfactory.

Sylvia Lyons, widowed at sixty-six, got a job—without experience—in a travel agency and has guided groups to China, Tuscany, Budapest, you name it, ever since. Sylvia is eighty-one. My favorite rich-girl-parted-from-her-riches, back-to-work story is that of Simone Levitt, wife of William Levitt, who created Levittown, the first inexpensive but *good* housing for GIs returning from World War II. Early in their marriage, Simone had a yacht named for her—*La Belle Simone*. I can see her out on deck of this floating palace in the Barbados sunshine, instructing her crew—about two dozen bronzed, white-shirted, Bermuda-shorted good-looking young people plus captain and engineer ... it was a *sight*. After Bill's fortunes changed, Simone went to work—I mean *work*. She searched job possibilities like any other hunter, finally persuaded the Cunard Line—boats were what she knew best—to let her create some special La Belle Simone cruises. You think that was *fun*—calling up people who were once your guests to see if they'd like to *pay* for a cruise?! The project prospered for one season. Simone is now buying for Janet Brown stores, starting a travel agency.

What about the ambivalent? My friend Elizabeth *thinks* she wants a job, speaks *longingly* of work ("I've got

to get a *job;* will you help?!"), seeing working-women
pals more life-involved than she, but since Elizabeth is
wealthy, social, married, and needs to be free to travel
with her husband on business trips, whatever any of us
comes up with is never pursued. I think she is deeply ambivalent, plus also deeply *scared.* The catch for many
older women somewhat like Elizabeth is that they want
Worthy. The job should be challenging, interesting, well-
paid, in pleasant surroundings not too far from home with
nice people just like them! Failing to find such a job—a
distinct possibility when you're starting out—they cluck
and fume and stay home. "Forget worthy, forget glamour,"
says Berna Linden. "Get the job. It will at least classify
you as a working woman. Get some experience and gradually trade up."

Betty Furness, who had plenty of experience looking
for work through a variety of careers—film and stage actress, television commercial spokesman, presidential assistant for consumer affairs—before becoming, as she was
until recently, consumer reporter for NBC, says, "Middle-
aged women should never turn up their noses at entry-
level jobs and should fake only one thing: confidence. No
one wants to know you're scared. It makes them scared
themselves. Appear to be absolutely sure of yourself and,
if you aren't, be an actress!" Is that wonderful? "I think an
entry-level job is just dandy," Betty says. "The important
thing is to get your foot in the door. Take a job, any job.
Gofer, file clerk, secretary. Whatever is offered. Once you
are inside, look around and see what else is available.
When you're job hunting, go back and go back and go
back, determined not to take no as a final answer. But if
rejection is all that you can get, don't take it personally. It
goes with the territory of looking for work. Expose yourself to as much humiliation as you can bear, then go home
and go at it all over again tomorrow!"

Liz Carpenter said in her book, *Getting Better All the
Time,* that you have to believe in yourself. Everybody says
that, but I never have. Not from earliest job days to now—
not for one hour! What I have believed in and still do is
that if you do the really best you can, put the ass behind

it, based on your talent, limits and liabilities, you will probably come out pretty good. What you believe in is the *record* that says you did it okay so you probably can again. Just an all-out, here-I-am-world, unadulterated belief in yourself as a real great little cookie—well, that condition has *eluded* me!

A very big field for women of *whatever* age is entrepreneuring. Nearly one third of small businesses in the United States today belong to women and many people predict that by the turn of the century, women will own 50 percent of small businesses in America. Women increasingly have been starting businesses in industries where they rarely owned businesses before, such as transportation, construction and manufacturing. We know restaurants, weight-loss and exercise programs, PR firms are started by women. And we all know the biggies: Estée Lauder, Liz Claiborne, Adrienne Arpel, Debbie Fields of cookie fame, Martha Stewart, Lillian Vernon, Diane Von Furstenberg, Eileen Ford, who have made millions or close to. Estée is said to be one of the twenty richest women in the world. Maybe you won't be a major tycoon, but if you want to start a company, lots of advice is available. You might start by writing to the Office of Women's Business Ownership, U.S. Small Business Administration, 1441 L Street N.W., Room 414, Washington, D.C. 20416 (202/653-4000).

Want to write a book? Hundreds get published every year by people who never wrote before. For a novel, it may be best to write the whole thing, so a prospective publisher can tell whether it hangs together to the end. You don't need to if your sample chapters are outstanding and your outline good, but these days, the chances for a first novelist are so poor, the more ammunition the better. With nonfiction, submitting a couple of chapters plus a complete outline may do it. That's how I sold *Sex and the Single Girl,* not ever having had even a magazine article published before. Quite a few agents will handle unpublished writers. Look in the *LMP (Literary Market Place),* found in any library. It's updated each year and includes a long section on agents in every part of the country, what kinds of properties they represent and how to approach them—query letter, full manuscript, outline, whatever.

If you want to try for a magazine assignment, you *could* send a query letter *or* the finished article to whoever is listed on the masthead as articles, managing or executive editor. If you are not a big-shot writer, you might offer to write on "spec"—paid only if the piece is accepted. Study several issues of a magazine to see what kind of stuff they *use:* Is what you are sending or suggesting anything *like* their usual articles in terms of theme or style? *Cosmo* gets lots of queries about gardening, medical malpractice, profiles of subjects only three other people have ever heard of—we don't profile "civilians" no matter how admirable. Don't go just for huge-circulation magazines; dozens of small magazines use free-lance material. In my opinion, anybody who can write a really good letter can write nonfiction—you *communicate.* For fiction, you need an advanced fantasy life or at least a good imagination. I'm always shocked at what writers, particularly of sexy material, *look* like. They don't look like sex and they don't look like *much.* When David's new secretary met me for the first time, after *Sex and the Single Girl* hit, she stood in our living room and said, "But, Mrs. Brown, you aren't sexy at *all!*" She *said* that! Of *course* the girl didn't last . . . she couldn't *type!*

So let's say you've got a job. This advice has worked for me all my life, can for *anybody.* Don't bother with dreams of glory, just do the (often grubby) work in front of you every day. Take on more work (and challenge) all the time and one day you will be better off than when you began. The plan is called "mouse-burgering," a term a lot of people think silly or don't understand (can you imagine?!). Mouseburgering means you just quietly get *on* with it and eventually your work makes you more confident and more noticeable . . . not really mousy anymore. Katherine Fanning, editor/publisher of the huge-circulation *Christian Science Monitor,* says the same thing. "Forget about advancement. If you sit around thinking about advancement you won't get there. The only thing that will get you advanced is to concentrate on your work."

You will undoubtedly be working *for* somebody and this advice, extrapolated from *Getting Along with Your Boss* by George Berkley, is the best I have ever seen: Really listen. Be concise. Don't criticize but ask questions. Be diplomatic about his/her plan. Accent the positive—be an optimist. Make the boss look good. Solve your own problems—don't bring them to him or her. Keep your promise. A boss can adjust to anything except not being able to depend on you. Know your boss and anticipate moods. Don't get *too* close.

What about charity work for keeping busy and useful? That's for *all* of us, whether we hold a job or not. During the treasured afternoon I got to spend with the late anthropologist Margaret Mead, she praised American *women's* gigantic contribution to philanthropy. "In Europe they don't have such a thing," she said. "Government has to take care of the indigent or the person's family does it or it doesn't get done. Here *women* do it." Efforts are made on behalf of everything from getting a nuclear-weapons dump removed from your neighborhood (don't get *too* obstreperous or you'll get arrested), to helping terminally ill kids realize a dream, to saving a whale or ancient tree, to counseling unwed pregnant teenagers, simply to "adopting" somebody lonely and out of it and spending time with him. I get two or three letters a week asking for an item to auction off to raise money for a children's camp, hospital, library, recreation center for the handicapped ... nearly always *women* seeking help for somebody *else*. Impressive. Women are terrific fund-raisers, can raise a million dollars in one night, having banged people on the head to buy tables for one of the New York or Los Angeles big charity dinners. Lilly Tartikoff, wife of a television and movie mogul, has raised millions for UCLA cancer-research programs (she got interested when her husband beat Hodgkin's disease fifteen years ago).

Pat Mosbacher raised giant sums for New York's Hospital for Special Surgery, Beverly Sills for March of Dimes, Dina Merrill, Mary Tyler Moore and Barbara Davis for diabetes and hundreds more like them. My friend Ann Siegel had artist Richard Giglio design a group of greeting cards—$50 per box, tax deductible and they're gorgeous—to raise money for the American Cancer Society. She worked on this project for three years and it's thrilling to see her get it launched. If these women were running *companies,* which they *could* if they'd gone that direction, you'd hear *more.* I find Barbara Bush's work to combat illiteracy totally inspiring. She did it long before George hit the White House and made her high-profile.

And what if the idea of such a project has never occurred to you before? Gloria Steinem reminds us that women in later years get energized, become bolder, do gutsy things we wouldn't have dreamed of doing earlier. She's talking about causes, of course, political activism, running for office, helping other women run for office, speaking *out!* Men, on the other hand, she says, get more conservative, less passionate. We come into our own while they slough *off,* so to speak. Gloria has a way of speaking truths about men's and women's roles better than anybody. I find this one so *encouraging.*

You don't have to deal in big-time or even small-time *money* raising if that makes you nervous. *Any* charity work is rewarding. Everybody needs you. Ask friends, co-workers, read the papers, call up a hospital or write to the American Association of Retired Persons (AARP) 601 E Street N.W., Washington, D.C. 20049, about volunteer programs.

On to another subject *not* age-related.

Why don't women very often become heads of companies (CEO, president, chairman, etc.)? I've studied this subject a lot and have decided two things keep us back: One: Women are still given choices. Yes, we're expected to work when we get out of school but if we marry and have children and our husbands can *afford* it, we may drop back or drop out of the work force for a few years or forever. Men aren't allowed that choice. The need to conquer and achieve is more ingrained in them. Give or take a few househusbands, the world pretty much expects men to work—and *hard*—until they retire. Not having the option of defecting surely solidifies resolve. Gloria Steinem has said, "I have yet to hear a man ask for advice on how to combine marriage and a career." They sure never ask about combining *fatherhood* and career. Two: Motherhood may change a woman emotionally in a way fatherhood doesn't change a man ... growing the baby inside you, then breast-feeding, but I think it's more likely society's brainwashing about motherhood that holds women back from wanting or gaining power. Motherhood is still considered a woman's most important work. Many companies tend to think a woman is not really serious about her career after she becomes a mother. We are afraid to *postpone* the career-slowing decision of motherhood lest the body won't cooperate. For men it's *never* too late. Television tycoon Norman Lear produced a baby last year at sixty-seven. My observation is that a woman can hold a pretty high-powered job with *one* child; with the second or third child, the going gets rough. She can't give work the same time and push she did before motherhood and she stays pretty much on her present plateau—no more big moves forward—or she drops back.

But after her family is older, a woman may get into high gear again or even get there for the first time. It sure happened to Eleanor Roosevelt after Franklin died—to go back a lot of years. She blossomed. Linda Wachner, CEO and president of Warnaco, one of two *Fortune* 500 companies run by a woman, was widowed before her biggest career moves took place. Liz Smith says menopause frees women to concentrate on their work, on *themselves,* instead of on pampering men and children. Listen, it *is* all out there, a lot of it waiting to be scooped up by *us (well* past forty), I'm convinced. Perhaps Abe Ribicoff, former governor of and U.S. senator from Connecticut, now special counsel at Kaye, Scholer, Fierman, Hays and Hander law firm, says best why you can still go on achieving to a late age. "When your mind works, it makes your body work ... your body goes along with what your mind tells it to do. I expect to work till I die." Abe is eighty-one. I expect to, too.

Would you like to hear from a few of the over-*sixty* working women I interviewed on how they feel about their jobs? Keep this in mind: *All* are in their sixties, seventies, eighties and *nineties!* True, this report is *rigged*—I didn't talk to women who hadn't worked since young womanhood (there could be some happy people in *those* groups), but I was thrilled to find not *one* of my interviewees said she would quit even if she didn't need the money. Jack LaLanne would approve of them *all* if I may quote him again. Jack says, "The minute you think retirement you might as well get in the casket and let them bury you." Many are going to *die* in their Chanel pumps rushing to a business lunch date or slumped over their word-processor. *Listen* to them!

Mary Garcia *(eighties)　Laboratory nurse for Dr. George Nagamatsu, urologist, New York*

"I retired for a while—started working for the doctor *again* when I was sixty-nine—that was eleven years ago." Of course the *doctor* is eighty-four, and *he* doesn't plan to retire either, so they're compatible.

Grace O'Reilly *(seventies)　Executive secretary to David Brown for the past twenty-five years*

"I wouldn't know what to do with myself at home. The best part of my job? Interesting people! I meet a lot of writers, directors, designers, actors . . . it improves your mind. Worst part? Don't ask!" We both knew it was darling David, who is sometimes cross and *always* demanding but, Grace says, always worth it.

Dorothy Caplin *(over sixty)　Executive assistant to the dean of the Dental School, Case Western Reserve University, Cleveland*

"I've had this job for eighteen years. The present dean is a teacher so I keep up with new procedures and scholastic curriculum. Retire? Why? I don't *have* hobbies . . . who wants to make afghans or hemstitch tea towels?!"

Glee Zuzi *(sixties)   Teaches eight-year-olds in second grade, Calhoun School, New York*

"I feel about as young as the kids! We play kickball, go on field trips all over New York. We've been to the Museum of Natural History, the Brooklyn Museum, the Metropolitan. Right now we're studying New Amsterdam and what it must have been like to be a native American . . . you have no idea how many different kinds of doughnuts there were. It would be nice to go shopping at Saks some days, but if I could only go shopping, forget it!"

Angela Lansbury *(sixties)   Actress*

"I like my work because acting is the one thing I believe I do reasonably well. I wish I had a clock inside me that told me, 'You can't do it another minute.' I don't and consequently I overwork and sometimes get headaches. I don't plan to stop acting. I think I'd miss it terribly."

Ann Landers *(seventies)   Syndicated columnist (over 1,200 papers)*

"My job often means ten- and twelve-hour days, thousands of letters that run the gamut from heartbreaking to hilarious. I've been called a saint, a savior, a crummy old bat, a male-basher and a woman-hater. I cannot imagine a career that could possibly give me more satisfaction or more of a sense of service. I've been asked from time to time when I plan to retire. I think one day when I'm about ninety-nine, they will find me slumped over my typewriter and that will be it."

Eileen Ford *(seventies)   Owner of the Ford Model Agency*

"Jerry [her husband and co-founder of Ford Models] does the business side; I'm better at sales. There's always the challenge of the next thing . . . we keep creating new stuff. Since we started the business in 1946, I've only been away from work long enough to have my three children and I was back again within weeks. The children [in business with her] are not trying to push me out. The cruddy stuff—that's life! I don't *have* any mornings when I think I can't do this anymore . . . can't face the day or have that 'Oh, God, I'm slipping' feeling."

Barbara Gillies *(sixties)   Real-estate broker, Westhampton, Long Island*

"In the real-estate business they don't care what age you are or what sex. If you can move the merchandise, nobody pays any attention to your looks or your ankles. No, I don't feel any pain or aches and creaks when I get up in the morning. If I didn't have someplace to go, I would go *crazy!*"

Mary Johnson *(seventies)   Opens new hotels for the Marriott chain (the Marquis in New York, the Marriott in San Francisco and Washington, D.C.)*

"Nobody has ever said, 'You're too old to be here.' They gave me a surprise seventieth birthday party. Sometimes I look in the mirror and say, 'My God, you're no baby chick,' but that's the only time I'm ever reminded of age. I work three days a week now—have *no* plans to retire."

Georgette Klinger *(seventies)   Skin-care specialist*

"My work aggravates me to death but I couldn't live without it. I really *care* about each and every client and people who aren't . . . skin is my passion. I want everyone who comes to me to be revived and beautiful when she leaves. I've had the Klinger salons—two in New York, Beverly Hills, Palm Beach, Bal Harbor, Dallas, Chicago and one coming in Washington—for fifty years. No, I will never pack up and move to my house in Phoenix."

Flora Lewis *(sixties)   Senior columnist for* The New York Times

"I shall continue to work as long as I'm physically able. I don't golf; I don't enjoy gardening or puttering. I feel I have had the greatest of all luxuries: a life in which most of the time it's hard to tell whether I'm working or playing. The special thrills are the sense of being close to history as it unfolds, and, once in a while, actually contributing to it."

Mathilde Krim *(sixties) PH.D., founding co-Chair of the American Foundation for AIDS Research, recipient of five doctorates honoris causa and many other honors*

"I've worked all my life, only took three weeks off to have a baby in 1958. I was an early feminist in Geneva. I have been helpful to this present cause because of my scientific background and previous work on medical projects ... this gives me credibility. My work is grueling, yes. I would like to spend more time gardening, traveling, but I can't let up now. We will have a vaccine (to prevent AIDS) before too long but right now the number of victims are still too great."

Cornelia G. Kennedy *(sixties) Circuit judge, United States Court of Appeals, Sixth Circuit: Michigan-Ohio-Kentucky-Tennessee*

"My work as a judge of a federal court of appeals is always intellectually challenging ... demanding. I usually put in over fifty hours a week—plus many hours on related activities such as judging moot courts, attending seminars, serving on boards or committees of law-related associates. I *don't* plan to retire. Hobbies and travel are fine but no substitute for work."

Frances Lear *(sixties) Founder/owner of* Lear's *magazine*

"I have had a complete metamorphosis since leaving Norman [her third husband] four years ago and getting a divorce. The magazine has been a serious investment of money, energy and guts ... expensive, thrilling, frustrating, grueling and the dream of a lifetime. In another year I expect to be in the black, and then I may sell but I'm sure I'll still be involved. You could say I've been liberated. . . . Betty Friedan is doing a whole chapter in her new book on me!"

Shirley Verrett *(sixties)   Soprano, has sung with the Metropolitan Opera, Royal Opera Covent Garden, Vienna State Opera and many others.*

"I don't *ever* plan to retire because that would be death! I will go on and do something in my own field or possibly another field entirely. [Shirley is a CPA and certified real-estate broker.] Of *course* I get weary but after a little R and R, I'm raring to go again."

Eleanor Lambert *(eighties)   Eleanor Lambert Public Relations, founder and director of the Best Dressed List*

"When I started, everybody said I was too young; now they ask how I can keep doing it. I forget how old I am and am annoyed when people mention it to me. I prefer just to go on working and forget age. I scream at my young employees sometimes but we get along fine. Work is a river which you go on being carried by."

Venita Van Caspel *(over fifty)   Senior vice-president/ investments of Raymond James & Associates, Inc., Houston*

"I find my profession still exciting. . . . Financial planning is such a dynamic world of change that every day is a new day. It doesn't happen often that I wish I didn't have to go to work. I have a wonderful husband and we take exciting trips and go on cruises on a regular basis. I'm fortunate to have a competent staff to keep everything shipshape while I'm gone. At present I don't plan to retire."

Sophie Masloff *(seventies)   Mayor of Pittsburgh*

"Being mayor is the best job in town . . . I love the challenges, the pace. There are stresses but there isn't a day I don't love being behind the mayor's desk. I start early and pace myself through meetings, community events, dinner meetings, speeches and other special Pittsburgh forums. I never get tired of talking to our citizens; that's what being mayor is all about . . . I love every minute of it."

Catherine Woolley *(aka Jane Thayer) (eighties)* *Author of eighty-seven books*

"I could no more live and not write than I could live and not breathe. I no longer produce two or three books or even one book a year, but an idea always rears its head and it's a comfort to know it's waiting to be worked on. Retire? I've just bought a new typewriter!"

Grace Mirabella *(sixties)* *Founder and editor of* Mirabella *magazine*

"I'd been at Conde Nast for thirty-five years when I was asked to leave. I could have stopped working, but when the offer came to start *Mirabella,* my husband [surgeon William Cahan] said, 'You can't *not* do it.' It's been terrific. As the editor of a fashion magazine you are part of the arts—music, ballet, literature—whatever interests you. It's like living theater . . . each month a new production . . . enormously fulfilling."

Marilyn Evins *(sixties)* *Owner of Marilyn Evins Public Relations (clients include* Architectural Digest, *Judith Leiber)*

"To get me to quit working they will have to carry me out. Work involves you with *life*—what is really going on out there. When I take a vacation—rarely—I am always thinking of work. If I'm *not* working in the evening (which I love to be required to do!), my mind is still on business. When I go to sleep, I'm thinking about the next morning and can't wait to get started . . . weekends are torture! I deeply resent the years I spent *not* working, raising a family. I pay absolutely no attention to aches and pains. I never look anyplace except to the future."

Berna Linden *(sixties)*   *Sales executive of Rodeo Realty, Beverly Hills*

"I know people who have retired and are now walking around like zombies! They don't like the people they now have to associate with—other people like them who also aren't involved! Charity doesn't do it. Now they have to spend a ton of money to have as interesting a life as they had as a working person—theater, travel, books, restaurants, movies—just stuff to keep them *occupied.*"

Barbara Walters *(sixties)*   *Broadcast journalist on 20/20, celebrity interviewer*

"I don't plan to retire though I don't want to do what Mike Wallace does . . . get on and off airplanes every ten days. It will be more difficult for me to stay in my work than for people in other fields—broadcasting is very aware of age and I don't know how long I can do exactly what I am doing [interviewing political leaders, celebrities]. People did use to ask a lot about how it was, getting older in this particular field, how long did I think I could go on. I don't hear that anymore. I'm optimistic."

Dr. Janet Davison Rawley *(sixties)*   *University of Chicago (uncovered chromosomal changes in leukemia patients, thereby breaking new ground in the field of cancer genetics)*

"This is very hot, exciting work. It needs to be thought about by young brains, but I seem to be able to attract them to the department. I have four children; my husband is an immunologist. He would like to slow down a bit but I'm not prepared to do that. I was hurt a couple of years ago in a ski accident and don't jog every day but I'm healthy. I live three quarters of a mile from the university and walk to work. I think you can choose to have a career early and kids later, as I did, or family early and career later."

Lillian Vernon *(sixties)*   *Chief executive officer of Lillian Vernon Corporation, publishers of nineteen editions of Lillian*

Vernon catalogs with circulation of over 147 million; employs over 1,300 people during peak Christmas season

"My work has been my third child for forty years. I've poured love and attention and detail into this company, but since the business is so successful, I've been paid back a thousand times. No, no, no, I don't *ever* plan to retire! Who *doesn't* get tired sometimes and long for a good laugh, some fun, but that passes and your job becomes the core again."

Katharine Graham *(seventies)* *Chairman of the Board of The Washington Post Company and often described as the most powerful woman in America*

"I think you think of yourself at a particular age and you just stay there. In my case—probably around forty-five. I'm not going to stay forever but I don't know just when the cutoff point is. I was brought up by a strong mother and father who believed people should work. I play tennis every weekend but now play doubles. My husband and I used to have older friends, most of whom are gone. You have to remember to keep making new young ones."

Mary Frances Borden Crisman *(seventies)* *Chief librarian for the Frank Russell Company (management consultants), Tacoma, Washington*

"You have to see the big picture, be able to adapt to change. I firmly believe that *not* having that kind of mental exercise is what makes one old, not the calendar. I drive to work in a great old '67 Buick Electra convert or a '68 Mustang Fastback 302 which I recently had restored to the envy of numerous male colleagues. I drive in in my Reeboks but work in (usually three-inch) heels. You bet I get tired and weary and wish I didn't have to go to the job . . . who doesn't? . . . but I know that someone is depending on me to get information, simple, or complex, brief or lengthy, which will help them or one of our clients. It's amazing how much energy that can inject, how it makes the time fly and the day seem too short."

Pauline Trigere *(eighties)   Couturier designer*

"You might say this business keeps you younger because you have to think months in advance. We turn out four collections a year and you are always thinking not in the past, not even in the present, but four months away. I get frustrated when something doesn't work. I get an idea at night or coming in in the car and begin to work with fabric when I get in—I have never done sketches. I start draping and then someone else takes over completion of the design. We may have worked on it for three or four days and it doesn't happen—very disappointing. I am more impatient now; perhaps my temper is a bit shorter. I scream a little. Some of my people have been with me forever, however, and actually I have a lot of patience. You *have* to have because you are always changing a hem, redoing a sleeve. I still have the same thrill with my work. I will keep doing this."

Lilian Seitsize, M.D. *(eighties)   Still a general practitioner at Northridge Hospital, Northridge, California*

"I keep office hours Monday, Tuesday, Thursday from nine to six, Fridays half day. Patients tell me they would like me to take a vacation but I have to come back—they don't want me out of their lives. Some I have treated their entire life. I went to NYU and later to Philadelphia Women's Medical College. When I was trying to get into Coney Island Hospital in Brooklyn for my internship—they now call this a residency—I was in line with three hundred men. One of them came up to me and said, 'Don't you know women should be in the kitchen?'—this was in the twenties. I was so astonished my coat fell to the floor. Another man picked it up, put it back on my shoulders and said, 'Don't pay any attention to him—he's a jerk.' I later married him—the man who picked up the coat."

Tynni Kalervo *(nineties)   Bartender at Little Finland, New York City*

"I lost my lease a few years ago but signed a twelve-year lease on a new site a few blocks away. I moved the polished mahogany bar to the new place, hung up the photo of my late husband and one of me with the president of Finland and began doing what I do best: dealing with suppliers, tending bar. I work every day. I hope to work till I'm one hundred years old."

Aline, Countess of Romanones *(seventies) Author of* The Spy Wore Red, The Spy Wore Silk, The Spy Went Dancing

"I love writing. Not only does it relax me and provide something to look forward to each day but it's given me the opportunity to live selfishly . . . like a student of twenty-one. I dress like one—all day in jogging shoes and short skirts and I forget entirely that I am seventy years old. Maybe the young can live without work but we adults keep young working. It keeps us learning and enriching ourselves. Usually my work is more fun for me than going to a party."

Mildred Newman, M.D. *(sixties) Psychiatrist, New York (many famous writers and entertainers are among her patients), author of* How to Be Your Own Best Friend

"I am just as excited going to my office every day as I was when I first arrived there in 1953, as interested in treating the next patients as I was the first. I might have thought the joy would have stopped but it hasn't. . . . It's okay getting older if you still have your feelings, the greatest lover in the world, the best dentist . . . and you need humor. I definitely still have a sex life. I think being happy with your work is even more important than love. It's great to know that you are helping people. I actually *feel* healthier than I did thirty years ago."

Erma Bombeck *(sixties) Author, syndicated columnist*

"It's a love/hate relationship with my work. On the days I have an exciting new idea, I can't wait to get to the typewriter and develop it. On most days, I convince myself I don't need this job. I can quit anytime I want. I can put my life together, have lunch with my friends whenever I want, and ultimately satisfy myself professionally by passing out free samples of sausage in a supermarket on Saturdays. I'm kidding myself. I am my job. It's the best of me. I am only alive when I'm producing. I am still in awe of a profession that begins with a blank sheet of paper and when I have filled it, it goes out to countries I have never seen, is read by people I have never met, and brings about laughter or tears from persons I cannot hear. It is an enigma and I feel flattered to be an instrument.

"Everyone pays a price for what he does. I pay for it in time, personal sacrifice, and discipline that rivals a prima ballerina's. After twenty-six years . . . it's still a challenge to discover some small chunk of the human condition, put it under a microscope, show its warts, and dare someone to laugh. God, this job is constant. Every Monday of every week of every year for twenty-six years, there must be three columns ready to file for seven hundred newspapers. I have written from hospital beds, the afternoon of my sister's funeral, on vacations, and during literary droughts. In the syndicate business we tell the story about the syndicated cartoonist who died and the head of the syndicate asked his wife, 'Does that mean he's going to file late?' I love the challenge of writing for a generation who has never heard of Adlai Stevenson or ironing boards. Happily, I'm in a profession where gravity and erosion don't limit me. I'm such a harsh critic of myself, I will be the first to know when I've said it all. Until then, as long as health, humor, and parts for my IBM prevail . . . I still meet my deadlines."

Jean Dalrymple *(nineties)   Formerly president of the Light Opera Company of Manhattan, producer of four hit Broadway plays including* The Four Poster *with Hume Cronyn and Jessica Tandy and* King Lear *with Orson Welles, recipient of six citations from mayors of New York, member of the National Council for the Arts*

"I think work is *more* important than play—I only ever went to Europe if it was connected with work. All through the years I took on too many things but people kept asking and I would say yes. Right now I'm working for the American Theatre Wing, trying to get stars to attend the opening of *Private Lives*—you always ask stars from other shows to opening-night parties. Nobody has ever mentioned age to me. I do everything I ever did except play golf."

Liz Smith *(sixties)* *Syndicated columnist, television journalist*

"The great anthropologist Margaret Mead once said there are no limits to what can be accomplished by 'menopausal women.' She meant there is a time in life when women become *liberated* from the ongoing tyranny of their bodies, sex, children, family responsibilities. That's the time a woman needs 'work'—her own work—and can accomplish *anything* through that work. Who wants to talk to anybody if they have nothing to talk about but recipes, baby talk and diapers? People want to talk to someone who has ideas, gossip and fun to contribute, someone who read or saw something to tell about, someone doing something.

"Concentrating on age isn't real, because age isn't important. If it seems to be—if agism exists—well, one has to rise above it. Ridiculous that so much is made of it. These days people all look *BETTER* ... DIFFERENT BUT BETTER. Alan King, Joan Rivers, Carol Burnett all looked great on the *Ed Sullivan* TV retrospective. They were a big improvement on their young selves. What you have *become* is what counts.

"Self-respect comes from our work. I'm not talking about planning a career to have something down the line 'to fall back on.' I'm talking about the energy and fun and effort of working at capacity on all levels for the *joy* of it. And if money, fame, success and power come along the way with the effort, so be it.

"No, I don't plan to quit working. I *need* to read five or six newspapers a day, look at every magazine, read

books, tell what I know and can synthesize. I love the
movies, TV, theater, opera, the great outdoors, animals,
friends and my family. I want it all. I've had it all. Now
I want the rest of it as well."

Joyce Carpati *(early fifties)* *Cosmetic and fragrance
marketing director,* Cosmo, *handles Lancôme, L'Oréal,
Pfizer/Coty, Calvin Klein, Elizabeth Arden, Chanel, etc.*

"Yes, I wear down sometimes and last year I was celebrating getting a big account, fell down the steps at the Great
American Health Bar and fractured my ankle. Crutches, a
walker, then a cane, but I always take a deep breath and
start again. Working is *living.* I actually *tremble* when I
think of not continuing to work!"

Joan Ganz Cooney *(sixties)* *Founder of Children's Television Workshop* (Sesame Street, 3-2-1 Contact), *on boards
of Xerox, Johnson & Johnson, Metropolitan Life and
Chase Manhattan*

"Freud said the two most important things are work and
love and, if you must choose, choose work. You simply
can't develop your brain or be a total person without work.
You cannot derive an identity through love or through
relationships—they are the frosting on the cake. I've seen
women try to do that and it doesn't work. Some are married to congressmen and work for their husbands. These
are real jobs, but if the man doesn't get reelected, you're
out of a job. Last year I stepped down from CEO to do
full-time creative work. I don't have much psychic energy
for repetitiveness ... don't want to deal any longer with
personnel and budgets. Fortunately, I was able to shift
within my own company to do something more agreeable.
When you play a seminal role in the development of a
company, as I did with *Sesame Street,* they are delighted to
have you stay on. When I decided to change positions at
age fifty-nine, they gave me a five-year contract—very
gratifying. We have a tremendous licensing business I'm
involved with and I'm developing a show now for eight-
to eleven-year-olds. Who would I be if I didn't work, if

not identified with this company? I never want to say to a man, 'I saw this cute suit, can I have a thousand dollars?' Some of us worked because we didn't have a choice. Somewhere along the line we probably got into the position of *having* a choice (with a wealthy husband) but we *still* feel we don't have a choice—we were brain-damaged early! I cannot *conceive* of life without work!"

Betty Comden *(seventies) Writer and lyricist (with Adolph Green) of* On the Town, Subways Are for Sleeping, Bells Are Ringing, *did book for* Applause, *lyrics for* Will Rogers Follies, *screenplay for* Singin' in the Rain, *also performs*

"As a writer for theater and movies and a performer, I am one of the lucky ones . . . doing exactly what I love. I plan to conk out slumped over a typewriter, with a long yellow pad, or at a rehearsal. I will never retire. Yes, I do get weary but much of the time I work at home and to go to work I just have to go to the next room. If it's a movie, I go to the studio; a show in rehearsal, I go to the theater. In any case, I *get* there!"

Laura Willi *(nineties) Assistant in a nursing home, New York City*

"I walk approximately three miles a day from my apartment at Seventy-fourth and Fifth Avenue to York and Seventieth—crosstown blocks in New York are long. I go there whether it's raining or snowing—those old people *need* me."

Sayra Lebenthal *(nineties) Broker, Lebenthal & Company*

Fortune magazine reports Sayra "still puts in a full day working the phones as a broker for the firm she and her husband, Louis, founded in 1925. Since then she has survived 12 recessions, three wars, two husbands, two market crashes and one Great Depression."

" 'On Saturday, Sunday and legal holidays, I have all

the aches and pains every old woman has. But on Monday I forget about them and come to work. Why not retire? I don't like what's on TV these days.' "

Katharine Hepburn *(eighties)* *Actress*

"You and I better not stop working because we'd go *mad!* I don't even call it work ... I think you are just lucky if you have something to do that you really can do."

Had enough? Okay, let's gallop around the clubhouse turn and move into the stretch.

chapter eleven

Money

After you're older, two things are possibly more important than any others: health and money. Sex, work, friendship, love have to be fitted *in*, of course, but if money and/or health are a shambles, you can't even think about much of anything else. Health, as we've already suggested, *can* be protected and enhanced when you're older. So can money ... if you've got the *knack*. Some people are geniuses at making money *grow* ... and then there are the rest of us.

I know how to stay on a payroll (fear and hard work), but through the years every tiny effort of mine to multiply funds has been a *disaster*. As a twenty-three-year-old secretary I invested a week's salary—$35.00—in a chemical compound which, added to pure-grain alcohol and let sit in a closet for two weeks, was supposed to produce—ta-ta!—Shalimar! You then decanted this Persian delight into little bottles and sold them to perfume bargain hunters in your office, apartment building, ballet class, wherever, at a Large Profit. Tragically, although I brewed my chemicals in the closet—talk about your fire hazards!—as directed, essence and alcohol didn't combine properly; what developed was an industrial-strength liquid that smelled as though you could scrub a gymnasium with it. Entrepreneuring (obviously) not being my forte, through the next few years I tried a few *other* routes to riches: deposited $1,000 with a Los Angeles swimsuit company labor union—yield one year later, $18.00. I bought two hundred shares of stock in an advertising agency that went public and then went bust—a wipeout. I *did* get good at liar's poker but your total take after working all night—$5.00;

311

you could also *lose* that much. Clearly untalented with making money grow, I quit trying and, for the next thirteen years, squirreled whatever I could from each paycheck into a Los Angeles Security First National Bank savings account—interest: 2 percent but it was *steady*.

When I married David at thirty-seven, having paid $5,000 cash from the savings account (where else would it come from?) for a used Mercedes-Benz 190 SL, which, as I told you, had a *marriage*-inducing effect on David (I'm *sure* of it!), I still had $8,000 in the account. David came to our marriage *without* money, although he made a big salary as a movie executive and that appealed to *me*. In the next six years, my husband miraculously learned not only how to *make* money but how to *save* it (if you stop getting divorced and paying alimony all the time, *that's* a saving), which he invested wisely.

Now, at age forty-three, with *Sex and the Single Girl* movie-sale money invested, I'm at *Cosmo* doing well, David is executive vice-president of creative operations at 20th Century-Fox, doing *more* than well—we are comfortable but not rich. One night I say to my beloved, "What would you think of my asking one of the executives at Hearst (my bosses) how *he* invests money—he seems to be good at it." "Go right ahead," David said. "You might learn something." Hearst executive took me to lunch at Burnham and Company (later to become Drexel-Burnham-Lambert, home of the legendary, now-jailed money genius, Michael Milken). Chairman Tubby Burnham, very cordial; account executive I am turned over to, also cordial. Subsequently I am put in—what else—the Burnham Fund, a collection of stocks Tubby Burnham and his people believed in. Two years later I left the fund with $8,000 less than I put in—exactly the amount of my original "life savings" (minus the Benz money) when I married David. You might say I am *still* not real talented with money.

Then, in the mid-seventies, David made a lot of money—whoopee! with a profit-participation in three box-office hits—*The Sting, Jaws,* and *Jaws 2*. He invested *less* conservatively and did *more* than well—he was written up in *Forbes* magazine as a gifted money maven. Fourteen years went by after that, during which time I behaved myself and stayed *away* from our funds except occasionally to buy a new dress and have my eyes done. Then something—the devil?—got into me or maybe it was greed who put his arms around me and took me off to tango. One night at a dinner party I sat next to a Wall Street player whom I found fascinating. More accurately, I found his ability to have made all that money—tons— fascinating and he ran it himself, i.e., no advisers. I asked this nice man, who is surely not coming on to me, if he would have lunch with me and at lunch asked if he would consider looking at David's and my portfolio. It was about the last thing he wanted to do—who needs to advise civilians when you aren't in that business—but he did take a look and, without any great fanfare or brow furrowing, suggested we sell half our I.B.M. and purchase Cray Computer, a new company, yes, destined for greatness. David again didn't question our doing this. I had been a good girl since the Burnham caper, kept my hands out of the till, and he said, *do* it ... it's your money, too—technically true though he had made most of it. It took two days to sell the I.B.M. and buy Cray—there wasn't that much Cray *around.* Denouement: A year later Cray has dropped from 14 to 2⅝ and we have lost a million dollars. The I.B.M. which we sold at 95 dipped a *little* but, as I write, is hovering at 96, *plus* I.B.M. pays a dividend, Cray does not. Okay, once *more* you'll be glad to know I am out of the "money-growing" business. (David is even more relieved than *you* are.) If Warren Buffett, a genius private investor, should offer me an interest-free loan to buy something he devoutly believed in, I think I would tell him to get lost. I feel a *little* sorry for the man who gave me the Cray tip. There was nothing in it for him and I'm sure he feels terrible about my loss (but not as terrible as *I* feel).

Are other (older) women as untalented with money as I am? Well, there *is* a lot of propaganda along that line and some of it is *true.* Until quite recently money management wasn't considered feminine. They plunked us into algebra and geometry classes with the Opposite Sex, some of whom couldn't do simple arithmetic, but you weren't really supposed to *understand* the Hypotenuse and Pythagorean Theorem, were you?, let alone Price Earnings Ratio and the Consumer Index later *on*. About as smart as a woman was supposed to be about numbers was to remember whether her partner had thrown down a six of spades in contract bridge so she shouldn't pick up the five. A male relative would worry *his* presumably wiser head *for* you. Three extremely successful career women my age say they *still* don't know a Treasury bond from a Persian rug except one is silky. "Alan does it *for* me," "Bernie is a lawyer *and* a C.P.A.—why would I worry?" "I trust Colin *totally*," they declare. What can you do? . . . These three have been lucky, but the horror stories of women who've let dumb (grabby) men get away with their funds . . . A so-in-love actress friend of mine's husband lost her savings from sixteen movies and a TV series when he was caught short in the 1987 market crash. Another husband, knowing he and his antique bride would be divorced, liquidated *everything*, said they'd lost it in the market, took the proceeds to Santa Fe to start a new life with a new wife. Wiser-*schmeizer!*

I think you have to be cautious to the point of paranoia about turning funds over even to a trusted male loved one or relative. A well-intentioned brother-in-law or copper-bright nephew can *destroy* you. If your husband is managing your funds, even if he contributes more than you do, he must be asked to explain his financial plan. What is he going to do, *hit* you? If the answer is yes, you *already* know you're in trouble. Some husbands—mine (still trusting after all that damage)—*welcome* a little interest, even if just to show you how smart they are and how wise their investments. If you're asking for the first time, you can say—whether true or not—you don't want to interfere but only to know what's *happening* . . . you don't want him married to a birdbrain. Not knowing what's going on with the finances in marriage is about as smart as a man expecting his wife to do all the disciplining of the children and being surprised one day when one of them goes up on a drug rap.

I've always had the feeling that being *around* wealthy people might cause some of the gold dust to sift down on me. Lunacy! I've finally decided all these people do is make you feel *poor!* At a party in Cannes last year a woman asked David and me, "Where are your houses?" *Houses?!* We have one city apartment with which we barely cope, that's *it!* When we joined Malcolm Forbes for his seventieth birthday party in Tangiers a few years ago, one question on the forms you filled out was "What is the number of your private aircraft or yacht, port of registry, number in crew?" I felt I let that questionnaire *down* . . . we came in on Air Maroc.

Twice before marrying David, I think I had a shot at (serious) money—from a *man.* I had already figured I was never going to amass it through investment; also I had been unhappily in love *twice* and the condition no longer appealed to me—why not a little common sense for a change? For six months in my late twenties I became a mistress—the serious, old-fashioned kind—car, apartment, clothes, everything paid for with the promise of Real Riches later. Financial security for Mary, Mother and me for the rest of our lives . . . not a bad idea! I think my benefactor *meant* to deliver on all the promises. He was from a prominent New York banking family, and many of his cousins and brothers *had* made a favorite minion wealthy . . . sort of in the tradition of British Royalty. I loved driving up to Gilcrest Drive in Bel Air to see *"my* lot"—across the street from Ginger Rogers's house. Alas, I was such an unsatisfactory mistress the arrangement couldn't work. Since he couldn't be with me *ever* in the evenings (why do you *think?* An in-residence wife with whom he had a heavy social life), I would occasionally have a date, yes, with a *man,* and idiotically tell him about it . . . why didn't I just shut *up?!* "Who can *trust* you?" he would moan. "But I didn't even *kiss* him," I would explain. "You shouldn't have been in the same *room* with him," he would counterexplain. Like all others, I guess "love games" have rules. I stopped dating but, a dedicated anti-Semite, my friend had serious objections even to my Jewish *girlfriends,* who at the time were my dearest and nearest. Bye-bye lot, bye-bye house on Gilcrest, bye-bye stock portfolio . . . not a single share of *anything* ever got put into it. I did get to keep the seven-year-old wooden station wagon, Appletrees, which had been loaned me from his estate on Long Island. The rain came through the roof. . . . I would drive around Beverly Hills with an umbrella up inside the car.

Second chance: A Swiss advertising man found me attractive both because he'd never met an American career girl before—career women in Zurich at the time were almost nonexistent—and because my taking care of my invalid sister and nearly fundless mother somehow appealed to him. Well, not being too long out of the Ozark Mountains of Arkansas and still a minor-league hick, I could *also* drum up a little bigotry—his guttural Swiss-German accent repelled me, plus he had a wife, child and another on the way. Wives never really bothered me—I had my problems, they had *theirs*—but this one I kind of *liked*. The less interested I was in the man, the more passionate he became—you don't have to be a *U.S.* male to have this predilection. One day he came to my office with a bankbook (maybe not his *principal* bankbook but it was very Swiss and official-looking) and said, to prove his devotion, he was transferring everything out of it into my name that *day*. Nice. I could have used the $50,000. Maybe I wasn't feeling well that morning. Maybe the wife, the child and a half, the accent, plus my previous failure as a kept-ee were affecting my judgment. For whatever reason I declined. A few years later, when he got to be a major advertising presence in Europe with offices in five cities, I would think about the offer. Maybe I made a mistake. He and his wife are now divorced . . . what *else?!*

Okay, being too dumb and inept to make money the *easy* way (learn about investing and do it well) and equally inept at making it the hard way (being kept), I went on grubbing away at secretarial jobs, getting slightly better jobs as years went on and saving little dribbles of money—enough to buy the sports car and pay bills, even fall in love occasionally with somebody penniless. I'm sure you have your own stories of how you could have married or been kept wealthily or maybe these possibilities never appealed or sought you out. They both did to *me* . . . how lucky can you be when things don't work out as you planned and you have to, however slowly and unspectacularly, do it yourself? It's highly unlikely *now,* at our age, that we are going to fall into money through a man we aren't married to, though I do know a sixty-year-old Danish nurse who helped a wealthy woman through terminal illness, stayed on to cheer the woman's widower, married the man herself and when *he* died—rather soon—was left 23 million bucks. Elapsed time: two and a half years. Happens.

Suing the socks off somebody, unless the cause is super just, has always seemed to me *another* hard way to make money. I read about a former United Airlines flight attendant who sued Rico Petrocelli, a Boston Red Sox third baseman, for $750,000 for putting his hands on her breasts in the aisle of a chartered jetliner bringing the team home from a game in Detroit. You read a lot of lawsuit stories. Two of Petrocelli's teammates testified that the third baseman did have his hands—briefly—on the women's *hips,* "trying to get through a crowded aisle," but that was the extent of his "transgression." Possibly the elapsed time of hands on hips—or elsewhere—*wasn't* so brief, and we know how we all feel about sexual harassment—not acceptable. A person also wants to recognize a good fundraiser when she *sees* one and take advantage of it—but isn't this a ton of money to expect for such "wrongdoing"? Probably the third baseman *was* rude and unruly, a not-so-unusual happening even for a civilian woman stuck in a plane with a bunch of victory-happy, semi- (or not so semi-) drunk ballplayers, but even if guilty, did that guy really do her breasts $750,000 worth of damage? (Checking *The Boston Globe and* Red Sox P.R. office, I haven't been able to find out how the case came out.) Yes, there are legitimate reasons to sue, but litigation mostly doesn't bring enough money—if any—to warrant the aggravation, don't you agree?

Switching gears, it's hard not to be nostalgic about what things cost *then* (in our youth) compared to what they cost now. I don't even *try* to resist ... the double-deck ice cream cone—banana *and* rocky road, chocolate revel *and* strawberry-peach—five cents; the cloud-soft angora sweater my mother skimped to buy me from her grocery money—$5.00. Movies were ten cents apiece; they changed the bill three times a week and gave kids a Milky Way at the Saturday matinee. Tonight I am unwrapping a package containing a white crepe skirt with rhinestone buttons, pink cashmere twin-sweater set Elizabeth Bixon of Adolfo has sent over to me ... doesn't weight much ... and I realize I am holding the equivalent of my father's entire salary for 1931—$2,400—in that tissue paper. This "truth" doesn't hit me a great deal harder than checking a recent Regent Food Market bill and finding two red peppers cost $7.98! Mary's, Mother's and my entire weekly food budget in 1947 was $10.00, including meat. Still, I think inflation jolts me hardest when I see the parking signs in the Times Square theater district—$6.59 for half an hour—or the one in Midtown—$29.05 for the whole day. My mind floats to Los Angeles in the late thirties when parking all evening cost 50 cents *or,* if you went as far west as Figueroa, 25 cents.

Shall we stop this nonsense? It's *now!* Things change though my being thrifty (cheap) *hasn't.* As I mentioned, it's handy when an oral and an anal person get together; David has *kind* of balanced things out for us. Occasionally I even play it his way. On the Amtrak to Baltimore recently I picked up the tab for five men who had just stiffed the bartender—I didn't know them. Guys had a round of drinks, were given the bill, jumped train in Philadelphia without paying—about $21.00, including tip, as I remember. I felt all glowy for about five minutes ... so *that's* why people do these things I philosophized ... but bartender wasn't all that appreciative ... sort of acted as though I was patronizing him. Fuck *you,* bartender. My personal thrifts continue: Recycle Baggies, tattered lingerie becomes exercise outfits, old D.B. shirts become night-gowns, memos to staff are written on backs of discarded manuscript paper; if near destination, leave cab at red light and walk half a block to keep from paying meter drop

while waiting for light to change. I cut open tubes to get
the last out, use up all food in the fridge even if the carrots
are *wrinkled,* put the money in navy gabardine rather than
lavender sequins. I've finally (regretfully) given up cheap
vodka (you can't tell it from *good* in vodka/tonic), but
whatever comes in the snack basket on U.S. Air or Delta
commuter flights, I take off the plane . . . lunch for Anna
(our housekeeper) or me. The worst thing I *still* do is put
tap water in the Mountain Valley bottle, put it back in the
fridge, pass it off as the Real Thing. One of these days David is going to catch me. He'll arrive in the kitchen at the
wrong moment and say, "Helen, what in God's name are
you doing?!," and I will say, "Oh, just washing out the
bottle," and he will say, "You're washing out a bottle that
contained *water?!,*" etc., etc. What keeps me perpetrating
this fraud is that although he will drink *"only* bottled water," I don't think he knows the difference. If I give him
a glass of fake Mountain Valley, he will beam and say,
"Oh, that's good spring water . . . from *your* state [Arkan-
sas]!" Sure I feel guilty but is that any reason not to save
the $1.98 per bottle? Once in a while I break out a new
real one if the old label is getting waterlogged.

I'm not *hopeless.* I don't accept a bus transfer somebody gives me on the street which they don't need so you
can get on the "transfer" bus free . . . poor old New York
Transit Authority. At my senior-citizen rate (60 cents) I
can pay. I don't take anything more serious from hotels
these days than the Q-Tip supply and maybe a bar of soap
(they *left* it for me, didn't they?). No shoveling Equal
packets from the Russian Tea Room into my purse though
I use several a day. If you are going to *steal,* this is too
pippypoo, but still I don't get great marks for generosity.
It takes me *weeks* to get my check to Public Broadcasting
during a fund drive, though *Masterpiece Theatre* and the
McNeil/Lehrer Newshour have brought me *years* of pleasure. I *admire* generous people. Elizabeth and Felix
Rohatyn, Saul and Gyfryd Steinberg, have both adopted
classes of underprivileged kids in New York schools
whom they will see all the way through *college.* Phil
Donahue takes his staff on some incredible South of

France vacation or round-the-world cruise every few years and gave them *all* the royalties from his best-selling book. David rarely says no to a charity or personal-friend request so *maybe* he makes up for me. *Maybe!* Since I don't have children, unless I sit next to another stock-market genius whose (terrible) advice I get the hots for—not likely— several charities some day will be benefited . . . except I'm planning to live forever.

I heard about a woman even cheaper than I am. A friend loaned her cleaning woman to a friend. Cleaning woman asked temporary boss for money for the Laundromat to wash sheets. New employer says, "This is a king-size bed and I have only slept on one side of the bed—I never moved over to the other side so naturally I am not going to pay to have the entire sheet laundered. . . . I barely even messed up *my* side. Cleaning woman said, "Ma'am, I got strength in my arms and all that but I cannot see how I am going to get hold of the other side of the sheet which you haven't slept on as it is whirling around in the washing machine to keep it from being washed. . . . I'd throw my back out." "Okay," said new employer, "but I don't want you nickel and diming me all week for washing machines and things like that." Story made me feel *almost* bountiful!

Whether cheap or generous (I'll bet you're the latter), smart or dumb about money (I'll bet the former), I hope you have collected some things that not only bring daily pleasure but are worth more than you paid for them if you want to sell. This knack I also haven't. I have stupidly concentrated on buying *wholesale*—clothes, household appliances, dishes—magazine editors are spoiled—plus I frequently order by phone and never get *near* a store to see what's in it. In the sixties and seventies when David began to make money I might have shopped a *little* for good furniture, paintings, antiques that would have increased in value as well as brought pleasure, but I didn't. David is not a collector, except of books, so *he* was no help. In 1976 we did buy a flat from Mike Nichols, who, mercifully, had acquired some nice things which he let us buy since they "went with the apartment," but not very many.

Our decorator Nathan Mandelbaum bludgeoned me into buying a few more antiques but again not nearly enough. I have a Dufy print of Epsom, for which I paid $20.00 in 1947, listed in our insurance appraisal at $75,000. Do those people occasionally smoke grass or something while appraising? If the apartment burns down, maybe I can collect—or possibly I could have it *stolen*. (I'll keep you posted.)

Well, your money personality—anal (thrifty/stingy) like me, oral (generous/extravagant) like David, or somewhere in between—will probably not change. You're basically stuck with yourself in your personal life, but investing is something else. Your money ought to be managed *impersonally*, even by *you*. We're coming to an investment plan in a minute. Maybe you don't have any money to invest, however, and are actually living close to the financial edge. Well, at whatever level you are squeaking by, solvent is *still* the most attractive thing a woman can be, forget monogrammed stationery, vintage wine for girlfriend-lunches, handmade shoes *or* investing (if you don't have it to invest). If you need to be super thrifty—and I certainly did and was from ages ten through thirty-five and could be *again*—here are some suggestions:

- Borrow or share books and newspapers, don't buy. Get a library card so you can keep up with good books.
- Walk. You don't even ride *public* transportation if your feet can get you there.
- Drive a car at least as old as your porch furniture. Old cars have character and, like older *people,* perform brilliantly if cared for.
- Don't drink, smoke, go sleepless, shovel in junk food. You can't afford the repair bills (you've heard this *before!*). Veggies and fruit in season are not only cheap but do the most *for* you. Beans can provide cheap protein; forget porterhouse steaks. You *know* to eschew expensive bakery goods, bar cocktails at $2.50 each.
- Elegant brand-name cosmetics are probably not for you. Can you *really* tell the difference?

- Go for your senior citizen (isn't that a loathsome term ... so patronizing!) discount on public transportation, commuter airlines, movie theaters, certain Broadway shows.
- Take in *all* the free concerts, art exhibits, lectures.
- If you've never clipped supermarket coupons, start.
- Encourage people to send food home with you. You don't out-and-out ask (tacky!) but you might try: "This is the best fudge cake I ever tasted but *dinner* was so divine I'd like to put the cake in a napkin and take it *home* if you don't mind (of course, you can't *also* eat it at table!). While she's wrapping the take-home cake, hostess *might* just throw in the rest of the cake or other things from diner.
- Keep clothes brushed, sponged, spots removed and not jammed in the closet. They hold up better.
- Put the money in woolen *basics*. (How many times do we have to be told?!) Get out of the habit of frittering away money. Instead of nonsense spending, save up those throwaway dollars for a fabulous suit, something that lasts and always lifts your spirits.
- Check out charity thrift shops. Rich women donate designer dresses after a season.
- Switch shoes daily; get new lifts whenever necessary. Shoes last much longer.
- Do your own hair and manicure, for God's sake. For fifteen years I never set foot in a beauty shop. Nobody bars you from the office or the picnic.
- If you're a city apartment dweller, don't be too stingy with the building maintenance men. They can make your life *possible* (plumbing, electrical repairs) or refer to you as "that stingy bitch in 16A" and get to you last or *never.*
- Grow some houseplants. Fresh greenery is a decorating bargain.
- Hang out with the wealthy when possible. Aside from making *you* feel a little *poor* (they don't mean to), they can provide great food, a visit to their country house, hand-me-down clothes (you don't *want* a two-year-old Valentino?). Your particular talent for compassion, lis-

tening, helping straighten out a family crisis *may* be a good trade-off for them.

- Shop for Christmas presents all year long—we're talking inexpensive here—or make them. Check out junky antique shops for sweet, small items. Learn to wrap well and buy gift paper whenever it's on sale.
- Buy staples (toilet tissue, paper towels, Kleenex) in bulk but only *those.* Buy sheets/towels only during the January white sales.
- Send personal notes (promptly) for birthdays, anniversaries, to say thank-you; skip bought greeting cards. You're still sending Christmas cards? The Christmas *note* will suffice. (I don't recommend not sending *anything.* We don't want you not getting Christmas greetings *back.* These things are reciprocal.)
- Book early or last-minute travel reservations. Both are generally well below normal prices. Example: A tourist ticket on the *QE2* from New York to Southampton costs $1,095 if you opt for standby, meaning they'll let you know if there's space four weeks ahead of sailing. Normal price is $1,795.
- Sponge as little as possible from your children; if you must, be gracious. You can't have *them* subsidize and you *criticize;* what kind of creep *are* you?
- Don't splurge on grandchildren gifts. Children don't know the price of anything; they just love presents.
- Drink tap water, chilled in the fridge, instead of *any* bottled beverage. Some of us have survived *endlessly* (even healthfully) doing that all our lives.
- Check your bank and credit-card statements carefully. Mistakes can be made, particularly with clerks trying to read our handwritten payment checks.
- Stop financially propping up your children or indigent relatives. Isn't it *your* turn?

How do you *make* extra money if you need it? You can sell your 78s record collection, make and sell special pecan pralines with Amaretto or better brownies than Famous Amos, hand-paint and sell T-shirts, tutor, teach

French, word-process a manuscript, research for a writer, organize somebody's files, closets or house, baby-sit, dog-sit, apartment-sit, personal shop, do alterations, cater. A group of fifteen young women and men in New York (Homebodies) charge $75 an hour to exercise with you at home and, by publication of this book, the price might even be *higher.* You may not be a pro like they are, and we don't want you helping somebody throw her back out, but some people need somebody to be there to make them *do* it and do it *with* them (huff puff) more than they need Jane Fonda. If you have a sports background, you can probably *develop* an exercise routine to take next door to a neighbor and charge. Listen, you'll have ideas of your own. Charge less than others until you get good and can fluff up your fees.

So here is an investment plan just in *case* you're interested. The plan doesn't come from *me.* Hanging on to your first dollar—well, *almost* your first, with a few slips—like a bald eagle with a mackerel in its mouth disqualifies you, I realize, to give financial advice, so I asked Liz Oberbeck, *Cosmo*'s smart financial columnist, for some thoughts, plus an investment plan. Cogent thoughts first. Liz checks with other experts of course, to write her column and give advice.

Says Liz, "It is simply *crucial* for a woman to learn about money. You can't start too early or too *late.*" You could begin your education by reading *Your Personal Financial Fitness Program* by Elizabeth S. Lewin, CFP (Facts on File), a Baedeker of practical wisdom. You might also want to buy this videotape: *The Wall Street Journal Video Guide to Money and Markets.* For nonsubscribers to *The Wall Street Journal,* send $14.95 (check or money order) to Dow Jones & Co., Inc., Ms. Nancy Travaglione, P.O. Box 300, Princeton, N.J. 08543; telephone 609/520-4258. They don't accept credit cards. For subscribers to the *Journal,* call 1-800-628-9320 to receive a complimentary copy of the tape.

"To get smart, you must talk, study, probe. If you are just beginning to manage your own money (you're widowed or divorced) or think you could do better with it than you now are, ask *everybody*—doctor, landlord, boss, friends, other women making investments—what *they* do, not necessarily toward doing the same thing yourself but to get an idea of what's *out* there. You may want to have a professional financial planner who will help you get a *grip* on your finances—how much money and other assets do you actually have, what are their sources, what are your fixed and fluctuating expenses, long and short-term financial goals? The International Association of Certified Planners, a group of whose members must have completed a number of courses to belong, and who are supposed to be reliable, will give you names of several people in your area. Phone 404/395-1005. You can ask whatever planner you call about her background and fees. Financial planners usually charge from $75 to $300 a session; you may decide one or two sessions are all you need.

"Shopping for a financial planner is a bit like being in a new city and tracking down a doctor. You'd spend possibly a month buying a fur coat or even a good cloth one, yet people make financial decisions in two minutes! A woman *alone* is vulnerable, not so much because people are trying to swindle her, although they might be, but because the financial world *is* a jungle. Investment options are as varied as trees; the price of the stocks, bonds, Treasury notes, Treasury bills, whatever you own changes by the month, the day, sometimes actually by the second (stocks). Nobody has a perfect investment formula. Even if some hotshots seem to have got it brilliantly right for the moment, stay tuned! Without proper research (and sometimes even *with*) stocks are a gamble. You might as well say somebody has the perfect formula for winning at Las Vegas. Observing superstar investors like Warren Buffett and Fayes Serafim and figuring you'll do just what *they* do can't happen—you haven't their resources. Gradually, if you research hard and don't get bored (I mean a lot of women are *not* fascinated with money management), with or without a financial adviser, a financial plan will develop.

"After you've invested, you need at least two people looking at your portfolio (stocks, bonds, money market, whatever you're in) every so often—just a little safety check. The person you deal with at one of your mutual funds (more in a minute) may be one of the people you check in with. If you are on good terms and a steady customer, they will do this for you. Another checker might be some conservative rich friend, maybe a boss if he's money-shrewd. A broker possibly *isn't* a good 'checker' because he makes his money getting people to buy and sell stock. Your 'check-up people' may not totally agree with what you're doing or with each *other* but will cause you to think and question even if you stay exactly with your plan. The first goal is to get your head out of the sand; the second is not to get it knocked off! You constantly adjust strategy. You aren't changing your entire portfolio *all* the time but you are always assessing and occasionally adjusting. You are healthily suspicious of what everybody tells you but not paranoid! Investments are like a living organism—they change texture, color and state of health almost like a gardenia plant."

Here is Liz's suggested investment plan for $100,000. Goal: reasonable safety *and* reasonable growth. You could invest a bigger or smaller amount. We've already said that most people won't have this much—or *any*—money to invest. We're just doing a hypothetical plan.

1. Start with 30 to 40 percent of your money in a conservative stock mutual fund such as Vanguard Conservative Equity Fund or T. Rowe Price Conservative Equity Fund. These and many others are listed in *The Wall Street Journal*. (As you become more comfortable with investing, you might consider raising the percentage.) A mutual fund is a *considered selection* of stocks, where your money, along with that of other investors, will be spread among stocks chosen by the fund managers. In a mutual stock fund your money can *grow*. As with all investments in the stock market, it is risky but not *very*, especially if you hold stocks over extended periods of time (three to five years), and mutual funds such as the ones mentioned have a good track record. Historically, with stocks held over a five-year period, 85 percent of the time you can make 10 percent on your money. Yes, investing in a con-

servative stock mutual fund is probably better than finding a broker and picking stocks yourself, at least until you get a little more knowledge and experience. For the moment, however, we are not talking about giving somebody "discretionary power" to invest your money except in the mutual fund.

Buying into a mutual fund you may want to take advantage of what is called dollar-cost averaging, a conservative investing plan whereby you don't invest, say, the whole $50,000 at one time but "phase in" a fixed sum of money at regular intervals over a twelve-month period, say $4,000 a month, regardless of market conditions. Stock prices do fluctuate and shares in a good company might be picked up for a particularly low price in a particular month.

2. Put 40 to 50 percent of your money in a high-quality government and corporate *bond* mutual fund which will incorporate Treasury bonds as well as high-quality *corporate* bonds. You won't be choosing the bonds yourself but, as in a stock fund, professional managers will select specific bonds to buy for the portfolio. The bond fund might be handled by the same people from whom you buy the *stock* fund but doesn't need to be. You generally don't buy bonds for growth, but if interest rates decline, you could earn a lot of money on bonds. Bonds are safe—municipal bonds almost *never* go into default and can produce 5 to 7.5 percent interest tax-free depending on the bonds' maturity date and credit rating.

3. Put the balance of your money in a high-liquidity money-market funding that concentrates on short-term government debt, on high-grade corporate debt, and passes interest payments on to shareholders. Money-market mutual funds are the safest of all investments because loans to the government are short-term and fully backed by the government—*this* government pays its bills. You could say this fund is your "emergency nest egg" but no more than that because money markets are a no-growth situation. Four percent is about all your money can earn at this time. That's still better than a passbook savings account, which brings 3.28 percent interest—used to be 4 but is now

lower. Money-market funds are also listed in *The Wall Street Journal*. A big mutual fund can handle stocks, bonds, *and* money-market investments, but funds should be selected based on their individual merit. Dealing with three different mutual funds rather than settling all your money in one place is probably a better idea. Convenience should never be an investment consideration.

There is a real danger of older women being too conservative, hoarding money the way a squirrel hoards nuts (under the mattress or in a savings bank, where they can easily get their hands on it). You also can never *lose* it (short of burglars and/or the U.S. government going bust), but because of inflation, the hoard gets "smaller" by the minute (have you ever seen inflation stop dead in its tracks and go in the other direction?).

Let me cite a woman who decided, after the 1987 crash, to stash her money in a savings bank "until the market is healthy again" and, from fall 1987 through winter 1989, let her money languish there, bringing in around 5 percent interest but not growing. Repeat: By being "safe," you are ignoring inflation, which, ten or twenty-five years later, will have eaten away your funds like acid. Even in a so-called down market, there are good investments to make, mutual funds to buy. At age sixty you still have another twenty years, maybe more, to live. You need your money to grow and keep you comfortable. Stocks outperform bonds in that department.

Beyond these three suggestions, if you are working, you should sock every dime possible into your 401-K account, especially any percentage your employer matches. The 401-K is an employer-sponsored retirement fund to which you and possibly your employer—some do, some don't—contribute. You don't pay taxes on the amount deducted from your paycheck until retirement, at which time, presumably, your income will be lower and so will the taxes on the sequestered money. You also won't have to pay taxes on your 401-K earnings. If you withdraw the money before age 59½, you will pay a 10 percent penalty. At present the limit you can contribute yearly to a 401-K account is $8,500.

Liz's plan certainly sounds sensible to *me*. Now just a few more thoughts.

PENSION PLANS AND SOCIAL SECURITY

If your company has a pension plan, obviously you will have been checking benefits. One sixty-year-old woman recently found that since she had been with the company just under five years, if she should be fired within the next six months, her pension would never begin. On the date of her fifth anniversary with the company she would become 100 percent vested in the retirement plan and collect a pension whether or not she stayed one more day after that—the longer the stay, the better chance of getting a *larger* pension. My friend is working hard to be especially valuable in the six months ahead. Every company's plan is different.

You'll certainly want to check your Social Security benefits. Ordinarily Social Security is paid at age sixty-five, but you can opt to collect at age sixty-two, in which case you receive 80 percent of what would be due you at sixty-five. Whatever amount they then compute for you to collect monthly is the *permanent* amount of your Social Security benefits from then on; it is *not* adjusted to reflect a higher amount at age sixty-five. If you collect Social Security at age sixty-two but continue to work, you can earn up to $7,440 annually (this amount changes every year to reflect cost of living). For every $2.00 over that amount (considered "excess earnings"!), they will deduct $1.00 from your benefits. If you continue to work from age sixty-five through sixty-nine, the amount you can earn is increased to $10,200. Then they will deduct $1.00 for every $3.00 from the "excess earnings." At age seventy there is *no* ceiling on earnings. Earn as much as you please *and* collect max Social Security!

REAL ESTATE

We haven't talked real estate as an investment. Well, it might be a little *late* for that . . . how many years can you afford to *wait* for the building to double in value? There have been fabulous real-estate booms—along with devastating real-estate busts—and your property can be worth *less* than you paid. Ugh! Unlike a stock that can float right off the exchange, real estate can't *disappear*—that's why it's called "real"—but you will have been paying taxes through the years, not deriving income unless it's rental property, so that for a woman over sixty, real estate for an *investment* seems a little capricious. You'll decide what you can afford to pay to *live* in, whether to rent or buy.

OTHER THINGS TO CONSIDER

You *know* you don't want to be without adequate health care as you get older . . . brrr! The health-insurance industry has worked out a plan for people fifty and over whereby for $500 to $1,200 a year you can take out insurance that covers catastrophic medical situations not covered by your company insurance plan and keep it after you leave the company. The Prudential and Equitable insurance companies are good places to inquire about long-term health-care insurance. A financial planner can also advise you.

ESTATE PLANNING

Make out a will, you silly goose. A regular will, along with bequeathing whatever you want bequeathed to loved ones and friends, will indicate who is to administer the will. In New York State a *Living* Will is a document that tells others, when you are dead, to donate your eyes to the eye bank, your kidney to whoever needs one at the time, your liver to the transplant patient, etc. In New York State, a document called a Health Care Proxy is used to appoint somebody as your medical guardian and to say that you want no extraordinary measures taken to resuscitate you. I assume most states have Living Wills, Health Care Proxies or their equivalents.

That's it, pussycat, I didn't know anything about money management when I started writing this chapter, had never taken any of the advice *in* it. I'm feeling a *little* more competent now ... that means there could also be hope for *you*.

chapter twelve

Joys, Sorrows, Compensations

You thought you were going to escape a wrap-up chapter? Don't be foolish! Cheer-up books (which this has "deteriorated" *into!*) always have a wrap-up chapter.

In the play *Tru,* Truman Capote says, "Cicero said life is a moderately good play with a badly written last act." Well, I want to deal with bad stuff in our last act for one minute. Aging *is* absolutely ghastly sometimes. We are often, as I have said, basically crazy. Yesterday I found myself talking to some mushrooms. Preparing pasta prima-vera, I sautéed mushrooms and onion, realized red pepper wasn't in the pan, quickly tossed some in, put several cooked mushrooms on top of pepper, said to mushrooms, "Listen, mushrooms, *you* warm up the peppers like a little blanket . . . just lend them your body heat real fast while I get the pasta drained." Nobody hears you, thank God.

We lose our tempers. You wouldn't have wanted to be in the cab with David and me in Washington, D.C., re-cently when the driver mistakenly took us to the Delta Building at National Airport instead of the old Pan Am Shuttle Building, now Delta's embarkation point. Mistake required an extra fifteen-minute drive on a wildly busy morning and, on *finally* delivering us to right place, the driver said, "Well, you folks got a nice ride around the air-port!" David put his hands over his ears.

Envy is not unknown . . . *still.* "If you could be any-body else, who would you want to be?" my psychology professor at a UCLA extension course asked the class a

hundred years ago. I didn't even have to *think* ... Lana
Turner! Not a year later Lana's daughter, Cheryl Crane,
had killed her mother's lover with a butcher knife, both
women were in court fighting to keep Cheryl out of prison
and *that* sort of took Lana off my envy list. But replace-
ments move right in virtually all your life. We don't want
to *be* those other people ... just have things they *have*
(Academy Award for best actress, bushels of pale blond
hair, Don Johnson mad about us). We love the big-time
downfalls of celebrities (Clark Clifford, Mike Tyson, Michael Milken, Robert Maxwell—though we didn't need
him to *die),* the smaller-time failure of friends. When people are on the way up, we're there cheering. They beat or
used the system and we're happy for them, if we're not
having too bad a time ourselves at the moment. But once
they're on top, envy creeps in and we're thrilled to have
them—someone we know or someone we don't—come
skidding right back down again. I don't know how we can
be so two-faced ... adoring of our big-time friends, bragging about knowing them, and also satisfied by their not
being there anymore, or at least in trouble. My pal, the late
Milton Gordon, calls to tell me he and Mara, his
ladyfriend, have had a rotten time in Paris. It rained, was
bitter cold, he *caught* a cold and they didn't have any fun.
How uplifting! When R., nearly the most perfect person I
have ever known, tells me her daughter hasn't found a job
yet and insists on sitting home trying to write a screenplay,
my spirits soar. It's high time R.'s daughter gave her a little trouble. Envy ... a staple even *now.*

What else isn't good about us survivors? We are not
always nice. Sometimes I *don't* go clear to the end of an
airport security-check line stretching from here to Klamath
Falls, Oregon. I may slither ahead of a real dawdler who
doesn't know her body from her shoulder bag or at least
is clinically unable to part with one and lay it on the con-
veyor belt while walking the other through the metal de-
tector. If I see somebody creeping in line ahead of me in
a department store, I *may* let him get away with it—
respect for a pro and all that—unless the line is *serious* or
I've been holding an eggbeater in one hand and my Visa

card in the other for twenty minutes; then there is no *way* that person is not going to get splattered, right there in Bloomingdale's.

We still know prejudice, the condition that lets people feel they are better than *somebody* else—Jews, blacks, women, Hispanics, etc.; it's not hard to find a target for our "superiority." Women have been so handy for *men* all these years (millennia), no *wonder* the feminist movement has been rabidly (if sneakily) resisted by a lot of them. If you aren't better than a *woman,* what kind of person *are* you? Men *control* women when they control our sex lives and say we may have sex only to create a family (i.e., if a young woman gets pregnant accidentally, she must bring the baby to term whether she wants to or not). That's *one* way of staying "superior" to us. Though legal abortion isn't an option anybody our age needs, I'm in there fighting to keep it. Patriarchal societies *always* try to keep women in the home. It's a yucky idea.

Do *women* need somebody to feel superior to? You bet . . . lots of prejudiced females out there. A black woman, already down on two counts, could maybe feel superior to her no-good sister-in-law. *I* feel superior to fat people, drinkers, drug users and real dummies (by my assessment). Hardly *anybody* deep down thinks we're all equal. Age doesn't make you really more tolerant, does it?

It's easy to get a bit "coarse" (what we called females in Little Rock in the thirties who didn't talk nice, mask their true feelings, dress ladylike or measure up to the silly, vapid standards for women of their time) when you get older. You've seen a lot, been *around.* You've toughened *up* . . . haven't got time for the simpering niceties. My language horrifies even *me* sometimes. If you had to choose between tough and direct and prissy and bland (at our age), I would choose tough, but once in a while I try to quiet down and be more silky, cool it with the four-letter words. I know Cleo in her grave, like Scarlett's mother, Ellen, in hers, would like that . . . a lady on the outside, tough underneath.

Ticking off other shortcomings of older people (I'm never going to call us *old),* we're not always as grateful as we should be. I not only see the glass half empty, I want what was in the other half returned . . . immediately! Two years down the line—or sooner—I will look back at this moment and think I was blessed . . . why can't I know that *now?* There is a picture of me having just got off a plane at Charles de Gaulle Airport in Paris—skinny pink-silk shirtwaist dress—long hair—a long-stemmed rose in my hand—zonked, pretty, sexy—about 1975, I'd say. Did I have a *clue* I looked good, was blessed and *Cosmo* was a miracle?! Of course not! And tonight . . . *any* night . . . can I actually *feel* gratitude for my blessings? Is Elvis playing Radio City Music Hall this evening? I don't *do* too well with grateful—are you somewhat better?

We lose things. My Cartier love-ring went last night at the Gotham Theatre. I slipped all my rings and bracelets into my purse to be more comfortable . . . love-ring must have fallen to floor (four ushers on hands and knees never found it). Last week my desk calendar, containing the entire history of my life for this year, disappeared. How do you lose a desk calendar? Who would want it? Where could it *be?!*

Recently at my sister Mary's house in Shawnee, Oklahoma, I lost one big plastic earring—cost about five dollars. I nearly went *mad*. We searched under every piece of furniture, heavy oak stuff had to be moved out from the wall . . . went through wastebaskets, shelves, drawers of cabinets in rooms I hadn't been *in*. The loss ruined the visit because my sister is as anal as I about parting with things she hasn't meant to and we couldn't quit *looking!* Earring finally turned up in Vuitton tote where I had looked three times before. Who put it there and forgot?— who do you *suppose?!* Lost earrings are my nemesis. In a restaurant I took off a pair of 18k gold and Sea Island pearl ones (already a line-for-line replacement of a pair lost earlier in *another* restaurant) and put them on the table to listen with unpained ears to Gene Hackman and Matt Dillon discuss a movie they were in. I left earrings on table, never got them back, ordered the *second* replacement pair.

And there was the jade bracelet that fell into the

kitchen trash can the exact moment I passed by . . . only place it *could* have gone. I was wearing it in the kitchen but didn't miss it soon enough to retrieve before garbage was collected. Speaking of trash, what about the David Webb emerald ring I hid in the toe of a shoe, later got the urge to get rid of some "marginal stuff," unmarginal emerald ring tucked in marginal-shoe toe went pouf, right into the garbage. On discovering loss around midnight, I kept baby browns open until 5:00 A.M. when one of the building men came in, took me to the basement and we went straight through one hundred big black body bags of garbage for one hundred apartments. Living in the penthouse where collection begins, ours was at the bottom, of course. I can't describe the joy of seeing *our* garbage— *Wall Street Journals,* Kitty Litter bags, No-Cal ginger-ale bottles . . . we were *reasonably* chic; ring was among the coffee grounds. I gave security man $100, took him back to my apartment and we had a belt of Scotch. I already told you about the David Webb pin lost in a taxi in San Francisco I never got back . . . it's all *disgusting* and I think age-related.

Other than *material* things go bye-bye, like your *memory.* My friend Connie went for a half-hour walk while garage fixed her car. On returning to the garage she asked, "Is my car ready?" "You took the keys *with* you," they said. Lunching with Bryant Gumbel of *The Today Show,* I misplaced Lech Walesa. He was in my memory bank somewhere; I just couldn't get him out. This was the first time I'd lunched with Bryant, quick as a lizard and very attractive, and you don't want to stop the conversation cold to inquire, "Who *is* the leader of Poland?" Not five minutes later I lost the Japanese people who bought MCA Universal—Mitsukoshi? Mitsobishi? Matsuhama? Close but I never got all the way to Matsushita! Never mind you forgot things when you were seven (of course, you had a lot less to remember), forgetting is such a specific reminder of *age* even though the forgotten names and words aren't gone forever. You can generally haul them up later in the day or next morning but who needs them *then?!* If it's any consolation—I find it *some*—men's brains deteriorate faster than women's as we age. According to a study by University of Pennsylvania researchers, "The gender related differences suggest that female sex hormones may protect the brain from atrophy associated with aging." Good.

Rejection isn't something they take off the menu because we are too old to digest it. I can't get Cher on the phone. I can't get Cher's *manager* on the phone. I can get Cher's manager's secretary—a sweetheart—but she can't get Cher's manager to take my call or call me back. Calling her manager's office twice a day every day without getting a return call for two weeks is making me *ill!* (We did finally get her.) Frequently the big-time writers I pursue say they are busy with their book, movie, TV script or have a contract with *Vanity Fair* (which pays more). Rats!

I think hurt feelings usually happen because you've "overreached"—asked people to do things you shouldn't ever have expected them to do—invited "over-your-head" people instead of those who'd be delighted to go out with you, show up at your event. It's okay to cultivate stars of your particular world and, with diligence, you may even get them occasionally to do what you want, but you can't pull in stars regularly, so you shouldn't be hurt when they decide to shine right there in their galaxy without you. As for wincing because you didn't get included in a party, I've decided getting excluded—and getting hurt over it—is probably going to go on *forever.* Life is endless lists, some of which you'd love to be on but didn't make the cut. *You're* probably excluding somebody from a tiny list of your own.

A well-known woman recently asked an even *more* well-known woman if she was attending a party that night. "I wasn't invited," said the famous one. "And I'm hurt!" "Are you crazy?!" asked her friend. "You are probably invited to more parties than any other person in this city ... if you say you'll be there, they'll *give* a party! How can you worry about some dippy little reception that's probably going to be a major bore?" "I want to be invited to everything," said the famous lady. "Then I can turn things down." Social insecurity in the famous ... isn't it heart-warming?

Sometimes rejection is silence ... you don't hear *anything*. As a minor celebrity you could go mad thinking of the newspapers, magazines, radio shows, television shows (local, network and cable) that need to fill hundreds of hours and thousands of columns and yet they aren't calling *you*. And how about the parties and lunches you don't get invited to and read about in the columns?

Some days *nostalgia* can engulf you so totally, be so intoxicating, there isn't any *now!* The snowflakes falling at a borrowed chalet in Lake Arrowhead, the peach cashmere scarf two yards long you looked so pretty in, mulled wine, your song ... "I Don't Want to Set the World on Fire" ... the man, always a man ... the second lieutenant who adored you and later married a Chicago girl. Strangely enough, the *details* in the nostalgia fit—clothes, food, music—are just as valid and vivid as the man making love to you and maybe as important in making up the vignette ... those bloody details you think may possibly kill you with longing when they start playing in your mind. For me it is always Los Angeles in the fall. How can people say Los Angeles has no seasons ... you stop going to the beach ... the daytime air crisps up ... driving Sunset Boulevard either direction near the Beverly Hills Hotel in October is for me quintessential glamour, and I "drive" there, in my mind, day after day ... I can do a full twenty minutes of nostalgia on Los Angeles in fall and another on Little Rock in the summer ... *that* air ... moist, hot, sexy, young, the sun not quite coming out, sultry as sin ... those incredible thirties when Mary and I wolfed double-dip ice-cream cones at five cents apiece (vanilla, chocolate, strawberry—no rum raisin or crème de menthe frappé then). I *worshipped* Jean Harlow, Clark Gable, Carole Lombard ... Gods, Goddesses ... and lived for the next issue of *Photoplay*.

All nostalgia isn't happy. Memories for me were tinged with sadness after my father died when I was ten and you remember the sadness but it's just that it was all *then*. Now, a thousand years later, anything that happened *then* seems somehow *sacred!* I recently made a lunch date with Gloria Vanderbilt *specifically* to do "nostalgia." I had read her book *Black Knight/White Knight,* and wanted to know *more* about her evil first husband who played poker with the boys on her wedding night and sometimes beat her, and *more* about Leopold Stokowski, her second husband, and how she felt when others worshipped him as a conductor but she was the one he came home to and I wanted to ask her about the Frank Sinatra romance which made it possible for her finally to leave the prototypal male chauvinist Stokowski but mostly I wanted to talk about Beverly Hills—*my* Beverly Hills—in the forties when we both lived there though we didn't know each other. Well, darlings, she gave me one quick minute on the past and wanted to talk about her *present* romance (*not* uninteresting—Gloria is sixty-eight and *never* without a romance). She was smart enough not to *do* nostalgia.

Can you somehow turn nostalgia into gratitude ... that lovely things *once* happened? It isn't easy! In a famous Broadway musical, the older, widowed (still beautiful) English nanny sings to some young lovers she sees strolling about the moonlit palace grounds that she's happy for them—really happy—because she's had a love of her *own,* you see. Jesus! That previous love was *then*—what possible good does it do me *now???* Good memories are better than bad probably, although bad memories can make you a *little* grateful for now because things aren't as bad *now* as they were *then.* Good memories to me are like a book you've enjoyed—it doesn't do much to cheer you in the dentist's waiting room this minute—what you need is a *new* book. So nostalgia is tempting, inevitable and, I think, essentially useless. I give it a quick three minutes when it crops up. Then over and out.

Another hazard of being semi-ancient: People remind you how old you *are.* A nurse says, "Oh, you're his mother!" when you are visiting a fifty-year-old art director in St. Luke's Hospital and you thought you looked so yummy in your slub-silk walking shorts and Armani T-shirt. I do wantonly, tirelessly, convince myself I'm handling looks at my age better than peers ... all that exercise, diet and self-discipline born out of fear and pain . . . but sometimes I'm not so sure. I am in London with a new wardrobe, no business assignments one afternoon, ready for a tiny adventure and I start out from the St. James Club on Park Place with instructions for getting to the Tate Gallery on foot. I get lost immediately. Someone on the street tells me how to get to the Tate on public transportation . . . surely more of an adventure than walking and I'm pleased. Just as I am getting final instructions, "my" bus comes hurtling to the stop about half a block away. I quickly thank new friend, sprint for bus really hard but I'm in flats and good shape so no problem. Get on bus, panting and victorious, just as it is pulling away. Bus driver says, "You're real proud of yourself, aren't you? Makes you feel young!" This prick . . . I *am* young!

To shift subjects totally and get more general, people who kill animals *pour le sport* (and that includes some otherwise okay people who have a pet Shih Tzu and you actually have dinner in their homes) are more serious transgressors than age-reminding nudgers. Bea Pickens, wife of big-time Texas raider T. Boone Pickens, said on the *CBS Morning News* she had come dangerously close to a leopard on a shooting safari—so close, in fact, "the leopard got part of my finger." "Good!" I yelled at the TV set. I am looking forward to the day when animal lover Cleveland Amory's vision of an equitable world for animals becomes reality: Giant elk is driving down Taconic Parkway with a hunter thrown over the hood of his Cadillac Seville.

Crossword puzzles. You don't *believe* somebody could complain about crossword puzzles? *I* think they are sadistic. Instead of the clue for "pig" being "swine" or "young hog," it's "tamworth." Have you ever *seen* a tamworth? When somebody eats a pint of Häagen Dazs butter pecan in one sitting, do you say he's tamworthing *out?* The clue for "opera" is "a Cherubini product." Sounds to me like boxed pasta . . . what is the matter with "musical drama"? "Colic" is the answer; "mulligrubs" is the clue. I wouldn't know a mulligrub if it came up and bit me but I would know "childhood disease," etc., etc., etc. Maybe you *like* your puzzles "challenging" but I would like to be able to finish one in less than a week *without* a dictionary.

Okay, these things aren't really age-related . . . they could have got on your nerves a long time ago, and you probably have your own list. Thanks for letting me unburden. Polling a girlfriend or two about things they specifically don't like about aging: Betty Furness (seventies): "It takes longer to get your makeup on, figure out what to wear, what to pack. I can't *walk* as fast as I used to . . . I used to pass up everybody on the street." Leonora Hornblow (seventies): "You've got to remember time is now finite and you'd better fit in whatever you really want to fit *in*. You think to yourself you want to take a trip to Greece or down the Amazon . . . if you don't get busy and do it, it may not *happen.*" The late Mollie Parnis (she died at 93): "I could always go to parties in other cities. Now I can't do that . . . I can't get up and down the steps and I'm too vain to get a wheelchair." Jackie Lehman (seventies): "Men not making passes, definitely. A man did in Greece recently and he was very attractive but it was all so clear he wanted me to use my influence with my husband to get a movie filmed 'near his marina.' " Ann Ford Johnson (seventies): "The worst thing about aging is not being able to wear strapless dresses."

Ginny finds it daunting that "we never quite get anything *fixed!*" Mortimer Levitt *(How to Start Your Own Business Without Losing Your Shirt)* says, "It took me a long, long time to understand that misfortune—loneliness, sickness, financial reverses, malicious gossip, shabby treatment by friends, problems with children, the untimely death of family and friends, the duplicity of lovers—is a permanent part of life and should be expected to continue with varying degrees of severity as long as one lives." Jane Fonda (fifties): says, "It's a constant struggle—you work every day of your life. You can be famous, wealthy, respected and it still doesn't stop."

I find everything can be going along smashingly and then life says, "Hey, you're getting a little grand there . . . I've been meaning to speak to you . . . swat!" You do get some dragons slain but at that very moment, baby dragons are being hatched, others going through their adolescence, all of them preparing to start breathing fire on you one day (do you like that metaphor?). We're not talking *major* pain necessarily, just the everyday rejection, disappointment, dealing with morons, yukky assignments we all get handed. I don't *think* I'm more negative than others ... I just don't experience unadulterated happiness more than four days at a time before the cutoff date.

Nobel Laureate Robert Frost put it this way: "Life is a painted piece of trouble" and "Trouble keeps overflowing the retaining wall of philosophy." Paula, *not* a poet, says, "Life is one third ecstasy, one third agony and one third I'll surely feel better when I get out of the house and get to the office!" Angela comes down the same way: "Life is being miserable and happy in turns—whichever one I wasn't last is the one I'll be dealing with next!" She also says, "It's the recidivism that gets me. You don't mind so much never having started your own company, working in a Third World country for a year, having a Pulitzer Prize–winning child, but it's the thinning out of stuff you have had and enjoyed that hurts. Going *backward* is tougher than never having got there or even *getting* there!" I was bellyaching about not ever getting it fixed to press agent Pat Newcomb, who explained it to me this way: "All you can be is basically happy," she said. "Happy-okay. That condition is your vehicle, then the problems or challenges that come along every day are the fuel that *power* you through life. Nobody runs without fuel." That's *one* way to feel not so irritated about continuing woes or I guess you could try to remember that a completely happy person would be *brain* dead???

How we were at other stages of our life in terms of happy and sad probably ought to be considered before complaining our heads off about aging *now* and thinking this gruesomeness is something *new.* Were you a bundle of joy in your teens and twenties? I *wasn't.* Money worries, concern about my depressed mother, invalid sister never left me. Were *you* a perfectly functioning sexual creature in your thirties? Maybe you were *physically* but were you emotionally secure and ecstatic with the men you were functioning *with?* I never was. Let's don't even *start* on my two—*two*—Don Juans! Did you know at forty that was the best age a woman could be or were you sniveling about being dumped out of your thirties? That's what I *thought!* You possibly weren't appreciative or grateful then *either* (like I wasn't). A hundred years ago I remember standing on the outdoor stairs of Music Corporation of America on Burton Way in Beverly Hills, that graceful, sun-dappled southern-plantation building, now Litton Industries, where I worked, and having a hissy because World War II was taking away all the boys. I was twenty. The boys were drafted at twenty-one, which left me only a few more months, I figured, to get the good out of them. And at twenty-four, at the William Morris agency, the boss Abe Lastfogel's secretary found me wandering down an *alley* in Beverly Hills one noon weeping my head off. She picked me up and took me home with her to dry me out.

I was frequently a *metastacized* case of the sads. One of my early bosses, Paul Ziffren, later head of the Democratic party in California and a major force in the 1984 Olympics, took me to lunch one day—I was twenty-six—and said he was hereafter going to call me Atlas "because you are obviously carrying the weight of the world on your shoulders. . . . Okay, Atlas. Let's get the check."

I was so wantonly depressed—and *careless*—I even told *men* about my sadness and problems at home (no money, invalid sister, melancholy mother). It didn't depress the men usually, just removed them from my side!

Summing up: It never *was* a whole lot different in terms of how some of us felt about life when we *were* young—twenty, thirty, forty, so who am I to think *now* that age is a problem, *the* problem, when *life* is simply the problem! This is what I've concluded: I'm basically no unhappier now at age seventy than I was at twenty-four. Of course, I'm not any happier *either,* even with all the financial burdens gone and my mother and her anxiety put to rest, but I do have lots of hours of pleasure that age doesn't seem to interfere with. One thing we have to notice is how swiftly *time* goes by. One week is like you put down the phone to answer the doorbell and when you come back to pick it up it's already Thursday. I haven't got one single philosophical thought about this except that when I have a frozen tush trying to hail a cab on Madison Avenue in January, I remember to say to myself this is *fun* because when the weather softens up—along with my tush—I'll be six months older. How fabulous it's only *now*—winter—and I'm still "young."

For a while I was furious that nobody *warns* us age is going to happen to us and be such a yukky bore. They *don't*, you know ... they just let us crash in like those poor dinosaurs that used to flop into the glop that is now the La Brea Tar Pits in Los Angeles. If we knew ahead of time, I reasoned, we could take steps not to be so traumatized by the loss of physical attraction (wrinkled *knees?!*), the need for more sleep, losing your car keys twice a day, going to a room for one thing, forgetting what you went for and doing something else entirely—how *could* they have let us come on this condition *cold?!* I now think I was wrong to want a warning. If they told us ahead of time what was coming, it would just take some of the joy out of not *being* old yet. We'd have to start battening down the hatches ("Oh, God, *it*—the Thing—is out there waiting!"). And if they started telling us at twenty-five to enjoy, ENJOY, it won't last, would we, could we actually start piping in more dawns, getting *more* bottles of cold champagne into us and getting in between *more* cool sheets with more hot young men? I don't know about *you* but *I* was dancing as fast as I could already! My tax man tries to warn me about "Later." "Helen," he says, "you and David are going to have to plan to put more of your money into *services.* You'll probable need nurses ... people to walk you around. You ought to *think* about it." Fuck off, Red (I don't quite say that but I *think* it) ... sufficient unto the day, etc., etc., etc.

So when *should* we start acknowledging and accepting that we are old and start planning? Never, in my opinion. Accepting yourself as *older* is different from accepting yourself as *old.* I started thinking "older" at sixty-four, as I mentioned. You may think "older" later—or *sooner.* Up until at least sixty I was one of *them*—the *young* crowd! When I'm eighty or ninety *maybe* I'll get around to thinking *old*—I doubt it.

Birthdays themselves don't really matter much—not the day *of.* The damage was done during the preceding year or years, giving birthdays a bad name. I never celebrate mine, though people keep *track* and send stuff, which is sweet. How well you are remembered on your birthday is in direct proportion to how many phone calls, prezzies, flowers, cards *you* have dispatched ... it is a very reciprocal deal.

Age demarkation is actually quite a recent thing; did you know that? We didn't always make such a fuss about *older,* separate us out of society and confine us to the sidelines. In a review of Howard P. Chudacoff's book, *How Old Are You?,* in *The New York Times,* Robert H. Binstock writes, "Until the mid-nineteenth century, Americans showed little concern with age. The one-room schoolhouse was filled with students of varied ages, and children worked alongside adults. Age-consciousness in the United States began in the late nineteenth century, when schools began to set age limits and pediatrics was established as a medical specialty. Celebrating birthdays only came along with the arrival of the first birthday cards and gradually age-consciousness intensified, especially for the young, as child psychology, organized sports, age-peer organizations such as the Girl Scouts, street gangs and legislation regulating child labor and the age of sexual consent were established. Chudakoff thinks certain advantages accrue to living in an age-conscious society. Individuals can derive a sense of belonging and sense of self from their age-based peer group. He says the major drawback of such a society is 'agism'—the attribution of certain characteristics to *all* persons in an age category and he is sensitive to discrimination. 'Like gender and race, age cannot be changed,' he says. 'To disadvantage individuals merely because they possess a particular characteristic, one for which they cannot be held morally responsible, offends traditional American sensibilities of fairness.' "

Executive Health Report says, "Sixty-five is considered the time when vitality and skills begin to fade away.

This myth has nothing to do with actuarial tables; instead it derives from the world of Machiavellian politics. Before the rise to power in the last century, German Chancellor Bismarck observed that all his closest political competitors were over the age of sixty-five. He cleverly orchestrated an ordinance that effectively retired all citizens who reached sixty-five. With his competitors sidelined by the new law, Bismarck rose to power. As other countries followed, age sixty-five became the benchmark for retirement." So *that's* how it got started and there's no *real* reason to push people out of jobs and companies at sixty-five. Great!

From *Newsweek:* "It now seems that, absent disease, loss of mental acuity has less to do with intrinsic aging than with mental activity. That's because neurons (the structural and functional unit of the nervous system) can sprout new connections when stimulated—and it is the connections, not the nerve cells themselves, that determine how well we think and remember. 'Right up to the end of life, the more you challenge your brain, the more you can increase the number of connections,' says neuroscientist Dr. Arnold Schneibel of the University of California, Los Angeles. 'With a good deal of intellectual challenge, you may be able to hold your own.' " From Dr. Stuart Berger's *Forever Young:* " 'Despite the common belief, thinking can actually improve with age.'—New York Hospital-Cornell Medical Center." Yippee!

John Bradshaw says in *Lear's:* "I regard a lot of the issues around aging as delusions that we impose on ourselves. Because if I decide that the bags under my eyes mark me with some magical sign of aging, then I start acting accordingly. I create a new kind of self-image for myself that goes with old age, that says there are certain things I can't do anymore because I'm too old. And sure enough, I stop exercising energetically. I overeat because I can't do anything about losing weight anyway, and who cares? Aging is inevitable—just look at my gray hair. And this way of thinking can cover up a sense of failure in life, can close the curtain long before the show should be over, can banish the optimism that a full life relies on, the optimism that says—correctly—that it's never too late for anything on your mind."

Betty Friedan (seventies): "It [the mystique of age] has the same kind of effect as the feminine mystique. It denies personhood to people over 60 just as the feminine mystique denied personhood to women ... seeing women only as sexual reproductive partners of men." Betty wants us to see "the really true unique possibilities for the new 25 years of life that now are available to Americans." I'm willing to have a *go* at seeing them.

At any rate there sure are a lot more *of* us these days. Statistics from *Women's Wear Daily:*

- Twenty-seven years of life expectancy have been added since 1900.
- During the next dozen years, the fifty-plus group will grow by 23 percent as compared with an 8 percent growth rate for the total population under fifty.
- People fifty-plus have 80 percent of the country's savings.
- The sixty-two million who are fifty-plus control half of the $260 billion discretionary spending power.
- The fifty-five-to-sixty-four-year-olds have the greatest share of per capita income.

So here we are mature at last with some real advantages. From the Op-Ed page of *The New York Times:* Maturity is simply "the ability to set our own goals, to tolerate frustration, to postpone gratification, to take responsibility for others, to be curious about people, events or ideas that are older than yesterday." Maturity is *good,* right?

Let's see what some people say they *like* about being older. Jackie Lehman (seventies): "My sense of humor. I didn't have much of one before but I practiced, like a tennis game. Now I get the shrieks sometimes. Phone rings in the bathroom ... it's my friend Heidi. 'Heidi,' I say. 'Guess what I'm doing—I'm sitting on the floor of the john dying my pubic hair auburn. I do the hair on my *head,* why not the hair on my pussy?" Gloria Steinem (fifties): "As you get older you are relieved of certain responsibilities—like falling in love! My research indicates that people fall in love the most who are least mature—they have to have a love fix constantly to feel alive. The most well-adjusted people do not fall in love easily." (I don't agree. I think millions of older people would fall in love if they had anybody to fall in love with but Gloria feels not needing to is a virtue.) She also says, "I would never want to be young again ... it was too painful!" Ann Ford Johnson (seventies): "I'm more kind ... wiser ... more thoughtful. You get everything you didn't have when you were younger. I'm still making new friends ... all younger than I. I meet them through my charity work. Young people are doers ... they don't complain ... they're terrific to work with. I have a much broader circle of friends now."

Betsy Carter, editor of *New York Woman* (forties): "Growing older means you've earned the right not to pretend, not to waste time with people or events that really don't interest you. You can do less of what you're supposed to and more of what you want to, be totally honest without worrying about the repercussions, have an appreciation of time passing that demands that you use it more fruitfully than you once did. And in this process, you become more of who you are. The fainthearted become more insulted and self-absorbed; the intrepid become more indomitable." Leonora Hornblow (seventies): "You don't have to worry about silly things like do you have a date Saturday night, are you popular? I'm so busy ... *too* busy. My son says I'm Ado Annie in *Oklahoma!* I haven't said no to anything since he can remember. I do say no to the boring stuff but yes to what *pleases* me." Kitty Hart (seventies): "I can say things I never could say as a young woman. I can tell a man he's good-looking, charming, interesting without being afraid he'll think I'm making a pass. I can compliment a woman wholeheartedly because there's no thought of competition and I can reprimand young people for rudeness and bad behavior and get away with it! I *like* being as old as I am as long as I can function as if I were twenty-five years younger."

Charlotte Salisbury (seventies): "I think about my family life and growing up with two alcoholic parents; two marriages by the time I was twenty-five; then World War II and struggling with children and practically no money; and after that a very happy existence until I was forty-five and somehow got the courage to leave. Everything up until then was so stormy that now, being married to Harrison and leading the wonderful life he has given me, with four grown children who are devoted and loving, ten grandchildren ranging from twenty-seven to three, who are by turns interesting, amusing and all pretty close . . . I am happy and content." Frances Lear (sixties): "I used to be nothing but aches and pains . . . I just don't have them anymore. Exercising your brain is what keeps you youthful—*nothing* keeps you *young* . . . the trick is to find something to be passionate about. It doesn't have to be a paid job *or* a man. You can be passionate about the environment, social issues, etc. You can work your ass off for a political candidate. You can care deeply about a group of children or drug addicts. Being able to exercise your creativity is all-important. . . . I find it hard to look at myself in the mirror . . . yuff! but I don't look in the mirror that much these days because I am frantically busy. Inside of me I don't feel I am any different than I was as a young woman. My ability to do a job is no less great now than when I was thirty. The reason I feel I can say I am happy now is that I am without angst . . . no *sturm und drang*. . . . I think I am almost into serenity!"

Mary Ann Wilson (sixties): "Walking home from dinner along Third Avenue on Friday night, you see young people pouring out of J.G. Melon's or Sam's or some other trendy saloon and realize a chasm of years (and fatigue!) separates you from them but you don't *want* to be in a goddamn bar drinking diet-Pepsi, talking in 130-decibel noise for three hours about color coordinating the ushers' cummerbunds so they don't clash with the napkins at the wedding and are Aruba trade winds absolutely the best for windsurfing? You feel wrestled to the ground just *thinking* about it. Life *is* really delicious now ... good food, good conversations, good books, good friends ... will I sound like an asshole if I say now *is* more satisfying?" Carrie, a popular New York "single girl" in her sixties, reminds us that older women do very well at *parties*. "They've got the experience ... arriving all coifed and pretty, greeting friends, then shamelessly guest-hopping ... *not* getting stuck with the nerds. They are very comfortable with men, even without one of their own ... charming, gracious, amusing, flirtatious but not *too*, making a much bigger impression on a man by *listening* than by talking. The old pros, putting younger women right out of the race with their vast party experience."

I've found—if I can get in on this up side of aging, having complained so earlier—that you can be a little gracious, or even grand at times. You can do it as a boss, of course—yes, you *may* be away the week between Christmas and New Year's; yes, you may bring Alice (her Dalmatian) to the office while your apartment's being painted. Yes *(very* grand), you may put that on your expense account. The graciousness can be part of you long before you're older, of course ... it's charm and good manners and kindness. *Grand* you have to go easy with even if you *are* older, but occasionally you can indulge. I love to sweep into the bar at "21" on a snowy night after the theater with a couple of friends to have supper. It's like a club, though it isn't officially one ... old New York at its best. I kiss at least half the staff, including the maître d'. You don't kiss the maître d' before you are fifty or sixty, I wouldn't think. For many years I could barely get into "21" and was seated somewhere near Ketchum, Alaska, not even in *sight* of the bar; then *Cosmo* started spending money there ... so did David; now it's "Hello Dolly" when I get there and, yes, I do feel grand. So many other "grand" over-sixty ladies eat at "21," I hardly stand out.

Okay, how *different* do we want to be from the person we now are, and can we change? I think the little stuff, yes. I can give away the dress I haven't worn in six years but would really like to stuff right back in the closet. I can stop saying shit around David, get to the airport only thirty minutes ahead of time instead of an hour and twenty minutes, but *major?!* My longtime shrink, Herbert Walker, used to say I was the most rigid person he'd ever met (how's *that* for a shrink compliment?!), though he *also* said, coming from where I came from I was a *miracle,* so *there!* I will probably forever drown myself in work, my chloroform from pain and what I "have" to do, while what I "want" is to spend more careless hours with friends. I see the *Cosmo* staff chatting away at each other's desks, going out for lunch, drinks, movies, weekending together, the top editors no less friendly and involved with each other than less pressured assistants. I'm friendly but don't fraternize for more than five minutes, and it isn't because me boss, they employees. It's to do with being a mouse who is more at peace tending her chores, doing what I "have" to instead of what I wistfully think I *"want."* As Tennessee Williams said, "I fear if I lost my demons, I might lose my angels as well." Katharine Hepburn says her mother used to say, "Don't forsake those duties which keep you out of the nuthouse."

Everybody says, change before the changes are made *for* you; I can't seem to get the hang of that. *Why* do we have to drive a new way to the office, wear florals if we like solids, rearrange the guest towels—I like them ivory, white, *then* peach, just as they are. Give me my five favorite restaurants, you can keep *trendy.* If you're about to plunge over a cliff, I guess you try to rein in the steed, change directions (another great metaphor, right?), but changing just to change seems overanxious to me. I'm trying to hang on to *this* husband, job, face, teeth, apartment, friends as long as possible; later I promise to adjust if I must.

Other "sound" advice I have managed to ignore: Believe in yourself. In times of challenge everybody says you just dip down into your inner core of self-belief and *mush.* Well, some of us don't *have* an inner core of self-belief to mush with. What I believe in is that you try not to go down the old drain by using whatever you've got to work with, work like a *rat* and hope everything will come out okay. It frequently does. All these years I have survived and that is what I am still doing. Surviving and sometimes winning. I think you start all over again every day, squirrel in on the next awful thing that awaits you, believe in hard work and *do* it. That is usually sufficient to get you through or *more* than through. (I call it the Mouseburger Plan.)

Can you at least *like* yourself even if you aren't a big self-believer-in? Certainly. On Debbie Kronenberg's *Cosmo* newsletter quiz I got an 86 (in self-like) out of 100 and felt quite perky. Want to take it? On a scale of 1 to 10, how would you rate yourself?

1.	Pretty	_____	6.	Faithful	_____
2.	Special	_____	7.	Feminine	_____
3.	Cute	_____	8.	Thin	_____
4.	Sexy	_____	9.	Generous	_____
5.	Powerful	_____	10.	Vain	_____

I don't know whether 10 for vain should have run the score up or down but I chose up.

New subject (I'm trying to cover everything): When people make bad things happen to you, can you get revenge? I don't think *you* can get it. Revenge is usually got *for* you by somebody else or by life itself. By using the Mouseburger Plan—keeping your blinders on and just doing the best you can—I have managed to get beyond most of the detractors in my life. Somehow I never got into a vendetta with anybody who totally wanted to do me in; then I'd have to do *them* in, etc., etc. Getting fired a couple of times I could have done without, but *life* took care of the executioners (most of them are dead!). Men . . . now that is something else. I have been so wounded in love that watching the pain perpetrators dissolve in hot grease (after being made to confess they were wrong to have cheated so flagrantly and did adore only me) would have been a delicious sight but they have all got seedy with time and I think that is revenge enough. I fired someone (never any fun) a few years ago who later wrote a book with me as the "heroine"—a thoroughly disagreeable character, I understand, whom everybody hated, who finally loses her empire, her money, her looks and her man. That girl must have had a lot of pleasure writing that book. I never read it. You see, it's just very hard to arrange revenge on a person *yourself*. Now if Sabrina happens to see a copy of *this* book, she can be cheered by learning that I *have* suffered here and there though not as badly as she may have had in mind and not from her *book*.

One thing I'm sure of. If you stick around long enough—I consider us now having stuck around that long—you mostly see your enemies *destroyed* ... DESTROYED! Example: My beautiful nemesis, Marybeth Lewis (not her real name), who was in my life from age ten through twenty-four, made me mildly miserable and what do I mean mildly?! We both grew up in Little Rock and Marybeth came to Los Angeles a few years after I did. She was ravishing and, though maybe not as smart as I, who needed *smart?* You couldn't go anywhere with Marybeth without men trying to pick *her* up when *we* were waiting in a wartime movie or restaurant line. On Elm Drive in Beverly Hills, where we briefly shared an apartment, Marybeth's other roommate and I *tried* to sympathize as she clucked away about the perils of being a transplanted Arkansas rose in the fertile gardens of Hollywood—"This man followed me all the way down Vine Street in a Cadillac convertible and tried to get me to get *in*" or "Oh, my God, he's sent *more* flowers ... I've already got two dozen yellow roses at the office!" or "Do you want to hear this poem he wrote?" (No, I didn't.) These tributes were all from *different* men ... demoralizing!

Alors, it is forty years later and Marybeth is visiting me at *Cosmo* with a friend from Albuquerque where she now lives—we haven't seen each other in all that time. I'm sure *I* look the same (naturally). Marybeth has been wiped *out!* In her place is this shorter person, a slightly tougher version of Humphrey Bogart's third wife, Mayo Methot, or perhaps just *any* crumbling housewife—we're talking *dowdy,* only dowdy is how you dress and these

changes were *structural*. The once long silken hair is
short, thin and dyed blond. Eyes still big—you don't
shrink eyes—but now a little bulging. Upper lip still curls
over upper teeth, à la Gene Tierney, but the curling looks
a little feral. We have here somebody whose once great
looks are not visible in the smallest degree. I want to say,
"Lord, she needed to be toned down, true, maybe to become a little faded or fat but did you have to wipe *out*
Marybeth?" (who was, incidentally, sweet, said she was
joyous about my success and I think meant it). I wished I
could go back and shake my silly twenty-four-year-old self
very hard and say, "Dummy, don't let anybody's charms
blur your vision about life or spoil your fun. Marybeth's
boyfriends who can't see you for peanut shells will probably all get gout or cirrhosis or look like peanut shells
themselves during your lifetime. Keep your cloudless
young eyes straight in front of you, for God's sake, and
get on with *your* life ... it's all out there for you, you
ninny!" Actually, these thoughts about envy and covetous-
ness are not bad right this minute. Marybeth died of lung
cancer—she was a heavy smoker—last year. She haunts
me.

It is a little hard to be philosophical about beautiful
young women in our lives right this minute who aren't yet
having any trouble—they're only forty! Yes, they *will* be
as old as we are someday "Just wait until *she* is sixty!" I
hiss to myself as I watch an impossibly pretty girl flinging
her body and her hair around the dance floor. The catch is
that when she's sixty, I'll be *ninety*—oh, please, let's don't
even *think* about it—and how much fun will it be to check
up on her *then?* Gradually, *very* gradually, you realize that
relief doesn't come from knowing she and all the other
now-fluffy ones will be where we are someday; we simply
have to get on with what's here for us *now*. I'm doing
pretty well these days.

May I now offer perk-up-your-life ideas though I
promised this wouldn't be an advice book? It *isn't* ... it's
just "we're in this together" stuff. Let's start with reaching
out.

Reaching out is simply saying yes. My darling friend, press lord Victor Civita, whose company Editora Abril, publishes *Cosmo* and dozens of other magazines and newspapers in Brazil, used to say to me, "When you're older, Helen, it's easy to say no. No, no, no . . . I don't *do* that anymore . . . get my name off the list! To say yes involves work and pain. I say yes most of the time." Why do you do that? I asked. "It keeps me alive and fighting," he said. He was alive and fighting—and vigorous—until his death last year at eighty-three. Steve Brookstein, vice-president and management supervisor at Young and Rubicam, puts it this way: "Every day I raise the bar." Forget the tycoons, I think *we* need to say yes to just ordinary offers, to take little risks as we get older. Inger Elliot, original founder and owner of China Seas Fabric Shop, says, "You must try things you wouldn't have dared when you were younger. I have always been terrified of horses but I have a good instructor and I am now riding. Always use an instructor . . . they will make it possible for you to do things you didn't know you could. I felt the same way about the horse as I did when I learned to use the computer . . . the old gray matter is still functioning." As Karl Lagerfeld, the prolific French designer, says, "The purpose of life is life."

I agree we mustn't be *easy* on ourselves. Katharine Hepburn, who swims in Old Saybrook, Connecticut, on five-degree winter mornings, says, "Not everyone is lucky enough to understand how delicious it is to suffer." In warm weather, she takes ice-cold showers. In New York City older—and *younger*—women are supposed to be terrified of muggers, avoid the subways like botulin poisoning. "Why would you do that?" asks my friend Claudia. "I pull my coat and sweater sleeves down over my bracelets and wristwatch. I don't wear rings or chains. I read a newspaper. I'm wherever I'm supposed to be in ten minutes. Either that or I walk. On a bitter cold night I'll get into flats, pull my beret over my ears, wrap up like a dogsled driver and *mush* to the party or restaurant or home. . . . It gives me a feeling of *power!*"

I'm not much for "doing what comes naturally." In a

speech to the cosmetics industry last year I said I visual-
ized someday that a newspaper or TV interviewer would
ask me what I thought of natural and I would say, "Not
much. Natural is dandruff, acne, headaches, tears, fungus,
earthquakes, forest fires, blizzards, burping, snoring, mos-
quitos, tarantulas and snakes. It's double chins and jowls,
having hair where you don't want it and having it fall out
where you do ... along with your teeth! It's wanting to
kill your husband because he won't stop at a gas station
and ask directions after you've been driving around lost
for two hours, etc. On the other hand, *unnatural,* as in
self-discipline, will get you *everywhere.* "

Brook Astor (nineties) credits her longevity to one
thing: "Discipline—in every way. You can have fun, but
don't eat so much, don't drink so much, don't go dancing
so much." The late great *Vogue* editor Diana Vreeland declared, "Naturalness is a form of laziness." My favorite
older person, Jack LaLanne, says, "Don't stew, *do!*" And
in Josephine Hart's terrific novel, *Damage* (Knopf), the
curmudgeon father tells his son, "Will. Man's greatest asset. Underused by the majority. The solution to all life's
problems. Make up your mind about it. Then do it." I love
that. I guess what we're all saying is that we shouldn't be
too comfortable later in life. You swim three more laps
than are pleasant, meet a friend for lunch in a blizzard,
work till you're pooped, talk to strangers.

I started doing *that* at age thirty-three, feeling it was
good discipline for a shy person. I was in Rome on my
first trip to Europe because everybody had gone but me—
the only time I ever borrowed money—totally alone and
lonely. Coming out of a store on the Via Nazionale one afternoon with a ton of packages—leather gloves were a dollar, gilt and painted wooden boxes were two dollars—I
just impulsively walked up to a young man with a motorbike and asked if he would drive me around Rome for a
few minutes. Was this crazy? Yes, but not *too.* He was
gentle-looking, not with an entourage, and he said sure,
hop on. We stashed the packages under the seat, I sat behind him with my arms around his waist, we took off for
the Colosseum, the Forum, the Arch of Constantine, up

through the hills and down into city streets just at sunset with a few storm clouds gathering to make it all more dramatic. Bless that darling person. Racing through Rome on the back of somebody's motorbike, clinging like a baby koala bear, managing somehow to realize *at the time* how deeply wonderful it was has kept me from playing it totally safe—just *reasonably* safe—ever since.

May I tell you one more "gutsy" story I've never told anyone? Barbara Walters and her then husband, Merv Adelson, were giving a dinner dance at the Pierre Hotel, and shortly before the party, Barbara asked whom I'd like to sit next to. Sweet. Somebody who can dance, I said. Wanting to dance and not getting to was a serious problem in my life for years. I had been sitting like crabgrass at charity dinners (sometimes still am), with Peter Duchin or Lester Lanin playing all that great music from the thirties and forties, dying to dance and nobody to dance with. Tables are for ten; you can dance with your husband seated next to you—more about that in a minute—or the man on the other side who, if *he* doesn't dance, shuts your options right *down.* You can't ask a man from the other side of the table to dance because he belongs to *his* seatmates who will kill you. You can't go pounce on somebody at another table—that would be pushy, poor-little-orphan time. So you sit like the widowed Scarlett O'Hara tapping her foot during the Virginia reel, *longing* to dance and going crazy. David gets out on the floor and shakes, rattles and rolls—he's wonderful—and other ladies *love* to dance with him but, being close to professional class myself—sorry, I used to *teach* dancing!—I'm not certain David even *feels* the music the way I think he should. What I have in *mind* is J.G. (Junior Grade) Fred Astaire!

Barbara does indeed place me next to a man (from *Time* magazine) who dances beautifully—hallelujah! Alas, the floor is bumper to bumper, plus I don't think his wife is all that crazy to have us out there on it. Sigh . . . next party it's back to frustration on the sidelines. Being a practicing realist, I decide to try to Do Something about my problem. I sign up for lessons at Stepping Out, a dance studio up the street from *Cosmo,* so I can at least dance once a week. Plan isn't a total success. Stepping Out's specialty is Latin which isn't mine and, though I'm dancing, it's a struggle . . . I'm working my tail off.

Here come the guts. I call up *Time* magazine man I've never seen except at Barbara's party and ask him to lunch. (I tell my young *Cosmo* editors to take advantage of their jobs—an editor can ask *anybody* to lunch and he'll usually accept.) New friend meets me at Barbetta, we chat amiably; during macaroons and cappuccino he wants to know if I had anything in mind asking him to lunch. Well, yes, now that you mention it. I bravely tell him, feeling like an asshole (I mean I'm *not* Cindy Crawford—I'm a sixty-seven-year-old businesswoman), my problem: Love to dance, never get to dance, and the plan: Would he like to take an hour off some afternoon and go dancing at Roseland, New York's venerable dance emporium on West Fifty-second Street? You're on, he says. It took three weeks for us to get together—he kept having to go to Washington. One day we made a date, I arrived at Roseland directly from an advertising lunch, he never showed—he'd been called away suddenly and couldn't reach me. I sat on Roseland's steps for forty minutes, feeling like a hooker. Finally we made it. I wore my twirliest skirt; we danced up a storm for two hours. He remembered being at Roseland as a young soldier in World War II. I think he enjoyed himself, I surely did, but we didn't do it again. I had exorcised a longing and was proud of myself. He may have figured Mrs. Time Magazine would kill him if he did this often and she found out. David wouldn't have killed me but I just never told him. My brief-encounter dance partner and I are still friends though I rarely see him.

Then "fate" came along and rewarded me as fate sometimes does if you've been a Good Person (the kid has tried hard, let's give her a break.) John Mack Carter, the editor of *Good Housekeeping,* turns out to be a dancer. We've been associates at the Hearst Corporation for seventeen years but I never knew he could dance! Now at company parties, John will fetch me and we dance ourselves silly. Sharlyn Carter puts up with us. David puts up with us. They *may* both be glad to get us off their hands.

Okay, here's the point. You can do *something,* you see, mildly inappropriate, but frequently rewarding. You just have to get in the habit of thinking up possible small pleasures that take *guts,* then go for it. You pick yourself up after possible rejection and try again. Spoils go to the not-faint-hearted.

Now let's skip to loneliness—a much more serious problem than not dancing and a staple for divorced and widowed older women. The 1990 census reveals 11.5 million widows, median age fifty-six; one out of two marriages ends in divorce—so presumably that's a lot of *lonely.* Paula Blanchard, a public-relations executive and former first lady of Michigan, divorced for five years, says, "I believe loneliness is one of the things people fear most when they contemplate divorce. I didn't fear it, but it is a reality I deal with every day. The house is empty when I return at night from my office, and evenings and weekends are sometimes lonely. As with all problems, each of us finds our own individual solutions. I prefer to face loneliness head-on and wither it with an unflinching stare than try to deny it or run from it. I also face it with the belief that it is lonelier to live in an unhappy marriage or unfulfilled expectations than it is to live by yourself."

I can think only of the cliché ways of coping with loneliness: Have some kind of work, preferably paid but charity and pro bono are okay, so at least your daytimes are spoken for. Be good to your friends so you'll have lots. Please don't anybody tell me she's lonely who hasn't had four or six people to lunch or dinner at her house in six months. Not just dear old high-school chums but people you'd like to know better will come if you cook well and sign them up far enough in advance. Salad, pasta and fruit are fine; practice till they're as good as at a good Italian restaurant. Not everybody will have you back, the creeps, but some will. Like work, entertaining uses the best of you, perks you up (of course, it *is* work). Take classes. You've heard that before. Go to lectures. You've heard that, too. Something might really grab you. Museums ought to be in the curriculum, I suppose. I don't have a good time at them—I always *want* everything (what good does a Van Gogh do me in the Metropolitan?). I have a less envious time at the Whitney. Is anybody really *sure* you couldn't do all those squares and lines and dots and have them come out not *much* less good than a Peter Haley? I'm going to get some pieces of canvas and a bucket of paint someday and have a go at it. Okay, off to the museum with you.

Travel should be in your life if you want and can afford it. If you can't find anyone to go with you, alone is better than not going—you can talk to people on the tour. I went to Europe alone for six weeks when I was single, as I mentioned, shy as a woodchuck (except for that motorcycle incident) and it was *almost* terrific. Churches are good about bringing newcomers into activities, never mind whether you're religious.

As Paula Blanchard says, face loneliness down . . . it's something you *can* get the better of unlike creaky joints and deteriorating plumbing. Sometimes, of course, you don't have the will or energy to get into *any* activity. Please check the chapter on exercise. It's there to lift your psyche as well as your bod . . . it really *will*. I don't have to tell you nothing is more attractive than somebody who is too busy to see you. You thought you were doing your recently divorced friend a favor to invite her to the movies . . . the creature is *booked!* That instantly makes her more interesting. You can't *fake* busy (you *could* but it's hard to keep *up*). The real item (and it doesn't much matter busy with *what*—bridge night with the girls, taking your niece to the ballet) is effective in causing respect, possibly bringing future invitations. Of course, if you aren't booked, say yes without fuss—you're an *easy* date. Get ready fast, be a dreamboat all evening, offer to *pay*.

Are you getting fagged out with all this activity? Perhaps you feel you *gave* already . . . work, discipline, never wasting a minute . . . and now these precious later years you want to play or at least let down. I guess there *is* no "right" way to program older us. Constant playing would

send me for the *cyanide*. You have to be true to yourself
if you've finally figured out what that *is!*

May I mention music as something the "players" as
well as the compulsives can enjoy? I recently went nuts-
crazy at the Barry Manilow concert at the reopening of
Madison Square Garden, two days later screamed it up for
my idol Tony Bennett in Greenwich Village. I've written
Michael Feinstein five fan letters this year. (Does he read
them? We don't know, but at Charlotte Ford Downe's
birthday party for her husband, Ed, I am yelping at him
from a table near the piano, " 'Better Luck Next Time,'
Michael, play 'Better Luck Next Time'!" and he said,
"Okay, Helen, this one's for you" . . . he *must* be reading.)

Is it tacky to be a groupie at such an age . . . all that
adoration appropriate in the young being unleashed by
somebody with white (dyed mocha) hair? Possibly, but the
cool contained ones give me a headache. You don't have
to jump out of the balcony or throw your bra on the stage
and I don't need to hug or clutch or even *know* the admired one. When you *do* meet, you usually stand around
making small talk, being awkward with each other, but
getting this much pleasure from somebody talented is one
of the lovely freebies (or close) available to us all. Tapes,
CDs, laser discs are wonderful but I love *live*. One of the
privileges of "older" is that you can resign guiltlessly from
music you *don't* like or like *anymore*. Pauline tells me she
can't listen to Frank Sinatra now, though she has hundreds
of his tapes, because "they make me sad. All that romantic
love that isn't part of my life anymore." (Pauline, you
could *try!*) Leila is revving up "for about the twentieth
time" to try to like classical. "I'm told you have to be
soul-dead not to be moved by Puccini so I'll give it a shot
. . . *again!* Maybe music is like a blind date . . . you give
the new guy a *chance* though you possibly won't be going
into the sunset together."

Bobbie Ashley, *Cosmo*'s brilliant executive editor
(sixties) likes it *all* . . . "soft-rock and blues (Mabel Mer-
cer, Bessie Smith, Billie Holiday, Ella Fitzgerald, Sarah
Vaughan). I like big bands to dance to. I love musicals
(*Pal Joey* and *Guys and Dolls* are my two favorites). I like

the symphonies and classical music I *know,* e.g., Vivaldi's *Four Seasons,* Stravinsky and Grieg. I also love cabaret music. Bobby Short, Steve Ross, who play the piano and sing. I always half fall in love with the men who do this." My seventy-five-year-old sister, Mary, in a wheelchair these fifty-five years, more housebound now than in previous years, keeps music going night and day, a wizard with electronic equipment if it involves the sound of people she likes to listen to. The good thing about music is that you *can* own it. Barbra Streisand on your CD is just as much yours as she is Princess Stephanie's or Warren Buffett's.

A man in your life? I wrote about having one "for purposes of sex" in Chapter Three. Having one as a steady beau or to marry is something else. Are you willing to settle for "not appropriate"? Sue Mengers assures me many Beverly Hills women are *not* alone on Saturday night; they are home with the dog groomer, the trainer, the masseur. The men are not *unintelligent* . . . they just happen not to be in the right profession, not chic enough to take to a *party.* It's the old package deal: The woman has looks, money, a beautiful house, a certain age and massive loneliness in her portfolio; he has relative youth, attractiveness, niceness, a shortness of serious money, social skills or stories anybody would want to listen to. That's *one* group of older women and their men. There are lots of other combos. The activities that give you a viable *life* in your fifties, sixties, seventies and later are the things that also may bring a man. The keys to his acquisition are: 1. Wanting one badly enough to "go for it." 2. Doing the things you have to do to attract him—which doesn't mean extending yourself like a slide rule but does mean being thoughtful, kind, pretty and interested. 3. Being *totally* realistic about who's possible. That's all I plan to say about man-finding . . . this is *it!*

Are you now, by any chance, in a real funk, deeper than lonely? We haven't talked about widowhood, the lingering or terminal illness of a spouse, deep racking trouble in our lives. I don't think I can say anything meaningful about that kind of pain. We survive. We think we are going to die; we don't. Maybe it's worse at our age but I'm not sure—you can suffer when *young*. If you are feeling pitiful for less federal reasons, you have to remember self-pity is the most destructive human emotion *and* the most seductive. Indulge and you will disgust your friends, give pleasure to your enemies (who always knew you were a jerk) and delay recovery.

Again, I think the *only* way to go when struck down is *"busy"*—busy doing *anything*. Meditation? Okay ... I just hope you aren't into *sobs* when it's over; I always think active is better than passive. Many people still believe we should solve our own problems without running out for professional help. Some can, some can't. We "can't" simply have too deep a reservoir of psychic pain—yes, from childhood—not to need extra help in our grown-up lives, especially in emergencies, especially when older. The shrinks I know are deeply sympathetic—they get *paid* to be but most genuinely are anyway. Also these days they are *practical*—and try to move things along ... nobody's got the patience or money for psychoanalysis. Shrinks won't let you get *away* with self-destruct. When you leave you feel cleansed, ready to get on with your life and survive ... at least that's been my experience. A friend may recommend one or your doctor can.

For many, the solace for life's problems is religion. I have these iconoclastic thoughts about it. I think religion may be just people's wish to be held in the night. They hope there is A Plan ... surely things couldn't have got this rotten without forethought on *somebody's* part, right? ... and surely a Higher Being can get us through (even though "It" presumably got you into this mess in the first place). Well, I don't see how one can seriously believe in a God (out there somewhere) any more than you seriously believe in Santa Claus after age ten. From ages three to ten you believe, sure, but around ten you begin to figure out *Daddy* put the bicycle on the front porch and said Santa told him to tell you to go out there and look for it and *Mommy* bought the little fur muff at Hick's Department Store. Much as you will miss Santa Claus, logic and observation tell you to let go. At some point, I think you recognize God as something we invented to believe in, not the other way around (that God created *us).*

I joined the Presbyterian church at age nine and *loved* it! Sunday school with those dramatic Bible stories illustrated on picture cards—Naomi and Ruth on their camel, Daniel with his lion, contests to see who could turn to Corinthians 8:14 fastest in the Bible (of such simple pursuits is the competitive spirit born!). Church after Sunday school, solemnly singing from heavy hymn books, Christian Endeavor back at church Sunday night, plus picnics, swimming parties, hayrides, new dresses for Palm and Easter Sundays but I really loved the *religious* part. I sang in the junior choir of the Winfield Methodist Church (my Presbyterian church didn't have one) in Little Rock, later in the choir of the Immanuel Presbyterian Church in Los Angeles, but then the Santa Claus (in reverse) syndrome got me. I decided God hadn't really grabbed my father and taken him away when I was ten and needed him so badly or given Mary polio . . . *life* did that. All you really have is your own ability to deal with problems, get up and try again.

Of course some people, indoctrinated early, go on believing *forever* or you may *become* religious (born again) when life is about to sweep you out to sea. Fine, whatever works for you. Seems to me the people who believe strongest are the ones who need religion most . . . the poor, the seriously kicked-around. "God" gives a "reason" to go on taking it . . . it is "His" plan. Listen, the church—just about *any* church—one has to admire for the solace it gives its believers and I *do,* although one might wish they would all be a little less denigrating of women but that subject is for another day. Religion also curbs crime, unites families, and provides those reassuring rituals that celebrate life's passages—birth, marriage, death. After I abandoned formal religion around age twenty, people used to try to sign me up for *theirs.* I was so waiflike, so obviously sign-uppable, but I remained, as I am now, an atheist (I know I've *really* lost you!). I don't allow myself to pray. If you don't think there's anything "out there" it is a little phony to pray. Once in a while I run through the

Lord's Prayer or 100th Psalm to go to sleep along with my word games (is that cheating?). I believe we are all part of the rocks and trees and dinosaurs which disintegrated into coal and may right this minute be Elizabeth Taylor's diamonds. We're all part of each *other,* but if there was/is a *plan,* it has to have been hatched too long (millennias!) ago and I don't think there *was* one.

I'm grateful not to have been born Iranian, Iraqi, Saudi Arabian, Pakistani or into other Third World countries where being a woman isn't so great, but next time—whoops, that sounds suspiciously religious!—if I am plopped into one of them, I'll manage. Afraid I *don't* mind being a WASP, though the Protestant designation, as I mentioned, has about as much to do with me now as being described as blond or Hungarian. Nobody ever seems to hold WASPness against you the way they do other religions except maybe a Jewish or Catholic mother who doesn't want her son to marry you. If you are willing to switch to his religion, you can still make the deal. Funny we WASPs never ask people to switch to *ours* (did Kathleen Turner ask Jay Weiss to become a Methodist?). Anyway, religion may be one of the solaces of *your* life. Fine.

If we *should* come back again I would like to come back twice—first as an actress, model or chorus girl who marries a rich man, has four children, mostly phases out her career to do charity work, run houses in three countries, has the whole world gaga with approval (Audrey Hepburn). I don't want to have been that at *all* this time, I like what I got, but perhaps it would be good to experience motherhood—something everybody raves about—plus have this glossy, if temporary, show-biz career—is that too much for one comeback? The second time I want to be a man. I surely don't want to be one of those *now* . . . eeeuuuckkk . . . but I would like to see what *makes* them so silly (four football games on TV on just one New Year's Day? Cleaning the carpet of the Ferrari with a toothbrush and bottled water but can't get the hang of a washer/dryer?). It'll be enlightening.

Does astrology do it for you? When somebody asks

me, what sign are you?, I am simply horrified and we all get asked all the time. I know astrology gives a lot of people pleasure, even direction in life, but can you take *seriously* a science predicated on Madonna and Herbert Hoover being born under the same sign (Leona Helmsley and John Sununu? Jackie Kennedy and Pee Wee Herman)? How can you determine who you are based on the month you were born in when you've got these two other biggies—genes and environment—to consider? Okay, if astrology speaks to you, I guess you listen. Psychics? Channelers? In her book *Dance While You Can,* Shirley MacLaine writes of two psychics and one channeler who predicted she *couldn't* open her show in Los Angeles because of an injured leg. She opened. She played. Shirley defends these people by saying, "It is understood that one's consciousness can change destiny." In other words, if the predicters get it wrong, you let them off the hook. I think those channelers and psychics ought to be held *accountable!*

When things get desperate, of course, there's suicide. Truman Capote once said, "Look, anybody in their right mind *thinks* about suicide." I think about it the way I would think of becoming a heroin addict ... absolutely out of the question! Its biggest drawback, it seems to me, is that you wouldn't be here to "enjoy" all the fuss ... people sodden with remorse, throwing up because they didn't treat you better and try to stop you plus you could only do it *once.* We all know about wanting to stir them up, the bastards, also about being *tired,* but suicide really is going too far. Again, I'd dump it all on the shrink.

What do we do about losing people, not necessarily by suicide? Every day just about, the obit column tells us of somebody we don't want to do without or the news comes by phone. Joan Bové, eighty-seven, wife of Lawrence Gelb, who founded Clairol, tells me, "Frankly, my dear, I don't have that problem. I have always surrounded myself with people younger than I." That's one solution. I mentioned earlier having always liked to be the youngest in the room; *that* is a little more challenging, to say the least! I was on a country weekend recently among wealthy, lively people all older than I, all of whom take good care of themselves, the women chic, the men smart, but there was something eerie about this collection of oldies. Far from keeping you young because you *are* technically younger, they make you vaguely unhappy because you can see what you are going to be like. I have just about given up my need for older people, not *just* because they're harder to find but because companions of *all* ages are best. Younger than we are, fine, but it's irritating to have them not remember Fredric March or Betty Grable.

We're all going to die, right? I think we can best mourn as well as celebrate the people we've lost by having helped them pack a lot in, if possible, and being nice to their families when they're gone. We should be packing a lot in *ourselves* right now.

So here we are, having faced the demons, reached out, fought lonely, filled up our lives—can we talk about something trivial? Here it is: Do you *tell* your age? So few people *do.* I've always rather enjoyed the stunned incredulity in an audience when you just let it pop: *"You???* Thirty-seven? Forty-nine? Fifty-three? Incredible!"* Of course, the flashy confession doesn't make you enjoy the actual *condition* or help you with what to *do* about it. I think more people will tell their age in the future. It is just too dumb to have to be ashamed of and punished for being the *age* you are—you *haven't* consorted with terrorists or canceled too many beauty-salon appointments in a row without twenty-four hours' notice ... you simply got plunked down on earth in a particular year and it should be honorable to say so. It is probably "protesting too much" to say very *often* how old you are, however, like bragging about being from old Virginia stock, but if the subject comes *up,* why *not?*

Whether you tell your age or not, here are some things I think we definitely should do at our age.

One: Try not to bore anybody. She is in my office telling me about the marriage of the parents of a boy with whom her son is rooming at Yale. My mind is *blowing.* I'm not even particularly interested in her *son,* whom I haven't seen since he was a crawler, only asked about out of politeness, but her screening-out mechanism—that part of your brain that says, STOP, don't do any more on this subject—doesn't function. Maybe it isn't even *there* in her case, like not having the mechanical skills to work a VCR *(moi!).* One *should* always think ... is this more than they want to know about how Uncle Phil met Aunt Clara at the Iowa State Fair and they go back there every year? If the stories are about *celebrities,* that's different; family stories are the deadly ones for people who don't know the family.

Two: As we age, I think we should try hard to fight anger. Regardless of the worthiness of their cause, angry people are hard to take. Norman Mailer says, "To me, one of the most miserable conditions in life is to be very very angry in old age—which I'm not at yet" [he's sixty-nine]. At a good-bye party for a longtime employee, the guest of honor spoke glowingly of the man who had "taught me everything I know ... the consummate salesman of our time, etc., etc., etc." Complimented one had already left the party when the words were said, so I called him next day to repeat the testimonial. "Sure, sure, all that from a guy they fired too soon!" He was furious. I realized this man, instead of being flattered by the words or grateful *he* was still employed (at seventy-eight), hadn't wrestled anger about aging to the ground. I don't want to be like that. Though I was angry when I began this book six years ago, I'm not now. True, the idiots who cause the anger are all *out* there waiting to pounce, but you can stay away from them a lot and nix your own complaining and whining because people won't want to be *around* you. (I've mentioned earlier in this book having a few temper flings but they were only flings, not part of a continuing angry condition.)

One small way to spare yourself anger on a daily basis is to say who you are when you ask for *anything* on the phone, never mind they don't know you from Clara Peller, the Wendy's hamburger spokeswoman, and all you want is how to spell the company name or what hours they are open. People are so suspicious! I call the Schubert Organization to get their address and they ask who's calling. If I'd said I was the mother of a twelve-year-old who would like to audition for *Annie II,* would the address have been withheld? I finally got it *without* sending over my driver's license and American Express card. I now say it's me every single time.

And here's something else that irks *some* people: All that kissing hello and good-bye folks you barely *know.* First it was kissing one cheek, now it's both cheeks; are we soon going for eyes and ears? Well, being touched is such a happy experience for some of us—the hello kiss, pat on the arm, bear hug—if it's got out of hand I, for one, am probably *helping* it! Sometimes I feel almost sorry for the people I am kissing, hugging, patting. Give those people a *break,* I tell myself, but I don't listen. There aren't any rules as far as I know about how well-acquainted you have to be for hello and good-bye kisses to be okay. Salespeople, headwaiters, bosses, employees, children and dogs are on my kissing list but you may be more selective. If people are backing away or wincing, I guess you let up. After numerous nose collisions, I have decided the best logistical plan is to go in on the left (that would be the right side of *his* face) or do I mean the other way around? Whether both cheeks or one, you kind of try to figure out what they *expect.*

One has to be careful about giving unflattering photos to friends. I proffered what I thought was a nifty picture from my new Fuji to my darling manicurist, Denise. "Oh, that nose," she cried. *"What* nose?" I asked. I'd never even noticed her nose, only the complete girl (she's only twenty-seven, for God's sake; how bad could *anything* be?!). "You don't *want* the picture?" I asked, crestfallen. "You keep it," she said. Why should I be astonished? I have just dumped in the trash (instead of jumping off the roof) and 8 × 10 color photo Liz Smith sent me of us together at a party. She looks like Ingrid Bergman. I look like Fester of *The Addams Family.* Even though you don't pay endless attention to people's looks, only your own—isn't that terrific?—you can use common sense about passing along pictures that are going to ruin their day.

Shall we do this? Stop expecting people to be passionate about the same things we are and give up some of the ludicrous things *they* are passionate about? A friend of mine is still seeking the perfect hair colorist. Although twenty perfect hair colorists *minimum* exist in New York City, my friend doesn't think anyone competent to high-light her elegant flaxen tresses and continues her search like Galahad seeking the Holy Grail. Another friend sat across from me in the MGM Grand en route to Los Angeles with a large container of chicken salad from E.A.T. Zabar on her knees later to be analyzed by her chef to try to duplicate the dressing. (It isn't the *first* chicken salad she has knee-nurtured cross-country.) More time-consuming than salad-dressing duplication is a not-young French journalist's need to rise to the top of the New York social scene. Having relocated here two years ago, she continues to write, but writing isn't her raison d'être. Social-mothing is. Without money, heavy professional cre-dentials or clout, she has ingratiated herself with one after the other of the *wives* of New York's rich and powerful men and is now invited, I would say, to 94 percent of whatever is going on in the city. Astonishing!

I'm not denigrating hers or anyone else's passion, just saying I think it's time we quit being sanctimonious about what makes other people "happy," no matter how silly. It's fun to gossip about them anyway, knowing they are also gossiping about *us*. (I can just imagine what they say about my hopping the #57 crosstown bus for the sixty-cent senior-citizen fare instead of getting into a cab or my own car.)

What else should we discuss? How about the three secrets of my success even though it isn't a major one like H. Ross Perot or Linda Ronstadt or somebody and why should you have to listen to *that*, for God's sake? Because it would mean something to me to tell you, okay? They are:

1. Being able to write a good letter. We won't go into details—you've got your own specialty.
2. Being a killer listener. To qualify, all you have to do

is shut *up* and, of course, have somebody who will talk. Most people will, so then you just keep asking questions and don't interrupt with your own stories and pretty soon they think you're the smartest person they ever met. You pretty much know what you can ask and there isn't that much you can't. I *don't* take it easy with questions about money, especially, how much did you pay for the Van Dongen or the Jaguar XJ5? People love to talk about their acquisitions. You might not ask about somebody's sex life though you may get told if the talker has got all warmed up. Save the equal time (they talk, you talk) for friends. But with anybody you might learn something from—cab drivers, bartenders, bus companions and airplane mates, a real M.A.S. (mover and shaker), *you* ask questions, *they* talk. Repeat: You can't get smarter with your mouth open. I guess I really listen to be liked. If you aren't entertaining or a great beauty or twenty-three, you listen. It certainly is a good idea with bosses.

3. Appreciating. Thank them not just when it happens or gets given to you but several more times during the year or years. You simply are ... *grateful.* First you ask for what you want—I'm talking casual stuff here—to buy the dress wholesale, to get your airline tickets upgraded to first class, same fare, for a table in the world's busiest restaurant on the world's busiest day, for somebody to come in an hour early or work an hour late, for an emergency dentist/doctor/hairdresser appointment, to cancel an appointment last minute, for theater tickets for the hit show, favors for your family, friends, bosses—and you appreciate them all to *pieces!* The thank-you note is written instantly or you call or you do both. You bring up the subject when you see whoever it is again ... I adored it, I needed it, you were so good to get it for me, give it to me at that price, fit me in, say yes when you should have said no—on and on forever ... it's so *easy!* Maybe this seems excessive to you. *I* like it when people "overappreciate" *me.* Appreciation costs

nothing except remembering to do it . . . a very good
thing for older people to do or people who want to
keep their jobs. The big three for me: letter writing,
listening, appreciating.

How much time do you spend with the people who
need you? Plenty. But with the losers—the ones who wear
you down, and that includes family, but never get their
problems solved? I think you can ration them pretty guiltlessly. Giving your everything doesn't make them whole,
just depletes *you*. How much time do you devote to people
who lost but aren't losers, they just had bad luck? (Maybe
nobody was around to help them grow up right.) Now they
can't seem to get *beyond* the bad luck we all get handed
because they haven't the basic equipment to fight back.
My friend who, since her husband died, has had one physical thing after another the matter with her, whose outings
consist only of trips to doctors and psychiatrist, who has
become a recluse comes to mind. Yes, she ought to entertain, get out at least for girlfriend lunches and art-gallery
openings or ought to have when she was *able,* but she
didn't have the emotional stamina; now she is ill and can't
go out. How much time with this nice person who needs
you badly? Some . . . but not endless. Allocating the "right
amount" of time for the needy—of which there are 157
varieties—and the "right amount" for yourself is a serious
decision. Some days or even weeks you give everything to
somebody desperate or seriously ill, but all of yourself all
of the time, we're talking martyr.
    Of course, some people love helping beyond all else
in life but that doesn't necessarily make them *selfless.*
Maybe there isn't any such thing as selfless. The givers
are getting the "selfish" good out of it, right? I'm just saying every "altruistic" act takes place because it brings a
certain feeling of relief or satisfaction to the altruist. Glad
it works that way. I don't think you have to feel guilty because you aren't torn apart by every needy person and
cause. You couldn't get your work done if all you did was
suffer. As long as you give (till it semi-hurts—money *and*

care), you don't have to *love* it; responsible is all you have to be.

So, I think I've told you everything *I* know about being older—the joys, sorrows, compensations—plus a few things I just slipped in. Could I now do a wrap-up list of what I think the pleasures are in our lives as of now, bearing in mind I don't have children so they aren't included.

SMALL PLEASURES

- Rubbing off dead skin
- Smelling your panties
- Combing out freshly laundered hair after the set—by God, it *has* fluffed up and amounted to something again
- Sneezing
- Napping
- Having a manicure
- Having nothing to do one day
- Eating a fresh peach (40 calories)
- Going to the polls and voting
- Toothpicks (How are you supposed to be happy with shreds of roast beef wedged between your teeth? I use toothpicks when people are *looking* . . . one of mankind's best inventions . . . *very* helpful in getting false eyelashes with glue attached pushed down perfectly on your *own* lashes.)
- Freshening up your feet (Can there be a sweeter, less pretentious little pleasure than scraping away dead cuticle from toenails with a nail file after you have soaked your feet for twenty minutes in hot water? Rolling dead skin off the body with Andrea Bleach Cream—leave on ten minutes, then rub off—is close to *major* pleasure.)

MEDIUM PLEASURES

- Getting some great new clothes
- Having fun (a movie, a walk, a talk) with a loved one
- Being in the middle of a great new book
- Reading and eating at the same time
- Keeping your weight down—reading the score with relief every morning
- Breakfast
- Turning somebody on
- Helping somebody and it's working out for them
- Going to the movies, then having supper
- Rice (Always delicious and satisfying ... you can hardly do anything bad to it. All those tiny fluffy grains that go together to make up just one bite and spell mother.)

BIG PLEASURES

(Never mind you think some of them don't belong in this category)

- Finding a lost piece of serious jewelry
- A one-hour massage
- Having a great conversation with a friend (She comforted you, you her ... you laughed your heads off.)
- Having an orgasm
- Working on a project with your business buddies that's going gangbusters
- Completing a good piece of work solo
- Having somebody you love not unhappy about something anymore
- Being so ready to sleep you're out cold to the count of ten
- Having a cat or dog respond to you with purring, tail-wagging, rubbing against you, yapping
- Eating Chinese or Japanese food (double the pleasure if you're starving)

- Being in first-class en route to Europe or anyplace out of the country and the meal service has just begun
- Room service in a great hotel when you aren't paying
- Friday night and Saturday morning
- A toasted raisin bagel with cream cheese ... does it *get* any better?

Okay, to sum up, we need to accept ourselves at the age we are. People who don't know us almost invariably treat older people "funny." They see our *outside* (ancient) and refuse to address the *inside*—this vibrant, passionate person, much the same as we always were. *You* still think you are cute; they don't see cute. Strangers barely see you at all, despite your being in your new Escada, coiffed and *seriously* made up; they glance away quickly if they bother to look. But, my dear, we didn't "appreciate" older people when we were young either ... we were just as uninterested. Appreciating "old" isn't what youth *does*. If we have played our cards right—glued some nice people to us—*they* will still think us cute (and even better than that), look into instead of through us. I'm a little worried because I didn't create any *children* to do that but then they don't always take on that role anyway. How we perceive *ourselves* is something else. On bad days it's hard to forgive "older" in ourselves the same way it was once hard to forgive not-beautiful as a younger person. Pretty was (still is!) expected of women and if you weren't, you had "failed" them. Everybody now "expects" *young*—have we failed again?

We are so hard on ourselves! It takes enormous courage to let yourself up off the mat for being sixty or seventy. Beauty was actually an easier rap to beat than age is now. You weren't beautiful but with need, guts, charm, chic, clothes, energy, and cosmetic surgery, you pretty much managed to rise above *that* blight and have a terrific life. But now there is no beating *this* rap: old. You will not get younger as you once managed to get prettier ... this is *it!*

Well, we forgive *them* ... husbands, friends, just

about anybody else for *their* age; let them get older without feeling disgust. My darling friend—you in this morass with me—I guess we have to be as forgiving of *us* as we are of them. It's called self-acceptance and may be the toughest order anybody ever gets handed. How *can* you accept this woefully inadequate, terrified, somewhat beaten-up person? You can't all the time. But you can quite a *lot* of the time. I think I may be going to settle for that. Older is what we *get*. And it's okay. It even has its seriously great moments.

Index

INDEX

INDEX

INDEX